THE SOVIET UNION AND THE VIETNAM WAR

The SOVIET UNION *and the* VIETNAM WAR

Ilya V. Gaiduk

Ivan R. Dee
CHICAGO 1996

 For information, address: Ivan R. Dee, Inc., 1332 North Halsted Street, Chicago 60622. Manufactured in the United States of America and printed on acid-free paper.

Library of Congress Cataloging-in-Publication Data:
Gaiduk, Ilya V., 1961–
The Soviet Union and the Vietnam War / Ilya V. Gaiduk.
p. cm.
Includes bibliographical references and index.
ISBN 1-56663-103-3 (alk. paper)
1. Vietnamese Conflict, 1961–1975—Soviet Union. 2. Soviet Union—Relations—Vietnam (Democratic Republic). 3. Vietnam (Democratic Republic)—Relations—Soviet Union. 4. Soviet Union—Foreign relations—United States. 5. United States—Foreign relations—Soviet Union. I. Title.
DS558.6.S65G34 1996
959.704'3347—dc20 95-52204

Dedicated to the Memory of My Grandmother

Anastasiya

Contents

Preface

FOR YEARS, Soviet policy toward the outside world was a combination of two interrelated but contradictory tendencies. Adopted by Bolshevik leaders after 1917, an image of their country as a bastion of revolution and the vanguard of struggle against capitalism determined Moscow's efforts to support insurrectionary movements throughout the world and made the Soviet Union, in Western eyes, a constant source of instability in the international arena. Public declarations about the world revolution and the eventual victory of communism resounded from Moscow along with the practical moves of Kremlin leaders aimed at creating and supporting pro-Soviet regimes and subversive activities in various parts of the globe. Western governments saw the "hand of Moscow" wherever the order and foundation of existing regimes were tottering.

Yet almost from the beginning Soviet foreign policy demonstrated a surprising level of common sense, manifesting Lenin's well-known concept of "peaceful coexistence" with the capitalist world. Having established relations with the leading Western powers—including Germany, Britain, and France—in the 1920s and the United States in the early 1930s, Moscow pursued a policy that was sometimes unorthodox and scarcely seemed compatible with inflammatory Soviet propaganda.

Soviet policy during World War II and after only enhanced the impression in the West that Moscow was guided by considerations which, if not free from the tenets of Marxism-Leninism, at least combined them with the rules and methods known as realpolitik. This seemingly impossible combination of revolutionary militancy and geopolitical reasonableness informed the pattern of Moscow's behavior in the cold war years. During that period the Soviets created crisis situations over Berlin, overthrew coalition governments in Eastern and Central Europe, instigated and supported insurgency in Greece, Iran, and some third world countries, and maintained a political and military alliance with Castro's regime in Cuba. At the same time they searched for terms of accommodation with nations on the other side of the iron curtain, were reluctant to risk a showdown with the West, tried to curb the zeal of some of their allies who dreamed about revolutionary upheavals, and avoided a last, possibly fatal step in their conflict with the West.

In this sense Soviet foreign policy reflected the reality of the Soviet world position. On the one hand, the Soviet Union was one of the great powers with its own self-interests and security considerations. It was involved in state-to-state relationships with other countries, relationships with rules of their own. Neglect of those rules may easily have brought damaging consequences for the Soviet regime, especially in a nuclear age. As they demonstrated during the Cuban missile crisis in 1962, Soviet leaders were conscious of the restraints imposed on their policies by reality and were prepared to act within limits.

On the other hand, since 1917 Moscow had been preoccupied with strengthening its image and position as the vanguard of the world Communist movement and of the revolutionary process. It sought to maintain its prestige in the eyes of its Communist allies, some of whom often tried to outbid the Soviets in revolutionary ardor and to challenge Moscow's position. As a result, Soviet leaders were compelled not only to declare their loyalty to communism but also occasionally to prove it by their actions, lest they be suspected of revisionism and betrayal of the common cause.

It was not easy for Moscow to reconcile these virtually irreconcilable directions of policy, and Soviet leaders faced an enormous problem in striking a balance that would satisfy allies and avoid dangerous showdowns with rivals. That they were not always successful was clearly revealed by the Vietnam War.

The conflict in Vietnam illustrated how the diametrically opposite ideologies, political and social structures, and priorities of the two rival cold war camps inevitably produced confrontation as a way of life. It seemed strange and inexplicable that the interests of the great powers could clash in this small country which played so minimal a role in the strategic balance of forces at the time. But the struggle between the two camps transformed the internal struggle of the Vietnamese people into one between democracy and communism.

Although the Democratic Republic of Vietnam was supported throughout the war by its powerful allies, the USSR and the People's Republic of China, these supporters have virtually escaped the attention of historians of the conflict in Indochina. There is a prodigious literature about U.S. policy, numerous analyses of the policy of North Vietnam, and even articles on China's policy.[1] But one can search vainly for a comprehensive analysis of Soviet activities in the war and Moscow's policies.[2]

The USSR was, after all, not a direct participant in the war. Moscow provided North Vietnam with the substantial economic and military aid necessary for Hanoi's struggle against the United States and the Saigon regime. It also lent propaganda support, publishing and broadcasting condemnations of the crimes of American imperialism. But in general the Soviets tried to maintain a low profile with regard to the war, acting behind the scenes and rendering indirect services, avoiding publicity in their diplomatic activities.

Then too, most of the documents in Russian archives that might shed light on Moscow's role in the conflict remain unavailable. The declassification of similar documents in U.S. archives has begun only recently. Publication of the "negotiating volumes" of the Pentagon Papers in 1983 served as a starting point for this process,[3] but not until after the collapse of the Soviet Union in 1991 were U.S. officials ready to release documents sufficient for a more or less complete picture of Soviet-American relations during the Vietnam War. And it is impossible from these documents alone to answer many questions about Soviet involvement in the conflict, such as the nature of relations between Moscow and Hanoi, Soviet officials' assessment of the war and its influence on international relations, and the place of Vietnam and Indochina in Soviet foreign policy planning.

Soviet and Russian historical accounts only add to the difficulties of those who are interested in Soviet policy. Writings in the Soviet Union about the Vietnam War have been far from objective.

Most of these books appeared during or soon after the conflict in Indochina, and were written by journalists who described events from positions of official ideology. They made no attempt at a comprehensive assessment of the war, let alone of Soviet policy toward it.[4] Other books by party and governmental officials justify the Soviet course in the Vietnam War, and are reminiscent of editorials in the old *Pravda*. More important in such books is what has been omitted.[5] Finally, Soviet scholars too have contributed to the study of the Vietnam War, but with rare exceptions they have been forced to use secondary sources, and their writings have remained within the limits imposed by official ideology and state interests.[6] What's more, soon after the Communist victory in South Vietnam and the fall of the Saigon regime, the attention of Soviet scholars to the war declined and has never been revived. The absence of documents and a marginal interest in the Vietnam War precluded a birth of serious literature about the conflict in Southeast Asia and the Soviet role in it.

The aborted coup d'état in August 1991 and the ensuing disintegration of the Soviet Union led to the fall of the Communist regime in Russia. In preparing for the trial of the Communist Party of the Soviet Union (CPSU), the new Russian leaders opened former party archives to find evidence against the Communist regime and its representatives. Since the Communist party controlled all spheres of policy and life in the Soviet Union, important documents on Soviet foreign policy stored in those archives became available for the first time, not only for officials of the new regime but also for scholars. Access for researchers was facilitated by a number of agreements between the Soviet archives and Russian and international scholarly institutions.

One such agreement was signed by the Storage Center for Contemporary Documentation (the postcoup name for the CPSU Central Committee executive archive located in the party headquarters on Staraya Square), the Institute of World History of the Russian Academy of Science, and the Cold War International History Project at the Woodrow Wilson International Center for Scholars in Washington. This agreement stipulated that Western and Russian scholars involved in the project would be provided with equal access to "declassified materials" in the CPSU archives, and that eventually these materials would be open to everyone who had a desire to study the history of the Communist regime in the

Soviet Union. I was among those involved in the project at the time.[7]

This was a unique opportunity for historians to read revealing documents from the party archives on Soviet cold war policy. As it happened, the process of declassification lagged behind the requests of historians for new materials, and the leadership of the TKhSD (the Russian acronym for the Storage Center for Contemporary Documentation) agreed on an unprecedented step: to open still-classified documents with the intention of later releasing them for the general public. As I was one of a few scholars concentrating on the Vietnam War, and the only Russian with such an interest, I received the bulk of secret and top secret papers on Soviet–North Vietnamese relations, diplomatic activities of the Soviet Union during the Vietnam War, and Moscow's assessment of the war and its influence on Soviet positions in Southeast Asia and in the international arena.

These documents, which included annual and quarterly reports from the USSR embassy in Hanoi, records of conversations between Soviet and foreign officials, intelligence reports from the KGB and the Main Intelligence Directorate of the Soviet General Staff (GRU), as well as memoranda prepared in the two international departments of the Central Committee (the department concerned with relations with Communist and Workers' parties in capitalist countries, and the department responsible for relations with ruling parties in socialist countries), literally shattered my previous views on Soviet policy toward the war and Moscow's relationship with its North Vietnamese allies. Soviet policy, it turned out, was not as straightforward and one-dimensional as Communist propaganda had tried to suggest. Instead it was complicated and controversial.

The idea for a book on Soviet policy toward the Vietnam War came initially from my colleagues. After reading my paper prepared for a conference on the new evidence in the history of the cold war held in January 1993 in Moscow, they urged me to continue my study of the problem and, toward this end, to use my six-month visit to the United States for research in American archives. In fact this combination of Soviet and American documents made the picture of Soviet policy in Southeast Asia in those years more complete and distinct.

Meanwhile, the scholarly honeymoon in Russian archives

abruptly came to an end in Moscow. A pretext for Russian officials' reversal of policy was found in documents on Vietnam, and the publication in the *New York Times* of a North Vietnamese report on the number of American prisoners of war. This led to a diplomatic controversy and a series of accusations and counter-accusations in official circles in Russia, the United States, and the Socialist Republic of Vietnam. More important, Russian leaders recognized somewhat belatedly that documents stored in the party archives might be used for their own political purposes and invoked at appropriate moments, instead of opening all of them. As a result, officials decided to close the whole TKhSD collection, including documents on the Vietnam War. Once again historians interested in the Vietnam War had to confine themselves to bits and pieces of information contained in Soviet official publications, books, presentations of the highest Russian archival authorities written for various conferences abroad, and some documents opened for visitors in the TKhSD.[8]

Under such circumstances the need for a book based largely on secret Soviet documents as well as recently released materials from U.S. archives seems to be more pressing. Twenty years have passed since the end of the second Indochina war, and we should be approaching an objective and comprehensive analysis of the results and consequences of this conflict which had such a terrible impact on the lives of thousands of people in the United States and Vietnam, as well as on cold war relations.

This book is not a comprehensive account of events during the years of the second Indochina war. Nor is it a general overview of Soviet policy in that period. Instead, in order to analyze Soviet diplomacy toward the conflict in Southeast Asia, I focus on factors, trends, and motives that influenced the Soviet decision-making process in those years. Such an analysis involves a complex of relationships between the Soviet Union and a number of countries. Clearly relations with North Vietnam and with the United States occupied an important place in Moscow's plans with regard to the war. Worsening relations with China and the growing rivalry between the two Communist powers also influenced the direction of Soviet policy and sometimes determined the Soviet leadership's perception of the war and its diplomatic settlement. In addition, in their Vietnam policy the Soviets also considered their Eastern European allies; Great Britain, cochairman of the Geneva Conference;

and France, a participant in the first Indochina war in the 1950s and host of the Paris peace talks on Vietnam in 1968–1973.

My book opens in 1964, a transitional year for both the United States and North Vietnam. Then it was still possible to avoid a military confrontation by initiating negotiations leading to compromise or at least an understanding between the two countries. There were no visible obstacles toward such a process, except for the strong cold war prejudices of American leaders and their determination to contain communism wherever it appeared. Later U.S. bombings against the DRV destroyed possibilities for an early peaceful settlement of the conflict.

1964 was a transitional year for the Soviet Union as well. Moscow's attitude toward the conflict in Indochina underwent a gradual transformation from a policy of nonengagement in events to the substantial support of the Vietnamese Communists and their struggle. The turning point in this policy shift was the Tonkin Gulf crisis of August 1964.

The study ends with 1973, the year the agreement to end the war and restore peace in Vietnam was signed by the hostile parties. This ended direct U.S. involvement in the war and opened a new stage of the conflict, this time between two Vietnamese forces without foreign intervention. The period after 1973 was also characterized by new developments in international relations and in bilateral relations between the countries that had been involved in the war—which certainly deserves another book.

I do not attempt to measure the guilt or innocence of each country involved in the conflict or to search for villains in the history of the Vietnam War. Participants in the war defined their actions by such different sets of values that it is sometimes impossible to find the slightest similarity between them. What was justifiable from one point of view was totally unacceptable from another. The U.S. government considered its actions righteous, since its alleged aim was to prevent the Communist suppression of the liberty of the people in South Vietnam. Hanoi declared its struggle just and moral on the basis of national sovereignty, unification of Vietnam, and liberation of the South Vietnamese from capitalist oppression. Chinese and Soviet leaders had their own motives, which were closer to those of the North Vietnamese but still not completely congruent. Each side in the conflict could provide thousands of examples of immoral behavior on the part of its enemy. But in truth the leaders of any country involved in the conflict were guided by far from ethical considerations. Particularly in the case of diplomacy, ethics served largely as a basis for propaganda.

In trying to understand the motives and policies of political leaders, I fully share the conviction of British historian F. A. Simpson: "It is the easiest method of writing history well to people it with complete heroes and authentic villains. Not only are such characters artistically invaluable when found, but the discovery of them is actually assisted by the restful process of ignoring evidence. The task of examining evidence is irksome; and its reward is the risk of losing one's hero and almost certainly of losing one's villain."[9]

To understand the motives behind Soviet policy toward Vietnam, I could not avoid several important questions: How much did Moscow's inclination to develop relations with the West, and with the United States in particular, influence decisions in the Kremlin to support North Vietnam in their resistance to American aggression? Did considerations of prestige in the world Communist movement and competition with China determine Soviet leaders' attitude toward the war in Vietnam? Was there an inconsistency between Moscow's military aid to Hanoi and Soviet efforts to promote a negotiated settlement of the conflict?

I do not pretend to offer definitive answers to these as well as other questions. Not all documents on the problem were available to me even when archives in Russia were more open than they are today. Some that contain direct evidence on top-level decision-making are located in the Kremlin and remain inaccessible. Those who expect more details on Soviet–North Vietnamese economic and military cooperation during the war, as well as on Moscow's propaganda campaigns in support of the people of Vietnam, may also be disappointed, for this book focuses on the diplomatic history of the conflict and leaves all other aspects for more meticulous studies.

In a sense, this book is an attempt to supplement the impressive historiography of the Vietnam War that exists in the West with a view from the "other side of the front line." This view is based, perhaps for the first time, on documentary evidence. But there are many questions, links, and gaps still to be addressed. As the opening of archives in Russia, as well as in Vietnam and in China, continues, more opportunities will arise to write a comprehensive international history of the conflict and to contribute to a better understanding of the cold war era with all its paradoxes.

While working on this book I enjoyed the support and inspiration of my friends, colleagues, and others to whom I am greatly indebted. I wish to thank Jim Hershberg of the Cold War International History Project who encouraged me to pursue research in Soviet policy toward the Southeast Asian conflict when I was still uncertain about it; his enthusiasm followed the course of my research and writing. The efforts of the Cold War Project to open Russian archives for public use, and its generosity, enabled me to find appropriate documents in Moscow, Washington, and Austin, Texas, and to devote six months to research in U.S. archives, a rare opportunity.

I am grateful to the Norwegian Nobel Institute for the fellowship provided me at the critical moment when I was completing the manuscript and looking for a quiet and amiable atmosphere. The staff of the Nobel Institute gave me all this. I am especially indebted to Geir Lundestad, the director, and Odd Arne Westad, his deputy, who were friendly but astute critics of the manuscript. So too was Shu Guang Zhang, whose expertise in China's foreign policy allowed me to clarify some questions about the situation in Southeast Asia in those years, and whose encouragement dispelled some of my gravest doubts.

I cannot adequately express my gratitude to those archivists who helped my research in the United States. Bill Burr of the National Security Archive in Washington was my faithful guide through documentary collections accumulated in the National Security Archive as well as throughout the United States; Claudia Anderson of the Lyndon Baines Johnson Library in Austin, Texas, and David Humphrey, who has now moved from the LBJ Library to the State Department's historical office, helped me to find my way through innumerable documents in the LBJ Library and rendered invaluable assistance in locating material on U.S.-Soviet relations. I am grateful to Ted Gittinger of the LBJ Library who arranged my visit to Austin in October 1993 to participate in a conference on the early decisions of the Johnson administration. Thanks to him I was able not only to take part in this important symposium but also to find several important American documents on Soviet policy toward the Vietnam War.

I wish to thank Alexander Chubarian, director of the Institute of World History, Russian Academy of Science, whose encouragement, support, and tolerance for my frequent leaves of absence always kept awake my sense of responsibility.

My special thanks are reserved for two people without whom this book would probably never have appeared—Lloyd Gardner, its godfather, whose recommendation led me to Ivan Dee, who has not been dismayed by my tentative English.

I owe most to my parents, Lidiya and Valerii, and to my aunts Anna and Vera, whose dedication, selflessness, patience, understanding, and confidence helped me immensely throughout the course of my writing.

I. V. G.

Moscow
January 1996

ABBREVIATIONS USED IN THE TEXT

CC	Central Committee
CCP	Chinese Communist Party
Chicom	Communist China
CIA	Central Intelligence Agency
CINCPAC	Commander-in-Chief, Pacific (U.S.)
COSVN	Central Office for South Vietnam
CPSU	Communist Party of the Soviet Union
DCM	Deputy Chief of Mission
DMZ	Demilitarized Zone
DRV	Democratic Republic of Vietnam
GDR	German Democratic Republic
GRU	Russian acronym for the Main Intelligence Directorate of the Soviet General Staff
GVN	Government of (South) Vietnam
ICC	International Commission for Supervision and Control in Vietnam
JCS	Joint Chiefs of Staff (U.S.)
KGB	Russian acronym for the Committee on State Security
NATO	North Atlantic Treaty Organization
NLFSV	National Liberation Front of South Vietnam
NSA	National Security Archive
NSC	National Security Council (U.S.)
NVN	North Vietnam
PAV	People's Army of Vietnam
PLAF	People's Liberation Armed Forces
PRC	People's Republic of China
PRG	Provisional Revolutionary Government of South Vietnam
PTV	Russian acronym for Workers' Party of Vietnam
SALT	Strategic Arms Limitation Talks
SAM	Surface-to-air missiles
SCCD	Storage Center for Contemporary Documentation

SVN	South Vietnam
TASS	Telegraph Agency of the Soviet Union
UN	United Nations
UPI	United Press International
USA	United States of America
USIA	United States Information Agency
USSR	Union of Soviet Socialist Republics
WPV	Workers' Party of Vietnam, or the Lao Dong Party

THE SOVIET UNION AND THE VIETNAM WAR

ONE

On the Eve

War, like tragedy, has its own prologue. Unfortunately, people are rarely able to recognize it until it is too late. Otherwise, who knows how many wars might have been avoided?

In early 1964 no one could have predicted that the world would soon witness a conflict in an Indochina jungle which would affect many countries and the entire system of international relations. Although many observers were anxious about the situation in Southeast Asia and warned of dangerous developments in the region, most politicians and political analysts hoped it would be possible to avoid a fateful turn of events. Among the latter were the leaders of the USSR, who had their own reasons for so hoping.

In the Soviet Union the year 1964 began with the publication of a letter from Nikita S. Khrushchev, chairman of the Council of Ministers of the USSR, to heads of states throughout the world. The Soviet premier intended, as he put it, "to draw attention to one of the problems which is, in our viewpoint, very important for the cause of strengthening peace," that is, the problem of territorial disputes between states and their means of settlement.[1]

The letter was a typical Soviet peace initiative aimed at portraying the Soviet Union as a persistent fighter for peace. At the same time it reflected Moscow's views on the current international situation. The document included passages on Vietnam, though this was not clearly a matter of territorial dispute. "One more problem," Khrushchev wrote, "is related, *to some extent,* to the territorial question. This is the problem of the unification of Germany, Korea, and Vietnam. Each of those countries in the postwar period has been divided into two states with different social systems. Their peoples' desire for unification merits understanding and respect. But, of course, the question of unification must be resolved by the peoples of those countries themselves and by their governments, without foreign military interference or occupation, as, for instance, occurs in South Korea and in South Vietnam."[2]

Although Vietnam was mentioned last in Khrushchev's letter, the situation in Indochina was of primary concern to Moscow, which saw it as principally different from developments in Germany and Korea. Khrushchev's letter confirmed this view: "In resolving this question, it is necessary to avoid the use of force, to allow the peoples of those countries to resolve questions of unification peacefully. All other states must promote this."

Evidently the unstable situation in Vietnam was in the minds of Soviet policymakers when they included these two paragraphs in Khrushchev's letter. But was this statement simply a tribute from one socialist country to another? In some respects, yes, for ritual played an important role in Moscow's politics. But the Soviet leadership seemed also to have in mind the course of events in Vietnam by 1964.

It was apparently no secret to Moscow that since 1959 the Vietnamese Communists had aimed at a military unification of the country. Official documents of the third congress of the Lao Dong party (the Workers' Party of Vietnam), held in September 1960, had been published in the Soviet Union in 1961, testifying to the party's definition of the twofold strategic task of the Vietnamese revolution: realization of the socialist revolution in North Vietnam, and the liberation of South Vietnam from the "domination of American imperialists and their accomplices" and unification of the country.[3]

According to a resolution of the fifteenth plenum of the Lao Dong party central committee of 1959 and a special meeting of the party politburo several months later, this task involved orienting Vietnamese Communists to a military struggle for unification. Hanoi believed there was a "revolutionary situation" in South Vietnam. As a result, it was decided to intensify military efforts in the South combined with an "offensive against the enemy on the political front."[4] The North Vietnamese central committee adopted a concrete plan of action to fulfill this task.

All these measures, along with the creation of the National Liberation Front of South Vietnam (NLFSV, also known as the Viet Cong—Communist-inspired and supplied by North Vietnam) on December 20, 1960, signaled to the Soviets that new developments were under way in the region. At first glance, events in Southeast Asia would seem of little significance to Moscow. The region had never been of primary concern to the Soviet leadership because of its remoteness and the weakness of its revolutionary movement. An exception was the assistance the USSR provided to the Viet Minh during the first Indochina war and to the Democratic Republic of Vietnam after 1954. But in both cases Soviet aid was inferior to that of China, with whom the Vietnamese leaders had stronger ties.

The same was true with regard to military cooperation between the Soviet Union and North Vietnam. During the Vietnamese struggle against French colonialism, the People's Republic of China (PRC) delivered to Vietnam the bulk of weapons and ammunition.[5] After 1954 the Soviet Union participated in the reorganization of the DRV armed forces and sent to Vietnam military advisers and arms, some of which were then channeled to the Viet Cong. But this assistance was negligible.

Thus before 1964 the Soviet Union remained chiefly an observer of developments in Vietnam. This role served Khrushchev's strategy of peaceful coexistence with the West and the avoidance of conflicts similar to the Cuban missile crisis of 1962. Such a role was possible while the situation in Indochina remained an internal struggle between various factions of Vietnamese society. Even the dispatch of American advisers to South Vietnam did not present as much a problem for Moscow as the growth of Chinese influence in the region. The Soviet Union could continue to issue statements and declarations appealing for a peaceful resolution of the problem of unification, could assure the DRV of its support in the struggle of South Vietnamese patriots, could provide them—through Hanoi—with token aid in the form of German arms[6] and medical supplies, and meanwhile could build stable relations with the West. But the 1959 and 1960 decisions of the central committee of the Lao Dang party challenged these Kremlin tactics.

Also contributing to the transformation of Soviet views in

early 1964 was the quickly deepening split between the USSR and the PRC. The conflict between the two Communist parties and the two countries had now developed into an open rivalry with periods of truce becoming more and more rare. The Soviet-Chinese split had a powerful impact on Moscow's considerations about Southeast Asia.

Chinese influence in that region had always been strong, and geography was not the only reason. In the early 1960s China's position in the area, and particularly in Vietnam, grew even stronger. Chinese and Vietnamese Communists discovered they had much in common in their approach to the world Communist movement, the role of the national liberation struggle, and coexistence with capitalist countries. And they shared a strong feeling of nationalism which united them in their attitude toward their Soviet "comrades." As to the prospects for a unified Vietnam, there was also consensus between Hanoi and Beijing that military struggle represented the principal means to achieve this goal. Minor disagreements over such questions as whether North Vietnam should send its armed forces to assist the NLFSV in its offensive against the Americans and their "puppets," or whether the Viet Cong should rely on its own forces, were played down.

The growth of Chinese influence in Southeast Asia coincided with the relative decline of Soviet interest in the region. Khrushchev appears to have been convinced that the best way to handle circumstances was to let them develop with minimum Soviet involvement, limited mostly to propaganda support. This view remained unshaken after the visit of the Lao Dong party delegation to Moscow in January–February 1964.

The Vietnamese delegation, which arrived in Moscow on January 31, was headed by Le Duan and included such prominent representatives of the Hanoi leadership as Le Duc Tho and Hoang Van Hoan (both members of the politburo and secretaries of the central committee of the Lao Dong party). *Pravda* published a brief article on the arrival of the Vietnamese as well as on their stay in Moscow without any hint of the purpose of the visit. A reader might have thought the Vietnamese came primarily to see the sights of Moscow—the Lenin mausoleum, the Pioneer Palace, the Bolshoi theater.

But on February 9 *Pravda* printed a front-page story about a meeting in the Kremlin between the Vietnamese delegation and

First Secretary Khrushchev, along with a photo of the smiling Soviet leader and his beaming guests. The article noted that the meeting had been held in an atmosphere of "friendly frankness" and that questions of mutual interest had been discussed.

More important, the next paragraph stated that "both sides spoke out for the unity of the socialist camp and of the world Communist movement, for the strengthening of friendship and solidarity of the CPSU and the PTV [Russian acronym for the Workers' Party of Vietnam], of the Soviet Union and the Democratic Republic of Vietnam on the basis of Marxism-Leninism and principles of proletarian internationalism. *Both parties base their policy on the principles of the Declaration and the Statement of Communist and Workers' parties.*"[7] This last sentence implied that there were no differences between the two parties toward the problems that were at the center of the Soviet-Chinese dispute. The Lao Dong party seemed to be, according to the *Pravda* article, a strong supporter of the Soviets.

The real situation was more complicated. A March 1964 cable from the secretariat of the central committee of the Communist party of the Soviet Union to the Soviet ambassador in Paris presented a detailed account of discussions during the visit of Le Duan and his colleagues to the Soviet Union.[8] From the text of the cable it becomes clear that the visit had been planned by the Hanoi leadership for the purpose of advising its Soviet counterparts on the decisions of the Lao Dong party made at the December 1963 ninth plenum of its central committee, and to sound out Moscow's position on these decisions. Toward this end, the Vietnamese had prepared a seventy-three-page statement to explain their positions on "questions of peace and war, the national liberation movement, and the unity of the world Communist system and the socialist camp." Moreover, Le Duan noted that his delegation would touch upon only those questions on which the PTV's views differed from those of the CPSU.

The ninth plenum of the Workers' party had voiced a strong determination to prepare a general uprising in the South and had offered a strategy for this uprising. The plenum stressed the need to form "powerful armed units" and defined the struggle in three main areas of the South: mountains, countryside, and cities. The Vietnamese Communists were convinced that the "correlation of forces" had become favorable to them and offered a strong possibility for the success of the revolution in South Vietnam, though its final victory could be achieved only after a transitional period.[9]

The decision of the ninth plenum to pursue a military struggle demanded not only mobilization of all DRV resources but also the support of allies, particularly China and the Soviet Union. The leadership of the Workers' party went to Moscow on a kind of reconnaissance mission, to determine the Soviet position.

During their meetings with Soviet leaders, the Vietnamese envoys did not confine themselves to problems of Vietnam and Southeast Asia. They wanted to know the Soviet position on a broad spectrum of issues, for they understood that any disagreement might thwart or seriously complicate cooperation between the two countries. Moscow's impression in these discussions was that their Vietnamese counterparts' views reflected the strong influence of Beijing but were more flexible.

Le Duan and his colleagues did not avoid criticism of the Soviet position on such issues as peaceful coexistence with the West, Soviet assistance to India in her conflict with China, refusal to help the Chinese build nuclear weapons, and the lack of support for national liberation movements. The Vietnamese believed there was a real danger of nuclear war and that peace could be defended solely by means of revolutionary struggle. Peaceful coexistence with capitalist countries worked against the intensification of this struggle "to throw back imperialism and overthrow it piece by piece." "In other words," the Soviets concluded, "the PTV leadership . . . actually exclude an opportunity to pursue a policy of peaceful coexistence."[10]

Expressing their views on national liberation movements, Le Duan, according to Moscow, exaggerated their role in the "world revolutionary process." The Vietnamese Communists placed the center of "revolutionary storms" in the third world and believed in the possibility of socialist revolutions in Asia, Africa, and Latin America earlier than in the developed countries of the West. Thus the main task of the socialist countries and the world Communist movement was to concentrate their efforts on a "breakthrough of this weak link in the chain of imperialism." The PTV leadership was convinced there were almost no conditions suitable for organizing national democratic revolutions and moving on to socialism peacefully.

Vietnamese leaders believed, the Soviets concluded, that national liberation movements, not the world socialist system, played the leading role in the "world revolutionary process." As a result, the guests from Hanoi "belittle[d] the importance of assistance the Soviet Union and other socialist countries provide[d] to the strugglers for freedom and national independence."[11] The DRV envoys also stressed the struggle against revisionism and the unity of the world Communist movement. They supported the idea of a new international conference of Communist and Workers' parties but insisted on preliminary negotiations between the CPSU and the Chinese Communist Party (CCP).

The Soviet leaders could not have been satisfied with Hanoi's position. Khrushchev let the Vietnamese understand that there would be no prospects for close cooperation between the two countries unless Hanoi changed its position. When he met with Le Duan and other delegates in the Kremlin, he emphasized "frankly and in a friendly manner" the discrepancy between statements of the Vietnamese leadership expressing sympathy toward the CPSU and the Soviet Union, and the real actions of the central committee of the Lao Dong party. Khrushchev warned his counterparts that such activity did not contribute to unity and cooperation between the PTV and CPSU, and did not correspond to the interests of the socialist camp and the world Communist movement. The Soviet leader openly expressed concern over decisions of the ninth plenum of the Workers' party and warned of possible repercussions of Hanoi's policy.[12]

Indeed, the impression created by *Pravda* on the meeting between Khrushchev and the Vietnamese delegation was misleading. There were more disagreements between the two countries than consensus. Nonetheless, Moscow remained optimistic about the visit. After noting that the Lao Dong party leadership had evidently adopted a pro-Chinese position, the secretariat of the CPSU central committee wrote in its cable to France, "Along with that, the behavior of the Vietnamese delegates, the tone of their presentations make it possible to conclude that the CPSU and other fraternal parties can maintain and develop contacts with the PTV while patiently explaining to them the general direction of the world Communist movement that was agreed to at international conferences in 1957 and 1960, and demonstrating the harmfulness of the present course of the Chinese splinters and those who support them."[13]

Apparently the Soviets, though dissatisfied with the views of their Vietnamese comrades, did not wish to exclude prospects for cooperation. But it was implied that this cooperation would depend upon a favorable change of attitude by Hanoi toward Moscow. Meanwhile the Soviets would confine themselves solely to moral support. And propaganda followed a few days after the visit, thus demonstrating to the world, but especially to Beijing and Hanoi, that the USSR remained a reliable ally. Of course, this vigorous propaganda may have been designed to compensate for Moscow's unwillingness to provide more substantive aid.

On February 12, 1964, only two days after the Vietnamese delegation left Moscow, *Pravda* published an article entitled "It Is Impossible to Overcome South Vietnam Patriots." It was signed significantly "Observer." The anonymous author assured "patriots" that the Soviet Union supported the just struggle of the Vietnamese people and that the Soviet Union remained "a reliable friend of all peoples who fight for peace, freedom, and national liberation."[14]

Two weeks later *Pravda* again published a piece on Vietnam, but this time it was an official statement issued by TASS declaring that "the Soviet people cannot be indifferent" to developments in Southeast Asia. It emphasized again that the Soviets were "loyal supporters of the policy of solidarity with peoples" who fought for freedom and independence, and that the USSR followed with "deep sympathy" the just national liberation struggle of the South Vietnamese patriots and would give necessary support to this struggle.[15]

This pledge of "necessary support" may have been designed for the consumption not only of Moscow's Vietnamese friends but also for the United States. Soviet leaders understood that dangerous developments in Southeast Asia could be prevented if restraint could be placed not only on Hanoi but on Washington. That is why Moscow repeated tirelessly that termination of the American involvement in Vietnam was essential for the normalization of the situation in Southeast Asia.

That promises of support for the Viet Cong were merely a propaganda chip designed to bolster the Soviet position vis-à-vis its Communist allies became evident during the July 1964 visit to Moscow of a delegation from the National Liberation Front of South Vietnam. South Vietnamese Communists had been invited by the Soviet Afro-Asian Solidarity Committee. This fact in itself testified that Soviet leaders were avoiding official contacts with the Viet Cong on the governmental level. During meetings with representatives of the committee, the South Vietnamese made a number of requests, including those for increased supplies of arms and ammunition. They asked in particular for antiaircraft artillery, antitank guns, medical supplies, and money in American dollars. They were also prepared to open a permanent NLFSV mission in the USSR, provided an invitation was forthcoming from the Soviet government.

The Afro-Asian Solidarity Committee proposed that the central committee of the Communist party receive the NLFSV delegation. This proposal as well as the requests of the South Vietnamese were considered by the International Department, which prepared a draft of the reply to the "patriots." It suggested that the Soviet Afro-Asian Solidarity Committee and other Soviet *public* organizations were ready to supply the NLFSV with medical supplies, to invite a new group of wounded soldiers for treatment in Soviet hospitals, and to allow children and young people from South Vietnam to study in colleges and universities in the Soviet Union. On the question of military aid, the department suggested informing the delegates that this issue was a state responsibility and must be decided on an official level between the USSR and the DRV, since shipments of arms for the NLFSV went through Hanoi. But the International Department recommended against receiving the delegation in the central committee, for in that case the "patriots" might "again raise the questions of aid with arms and money and it would be necessary to give them a definite answer." Accordingly the department suggested evading the problem of a permanent NLFSV mission in the USSR.[16] Soviet leaders agreed with these recommendations.

Soviet policy toward Vietnam—that is, propaganda support but restraint in all other spheres of activity—had its limits. Certainly Hanoi was not satisfied with Moscow's position. To realize their plans for unification of the country, the North Vietnamese needed substantial assistance in the form of arms, ammunition, food, and transport equipment from their allies. By the summer of 1964 only Communist China was prepared to provide such aid, which at least partly coincided with Beijing's own views on developments in Southeast Asia. As a result, Soviet positions in the DRV and in the NLFSV quickly eroded while Chinese influence steadily grew.

Moscow would have reconciled itself to this position had the situation in the region remained stable. But the course of events in Indochina gradually led to war. If the Soviets hoped to dissuade the North Vietnamese from a military solution of their problem by refusing to lend them all-out support, they failed. Hanoi persisted in its determination to achieve its goal by all means, including military ones. Hanoi's stance was confirmed, for instance, by Spasovski, the Polish representative to the International Control Commission (ICC) on Vietnam. In a conversation with Konstantin Krutikov, Soviet ambassador to Cambodia, Spasovski, who had just visited Hanoi, told his Soviet colleague that the North Vietnamese were ready to fight the Americans and the Saigon regime for total victory, even if it meant a war of many years.[17]

Beijing stimulated the North Vietnamese leadership's determination to wage a long war. As early as 1956 Mao Zedong had told Vietnamese leaders, "It is impossible to resolve the problem of the division of Vietnam during a short period of time. It may demand a long time. . . . If ten years prove to be not enough, we must be ready to wait one hundred years."[18] Chinese officials later repeated this idea over and over again.

Likewise, the hope of Soviet leaders that their militant declarations in support of the National Liberation Front might deter the United States from escalating its involvement in the conflict in Indochina turned out to be futile. In the same conversation with Krutikov, Spasovski quoted DRV Premier Pham Van Dong as saying that the North Vietnamese could create favorable conditions for an American withdrawal with honor, provided the U.S. government wanted it. Unfortunately, noted Spasovski, the Americans did not yet show such a desire.[19]

Moscow's unease grew as the situation in Southeast Asia became more and more complicated. It showed itself in the demarche of the Soviet government on July 27.[20] The threat to resign as a cochairman of the Geneva Conference on Laos was a clear warning from Moscow to the participants of the conflict in Indochina. But even this demonstration could not slow the pace of the conflict, which became dangerously visible several days later in the Gulf of Tonkin, when the United States charged that two of its destroyers on patrol duty had been attacked by North Vietnamese torpedo boats.

On August 3 *Pravda* published a short piece on the events in the Tonkin Gulf with reference to its source: the headquarters of the U.S. Commander-in-Chief, Pacific (CINCPAC).[21] Scarcely anyone among ordinary readers of the newspaper paid attention to this paragraph. Few of them even knew where the gulf was. But for the Soviet leadership the news was significant: the situation in Southeast Asia had reached a danger point. While Vietnam was an internal struggle with limited participation by American advisers, Moscow could afford to confine itself to the purely symbolic support of North Vietnam and the NLFSV without deeper involvement in the complicated situation. Under these circumstances it could stand against the vigorous criticism of the Chinese who claimed that the Soviet Union sought to reach an understanding with the West at the expense of its allies. But once there was all-out war in Vietnam, the Kremlin would have to take a sharper position, even perhaps to the detriment of détente.

Such a contingency was not in the interests of Moscow policymakers. While they would not be reluctant to draw dividends from the U.S. entanglement in a serious conflict, Vietnam would be the wrong case—the USSR would have to deal with too many unknown factors and with too unreliable an ally. Thus the Soviets reacted to the Tonkin Gulf incident in a somewhat contradictory manner.

On August 5 TASS issued a statement which, along with its account of events, contained a warning to the United States that its actions could lead to a broad military conflict.[22] As observers noted, the tone of this statement was mild. The same day Chairman Khrushchev sent a letter to President Lyndon Johnson. Again, the wording of the letter was cautious and restrained. "From the very outset," the Soviet leader informed the president, he knew about events in the Gulf of Tonkin "solely from those statements which have been made these days in Washington, from the published orders to the American armed forces, from the reports of the news agencies and also from the statement . . . by the spokesman of the High Command of the Vietnamese People's Army. . . . We have no other information as yet."[23] By drawing Johnson's attention to his sources of information about the crisis, Khrushchev apparently wished to underline the fact that the Soviets were in no way behind the Tonkin Gulf skirmishes.

Then the Soviet premier put forward his arguments criticizing the militant response of the United States against the DRV, and noted the dangerous consequences the incident might have for the international situation. This seemed to be the Soviet leader's main concern. Khrushchev did not specify "those quarters and persons who do not conceal their desire to inflame passions, to pour oil on the flames, and whose militant frame of mind one should regard with great caution and restraint. . . ." Probably Khrushchev was referring to Republican presidential candidate Barry Goldwater, but the Soviet leader may also have had in mind Beijing with its support of the struggle for the violent unification of Vietnam.

Interestingly enough, in the same issue of *Pravda* that published news of the Tonkin Gulf incidents, a writer named Ivanov (a very common name in Russia) contributed an article entitled "War? Not Bad." The author cited statements made by high-ranking members of the Chinese government, namely Chen Yi, foreign minister of Communist China, and another, anonymous official, to the Austrian newspaper *Kurier.* "What are the high-ranking Chinese representatives speaking about?" asked Ivanov, and continued, "The world public is now anxious about the tense situation in Southeast Asia. The Soviet Union and other peace-loving countries make every effort to prevent inflaming conflict in this region of the globe. But the 'high-ranking member of the government of the PRC,' after vague reasoning, stated during the interview that 'war in Southeast Asia would not be such a bad thing.' "[24]

In any event, Khrushchev tried to persuade the American president to show composure and restraint toward developments in Indochina. His reference to the "enormous responsibility" of the two great powers "in ensuring that dangerous events whichever area of the globe they begin with, would not become first elements in the chain of ever more critical and maybe irreversible events" was bolstered by the Soviet Union's publicly impartial posture toward the conflict. He emphasized that no one had asked the Soviet government to address the president in connection with developments in the Tonkin Gulf. "If there appears a threat to peace, I am deeply convinced that we should not wait for requests and appeals from anybody but must act so as to remove that threat without delay."[25]

Khrushchev's appeal, however, did not alter U.S. determination to counter the North Vietnamese "aggression" against the Saigon regime. Johnson's reply to the Soviet leader's letter left Moscow small hope that developments in Southeast Asia would change radically for the better. The president emphasized again that his country "will always be prompt and firm in its positive reply to acts of aggression, and our power is equal to any such test."[26]

With Johnson's negative response, it became clear to Soviet leaders that the Tonkin Gulf incidents marked a new turning point in Indochina. As Douglas Pike put it, "While in itself not particularly important, the Tonkin Gulf incident symbolized the new relationship that Hanoi required with Moscow. The nature of the war was changing, as was its image: from barefooted Viet Cong with their homemade shotguns to Vietnamese Communist armies equipped with the best weapons the Communist world could produce."[27] But some time would pass before both the Soviet Union and North Vietnam arrived at full-scale cooperation in the war against "American imperialism."

Meanwhile, Moscow took the first step on the road to rapprochement with Hanoi. A new Soviet ambassador to the DRV had been appointed in the last days of August 1964. Ilia S. Shcherbakov was a prominent figure in the Soviet Communist party hierarchy. Since the 1930s he had enjoyed a career as a party functionary, and in 1949 he had been named to a post in the central committee's International Department. He was a graduate of the Military-Diplomatic Academy, a well-known Soviet institution which trained intelligence cadres for the USSR foreign service. In the central committee Shcherbakov rose quickly; by 1953 he had become chief of a division of the International Department that supervised relations with Communist parties in socialist countries. Just before his appointment to Hanoi, Shcherbakov had been sent to Beijing as minister-counselor. Thus the new ambassador was proficient not only in party activities but in international politics.

In fact, Shcherbakov possessed all the necessary qualifications for the post of Soviet ambassador to the DRV. As the United States Information Agency noted in its report "Soviet Relations with North Viet-Nam Strengthened in Last Quarter of 1964," "What was needed in Hanoi was a man who thoroughly understood the situation, one who had experience in the area and one who retained the confidence of Kremlin leaders."[28] Shcherbakov's connections in the central committee allowed him not only to feel comfortable implementing Moscow's policy but also to express more or less freely his opinion on Soviet–North Vietnamese relations without fear that someone in the "Center" (i.e., the Kremlin) would object to his viewpoint. These factors had apparently been taken into consideration by Soviet leaders, who needed an accurate picture of events in Vietnam.

Shcherbakov arrived in Hanoi on September 23 and found Soviet influence in the DRV at low ebb. A pro-Chinese mood seemed overwhelming among North Vietnamese officials. Chinese propaganda swept the country. Articles in newspapers and journals hailed the North Vietnam–China friendship. Participants in public meetings greeted Beijing's demonstration of solidarity with the "just struggle of the Vietnamese people against imperialism and its puppets in Saigon." Various delegations traveled back and forth between the two countries. In the third quarter of 1964 there were thirty-two PRC-DRV exchanges against only three between the DRV and the Soviet Union.[29]

Particularly important was the development of China–North Vietnam military cooperation. In 1960 Hanoi and Beijing had allegedly agreed on a general direction for military cooperation. According to some sources, this agreement prohibited assistance from a third country without the approval of one of the two signatories.[30] Although the Soviet Union did provide military assistance, after 1960, the Chinese obviously made attempts to thwart Soviet aid to Vietnam. They are confirmed in a pamphlet Hanoi issued in the late 1970s, when relations between Communists in Vietnam and China had significantly deteriorated. According to the pamphlet, Deng Xiaoping offered Hanoi one billion Chinese yuan in exchange for a North Vietnamese refusal to accept any form of assistance from the Soviet Union.[31]

In 1964 the DRV and China began negotiations on a new military agreement. After the decision of the central committee of the Workers' Party of Vietnam to pursue military action, a delegation headed by Minister of Defense Lin Biao was invited to Hanoi. A new agreement signed in December 1964 included provisions for dispatching up to 300,000 Chinese troops (five infantry divisions and five antiaircraft divisions) to the northern provinces of the DRV in order to allow additional regiments of the Vietnamese People's Army to be sent to South Vietnam.[32]

Meanwhile, Soviet influence in the DRV armed forces weakened. The People's Liberation Army of Communist China, not the

Soviet army, gradually became a model for the North Vietnamese, and the role of Soviet military advisers in the DRV became more and more symbolic. Finally, in November 1964, the Soviet military attaché was told by the Vietnamese general staff that the DRV armed forces had "its own views" on strategy and tactics in the region, and they differed from those of the Soviets. Therefore the DRV Ministry of Defense informed the attaché that there was no longer any need for Soviet military experts in the country, and as soon as their term of business ended, they should leave. No replacements would be requested.[33] This was the clearest illustration of the diminished Soviet role in Vietnam in 1964.

Ambassador Shcherbakov presented his credentials to DRV Vice-President Ton Duc Thang on September 26. A little more than two weeks later, radical changes took place in Moscow. On October 15 the plenum of the central committee of the Communist Party of the Soviet Union replaced Khrushchev as its first secretary and elected to this post Leonid I. Brezhnev. Khrushchev was removed as chairman of the USSR council of ministers as well, and the plenum approved Alexei N. Kosygin's appointment as Soviet premier.

It has become a commonplace in the historiography of the Vietnam War to link the ouster of Khrushchev with a decisive turnabout in Soviet policy toward Vietnam. Some observers even claim that Khrushchev's removal was caused chiefly by his colleagues' dissatisfaction with his policy toward China and Vietnam.[34] But this is an exaggeration, based on ignorance of the real situation in the Soviet leadership by October 1964. In fact, the causes of Khrushchev's resignation had their roots primarily in the Soviets' domestic situation, with problems of foreign policy playing only a secondary role. Changes in the Soviet attitude toward the Vietnamese conflict after Khrushchev had less to do with prospects for cooperation with North Vietnam than with the changing situation in the region.

After the Tonkin Gulf incident, Moscow recognized that both North Vietnam and the United States were adamant in resolving the problem of Vietnam by military means. Events that followed confirmed Soviet misgivings. Moscow now faced a problem of reconciling its Communist prestige with its geopolitical interests. The former dictated that Moscow become deeply entangled in the war while the latter demanded complete disengagement—and thus a serious risk to Soviet influence in the socialist camp and the world Communist movement. Once war between the DRV and the Americans began, the question of support for a fraternal socialist country would become unavoidable. In addition, Moscow understood that Hanoi would inevitably seek aid from the Soviet Union as an international responsibility. As Ambassador Shcherbakov put it in his memorandum to Moscow, "It is believed here [in Hanoi] that socialist countries, especially China, will provide all-out support to the DRV. The USSR also will not be able to hold itself aloof and will receive requests for assistance which will be regarded, as always, as very important."[35] A Soviet refusal to provide assistance to the DRV would open Moscow to sharp criticism from China, which the Soviets would prefer to avoid.

But there was another reason why Moscow could not accept a course of "noninvolvement" in the Vietnamese conflict. Soviet leaders did not wish to abandon prospects for strengthening USSR positions in Southeast Asia. They hoped to use the DRV as a channel for Soviet political penetration into this strategically important region so as to attempt to swing such countries as Thailand, Malaysia, and the Philippines from pro-American positions to a more neutralist, if not pro-Soviet, course. If this initiative failed, Moscow would apparently be satisfied with some kind of understanding with the United States that divided the region into spheres of influence. Soviet leaders also had in mind their relations with European socialist countries. Moscow's failure to defend the DRV might make suspect its ability to protect such regimes as East Germany, Czechoslovakia, and Poland in a similar encounter with the West.[36]

Yet Moscow feared a deep commitment to a conflict in a remote region. The war in Vietnam threatened unpredictable consequences. The Soviets would have to deal with the highly independent and nationalist-oriented Vietnamese Communists who, moreover, were under the strong influence of Beijing. These unpredictable allies were likely to bring more difficulties than benefits. Then too, the Kremlin was reluctant to sacrifice its relationship with the West, particularly Soviet-American cooperation. And the possibility of the conflict spreading over other areas of the world might be fatal for Moscow's plans for détente.

Caught in this cross fire, Soviet leaders began to search for a way out. Changes in the Kremlin only intensified this process; they were not its starting point. This explains why Soviet policy shifts toward the Vietnamese conflict appeared so soon after the new "collective leadership" came to power.

New leaders in the Kremlin nonetheless announced that Soviet foreign policy would not be changed. They did it publicly from various podiums as well as privately in conversations with Western politicians. The Soviet ambassador in Washington, Anatolii Dobrynin, for instance, met with President Johnson to assure him that Moscow remained committed to its international obligations, and *Pravda* promptly reported to the Soviet people about this meeting.[37]

Regardless, by November Moscow was ready to move from purely propaganda support of Hanoi and the NLFSV to more substantial aid. Soviet leaders did not withdraw from their relations with the United States, but after November these were linked to the course of U.S. policy in Vietnam. One new important feature was added to Soviet policy in this crucial period: efforts by Soviet leaders to find a peaceful means to settle the conflict in Southeast Asia.

Thus, as Douglas Pike has noted, Soviet policy during the Vietnam War had three dimensions. First, Moscow decided that within limits Hanoi would be provided with all the necessary military and economic assistance needed to pursue its war. Second, the USSR would not sacrifice a strategy of détente in its relations with the West but instead would adjust Vietnamese policy to this course "if and when necessary." Third, the Soviet Union "would place great emphasis on a negotiated settlement outcome of the war as the best insurance against being drawn further into it (since it could always counter a Hanoi appeal for intervention with a new proposal for political settlement), even though it recognized that this policy would not go down well in Hanoi. . . ."[38]

Contours of the new Soviet attitude became evident in November. On November 9 Soviet Premier Kosygin received a DRV delegation headed by Pham Van Dong that had come to Moscow to participate in festivities for the forty-seventh anniversary of the October Revolution.[39] It was the first public visit of Hanoi leaders after the ouster of Khrushchev, though a secret one had occurred in October, soon after the Soviet Communist party plenum, when

Hanoi, anxious to maintain relations with the new Soviet leaders and get from them what they had failed to get from Khrushchev, had sent the DRV premier to Moscow.

In November, as in October, Soviet cooperation with Hanoi was clearly the main subject of the talks. There is good reason to believe that the parties reached an understanding in principle on Soviet aid to the DRV, including military, and that a Soviet leader would shortly visit North Vietnam to work out details. A TASS statement of November 27 contains, for the first time, a promise of aid to North Vietnam coupled with a warning: "Those who nurture adventuristic plans in the Indochinese peninsula must be aware that the Soviet Union will not remain indifferent to the fate of the fraternal socialist country and is prepared to extend to it the necessary assistance."[40]

Moving ahead, on December 24 the politburo invited the NLFSV to open a permanent mission in the Soviet Union. Moscow agreed on this step in the wake of similar decisions by China and other socialist countries, so that its invitation might appear more significant. In December Soviet leaders undertook one of their last attempts to restrain the United States from direct involvement in the war in Vietnam. On December 9 Soviet Foreign Minister Andrei Gromyko, who was visiting the United States to attend the UN General Assembly, met at the Soviet embassy in Washington with U.S. Secretary of State Dean Rusk. Vietnam was a subject of their conversation. Gromyko tried to convince his counterpart that "the U.S. had made a great mistake by getting involved in South Vietnam, because there were no U.S. interests involved in that area." He also wondered "what the real U.S. intentions were."[41]

Rusk put forward Washington's usual arguments about the Communist threat from Beijing and Hanoi, U.S. obligations to the Saigon government, and the justifiability of U.S. goals. Gromyko must have noted Rusk's emphasis on U.S. determination to meet its obligations. "The Secretary repeated that if Hanoi and Peiping left their neighbors alone, we would not be there; otherwise, he stressed, we were in a serious situation. . . . Again, he could only say that if Hanoi and Peiping left the area alone, we would come home; otherwise, *there would be a real scrap*."[42]

These American statements reached Moscow along with similarly unpromising information from Hanoi. Shcherbakov wrote from the DRV capital, "Considering decisions of the Politburo [of the central committee of the Workers' Party of Vietnam] and other events, it is possible to suggest that plans of the Vietnamese leadership will be focused to the gradual augmentation of the NLFSV forces and intensification of military operations along with simultaneous activity to undermine the puppet regime from the inside. . . ."[43]

Pulling together these and other facts, Soviet officials hurriedly made final adjustments in their policy toward Vietnam while war seemed not months but days away.

TWO

Turning Points

If it is not necessary to be skillful to start a war, events in early 1965 would seem to support this notion. It was enough for political leaders blindly to follow developments in Southeast Asia in order to find themselves in a situation where war became the only choice. This was particularly true for the Johnson administration, though Soviet leaders faced a somewhat similar problem.

The U.S. position in South Vietnam deteriorated rapidly during the last months of 1964. The government in Saigon remained unstable, and various pacification programs designed to strengthen it in the countryside proved ineffective. The South Vietnamese army was passive before the growing activity of the Viet Cong. Between December 26 and January 2, well-armed and well-trained South Vietnamese army units, supported by American advisers and equipment, were defeated in a battle at Bien Gia.[1] According to the CIA, the National Liberation Front of South Vietnam had now "extended its influence, if not its control, into nearly every corner of South Vietnam." The NLF claimed to control three-quarters of the country and eight million of its fourteen million people.[2]

Reports from the American embassy in Saigon concurred with the CIA's estimates. U.S. officials in South Vietnam believed that North Vietnamese leaders could look back on 1964 "with some measure of satisfaction." Armed insurgency in South Vietnam had developed favorably. The Viet Cong had expanded the area and scope of its operations and enjoyed a number of military successes. The failure of the United States and the Saigon regime to put down this insurgency had resulted in the further demoralization of the army and the growth of political instability in the country—in contrast with the domestic political scene in the North, where there was "no change apparent in top-level leadership or in major policies. . . ."[3]

Heightened concern in Washington over the course of these events led President Johnson and his advisers to lean increasingly toward a military solution in Vietnam. In late November 1964 a two-phase plan was worked out in Washington which included air strikes on the North as an ultimate measure to force Hanoi to cease its support of the NLF. Although these strikes were not on Washington's agenda at that time, their approval by President Johnson reflected the mood of the administration.

The success of the NLF in early January 1965 reinforced the mood of American policymakers. Toward the end of that month they viewed retaliation against the DRV as the only appropriate way to resolve the Vietnam problem. This was the principal idea expressed in National Security Adviser McGeorge Bundy's memorandum to the president on January 27, known as the "Fork in the Y Memo." The author, who also spoke for Secretary of Defense Robert McNamara, saw only two alternatives for Vietnam. "The *first* is to use our military power in the Far East and to force a change of Communist policy. The *second* is to deploy all our resources along a track of negotiation, aimed at salvaging what little can be preserved with no major addition to our present military risks."[4] Clearly the second alternative was not on the U.S. agenda.

Washington understood that moving toward a military solution of the conflict in Indochina involved certain risks and a number of unknown quantities, among them a possible Soviet reaction to a U.S. military attack on the Democratic Republic of Vietnam. American leaders seriously considered this prospect during January and early February, pondering their arguments in support of or against military involvement.

Three main questions arose in the minds of American leaders. The first touched upon forms of Soviet involvement in the conflict. American leaders also discussed the effect of American escalation on Sino-Soviet relations. Finally, prospects for détente in general and Soviet-American relations in particular were also considered in Washington.

American leadership did not expect the Soviets to stand aside in the event of a U.S. attack on the DRV. But what would be Moscow's attitude toward the prospects of war in Southeast Asia, and what kind of assistance would they be ready to provide North Vietnam if the United States implemented its plans for retaliation against Hanoi? These questions seemed to concern Secretary of State Rusk when, on January 8, he appeared before the Senate Foreign Relations Committee to talk about the situation in Southeast Asia. According to Rusk, the Soviet Union wished to avoid engagement with the United States in the struggle in this region. Moreover, the Soviets feared the consequences of a conflict between North Vietnam and Communist China on the one side, and "the leader of the capitalist world" on the other. "We have had some indication that they are worried about that particular prospect down the long trail here in this situation," Rusk claimed.[5]

The CIA shared this view when it reported in January that the "Soviet Union appears to be increasingly concerned over the possibility of escalation of the fighting in both South Vietnam and Laos and is searching for some means of inhibiting the actions of both the US and North Vietnam."[6] As to Moscow's plans for supporting its Vietnamese allies, the CIA suggested that the "Soviet response to the US program of air attack would consist both of a vigorous diplomatic and propaganda effort" coupled with military assistance to the North which "would almost certainly include antiaircraft artillery and radars." American intelligence was also convinced that North Vietnam would press the USSR for surface-to-air missiles and advanced jet fighters.[7]

By this time the Soviet Union had already begun its shipments for the DRV air defense system. In a February 3 memorandum, the CIA reported that Soviet antiaircraft weapons had recently shown up in North Vietnam.[8] On February 9 William Bundy, then assistant secretary of defense for international security affairs, supplied members of the Subcommittee on Far Eastern Affairs of the Senate Committee on Foreign Relations with information that Moscow had furnished "substantial" antiaircraft equipment for the key airfield in the Hanoi area.[9]

At the center of discussions in Washington in January and early February 1965 were two closely interrelated concerns over possible Soviet policy toward the United States and China. American policymakers believed that China was a major problem for the Soviets, considering the growing rivalry between the two powers for leadership of the world Communist movement. Because of this, according to the president's advisers, Moscow was prepared to strengthen its position among the socialist countries and even sacrifice some of its goals for détente with the West.

This notion was pronounced, for instance, by Llewellyn Thompson, a Soviet expert and ambassador at large, before the Senate Foreign Relations Committee on January 14. "Certainly in the next months, almost their [the Soviet leaders'] greater preoccupation is going to be their relations with Communist China," Thompson observed. "Since they are contending with the Communist Chinese for influence over other parties, everything they do will be looked at as to how it will affect that problem."[10] Thompson thought Soviet relations with the West would be "very low on their agenda."

Several days later Secretary Rusk expressed the same view even more bluntly while reporting to the committee on the situation in Southeast Asia. "My own present thinking," he stated, "is that the Chinese problem is a major preoccupation in Moscow and that anything that they and we are doing or talking about is going to be simply a part of their problem with Peiping, that in the most basic sense the Peiping problem is their No. 1 foreign policy problem."[11]

U.S. intelligence memoranda supported (and in some ways inspired) this viewpoint by analyzing the development of Soviet policy in Southeast Asia from the perspective of the Sino-Soviet rift. The outcome of this preoccupation with the Chinese, according to American analysts, was a more irreconcilable position for Moscow in the sphere of Soviet-American relations, especially in the case of U.S. planned actions against North Vietnam. In a Special National Intelligence Estimate just after U.S. retaliatory air strikes against North Vietnam, the U.S. Intelligence Board, after speculations on China's efforts to sharpen the Soviet dilemma, predicted that "general Soviet policy would harden against the US. This would tend to preclude moves toward a relaxation of tensions and to increase the USSR's verbal ugliness on other East-West issues." At the same time intelligence stated that the Soviets would not wish to provoke a major crisis elsewhere—for example, Berlin or Cuba—as a reaction to U.S. actions.[12]

Although Washington was concerned over a possible deterioration of Soviet-American relations, the prospect of a Sino-Soviet alliance was the real nightmare for American policymakers. Rusk believed that if the United States failed to take strong action to counter the Chinese threat in Southeast Asia, the Soviets and the Chinese would be inspired to unite their efforts to make "American imperialists" retreat in other regions of the world as well. As he put it in testimony before the Foreign Relations Committee, "If Peiping can demonstrate that their course of policy is paying substantial dividends, as successes in Southeast Asia and Indonesia would indicate, then there is a much greater possibility that Moscow would attempt to close the gap between Moscow and Peiping by moving toward Peiping's more militant attitude toward the world revolution."[13]

The secretary demonstrated this conviction again several days later before the same committee: "I do think that if Peiping achieves a stunning success in Southeast Asia or against India, it would increase the prospect that the Soviet Union would tend to close the gap with Peiping by moving toward Peiping's ideological orientation and tactical orientation. On the other hand, if the Red Chinese are stopped along their present frontiers, the chances are improved that Peiping, at least by stages, will move further toward more of a line of peaceful coexistence. *I don't expect that any time soon.*"[14]

An opposing view on the possibility of rapprochement between Moscow and Beijing was presented by Senate Majority Leader Mike Mansfield. In his letter to President Johnson after a discussion in the White House in early February on the retaliatory strikes against North Vietnam that followed the NLF attack at Pleiku, Mansfield argued that direct U.S. involvement in the Vietnam conflict would bring a "closer degree of cooperation by the Soviet Union and the Chinese. . . . It may well express itself in this situation by a resumption of major Russian military aid to China and transference through China of Soviet aid to North Vietnam. This would be most unfortunate because *one of the hopes of Western policy was to encourage the split between the two great communist powers, a hope which will now, I believe, lessen to a considerable degree.*"[15]

From the numerous discussions in Washington in early 1965 that would affect Soviet-American relations during the Vietnam

War, it is possible to discern two conclusions. First, that the Soviet Union was not pleased with the military conflict in Indochina and would prefer a peaceful settlement, the sooner the better. And, second, that in the long run the Soviets would not be willing to jeopardize their relations with the West in general, and with the United States in particular, because of this clash in a remote corner of the world.

While American analysts unraveled the threads of the international situation as it might be affected by U.S. actions in Vietnam, two events in February radically changed the situation there and marked another turning point in the conflict. On January 31 it was announced in the Moscow press that Soviet Premier Kosygin would visit Hanoi in early February. This visit must have represented a step forward in Soviet–North Vietnamese relations after the meeting between Soviet leaders and Pham Van Dong in October and November 1964.[16] The interval between these meetings and Kosygin's trip was marked by changes in the character of USSR-DRV bilateral relations. In addition to the opening in Moscow of a permanent NLF mission in late December 1964, the Soviets in January visibly increased their efforts to defend Hanoi from possible air strikes by delivering to the DRV antiaircraft weapons. And they intensified their propaganda support by condemning U.S. policy in Vietnam and in Southeast Asia. These shifts in Soviet policy had been welcomed by the Vietnamese comrades. Soviet diplomats informed Moscow that the NLF regarded with satisfaction news about Soviet support of their struggle.[17] At the same time they emphasized that Moscow's position in the region would depend on the scope of aid provided for the struggle.[18]

Doubtless Kosygin's visit was intended to consolidate the new basis of USSR-DRV relations and to define details of cooperation between the two countries, with military matters at the center of discussions. Thus the delegation included USSR Deputy Minister of Defense Marshal Konstantin Vershinin, Deputy Chairman of the State Committee on Foreign Trade General G. S. Sidorovich, and Minister of Civil Aviation Eugenii Loginov.

The CIA noted the importance of the Soviet visit in its intelligence memorandum on February 1. It observed that one of the main purposes of Kosygin's trip was to "strengthen the credibility of repeated public statements since November that the USSR 'cannot remain indifferent to the fate of a fraternal socialist country' and that it is ready to give Hanoi the 'necessary assistance.' " The agency viewed the visit as the "culmination of an exchange of views since Khrushchev's downfall."[19] But, according to American intelligence, Moscow was also pursuing other goals by sending a top-level delegation to Hanoi. Two months later the CIA, with the advantage of new evidence since the visit, suggested that "Kosygin probably intended to warn the North Vietnamese not to underestimate US determination to prevent a Communist victory in the south; his mission presumably was to urge Hanoi to avoid actions which might provoke US retaliation and alter the terms of the conflict and to play for time to allow political disintegration in Saigon to ripen."[20] Taking into account the delegation's two stopovers in Beijing, it became clear that the Soviets planned to come to an agreement with the Chinese as well.[21]

However well calculated were the aims of Kosygin's delegation, the Soviets soon discovered that at least some of their goals were unattainable. First, their desire to convince the Vietnamese to avoid provocations against the United States proved to be in vain. Just after Kosygin's arrival in Hanoi, NLF units raided a U.S. base at Pleiku, killing eight Americans and wounding sixty or more. That attack became a long-awaited pretext for U.S. retaliation. President Johnson approved immediate air strikes against DRV territory. Although Washington had earlier canceled a De Soto patrol (an intelligence-gathering mission in the Gulf of Tonkin along the coast of North Vietnam) until after Kosygin's visit in order to avoid harming Soviet-American relations, the attack at Pleiku provided such a wonderful opportunity to punish the North Vietnamese that the Soviet premier's presence in Hanoi could not deter Washington from such a move.[22]

There is no evidence that the Soviets knew in advance of the attack on Pleiku, notwithstanding arguments to the contrary.[23] Relations between the two countries had not yet reached a level where Hanoi was prepared to inform Moscow of its plans and actions in the South. For example, in early January an official of the Soviet embassy in the DRV, in a conversation with a representative of the North Vietnamese Committee on the Unification of the Country, tried to learn about forthcoming operations of the NLF, but to no avail. The diplomat concluded that "the Vietnamese comrades, as before, do not want to share with us any information, particularly concerning specific questions of the situation in South Vietnam, the NLFSV's activity and its plans for the future."[24]

Nor was Moscow interested in inspiring incidents in the South in order to provoke the United States, as R. B. Smith claims in his study of the Vietnam War.[25] The behavior of Soviet leaders before the event as well as their weak (even lack of) influence in Hanoi testifies that they scarcely had such intentions. American officials understood this quite well. There was not the slightest suspicion in Washington at the time that the Soviets might have known about the NLF's plans. Quite the contrary, all statements and documents confirmed the conviction of U.S. policymakers that Kosygin may have been "mouse-trapped by Hanoi."[26]

Nevertheless, President Johnson was aware of the likely effect on Moscow of U.S. reprisals. During discussions in the White House just after news of the attack on Pleiku had been received in Washington, not all the president's top advisers supported retaliatory strikes on DRV territory, primarily because of the damage they might cause to Soviet-American relations. Among the dissenters were Under Secretary of State George Ball, Mike Mansfield, and Llewellyn Thompson. In order to at least minimally repair this damage, Johnson approved measures to keep the Soviets informed on U.S. intentions in Vietnam. On the eve of a National Security Council (NSC) meeting on February 8, Thompson met with Soviet Ambassador Anatolii Dobrynin and tried to convince him that the United States had been forced to react to the Viet Cong attack. Johnson himself authorized the discussion with the Soviet ambassador, as he explained to congressional leaders, "because of the importance of conveying our views to the Russians."[27]

But these administration efforts could not prevent Moscow's negative reaction. On February 9 the Soviet government issued a statement recounting and explaining events in Vietnam, with a warning that the Soviet Union "along with its allies and friends" would have to take "further measures to protect the security and strengthen the defense of the Democratic Republic of Vietnam." More significant was a paragraph on Soviet-American relations. Soviet leaders emphasized that the development of bilateral relations was a mutual process, incompatible with "aggressive political actions that may negate steps toward the amelioration of Soviet-American relations."[28]

The next day Kosygin and Pham Van Dong published a joint statement that stressed the importance of the DRV as the "outpost of the socialist camp in Southeast Asia," its role in the struggle against "American imperialism," and its contribution to the defense of peace in Asia and throughout the world. The statement reaffirmed that the USSR would not "remain indifferent to ensuring the security of a fraternal socialist country" and would "give the DRV necessary aid and support."[29] The statement also revealed that the two countries had reached an understanding on steps to be taken to strengthen the defense capabilities of North Vietnam.

The Soviet propaganda campaign clearly stemmed from a feeling of indignation at the aggressive U.S. actions against North Vietnam during the visit of the Soviet premier to Hanoi. Moscow did not conceal its view that the timing of U.S. air strikes on DRV territory was an insult to Kosygin, the very outcome some of Johnson's advisers had feared. On February 10 a Soviet official in the United Nations affirmed that the Soviets considered U.S. bombings during Kosygin's visit to Hanoi an "unfriendly act."[30] Kosygin himself could not forget this "humiliation" and even a year later brought it up during a conversation with Vice-President Hubert Humphrey in New Delhi.[31]

But there were more substantial reasons for the exasperation of Soviet leaders. The Pleiku incident and U.S. retaliation destroyed what was left of Moscow's hope to avoid an internationalization of the conflict in Vietnam. As a result, the Soviet Union would be forced to set aside its policy of propaganda and noninvolvement and plunge into a war with unpredictable consequences.

The Soviet foreign policy dilemma was aggravated by worsening relations with Beijing. Kosygin's stopovers there demonstrated the irreconcilable aims of the two Communist giants. On his way back to Moscow the Soviet premier saw Mao Zedong on February 11, a meeting that did not produce positive results. The Chinese leadership rejected Soviet offers for reconciliation as well as a concrete proposal to coordinate assistance to the DRV.[32]

In this situation Soviet leaders adopted a policy that had begun to take shape late in 1964. First, Moscow would not risk a showdown with the United States. Although it condemned the latest actions of "American imperialism," its pronouncements were distinguished by a somewhat restrained tone. Likewise, Soviet leaders refrained from further warnings about the effect of American actions on bilateral relations, thus avoiding the notion of a possible future breakdown. Moscow was also relatively measured in its promises of support to Hanoi. In his televised speech on February 26, as State Department analysts noted, Kosygin said enough "to cover the Soviet rear against Chinese Communist allegations of Soviet infidelity to Hanoi, but far from committing the USSR to carte-blanche support for North Vietnam."[33]

Certainly this did not imply that the Soviets aimed to avoid providing substantial support to their Vietnamese friends. Indeed, the amount of Soviet aid to North Vietnam was impressive and was growing every year. But the restraint evident in Soviet statements at the initial stage of the conflict in Vietnam demonstrated Moscow's reluctance to make this aid a stumbling block in its relations with the West.

In addition to disguised signals, Moscow was eager to give the United States more obvious evidence that the Soviets would like to keep their channels of communication with the West open. On February 12 the CIA sent information to the State Department that a medium-level Soviet diplomat had advised his American interlocutor of the usefulness of unofficial contacts between the two powers in attempting to settle the conflict peacefully.[34]

Toward the end of March the CIA summarized private approaches by Soviet officials during the first days of the war's escalation. According to the CIA, these approaches continued "to stress Moscow's desire to avoid involvement in the Vietnam conflict and to cooperate with the US in moving toward a political settlement." A "consistent theme in the conversations," the CIA noted, was an emphasis on the mutual interest of the United States and the Soviet Union in reaching a peaceful settlement of the crisis.[35] Everyone acquainted with the methods of the Soviet hierarchy would understand that such approaches could not be made without instructions from above. Therefore these feelers reflected the position of the Soviet leadership and its desire to avoid an unnecessary aggravation of relations with Washington.

Moscow's highest officials themselves made it clear to American diplomats how their public stance should be perceived. American Ambassador to Moscow Foy Kohler informed the State Department on March 4 that despite the toughness of the Soviet line, the situation in the Soviet capital seemed "fluid," which meant that all channels of communication with the Soviets should be kept "in good working order in immediate future." The ambassador had been convinced by Gromyko's "almost flat admission," in reply to Kohler's question, that another Soviet "declaration" handed to the American ambassador was just a "propaganda piece" and could not be considered a reply of the Soviet government to Secretary Rusk's statements to Ambassador Dobrynin.[36]

In Washington these Soviet overtures were met with satisfaction in two respects. First, contacts between Soviet and American officials helped to keep each other informed on views and intentions and served as a guarantee against misunderstandings which might endanger bilateral relations. Second, the Soviets might provide a channel for communication with Hanoi or at least a way of informing Hanoi about American plans in Vietnam without the risk that this information would be deliberately distorted by, for example, Beijing.

These considerations helped to form recommendations on the importance of communication with the Soviets worked out by American ambassadors in Southeast Asia. On February 26 Maxwell Taylor from Saigon as well as U. Alexis Johnson, his deputy; William Sullivan, U.S. ambassador to Laos; and Graham Martin, U.S. ambassador to Thailand, sent to Washington their views on the possible role of the Soviet Union in the conflict.

Taylor was worried about the quality of information about U.S. objectives that Hanoi was receiving. He surmised that it might be considerably distorted by the Chinese. "To avoid this danger," Taylor argued, "we suggest possibility of communicating to Soviets exact and limited nature of our objectives, not with any request from us that they pass them on to Hanoi, but rather in hope that Soviets will do so in insurance of their own interests."[37]

Then he added his voice to a joint cable from the four ambassadors which discussed at length various problems of the Vietnam conflict. They stressed the strong influence the Chinese wielded in the DRV. The only *acceptable* alternative to the Chinese, according to the message, was the Soviet Union. "It is, therefore, important, that Soviets receive accurate indications that we would not oppose continuing Soviet role in DRV, to replace dominant influence of Chicoms [Chinese Communists]." At the same time the ambassadors were reluctant to *force* the Soviets to support the DRV. Although the American diplomats believed that the time for negotiations with the DRV had not yet come, they acknowledged such a possibility when the DRV, "presumably with Soviet support," accepted the division of Vietnam and agreed to its status as a "small, independent Communist nation north of 17th parallel."[38] Thus the document indicates that in February 1965 Washington was prepared to negotiate with North Vietnam only on its own terms, and that in doing so it did not exclude the help of the Soviet Union.

For Soviet leaders, the onset of U.S. military action against the DRV shrank their space for maneuver. "Proletarian solidarity" with the struggle for independence and against imperialism dictated its own rules. Despite its desire to settle the conflict peacefully, Moscow had to consider the wishes of its North Vietnamese ally. If, as Rusk claimed, Hanoi and Beijing were writing a scenario for U.S. actions in Southeast Asia,[39] the Soviets too were contributing, at least officially. Kosygin stated this in plain words in a conversation with a Western official in late February,[40] at a time when North Vietnamese leaders obviously intended to wage war for victory.

Still, American leaders could be satisfied with the situation following escalation of U.S. involvement in Vietnam. All their fears turned out to be exaggerated. Retaliatory strikes against North Vietnam as well as a program of continuing bombing of the DRV (code-named Rolling Thunder) and the ensuing deployment of American combat forces in South Vietnam had not led to a major world crisis or to a war with China and the Soviet Union. Moreover, Moscow seemed eager to help resolve the situation.

McGeorge Bundy, evaluating results of these first days of war, noted in his memorandum for the president that U.S. actions had not driven the Chinese and Soviets together. Although Hanoi was not yet persuaded to "leave its neighbors alone," the United States might have made a beginning. Most important, according to Bundy, Washington might "be moving, with less friction than we anticipated, toward a situation in which international opinion may regard our actions against the North as a natural reply against Viet Cong operations in the South." This was, wrote Bundy, reflecting the prevailing mood in Washington, "a new and important change; it will be most helpful to us against guerrilla infiltration over the long run, *whatever the eventual result in Vietnam.*"[41] Unfortunately Bundy did not know what the "eventual result in Vietnam" would be.

In Moscow, a degree of confusion and embarrassment during the first days of the escalation of the conflict had given way to earnest deliberation. Although they had expected an outbreak of hostilities in Vietnam, Soviet leaders had not yet settled on a course of policy. For months to come, the Soviets would improvise a policy toward the war while trying to measure their involvement in the conflict.

THREE

War in the Saddle

With President Johnson's decision to begin sustained reprisals against North Vietnam, the conflict in Indochina entered a new phase. Now military actions on both sides dictated a logic of their own to the participants. From March 1965 on, scenarios were already being written on the battlefield. Events between March and July 1965 proved that both Washington and Hanoi, contrary to their declarations in support of peaceful negotiations, saw military conflict as the only means to their ends.

The eleventh plenum of the Lao Dong party, held in March, confirmed the course of Vietnamese Communists on a military victory over "American imperialism." Meanwhile, decisions of the Johnson administration on the deployment of U.S. combat forces in South Vietnam, and the expansion of the air war against the DRV, showed American determination to suppress insurgency in the South and its supporters in the North. And new developments in Southeast Asia had repercussions in the capitals of friends and allies of the participants of the conflict; Moscow was among those who viewed events in Indochina with apprehension and uncertainty.

Because Soviet efforts to achieve a diplomatic settlement of the conflict had failed, Moscow was apparently inclined, at least for the time being, to concentrate instead on consolidating DRV defenses and meeting Chinese accusations of "betrayal" of the interests of socialism. In March Beijing intensified its campaign against the Soviet Union as a response to the conference of Communist and Workers' parties held in Moscow at the beginning of the month and to the first signs of rapprochement between the Soviets and the North Vietnamese after Kosygin's visit to Southeast Asia. The discontent of Chinese leaders had been demonstrated in an incident near the American embassy in Moscow on March 4. The next day *Pravda* informed its readers that a demonstration by foreign students who were studying in Soviet universities had been held in front of the American embassy, reportedly protesting U.S. aggression against Vietnam.[1] The report was brief and would have gone unnoticed if a week later, on March 13, *Pravda* had not published a note from the USSR Ministry of Foreign Affairs to the Chinese ambassador, in which Soviet authorities condemned the "vociferous propaganda campaign" unfolding in China and related to the March 4 demonstration. The note presented the Soviet version of that day's events and called the behavior of Chinese students during the demonstration an "attempt prepared in advance to provoke violent actions directed both against a foreign embassy and representatives of the Soviet authorities."[2] *Pravda* claimed that more than thirty militia and military had been beaten and four seriously injured by the Chinese.[3] When the Chinese government honored the students who were involved in this and a later incident, in ceremonies in Beijing after the students returned home, it seemed clear to Soviet leaders that Chinese authorities had been behind this "provocation."[4]

These events demonstrated that the rift between the two Communist giants not only had not been repaired after the American escalation in Vietnam, it had broadened despite Soviet efforts to create a "unified front" of socialist countries. The Soviet leadership now began to take vigorous steps to develop Soviet–North Vietnamese relations.

First, Moscow undertook to strengthen cooperation between the two countries in economic and military areas. The first important shipments of Soviet aid to Hanoi evidently took place in March as a consequence of agreements concluded during the February visit of the Soviet delegation to the DRV. Moscow initially used sea transport and confined its aid to supplies of food and equipment, but after a protocol between the USSR and China on the transit of Soviet aid through Chinese territory was concluded on March 30[5] (a minor concession by Beijing to the demands of the "united front"), growing amounts of arms and ammunition were moved from the Soviet Union for the People's Army of Vietnam.

Moscow meanwhile maintained a hard public line on the situation in Southeast Asia. Soviet propaganda intensified during March as the Kremlin spared no opportunity to declare its adherence to the "just cause" of the Vietnamese people and issued numerous statements condemning U.S. aggression. Moreover, Soviet leaders added a new wrinkle to their pronouncements in support of Hanoi. On March 24 Brezhnev spoke on Red Square to honor the just-returned Soviet cosmonauts of Voskhod II. Suddenly turning to the problem of the Vietnam War, Brezhnev routinely condemned "American imperialism" for its assault on the independence and territorial integrity of a socialist country. Then he noted that many Soviet citizens had volunteered to go to Vietnam to fight for freedom. The Soviet leader assured his audience that he understood "feelings of fraternal solidarity and socialist internationalism" which were finding their expression in these appeals of the Soviet people. His country, he emphasized, would fulfill its international obligation toward the DRV.[6]

Brezhnev's statement alarmed officials in Washington who feared nothing more than direct Soviet participation in the war. U.S. Ambassador Kohler in Moscow assessed the speech as the "opening gun in political and propaganda campaign designed to undermine U.S. position in Vietnam before the world, to alarm world opinion as to imminent escalation of hostilities . . . and thus persuade the world that the only alternative to serious deterioration of the situation is a conference on Soviet terms." Yet Kohler perceived the reference to volunteers only as a cover to allow Moscow to dispatch Soviet personnel to man sophisticated weaponry sent by the USSR to Hanoi.[7]

But this was scarcely Brezhnev's only purpose. While his principal motive was to demonstrate Soviet readiness to assist a fraternal socialist country by all possible means, his claim about Soviet volunteers was also aimed at Chinese accusations that "revisionists" in Moscow were ready to provide only halfhearted support to their allies so as not to spoil their relations with the "imperialists." And another clear objective was to strengthen the Soviet position in Hanoi, which called for a whole complex of Soviet efforts, not just "volunteers."

Sending volunteers to Vietnam was certainly not considered practical by Moscow in March 1965 (and, as we shall see, later as well). Brezhnev's reference was a response to the appeal of the National Liberation Front of South Vietnam on March 22 for assistance—including volunteers—from socialist countries in its struggle against "American imperialism." The real meaning of this appeal was revealed four days later in a conversation between the Soviet ambassador to Hanoi and DRV Deputy Foreign Minister Hoang Van Loi. Hoang confirmed that the campaign for volunteers played a "political role of expressing revolutionary solidarity and friendship of the peoples of the socialist countries." The NLF was grateful for Soviet support but did not yet need volunteers. They would be requested when necessary.[8]

For Hanoi, however, such a "necessity" was complicated by the Chinese factor. North Vietnamese leaders understood that they would be obliged to invite volunteers from the People's Republic of China as well as from the Soviet Union and other socialist countries. Despite close relations between the two Asian countries, there was an undercurrent of suspicion in Hanoi toward its "great northern neighbor" conditioned by experience. The North Vietnamese tried to cloak this "credibility gap" by referring to the rivalry between Moscow and Beijing as the principal obstacle in the question of volunteers and other logistical problems. One North Vietnamese expert also mentioned the question of subordinating volunteers to the Vietnamese command.[9] Though important, this problem could be resolved much more easily than Hanoi's fear of finding itself under Beijing's command.

Soviet volunteers and other aspects of Soviet–North Vietnamese relations were discussed during the April 1965 visit to Moscow of a DRV delegation headed by Le Duan. This visit appeared to be the last in a series of high-level meetings of leaders of the two countries that determined the direction and forms of cooperation under wartime conditions.

Information about the arrival of the North Vietnamese delegation was withheld by Soviet media until after the delegation left Moscow, attesting to the secret nature of the visit. Instead Soviet newspapers were filled with reports about the visit of a high-level delegation from Mongolia. Only on April 18 did *Pravda* publish the joint Soviet–North Vietnamese communiqué with information about the visit.

The communiqué informed the Soviet people that Le Duan, with DRV Minister of Defense Vo Nguyen Giap and Foreign Minister Nguyen Duy Trinh, had met with the highest Soviet authorities from April 10 to 17. The agenda of these negotiations was not revealed, but it could be inferred from the communiqué that the main item was Soviet-DRV cooperation in the North Vietnamese struggle against "American aggressors."

The communiqué contained two paragraphs that were important for an understanding of the negotiations. The first was a clear warning that, in the event U.S. aggression against the Democratic Republic of Vietnam continued, the Soviet government, "in accordance with the feelings of proletarian internationalism," would permit the departure to Vietnam of those Soviet citizens who expressed a desire to "fight for the just cause of the Vietnamese people, for preservation of socialist achievements" in the DRV, provided the government of North Vietnam requested volunteers. Second, the parties noted "with satisfaction" that the "earlier understanding" on "strengthening the defense potential of the DRV" was being carried out according "to the envisaged extent and procedure."[10]

Soviet leaders' satisfaction with the results of the negotiations was confirmed by Premier Kosygin several days later during a meeting honoring the Mongolian delegation. Kosygin told his audience about the visit of the North Vietnamese to Moscow and emphasized that negotiations between the Soviet and Vietnamese leaders had been a success. "They brought about positive results and helped to work out coordinated positions on the problems of forms and means of the struggle against the aggressive policy of American imperialism, of further strengthening the defense capacity of the socialist Vietnam as well as of a settlement of the problems of Indochina on the basis of the Geneva Accords."[11]

The April visit of the North Vietnamese to Moscow did not go unnoticed by Washington. The Johnson administration was anxious to learn of the outcome of the talks; the principal question was Soviet–North Vietnamese military cooperation. According to a special memorandum from the Board of National Estimates, the

USSR would "almost certainly" provide Hanoi with weaponry for antiaircraft defense. It would include surface-to-air missile batteries for areas around Hanoi, Haiphong, and other vital centers, and fighter aircraft—though the planes would be difficult to ship by rail without Chinese collaboration. As to military personnel, U.S. intelligence assumed the Soviets might dispatch "some pilots and technicians" under the guise of "volunteers." It questioned the likelihood of the Soviets deploying to Vietnam military forces that would include air defense units, ground units, a variety of other technical personnel, coastal naval vessels, and even submarines. Rather, the CIA and other intelligence suggested, the Soviet Union would choose a middle course between full-scale involvement and total disengagement, and "some sort of middle course" was "probably what emerged out of the April meeting in Moscow." But, the memorandum warned, if the crisis persisted at current or higher levels of risk and complication, "the middle way may not survive."[12]

The visit of Le Duan and his colleagues to Moscow may also have helped to resolve problems of transportation of Soviet aid through Chinese territory, and the stopover of the DRV delegation in Beijing on its way home probably had to do with arranging delivery of the aid. In fact, the CIA informed authorities in Washington in May that most of the problems relating to the Soviet aid had been settled and that "the arrival of the long expected Soviet military aid in North Vietnam may be imminent."[13] Later that month, on May 25, American intelligence reported the first signs of Soviet modern weapons in Vietnam: fifteen MIG 15/17s, probably sent to Vietnam by rail through China, in addition to one hundred armored personnel carriers equipped with antiaircraft guns.[14] Next day the State Department informed the American embassy in Moscow about the arrival in Vietnam of IL-28 light bombers, which the U.S. military had considered an offensive weapon during the 1962 Cuban missile crisis. Although State Department officials believed that the "preferred role of the aircraft in Moscow's view would be deterrence for the time being," they noted the determination of Soviet leaders to support their allies in North Vietnam by all possible means, even to the detriment of détente.[15]

Indeed, in the spring of 1965 Moscow demonstrated an unwillingness even to discuss prospects of a peaceful settlement in Vietnam. It seemed that Soviet leaders had renounced their earlier efforts to find a political solution to the dangerous situation. They flatly rejected any proposals that did not include the total cessation of American bombing of North Vietnamese territory.

While visiting London from March 16 to 20, Foreign Minister Gromyko, though he was "friendly and reasonably constructive" on problems of Soviet-British relations, was equally adamant with regard to a Vietnam settlement. He stonewalled every proposal to recall the Geneva Conference or any type of conference with the participation of the Soviet Union. His response was a "flat repetition" of the Soviet denunciation of the United States and a demand for unconditional withdrawal of American troops, equipment, and advisers.[16] Doubtless this attitude took into account the position of North Vietnam. Hanoi was ready to negotiate only on its own terms and was in no hurry to go to the conference table, preferring to gain military advantage and then to negotiate from a position of strength. The U.S. attitude was essentially the same.

Soviet leaders had been informed of the decisions of the eleventh plenum of the Lao Dong party as well as the intention of the United States to expand the presence and role of American forces in Vietnam. Soviet newspapers regularly provided their readers with the details of American plans during March and April 1965. In this situation Moscow apparently chose to strengthen its positions in the DRV and await further developments—a policy that seemed inadequate to Washington. While members of the Johnson administration believed the United States could always get to the conference table when necessary, and that there was "no great hurry about it right now,"[17] they felt pressure from various circles at home and abroad "to make explorations toward the possibility of talks" and considered the Soviet Union a potential ally in these explorations. Furthermore, American leaders hoped to keep channels of communication with Moscow open and get the Soviets involved in various peace initiatives as a guarantee against Soviet military involvement in the conflict. Finally, Washington viewed the Soviets as a welcome counterweight to Beijing in Southeast Asia and thus was ready to take some steps, however symbolic, to meet Soviet desires for a peaceful settlement of the Vietnam War. In this vein James Thomson and Chester Cooper of the National Security Council staff argued the case for a conference on Cambodia, proposed by Prince Sihanouk and supported by Moscow, in their memorandum to McGeorge Bundy on April 21.[18] These recommendations as well as those of other presidential advisers were clearly taken into account by the administration in April and early May as it pondered a bombing pause.

The May 1965 attempt to find a diplomatic solution of the conflict went forward when neither Washington nor Hanoi was ready to agree on a serious compromise of its objectives. From the outset it was thus doomed to failure. Nevertheless it proved useful as the first substantial test of attitudes of the countries involved in the conflict.

Project Mayflower, the code name of the first U.S. bombing pause, has been analyzed extensively by many scholars.[19] Here our analysis is confined to a brief account of the principal events of May 10–18 with emphasis on the role of the Soviet Union.

As mentioned earlier, pressure on the Johnson administration to move toward a peaceful settlement of the conflict in Indochina had mounted since the escalation of the war in February–March 1965. Not only was public opinion in the United States and abroad clamoring for a bombing halt and negotiations, but leaders from various countries were also calling for decisive peace moves. In Washington there was no consensus either. As Brian VanDeMark has noted, demands for a bombing halt came from the left as well as the right, for different reasons. While the left opposed further bombing in order to facilitate peace talks, "military and especially intelligence officials, doubting Rolling Thunder's ability to coerce North Vietnam into a settlement, began prodding LBJ to halt bombing briefly to test Hanoi's interest in negotiations, only to resume even more intense bombing thereafter."[20]

Johnson responded to this pressure by deciding on a bombing pause and ordering a simultaneous approach to the North Vietnamese with an offer to negotiate. He explained his decision in a May 10 cable to Ambassador Maxwell Taylor in Saigon. "You should understand," the president declared, "that my purpose in this plan is to begin to clear a path either toward restoration of peace or toward increased military action, depending upon the reactions of the Communists. We had amply demonstrated our determination and our commitment in the last two months, and I now wish to gain some flexibility."[21]

In its attempt to contact Hanoi, Washington counted on Soviet help. Moscow was to be approached in order to sound out the Kremlin's position toward diplomatic contacts between the warring parties and its possible role in arranging them. With this in mind, Secretary of State Rusk summoned Soviet Ambassador Dobrynin to his office on May 11 and informed him of the U.S. initiative along the lines of a message he planned to send to Kohler in Moscow the same day.

The cable to Kohler instructed the American ambassador to deliver a message to the North Vietnamese ambassador in Moscow, explaining that the United States was suspending its air attacks on North Vietnam for seven days beginning May 12. The ambassador was to emphasize the U.S. conviction that the "cause of trouble" in Southeast Asia was armed action against the South Vietnamese government by forces directed from North Vietnam. The American government would note whether during the bombing pause there were "significant reductions in such armed actions by such forces." Only in this case would an opportunity arise to bring a permanent end to American attacks on North Vietnam.[22]

Dobrynin's reaction to this information from Rusk reflected the attitude of the Soviet government at the time. According to Rusk, the Soviet ambassador *"was clearly relieved we [were] not asking them to act as intermediary."*[23] Apparently Soviet leaders were not eager to act as mediators between Hanoi and Washington, and Dobrynin knew this full well. Events confirmed this attitude.

When Kohler failed in his efforts to transmit a message to the North Vietnamese ambassador, he tried to reach any high-level official in the Soviet Foreign Ministry to ask for help in communicating with the North Vietnamese. The only official Kohler was able to meet with was Deputy Foreign Minister Nikolai Firyubin, who flatly declined his government's role as an intermediary and went on to lecture Kohler about the aggressive policy of the United States in Vietnam. Firyubin, who was responsible for Soviet relations with Asian countries, was acquainted with reports that the Soviet embassy in Hanoi sent to Moscow and therefore was acutely aware of North Vietnamese views on the prospects of the war and the Soviet role. These views were similar to those expressed in a later conversation between a member of the Vietnamese politburo, Le Duc Tho, and a French journalist. Le Duc Tho did not conceal his satisfaction with the economic and military aid and moral support rendered to the DRV by the Soviet Union. He noted, however, that Soviet leaders did not seem to believe in an ultimate victory of North Vietnam in the war, ". . . and this encourages them to search for a solution of the South Vietnamese question by means of negotiations; as to us, we think that conditions for negotiations have not yet ripened."[24]

Moscow could not fail to consider North Vietnamese suspicion of Soviet intentions with respect to a settlement of the Vietnamese conflict, and Firyubin was especially cautious not to jeopardize Moscow's efforts in March and April to create a solid ground for the Soviet position in Vietnam. Accordingly, his attacks on the U.S. position during his conversation with Kohler, his warnings that the American aggression would not "go unpunished, without response," his defense of the struggle in South Vietnam as a natural outcome of popular protest against oppression by the "Saigon puppets," seemed to be part of a ritual designed to avoid possible blame for "softness" on the part of Moscow.

But Firyubin, while refusing to be a "postman" between the two warring parties, "made no effort to return" the text of the oral communication which Kohler had handed him at the beginning of the conversation.[25] It may have been a deliberate move by the Soviets to see that Hanoi would eventually receive the U.S. offer, at least from the hands of Soviet comrades.

This was Kohler's understanding of Firyubin's behavior, and the ambassador remained surprisingly optimistic after his conversation. In a message to the State Department he confessed that he "could understand, if not sympathize with, Soviet sensitivity. . . ." He expressed a hope that Firyubin's reaction would not be viewed in Washington as evidence of a conscious hardening of the Soviet attitude. "It may simply be reflection of bind Soviets find themselves in at moment." Kohler was sure the U.S. message was already in DRV hands and that Washington should be on the alert for reaction from the other side.[26]

The ambassador's optimism had some basis. Just one day before the bombing pause, the Soviets had authorized a contact between "two somewhat shadowy officials" and Pierre Salinger, former press secretary to Presidents Kennedy and Johnson, who was in Moscow at the time on private business. Salinger was invited to dinner by Mikhail Sagatelyan of the Telegraph Agency of the Soviet Union. During the dinner Sagatelyan speculated at length on possible solutions to the conflict in Vietnam. Two nights later Salinger and Sagatelyan again met for dinner, this time joined by a Soviet Foreign Ministry representative identified only as Vasily

Sergeyevich. The Soviets confirmed their interest in a resolution in Vietnam and informed Salinger that the Soviet government had received the U.S. proposal to North Vietnam but would not answer it or act upon it until Soviet leaders were sure that something substantive would come from these meetings with Salinger.

"Throughout conversation," Kohler reported to Washington, "Soviets made clear to Salinger that because of sensitive Soviet position any progress toward political settlement Vietnam problem must be initiated and carried through, at least in preliminary stage, on basis unofficial contacts, clear implication being if leak should occur or if scheme should go awry, Soviet Government would be in position to disavow whole affair."[27] Sagatelyan clearly acted with the knowledge of the Soviet leadership, otherwise there was no reason for a Soviet journalist to touch upon the subject of Vietnam during a meeting with Salinger. Since Soviet officials were obliged to report on all meetings with Westerners, it might even be dangerous for Sagatelyan to raise this subject without prior authorization by his superiors.

One may therefore wonder about the purpose of Soviet officials who authorized the meetings with Salinger. Apparently Sagatelyan's task was twofold: to convey to the Americans Moscow's concern over developments in Vietnam and its desire to see the conflict settled, and to let Washington know that under the circumstances the Soviets had little room for maneuver, though the situation might change for the better. Perhaps the Kremlin was also probing the substance of the American proposals to North Vietnam. In any event, their interest in Sagatelyan's contacts waned.

A "brief Kaffeeklatsch" between Secretary Rusk and Foreign Minister Gromyko in Vienna on May 15 rounded off Soviet interest in Project Mayflower. During this "chat" Gromyko stated plainly that Moscow would not negotiate on Vietnam, that it viewed the temporary suspension of bombing as "insulting," and that the United States itself would have to find ways of establishing contact with North Vietnamese leaders. In light of the foreign minister's words, Rusk concluded that "Gromyko wanted me to believe that they are not prepared to work toward a settlement in Hanoi and Peiping and that, indeed, unless we abandon our effort in South Viet-Nam there will be very serious consequences ahead."[28]

Meanwhile, as officials in Washington had expected, Hanoi's

response to the American initiative was far from positive. Yet there were encouraging steps by Hanoi, notably a statement of the North Vietnamese National Assembly and an approach by the head of the DRV economic delegation in Paris, Mai Van Bo, to French diplomats. This approach, however, was made after the bombing resumed and was therefore too late to influence American decisions.[29]

Considering that Washington's objectives in the bombing pause were negative—to prove that Hanoi was not inclined toward a peaceful settlement—the results of the pause were confirming. Some months later Defense Secretary McNamara admitted: "Our first pause was a propaganda effort."[30] The substance of motives determines the substance of results in a situation where, to paraphrase Ralph Waldo Emerson, "war is in the saddle and rides mankind."

Meanwhile the scope of Soviet aid to North Vietnam was continuing to expand. The war's increasing demands forced Hanoi to ask for additional help from its socialist allies, first from the Soviet Union and China. The North Vietnamese thus sent a new delegation, headed by Pham Van Dong's deputy Le Thanh Nghi, to Moscow, Beijing, and the capitals of the Eastern European countries.

Pravda reported on the DRV delegation's arrival in Moscow on June 5, 1965, without referring to the goals of the visit.[31] But its importance became clear when news spread that Le Thanh Nghi was received first by Kosygin and then by Brezhnev. The talks, which took place between Kosygin's deputy Vladimir Novikov and the North Vietnamese, extended until July 10, with a break to allow Le Thanh Nghi to travel to Eastern Europe with the clear intention of coordinating socialist aid to the "fighting people of heroic Vietnam." In a communiqué issued after the visit and published by *Pravda* on July 13, the participants proclaimed that agreements had been reached on Soviet assistance in developing the people's economy and strengthening the defense capability of the Democratic Republic of Vietnam. They contained provisions on additional Soviet aid to North Vietnam beyond that already in the pipeline.[32]

Neither the amount nor the conditions of this aid were revealed by the negotiators, but the DRV council of ministers was "glad to note significant results in many areas achieved during these visits and negotiations."[33] Clearly North Vietnamese leaders were generally satisfied with the socialist countries' attitude toward aid to the DRV.

These negotiations in Moscow in June and July demonstrated that the Soviet Union was becoming more and more deeply involved in the conflict in Southeast Asia. Moreover, this involvement was not confined to defending North Vietnam in its encounter with the United States. Soviet leaders were fully aware that arms and ammunition produced in the USSR were being channeled to South Vietnamese "patriots" in direct conflict with Washington.[34] They seemed ready to take this risk. At least the Kremlin did not conceal its well-disposed attitude toward Viet Cong representatives in the Soviet capital.

The Soviet Union had agreed in December 1964 to open a permanent NLF mission in Moscow, but only in late April 1965 did the mission's staff arrive in the city. Kosygin received Dang Quang Minh, the head of the mission, on June 3, emphasizing the importance which the Soviet leadership attributed to its relations with the NLF.[35] At the same time this was a clear demonstration of Soviet determination to support the war in South Vietnam.

Yet Moscow was not willing to exceed certain limits of that risk. Soviet leaders could not fail to perceive the danger of an encounter with the United States, especially if Washington chose to resort to nuclear weapons to suppress the insurgency in South Vietnam. This seemed to be a real nightmare for Moscow because in the summer of 1965 reports on such a possibility reached the Kremlin regularly. For example, in June Soviet intelligence informed the Kremlin that in a conversation with Italian Foreign Minister Amintore Fanfani, Secretary of State Rusk had admitted that the prospect of using tactical nuclear weapons in Vietnam was on the agenda of American policymakers.[36] The USSR ministers of defense and foreign affairs and the KGB, in their report for the Soviet leadership in August, seriously considered the question of U.S. readiness to wage a thermonuclear war and the Johnson administration's intentions in this regard.[37]

Moscow could not neglect other pitfalls inherent in the USSR's involvement in Vietnam, such as the financial burden of aid to the DRV, aggravation of relations with the West, and incorrigible waywardness of the North Vietnamese comrades who viewed support of their struggle as the only duty of the Soviet people. All these factors pushed Soviet leaders to turn their eyes once again to relations with the United States—easier to do after Moscow had proved its adherence to the cause of North Vietnam.

For their gesture toward the United States, Soviet leaders used a reception arranged by the American embassy in Moscow in honor of a prominent diplomat and scholar, godfather of the cold war doctrine of "containment," and former ambassador to the Soviet Union, George F. Kennan, who was visiting in June apparently for his usual "sentimental journey" to the place of his youth. Foy Kohler invited to lunch at his residence, the famous Spaso House, several well-known Soviet officials, historians, and academicians, among them Foreign Minister Gromyko. Gromyko initially declined the invitation but then "suddenly" changed his mind and accepted while other invitees "suddenly" declined.

The conversation that took place on June 25 was significant from many points of view. According to Kohler, it "ranged over wide spectrum and throughout Gromyko was affable and gave impression of genuine desire to resume dialogue on basic issues which initiated in post-Cuba period."[38] After general discussion with Kennan on the problems of national liberation movements, Gromyko somewhat unexpectedly expressed a desire to convey to the American ambassador "two basic points": first, that the Soviets were not authorized and could not negotiate on behalf of North Vietnam, and, second, that it had been and continued to be "fundamental Soviet policy to seek improvement in U.S.-Soviet bilateral relations."

Developing the first statement, Gromkyo stressed that the Vietnamese situation had to be discussed directly with the DRV. The Soviet position was to support the four-point statement of Pham Van Dong of April 8. As in his conversation with Rusk in Vienna, Gromyko "cautioned" the Johnson administration that no progress could be made if future approaches to the DRV were cast in such "insulting" terms as they had been earlier.

As to Soviet-American relations, Gromyko noted that the Soviet government was disappointed by the "drastic change" in U.S. policy since the 1964 elections. He compared some measures of the Johnson administration to those that had been endorsed by Barry Goldwater in his electoral campaign.

Kohler tried to convince his counterpart that Washington understood quite well the difficulties faced by the Soviet government in dealing with the Vietnamese situation, first of all because of the attitudes of Hanoi and Beijing. But the Johnson administration remained hopeful that Moscow "would be prepared to bring its influence to bear on Hanoi in effort to bring about peaceful settlement of Vietnamese problem" which the United States did not wish to see escalated to a dangerous degree. The ambassador defended his country's actions in South Vietnam as consistent with previous U.S. policy and assured Gromyko that thus far there had been no change in the U.S. attitude toward relations with the Soviet Union. "We have consistently taken the position," stated Kohler, "that despite current difficulties, particularly in Vietnam, we desire continuing improvement in U.S.-Soviet relations on which such a significant start had been made in 1963."[39]

Gromyko apparently came to Spaso House not simply to reiterate that the Soviets were not in a position to play the role of intermediary between the United States and North Vietnam. His intention was also to reaffirm the Soviet interest in maintaining good relations with Washington. Kohler understood this and received the Soviet foreign minister's assurances enthusiastically, promising Gromyko that the U.S. government would do its part in developing relations between the two countries. In Kohler's report to Washington, he noted the fact of Gromyko's appearance at Spaso, his positive remarks on the U.S.-Soviet relationship, his affable mood, and his "almost wistful" recall of the atmosphere in 1963. Kohler concluded that there was "perhaps some new flexibility in Sov[iet] posture."[40]

Kohler's cable was received in Washington with mixed feelings. On one hand, as a staff member of the State Department's Bureau of Intelligence and Research observed in a memorandum to Llewellyn Thompson, Gromyko's visit as well as "other recent talk about channels of communication" suggested that "at the very least the Soviets might be getting worried that our relations are drifting out of control."[41] The fact that Gromyko refrained from objections during Kohler's pleas for Soviet pressure on Hanoi to negotiate was seen in Washington as another positive indication.

On the other hand, U.S. policymakers also noted Soviet efforts to outdo the Chinese in Southeast Asia in "revolutionary militancy" and some signs of Soviet hardening toward other international problems. Some members of the Johnson administration believed that the time had come for the USSR to move responsibly to reduce tensions in sensitive areas, primarily in Vietnam.

In light of Gromyko's assurances in his meeting with Kohler, Washington decided to probe the Soviet position more fully. This task was presumably in Secretary Rusk's mind when he called in Dobrynin on the eve of the latter's departure for Moscow, since this was a good opportunity to use the ambassador to carry home with him the American government's ideas on cooperation toward resolution of the conflict in Southeast Asia. This was all the more urgent for the Johnson administration because it was seriously considering plans for further Americanization of the war in Vietnam. Thus a discussion with Dobrynin could avoid a "misunderstanding" on the part of the Soviet leadership and could persuade the Kremlin that Washington was eager to find ways to end the war as soon as possible.

Rusk began his conversation with Dobrynin by restating his government's desire to see relations with the Soviet Union improved, a desire that remained unchanged despite sharp personal attacks on President Johnson in the Soviet press. The secretary of state then noted that "in the broadest sense" the key problem between the two countries was that of Southeast Asia. The U.S. government was ready to discuss this problem with the Soviets but was uncertain about the other side's attitude toward such a discussion.

After these introductory remarks Rusk speculated on the possibility of maintaining an "informal channel" of communication between Washington and Moscow on the problem of Vietnam. He understood Soviet concern about a possible disclosure of secret contacts between the two countries, Rusk said, but he was positive that private talks could be arranged and secured. Rusk concluded: "We understand that it is difficult for Moscow to bring this matter [i.e., the war in Vietnam] to its peaceful conclusion. There are also difficulties on our side. However, despite the existence of millions of Chinese, *there are only two countries, the Soviet Union and the United States, that can keep the peace.* We are puzzled as to how to proceed, assuming that both of us really want peace."[42]

To reinforce this conversation with the Soviet ambassador, Washington was planning to send W. Averell Harriman to Moscow to persuade the Soviets to take a more active role in negotiations. Harriman's name meant much in the history of Soviet-American relations. His experience in dealing with the Soviets went back to the early twenties when, as a young businessman and heir to one of the great American fortunes, he had received from Stalin's regime a concession for mining manganese in Soviet Georgia. Harriman's Georgian Manganese Company was an important part of the Soviet plan to win American recognition of the USSR through economic relations with the world's most developed capitalist country.

Harriman had come to Moscow for the first time in 1926 to meet with such famous Bolsheviks as Maxim Litvinov and Leon Trotsky. His next trips to the Soviet Union occurred during World War II, first as a special envoy of President Roosevelt, then as American ambassador to the Soviet Union. Harriman met with Stalin several times and gained vast experience in dealing with the dictator and his minions. Indeed, he won such respect in the USSR that his name became forever linked with the Soviet-Western alliance and victory over Hitler. Stalin himself paid special attention to the U.S. ambassador.

After the war Harriman remained a prominent figure in Soviet-American relations. He knew personally Khrushchev and Mikoyan. He met Kosygin when the latter was only one of Stalin's functionaries. As Harriman noted in a letter to President Johnson just after the 1964 election, "Presidents Roosevelt, Truman, and Kennedy used me as a pinch hitter for special negotiations, in addition to my regular duties. By luck or good fortune, my batting average has been surprisingly good."[43] Thus when the problem of finding appropriate channels of communication with the Soviets arose, Harriman seemed a logical candidate to be sent to Moscow—and he himself vigorously promoted this decision.

Harriman privately doubted the wisdom of U.S. involvement in Vietnam and believed in the need for a political settlement of the conflict. In his view, the road to peace in Indochina led through Moscow.[44] Harriman's confidence was based upon his estimate of the new Soviet leadership. Just after Khrushchev's ouster, Harriman confided to John McCloy, one of Johnson's close associates, that he knew Kosygin well and believed the new Soviet premier to be pragmatic.[45] This implied that for Kosygin, who was preoccupied with problems of the Soviet economy, the war in Indochina was an irritating obstacle that diverted money and other means for a needless imbroglio. Therefore, Harriman believed, Washington's desire to resolve the conflict as quickly as possible was in the Kremlin's interest, and it would be useful to maintain reliable channels of communication with Moscow and to ask the Soviet leaders for assistance in this matter. He was ready to go privately to Moscow on a reconnaissance mission.

He broached this subject with Ambassador Dobrynin in June and asked him to find out whether Moscow would approve his trip. Gromyko's conversation with Kohler and Kennan strengthened Harriman's determination to visit the Soviet Union, though, as he stressed in his telephone conversation with the Soviet ambassador, he did not wish to go unless Soviet leaders welcomed him.[46] Finally Dobrynin called on Harriman on July 1, 1965, and informed him that Soviet leaders had consented to meet with the former "special envoy to Churchill and Stalin."[47] Harriman, unlike Kennan, did not intend to take a "sentimental journey." In order to preserve the confidential nature of his visit, however, he announced his trip as an ordinary vacation.

Apparently this venture was wholly Harriman's initiative, but Johnson and Rusk then supported the idea of the ambassador at large (Harriman's official State Department title, though he preferred to be called "Governor," a legacy of his tenure as governor of New York). Rusk defined the goals of Harriman's visit in his conversation with Dobrynin on July 3. "The Secretary said he wished to make clear that he was not suggesting that Governor Harriman intended to get into formal negotiations" on the problems of Vietnam. "He said that Governor Harriman was, of course, aware of the United States position and familiar with our bilateral relations and would be glad to discuss them with the Soviet authorities." But his main task, said Rusk, was to determine Moscow's attitude toward contacts between the two capitals regarding U.S. involvement in the Vietnamese conflict.[48]

Neither the administration nor Harriman intended to reveal the true purpose of the mission. On the eve of the ambassador's departure, the State Department reminded him of the need to "discourage press speculation" about the trip, especially the Moscow portion, "as much as possible." Officially Mr. and Mrs. Harriman were on vacation. If the question arose as to whether Harriman expected to meet with Soviet authorities during his visit, the reply would not exclude such a possibility "in view of his position and personal acquaintance with officials of the French, Soviet and other governments."[49] The itinerary included Paris, Moscow, Brussels, West Germany, Rome, Belgrade, and London.

On July 8 Harriman arrived in Paris. There he discussed the principal aim of his trip with French Foreign Minister Couve de Murville. As soon as the French learned of the background of Harriman's mission, Couve drew the ambassador's attention to Moscow's difficult position. He noted that the Soviets "sincerely wanted peace but had no way to exercise any influence in this direction." They could not let the DRV down, Couve explained, but, on the other hand, they did not wish to risk increasing conflict.[50] With this discomforting information, Harriman left Paris for Moscow on July 12.

Harriman's announced purpose in Moscow was to attend an international film festival, though he had not entered a movie theatre in years and could barely remember a few films that had been shown for Stalin after banquets in the Kremlin.[51] As might be expected, this incongruity in the governor's behavior evoked interest among journalists, who asked administration representatives and even President Johnson about it. At his news conference on July 13, the president was asked whether Harriman's trip to Moscow had any connection with the Soviet position in Vietnam. Johnson stressed that Harriman was on vacation and had not been sent by the administration, though the president "approved heartily of his [Harriman's] statement that he would be glad to visit with any people that cared to visit with him."[52] Not surprisingly, Premier Kosygin was among those people.

Two meetings between Kosygin and Harriman took place in Moscow on July 15 and 21. On both occasions *Pravda* published brief information about these meetings without revealing details. Harriman, said the reports, was in the Soviet Union as a private citizen and had initiated these conversations.[53] Unlike *Pravda's* dreary prose, however, discussions between the two men seemed to be lively and emotional.

According to Harriman's report to Washington, Kosygin struck him as a sincere believer in communism and its ultimate victory. The premier "looked me squarely in the eye," wrote Harriman, when he talked about communism, liberation movements, and the U.S. endangering world peace. At the same time the American envoy found Kosygin pragmatic and not doctrinaire. He had enormous concern for the success of the Soviet economy. He made frank and sober statements about the international situation and how the Soviets understood it. In all, Harriman concluded that the premier had "conviction, determination, and courage."[54]

The subject of the talks ranged from Vietnam to Berlin to problems of nuclear weapons and bilateral relations. The Soviet premier complained that Johnson had changed course after the 1964 election, a recurrent Soviet remonstrance that showed itself in the depth of disappointment Moscow felt with regard to developments in Vietnam. The Soviets had figuratively voted for Johnson in the last election, Kosygin said, but the American president had not come up to their expectations.[55] Harriman tried to change this opinion of Johnson and may have succeeded, for Kosygin became "increasingly cordial in his expressions of desire" to meet the president.[56]

But the principal theme of the discussion was the Vietnamese conflict. Kosygin made it clear that the situation in Vietnam, though small in itself, affected relations between Moscow and Washington. However much Kosygin wished to see the Vietnam problem disappear, he nevertheless supported Pham Van Dong's four points and remained unconvinced by Harriman's assertions that the National Liberation Front was not the voice of the people of South Vietnam. He was clearly concerned about the Soviets' delicate position and sought to convey to Harriman that the row with Beijing was a most serious influence on Soviet policy toward Indochina.

Although he rejected the role of intermediary in the U.S.-DRV dispute, the Soviet premier was positive in his desire for a settlement in Vietnam and the retention of the 17th parallel as the demarcation line. This suggested that the Soviets did not object to the existence of two Vietnams, one of which would remain nonsocialist and perhaps with limited American forces on its territory.

His conversations with Kosygin left Harriman with contradictory feelings. As he stated in his report to Washington, "Visit to Moscow achieved somewhat more than the minimum I had expected and less than my highest hopes."[57] Certainly Harriman's arrival in the Soviet capital and his meetings with Kosygin proved to be useful in themselves. As Harriman noted, this was the first meeting of a representative of the Johnson administration with a member of the USSR ruling triumvirate since its coming to power in November 1964, except for incidental talks at receptions. The discussions helped clarify some problems of bilateral relations and of the world situation, and American leaders "gained some insight" into Soviet leaders' thinking, attitudes, and foreign affairs objectives.

What Harriman had not achieved was a firm Kremlin guarantee to exert pressure on Hanoi to negotiate on American terms. Special Assistant McGeorge Bundy remained skeptical about Harriman's accomplishments. It seemed "striking" to Bundy that Kosygin's comments were "rather routine": a standard list of disarmament objectives, a standard speech in favor of national liberation movements, a standard exchange on Vietnam.[58] The premier had apparently expressed an agreed Soviet position. But even in this position there were promising nuances for the United States.

The State Department's director of intelligence and research, Thomas Hughes, cited such nuances in a memorandum to Rusk. "Most suggestive" were Kosygin's remarks that the United States had to "counterpropose" something to Pham Van Dong's four points. This suggestion had "no precedent in authoritative Soviet or North Vietnamese comment." Hughes evaluated the Soviet premier's phraseology on Vietnam as a "serious suggestion and not simply as a means of washing his hands of the subject."[59] Kosygin implied that Hanoi did not rule out a political settlement and that its four points might be open to adjustment.

In a broader sense, Hughes wrote, the Soviet premier demonstrated that Soviet leaders were ready to discuss with Washington any problems which might seem appropriate. A "standard list" of Soviet declarations did not mean that it would remain unchanged forever, and Kosygin's apparent wish to see the Vietnamese conflict resolved, as well as his urging the United States to get together with North Vietnam in disregard of Beijing, implied that Moscow would move toward this end. But Washington had to take steps to facilitate this Soviet movement.

This idea of a U.S. adjustment dominated Harriman's conversation with Yosip Broz Tito, the Yugoslavian leader, when the old negotiator arrived in Belgrade after visits to Moscow, Brussels, Bonn, and Rome. Tito told Harriman that his impression from Moscow leaders was that the Indochinese situation was particularly difficult for the Soviet Union because of the U.S. bombing of North Vietnam. "The Soviet Union cannot fail in its stand of solidarity with Hanoi since it would otherwise expose itself to the danger of isolating itself in Southeast Asia and Communist parties elsewhere," explained Tito. As a Communist dictator, though an independent one, he understood Soviet concern full well. If the United States wanted Moscow's assistance, Tito stressed, it was first necessary to cease bombing the DRV.[60]

But the Johnson administration was not inclined to slow its military action against Hanoi. On the contrary, in July it was planning further escalation of the war in Vietnam. The same day Harriman met with Kosygin, Johnson held a meeting in the White House to discuss McNamara's recommendations to send an additional 200,000 U.S. troops to Vietnam.[61] These discussions among the administration and congressional leaders lasted until July 28 when the president announced his decision to raise the total of American forces in Vietnam from 75,000 to 125,000, stressing that additional forces would be sent later as requested.[62] The air war against North Vietnam was likewise to be intensified.

Although Kosygin could not have known of these plans when he spoke with Harriman, his posture took into account the possibility of further escalation of the war. Under such circumstances, Soviet leaders could not afford to take on any obligations with regard to settlement of the conflict. Besides, the Soviets knew that Hanoi's irreconcilable position was only strengthened by aggressive U.S. actions. The Johnson administration sought Moscow's assistance while undermining the basis for it.

Moscow's irritation showed itself on August 6 during a reception at the Kremlin honoring the Afghan king. Kosygin's speech included "unacceptable remarks about 'American imperialistic aggression in Viet-Nam,' " according to Kohler's report to Washington.[63]

Thus in the spring and summer of 1965 the war in Indochina approached a new, more dangerous phase despite attempts to prevent the fatal course of events. Peace initiatives failed to bring the warring parties to the negotiating table—and even some of those initiatives were little more than propaganda. Hanoi and Washington had not yet exhausted their bellicose potential.

FOUR

"A Rear Area of Vietnam"

In its war plans against the United States and the Saigon regime, the North Vietnamese leadership regarded the massive support of the "socialist camp" as an important condition of the victory of the "Vietnamese revolution." In his April 1965 speech setting forth the tasks facing the DRV after the start of the U.S. bombing of the North, Pham Van Dong stressed that the "more" the Vietnamese were "supported and assisted in all fields by the socialist camp, the more they will be able to struggle vigorously and resolutely" against their enemies. A year later the DRV premier reemphasized the importance of socialist aid, remarking that the "victories" of the Vietnamese people were the results not only of their own efforts but "of the infinitely valuable sympathy, support and assistance by the fraternal socialist countries."[1]

This was not simply a formalized declaration by Hanoi but an objective demand of the situation in Vietnam. Even relatively unbiased observers noted this fact in their conversations with Soviet officials. For example, the deputy chief of the Polish delegation to the International Control Commission on Vietnam told a Soviet diplomat in Cambodia that victory in South Vietnam would depend not only on the Vietnamese or the Americans but on the support of each country from the outside.[2]

In North Vietnam, the need for military and economic aid

from other socialist countries was conditioned by a primitive economy with the capability of producing only minor items of military equipment. The DRV relied on other countries for all its heavy weaponry and most of its small arms and ammunition.[3] It could not provide the most sophisticated weaponry, including supersonic jet aircraft, missiles, rockets, and radar, or sufficient quantities of even more simple arms. At the same time the war against such a powerful enemy as "American imperialism" demanded an efficient home front, capable of delivering every means for winning the war. And it was necessary to feed the army and the people and to repair damage inflicted by American air strikes. Undoubtedly Hanoi could not solve these problems without the help of its socialist allies, chiefly the Soviet Union and Communist China.

The Soviet Union stood at the top of the list of the DRV's suppliers. The character of Soviet economic and military aid was determined in the spring and summer of 1965, though first shipments from the USSR took place in January and February of that year. The amount of Soviet assistance grew steadily from 1965 to 1968. Moscow sent to North Vietnam industrial and telecommunications equipment, trucks, medical supplies, machine tools, iron ore, and nonferrous metals. In supplying its Vietnamese comrades the Soviets initially lagged behind the amount of aid from China. By 1967 overall socialist aid to the DRV accounted for approximately 1.5 billion rubles (more than $1.5 billion if converted to dollars at the Soviet official exchange rate of US $1=0.90 rubles). Moscow's share was 36.8 percent, or 547.3 million rubles ($608.1 million).[4] As the year passed, Soviet assistance grew to 50 percent of all socialist aid, and in 1968 it accounted for 524 million rubles ($582.2 million). This aid was entirely financed by long-term credits and grants.[5]

However important Soviet shipments were for DRV industry, telecommunications, and agriculture, the North Vietnamese were much more interested in Moscow's military aid. Military cooperation between the two countries received most of the attention of leaders in Moscow and Hanoi. The Soviets began to supply their Vietnamese allies with arms and military equipment in 1953, the year that appears in reports of Soviet officials. The amount of Soviet military aid prior to 1965 was insignificant; most was supplied by Communist China.[6]

The situation changed radically in 1965. The Soviet Union increased its military support of the DRV and gradually became the principal supplier of modern weaponry and equipment to North Vietnam. According to a Department of State memorandum of October 26, 1965, since the beginning of 1962 Moscow had provided the North Vietnamese government with approximately $200 million in military equipment, including aircraft. More than half of it had been delivered in 1965.[7]

In 1966–1967 Moscow assumed an obligation to deliver 500 million rubles in equipment for the North Vietnamese armed forces (approximately $550.5 million) and to reach a total of one billion rubles for military shipments since 1953.[8] But the Soviets actually exceeded this limit by 1968, reaching a figure of 1.1 billion rubles.[9] In 1968 military aid to North Vietnam comprised two-thirds of all Soviet assistance to the DRV and accounted for 357 million rubles ($396.7 million).[10]

The Soviet Union tried to satisfy requests from Hanoi for a wide variety of armaments and ammunition. Its main concern was to defend the DRV against American air attacks and to increase the air-defense capability of North Vietnam. Moscow sent to the DRV surface-to-air missiles, jet fighters, rockets, antiaircraft guns, and other hardware for air defense. American intelligence reported the first signs of this Soviet weaponry in the summer of 1965, though construction of air-defense sites around Hanoi and most important North Vietnamese airfields began in the spring of that year.[11] Almost at the outset air-defense equipment from the USSR demonstrated its effectiveness. On July 24, 1965, Soviet-made surface-to-air missiles were fired at U.S. aircraft for the first time and downed one of four F4Cs on their way to attack a target northwest of Hanoi.[12] During the Vietnam War highly mobile and virtually undetectable surface-to-air missiles often proved their potential in the fight against American air forces.[13] With jet aircraft, field artillery, and radar, they became a serious obstacle to U.S. plans to suppress North Vietnam by military efforts.

Modern armaments in themselves could not satisfy all of North Vietnam's needs. Hanoi also required well-trained military cadres who were experienced in manning modern weapons delivered from the USSR. This made the DRV dependent on Soviet advisers and demanded that North Vietnamese servicemen be sent to the Soviet Union for training. Each year during the Vietnam War several thousand soldiers and officers from the DRV were trained in Soviet military colleges. In 1966, according to a Soviet embassy's report, 2,600 Vietnamese were dispatched to the USSR to be schooled for service in the air forces and antiaircraft defense. In 1966 this training produced cadres for four antiaircraft regiments and technicians for an aircraft regiment as well as tens of pilots among those North Vietnamese who joined the People's Army of Vietnam.

Apparently some of those who trained in the Soviet Union then assumed command of NLF units in the South. Moscow knew of this, for the Vietnamese did not conceal from Soviet diplomats in Hanoi that they were sending increasing numbers of their soldiers to South Vietnam. Moreover, North Vietnamese regular troops were incorporated as the "main mobile forces" into the Viet Cong army which also consisted of "local armed forces" and "guerrillas." The "main mobile forces" were armed with modern submachine guns and mortars and were capable of participating in offensive combat operations and defending captured territory. They were responsible for assaults against American bases and airfields and for actions in various provinces of South Vietnam.[14] The number of DRV regular troops in the South was estimated by the USSR Foreign Ministry in 1967 at as many as 120,000 out of a Liberation Army of more than 300,000.[15] Since the presence of North Vietnamese regular units in the South was a secret to no one, least of all to the Americans, Hanoi officially acknowledged this fact by mid-1967.

Still, Moscow was not happy with this announcement. Soviet leaders were probably worried about their role in equipping units in the South with modern weapons and trained cadres. Moscow preferred to avoid disclosing some details of its relationship with North Vietnam and the Viet Cong, and among such details was the participation of Soviet advisers. It was expected that the Soviet Union would dispatch its military experts to Vietnam once the conflict in Southeast Asia expanded. In February 1965 the U.S. Department of Defense forewarned against such a possibility in its memorandum on Soviet delivery of surface-to-air missile equipment to the DRV. The missile launch sites, said the American military, "would almost certainly have to be manned by Soviet troops since no North Vietnamese are believed to be trained in SAM [surface-to-air missile] operations."[16] Thus when U.S. intelligence reported in September 1965 that 1,500 to 2,500 Soviet military personnel might then be in Vietnam, it came as no surprise to the administration. The report speculated that the bulk of Soviet military personnel were SAM operators in addition to Soviet training and support experts. Intelligence did not exclude the possible presence of some 150 Soviet pilots and maintenance personnel in the air training group and another 300 technicians engaged in administrative, communications, and logistical support activities.[17]

The information obtained by U.S. intelligence was highly detailed and found corroboration in a later 1967 report from the Soviet embassy in Hanoi. It counted 1,165 Soviet military experts in Vietnam who were responsible for the maintenance of various kinds of armaments and radar. Apparently these were chiefly technicians and SAM operators. But the report noted that these experts also took part in combat missions, suggesting a more active role. In its report the embassy stated that SAM operators and pilots were a majority among the Soviet specialists.[18] But one group of Soviet military experts escaped the attention of American intelligence.

Along with technicians, pilots, and SAM operators, Moscow sent to Vietnam a special group responsible for obtaining samples of American weapons captured during combat operations in Vietnam. In their plans for Soviet involvement in the conflict, Soviet leaders had in mind not only political and morale benefits but also the opportunity to battle-test the latest models of Soviet military hardware and a chance to obtain information about up-to-date U.S. arms by inspecting war booty.[19] Toward this end Moscow signed an agreement with Hanoi which obliged the DRV to assist the Soviets in obtaining and examining samples of American military equipment and weaponry, and sent a special group of military experts to Vietnam.

Members of this group were instructed to obtain parts of downed American aircraft and captured weapons, to examine instances where Soviet arms failed to work properly, and to send their conclusions with the most useful samples to Moscow. On the basis of this material, military experts in the Soviet Union prepared recommendations for adjusting Soviet weaponry to new American military hardware. The effect of this activity was significant in the first two years of Soviet involvement in the war. From May 1965 to early 1967, Soviet "special" experts delivered to the Soviet Union more than seven hundred samples of American military equipment, including parts of jet planes, missiles, radar, and photo reconnaissance equipment. They prepared a number of reports analyzing U.S. weaponry. As a consequence, the Soviet government decided to copy some American models—for example, Sparrow-3 guided missiles, aircraft engines, and electronic equipment—in Soviet industry.[20]

Soviet experts also worked out methods to defend North Vietnam against American air raids. Despite the recognized effectiveness of the Soviet antiaircraft complexes, Soviet experts made improvements to this weaponry, adjusting it to new capabilities of U.S. aircraft. For instance, when the Americans began to use F-111A planes in raids against the DRV, the Soviets perfected their Dvina antiaircraft complexes so they would be capable of shooting down planes with a speed of up to 3,700 kilometers per hour. These improvements proved to be effective on March 30, 1968, when an F-111 was brought down by a Dvina complex not far from Hanoi. USSR Minister of Defense Andrei Grechko reported this event directly to Brezhnev.[21]

Undoubtedly the presence of Soviet advisers in Vietnam was an ambiguous feature of Soviet policy toward the Vietnam War. While Soviet leaders were trying to create an image of seeking the earliest peaceful settlement of the conflict, Soviet advisers in Vietnam served as evidence to the contrary and might be perceived as an escalation of commitment. Thus Moscow was eager to avoid publicizing this aid and to divert world attention from it. To achieve this aim, the Soviets threatened to dispatch volunteers to Vietnam. By comparison, the deployment of a limited number of Soviet advisers to Vietnam seemed the lesser of two evils.[22]

Moscow revived the threat of volunteers from time to time during the Vietnam War. After Brezhnev's speech in Red Square on March 23, 1965, and the Soviet–North Vietnamese communiqué a month later, Soviet leaders included this idea in a number of their statements and declarations. Assurances of Soviet readiness to send volunteers were voiced during the twenty-third congress of the Communist Party of the Soviet Union and in an appeal of the fifteenth congress of the Soviet Young Communist League in the spring of 1966. But the loudest propaganda volley about volunteers occurred on July 6, 1966, when Warsaw Pact countries issued a joint declaration in Bucharest expressing readiness to allow their volunteers to go to Vietnam "in order to help the Vietnamese people in their struggle against the American aggressors."[23]

The West noted that for the first time this commitment on volunteers was undertaken by all European socialist countries. Previously the Soviet Union had declared such a commitment only with North Korea and Cuba. Still, Western analysts drew attention to the difference between the Bucharest declaration and the private reticence of socialist officials and concluded that "the increasing explicitness of the commitment does not necessarily reflect decisions as to its implementation."[24]

There also seemed to be self-restraint on the issue by China and North Vietnam itself. Both Hanoi and Beijing remained "relatively silent" about volunteers. A State Department memorandum cited Ho Chi Minh as saying that while Hanoi was grateful for the offer of volunteers, "the proposed help is not needed at present. But it still remains to be seen whether we shall require this aid in the future."[25]

Western analysis reflected the real situation in socialist countries. The sending of volunteers remained mostly a propaganda campaign, notwithstanding the public assurances of Communist leaders. It was included in the Bucharest declaration at the request of Pham Van Dong who linked the statement with American air raids against Hanoi and Haiphong. The principal goal of the declaration, according to North Vietnamese leaders, was to demonstrate socialist countries' solidarity with Vietnam.

The issue of volunteers was also clarified repeatedly during negotiations between Soviet and DRV officials. The North Vietnamese said they needed, first of all, weapons and military equipment. As to "human resources," there were enough of them in Vietnam.[26] Additional evidence of no serious intention to send volunteers to Vietnam was noted in July 1966 when Marshal Aleksei Yepishev, chief of the main political directorate of the Soviet armed forces, confided to a Western diplomat that Hanoi had not requested "volunteers" and the Soviets were not preparing to send any. Instead the USSR might consider increased deliveries of MIG jet fighters which had proved more useful in the war in Southeast Asia.[27]

Whatever the real intentions, the Soviet people took the propaganda about volunteers at face value and wrote to authorities with expressions of their readiness to go to Vietnam. The USSR Ministry of Defense informed the Communist party central committee that during 1966 they had received 750 requests from Soviet officers and soldiers to be dispatched as volunteers to Vietnam. One hundred eighty-eight entire units had sent such a request.[28] Thus the volunteer question served chiefly as a propaganda ploy, as a means of putting pressure on the United States, and in some respects as a smoke screen for the introduction of Soviet advisers into Vietnam.

As the Soviet Union increased its aid to North Vietnam and in 1968 became the principal supplier of arms, ammunition, and equipment, its influence in Hanoi did not grow accordingly.[29] Chinese influence in the DRV remained strong. China was a longtime ally of Ho Chi Minh's regime, having assisted the Viet Minh during the first Indochinese war against the French. It had sent weapons, food, and advisers to the Vietnamese Communists and had every right to share with them the victory at Dien Bien Phu in 1954.

After the war against the French ended, China provided the fledgling Communist state in North Vietnam with the assistance necessary to consolidate its power and to accumulate the means for war against the Saigon regime and its American supporters. In the early 1960s it was China, not the Soviet Union, that supplied the DRV with the bulk of aid, including arms and military equipment. By the end of 1964 China had provided its North Vietnamese allies with $457 million in material aid (48 percent) while the USSR accounted for $370 million, or 40 percent.[30]

When the escalation of the war began in 1965, China remained the leading supporter of the DRV. According to Soviet estimates, from 1955 to 1965 the People's Republic of China provided North Vietnam with 511.8 million rubles in economic aid (roughly $569 million). Of this amount, 302.5 million rubles ($336 million) were provided in the form of grants.[31]

Although China lost its lead in the supply of aid in 1968, it nevertheless continued to provide substantial assistance to the North Vietnamese. For example, Beijing was a chief supplier of hard currency to the National Liberation Front. In 1966 the Chinese sent to the Viet Cong $20 million; in 1967 the sum reached $30 million.[32] And the PRC continued to provide North Vietnam with food and arms.

No less important, China maintained troops in DRV territory.

Chinese military units were deployed in the northern provinces of North Vietnam by a secret agreement between the two countries signed in December 1965. The size of this force was estimated at 60,000 to 100,000 in mid-1967.[33] Most of it consisted of railway engineer units or conventional engineer units as well as military support units. But there were also a number of regular troops who were responsible for the antiaircraft defense of the DRV's northern provinces. In addition, the Chinese charged three aircraft regiments of MIG-17 jet fighters to defend North Vietnamese territory against possible penetration by American planes.[34]

The first Chinese regiments were introduced into North Vietnam in 1965.[35] This deployment of Chinese troops allowed the North Vietnamese, after the arrival of American forces in South Vietnam, to concentrate their combat troops in the southern DRV. At the same time North Vietnamese leaders surely understood that the presence of Chinese troops was fraught with the danger of greater dependence on Beijing, especially since the numbers of Chinese and Vietnamese forces in the northern provinces of the DRV were virtually equal.[36] Hanoi resisted Chinese proposals for still more PRC troops in North Vietnamese territory.[37]

Other factors determined China's strong position in North Vietnam. The DRV depended on China's collaboration in securing aid from other countries, including the Soviet Union. Since the bulk of aid from socialist countries came through Chinese territory (according to a Chinese source, every month eight thousand to nine thousand tons of goods were transferred to the DRV through the railway station at Pinghxiang[38]), Hanoi was careful not to close this channel of supply by spoiling relations with its "great northern neighbor." And of course geographic proximity played its role in the relationship between the two countries, for China was a next-door neighbor to North Vietnam.

Yet geographic proximity and Chinese aid could not have such importance for North Vietnamese leaders unless there were also close ideological ties between Beijing and Hanoi. The Vietnamese Communists shared with their Chinese counterparts a view of the conflict in Southeast Asia and of the international situation, of the role of the world Communist movement and of national liberation struggles, of détente and of the prospects for peaceful coexistence between socialism and capitalism.

A strong pro-Chinese feeling pervaded the top leadership of

the DRV. While politicians sympathetic to the Soviet Union had been removed from their posts during the period of estrangement between Moscow and Hanoi in the early 1960s, pro-Chinese leaders were powerful enough after 1965 to overcome the inclination of some members of the Vietnamese politburo for a more evenly divided approach to the two allies. This trend manifested itself in the relative abundance of Chinese propaganda in North Vietnam. While Soviet propaganda was confined to exhibitions and film screenings on the occasion of national holidays, Chinese anti-Soviet campaigns continued despite vigorous protests of the Soviet embassy in Hanoi. Chinese diplomats and other officials enjoyed more freedom in North Vietnam than their Soviet colleagues. And DRV leaders visited Beijing frequently to ask the advice of Mao Zedong or Zhou Enlai on important problems of DRV foreign policy. By and large, according to the not very comforting conclusion of the Soviet embassy in Hanoi, in North Vietnam there was more sympathy for China than for the Soviet Union.[39]

The Soviets kept abreast of developments in North Vietnam–China relations. They noted every sign of disagreement between the two countries and sought to exploit it in their own interests. Moscow first received such signals in 1965 with reports from diplomats and journalists of increasing discontent in Hanoi with Chinese Communist policy. According to this report, North Vietnamese leaders had become suspicious of Beijing's goals in Southeast Asia and questioned Chinese leaders' sincerity in cooperating with the DRV.[40]

This changing mood of DRV leaders can be explained by new developments in Soviet–North Vietnamese relations. Cooperation with Moscow provided Hanoi an opportunity to rid itself of China's excessive wardship and to occupy a more independent position in its relationship with Beijing. Although this shift in North Vietnamese policy did not promise Soviet leaders immediate success, they were ready to capitalize on it.

The Kremlin counted on a group of pragmatic politicians in the North Vietnamese leadership who were not happy with powerful Chinese influence in the DRV and wanted a more nationalistic policy. The Soviets had been informed that such a group existed in Hanoi and probably included such prominent figures as Le Duan, Pham Van Dong, and Vo Nguyen Giap, with the tacit support of Ho Chi Minh.[41] The Soviets also had a number of sympathizers among middle- and low-level bureaucrats and party functionaries who opposed a China-oriented course and were ready to support moves toward the USSR.

Apparently Moscow could not exert direct pressure on North Vietnamese leaders for fear of alienating them. Instead the Soviets used more subtle measures in pursuit of two interrelated goals: (1) to help the Vietnamese leadership occupy an independent (from China) position in its foreign and domestic policy, and (2) to "drag the Vietnamese comrades toward greater friendship and cooperation" with the Soviet Union.[42]

To achieve these objectives, the Kremlin mobilized its propaganda arsenal. During various meetings between Soviet and North Vietnamese officials, as well as during high-level talks, Moscow spared no opportunity to "unmask the treacherous nature" of Beijing, and to encourage Hanoi to take independent steps in its sphere of foreign policy. The Soviets tried to bring China and the DRV into conflict by letting Hanoi itself discuss with Beijing the problems of aid to Vietnam, particularly the transit of socialist aid through Chinese territory.[43]

Soviet efforts to promote dissension between Communist China and North Vietnam intensified during the "cultural revolution" unleashed by Mao's faction in the Chinese leadership. Hanoi was concerned over the struggle for power in Beijing and over Chinese attempts to involve the DRV in this struggle. In 1967 the Lao Dong party politburo sent one of its members, Hoang Van Hoan, to Beijing to assess the situation in China and its consequences for the DRV. The results of this fact-finding mission alarmed North Vietnamese leaders, who feared that Mao's imminent victory would lead to increased Chinese pressure on Hanoi. Hoan's report also alerted a group of former prominent Vietnamese politicians who had opposed the policy adopted by Hanoi in the early 1960s and had been removed from their posts because of their dissenting views. This group decided to support Le Duan in his desire to limit Chinese influence in the country and prevent the dominance of pro-Chinese elements in the DRV leadership.[44]

Members of the opposition group counted on Soviet support for their efforts. In contacts with Soviet officials, the Vietnamese advised their Soviet friends to put pressure on Hanoi to quit its unqualified support of Beijing's plans in Southeast Asia. They warned that such pressure should be carefully exerted, without insulting the self-esteem of North Vietnamese leaders, and should not repeat Khrushchev's mistakes with Tito and the Albanians. It would be better, the dissenters pointed out, to send a written appeal to Hanoi expressing the Soviet view. As for practical steps, the North Vietnamese leadership would have to take them.[45] Moscow clearly acknowledged these recommendations in its efforts to woo Vietnam away from China.

Aware of the USSR's guaranteed support and of competition between the two Communist powers for influence in Southeast Asia, the North Vietnamese leadership found itself with a unique opportunity to play both ends against the middle. Hanoi was ready to maintain friendly relations with both rivals and thus to receive all possible support from Soviet "revisionists" as well as from Chinese "hegemonists."

This prospect was discussed by various American analysts even before U.S. escalation against the DRV. It was obvious to the American ambassadors in Southeast Asian countries, in the forecasts they sent to Washington in early 1965. The American intelligence community also predicted that the USSR and China would compete in supporting North Vietnam, and would therefore provide Hanoi with an opportunity to get more aid from both countries.[46]

In fact, DRV policy justified this prediction, though it was much more complicated than Washington foresaw. The policy was not simply a result of a sober calculation but was strongly influenced by the sincere beliefs of the Vietnamese Communists and by their views on the struggle against "American imperialists." As Douglas Pike put it, throughout the war the Vietnamese Communists maintained an "ultra-hardline, fundamentalist view" of their enemy in the South, of their contribution to the "world revolutionary process," and of other socialist countries' responsibilities to them. "Each Communist nation, large or small, said the Hanoi theoretician, has both national interest and international duty. In dealing with these, the small nation (read DRV) must be free to decide its interest or obligations, which should never be forced on it by a larger nation (read USSR or China). However, the small nation also has the right to expect support from the big nations. Thus staked out was the claim that the USSR (and China) must support the DRV in the name of international proletarianism but—in the same spirit—may not levy requirements on the DRV, as that would violate the principle of self-determination."[47]

Where in this conception was pragmatic calculation and where was sincere belief? Intertwined, the two formed a basis for the foreign policy of the Democratic Republic of Vietnam. They also determined North Vietnamese behavior toward the Soviet Union. The Soviet embassy in Hanoi characterized this behavior as a "narrow national" approach to the role of the USSR in the world arena and in Vietnam.[48]

Further describing this approach, the embassy explained that the DRV considered the Soviet Union and other socialist countries a "rear area of Vietnam." North Vietnamese leaders were convinced that only the Lao Dong party could correctly assess the situation in Southeast Asia and find proper methods to solve the Vietnamese problem; therefore all socialist countries were obliged to support Hanoi's course.[49] In other words, from the Soviet point of view the North Vietnamese were proving to be independent and unmanageable.

This attitude showed itself in almost all areas of Soviet-DRV relations. North Vietnamese leaders were reluctant to share with their Soviet colleagues information on the political situation in Vietnam and in Indochina. They concealed facts about the internal affairs of the Lao Dong party and developments in its relations with Beijing. Hanoi was unwilling to share with Moscow its war plans or its views on possible means of settling the conflict. In response to insistent Soviet queries in 1967 about DRV war plans, Pham Van Dong even claimed that the North Vietnamese leadership had no such plans and acted according to the developing situation.[50]

Undoubtedly Hanoi's secretiveness was influenced by a fear of jeopardizing relations with China. But it remained a persistent characteristic of the North Vietnamese attitude even after friendship between the two Asian countries waned. As a result, Soviet diplomats in North Vietnam concluded that "even the manifestation of a more serious discord between the WPV [Workers' party] and the Chinese Communist Party will not probably mean automatic or proportionate Soviet-Vietnamese rapprochement."[51]

Nor was Moscow satisfied with the North Vietnamese attitude toward economic and military cooperation. Regarding Soviet aid to Vietnam as an international duty to the "heroic Vietnamese people," Hanoi acted exclusively in its own interests. North Vietnamese leaders spared no opportunity to ask Soviet comrades to expand their support, but they were in no hurry to pay in the same coin, refusing to take into account the interests and risks of their ally and to respond positively to Soviet requests.

The DRV received huge amounts of industrial equipment, machine tools, electric turbines, and trucks. Most of this equipment could be used for the reconstruction of factories, electric power stations, railways, and farms destroyed by American bombing. And Hanoi constantly begged for additional supplies of such equipment. But only part of the supplies were actually used in restoration work. The remainder was stored by the Vietnamese for future use. This tactic made no sense to the Soviets, since, aside from the problem of obsolescence, the equipment was usually left without care. Stored outdoors not far from ports and railway stations, because of the climate it soon became rusty junk. But demands for additional supplies persisted. According to Soviet embassy figures, 26 million rubles (more than $29 million) in unused industrial equipment had been piled up in the DRV by the end of 1966.[52]

The Vietnamese "friends" were no more thrifty with respect to Soviet military aid. They demanded from Moscow more missiles, shells, and radar equipment but wasted them in countless numbers. Soviet military advisers reported incidents when, for instance, the Vietnamese launched antiaircraft missiles without preparing necessary data, simply to scare off American planes. They called such launches a "realization of tactical tasks."

North Vietnamese troops violated storage rules for Soviet military hardware and neglected Soviet advice on the use of equipment, both of which led to spoilage. One adviser complained that despite providing the Vietnamese with sufficient radars, refusal of army commanders to use them according to the recommendations of Soviet specialists reduced the efficiency of the DRV's antiaircraft defense.[53]

Vietnamese authorities sought to explain away such incidents by blaming defective Soviet armaments. They spread rumors that the USSR provided North Vietnam with outdated arms and equipment that the Soviets no longer needed. They minimized the number of American planes brought down by Soviet missiles while losses of Vietnamese aircraft of Soviet origin were explained by their poor quality. At the same time Hanoi's leaders continually stressed the importance of Soviet moral, political, and material assistance and praised the USSR's support of their struggle.

Vietnamese officials repeatedly violated their agreement with the Soviet Union on the inspection of American military hardware. The special group of military experts sent by Moscow for this purpose encountered many problems, most of them created by Vietnamese officials who fabricated multiple excuses to deny the experts a chance to obtain this or that American missile or gun. Among official explanations were that Vietnamese museums and exhibitions needed the samples, that DRV provinces had a right to captured arms, and that Vietnamese experts needed to inspect this captured material.[54] Sometimes the highest Soviet officials had to raise the question of access to samples during their negotiations with Pham Van Dong and Le Duan in order to resolve it.[55]

The secretiveness and duplicity of the Vietnamese comrades was experienced by all Soviets who worked in the DRV. Diplomats and other specialists were under the close scrutiny of the DRV security service. They lived in an atmosphere of mistrust and suspicion. DRV authorities tried to prevent contacts between the Soviets and the Vietnamese, suspecting that their allies might obtain restricted information by means of such meetings. In early 1968 Moscow received news of the arrest of people in North Vietnam for leaking secret information to foreign diplomats.[56] In March 1968 the DRV adopted a law to punish counterrevolutionary activity. The Soviet embassy complained that in reality this law "had led to the serious reduction of our contacts with Vietnamese citizens who [now] feared possible consequences." At the same time DRV authorities imposed severe restrictions on the Soviets, who could not move freely even in Hanoi.[57]

The most telling example of the Vietnamese attitude toward the Soviet Union was provided in a letter from the USSR Ministry of Commercial Shipping to the central committee of the CPSU on July 18, 1966. Describing actions by the Vietnamese in the port of Haiphong, the ministry said that port authorities had deliberately delayed the unloading of Soviet vessels and held them in port because they would discourage bomb damage to the port in the event of U.S. air raids. Moreover, port authorities usually placed the Soviet vessels close to the most sensitive areas, as, for instance, near antiaircraft guns, in order to ensure those guns' safety during air strikes. And during U.S. air raids Vietnamese military boats used the Soviet vessels as cover while firing at enemy bombers.[58]

Thus Soviet–North Vietnamese relations were far from idyllic in 1965–1968. The Vietnamese Communists turned out to be unreliable and selfish allies who often caused difficulties for their Soviet comrades. Soviet influence on Hanoi's policy failed to measure up to the scale of Soviet assistance to North Vietnam. This fact was no secret to both the Soviets and the Vietnamese. "Do you know," a Vietnamese journalist asked Mikhail Ilyinski, an *Izvestiia* correspondent, "what is the Soviet Union's share in total assistance, received by Vietnam, and what is the share of Soviet political influence there (if the latter can be measured in per cent)? The respective figures are: 75–80 per cent and 4–5 per cent." The Soviet journalist noted, "If the Vietnamese journalist has exaggerated the former figures (by 15–20 per cent), the share of Soviet influence is probably correct."[59]

Moscow could not continue with such an unfavorable relationship. It needed greater influence in Vietnam in order to realize its foreign policy goals—to reach an appropriate settlement of the war and to make the DRV a reliable Soviet ally in the world Communist movement. Although the USSR was gradually improving its position there because of its assistance to North Vietnam, the process was still ongoing in 1966–1967 when the United States decided to seek direct contacts with the DRV in order to find ways to settle the conflict.

FIVE

Wilted Flowers

The Soviet Union's role in various U.S. attempts in 1966–1967 to resolve the conflict in Southeast Asia by inducing Hanoi's leaders to negotiate cannot be understood without analyzing Hanoi's attitude toward negotiations and without exploring Soviet–North Vietnamese diplomatic cooperation. The latter was an integral part of the alliance between the USSR and the DRV during the Vietnam War. Moscow had to prove its reliability not only by delivering economic and military aid to the "fighting people of Vietnam" and by declaring its solidarity with Hanoi, but also by rendering more subtle but no less important services on behalf of its ally through diplomatic channels.

In this sphere of Soviet activity, Moscow's inclination toward a peaceful settlement of the conflict seems most evident. It could be said that this goal permeated almost all steps by the Kremlin, either on its own initiative or on behalf of the North Vietnamese. As always, the danger of global conflict and a showdown with the United States was in the back of Soviet leaders' minds. Consequently they were anxious to avoid any turn of events that might lead to such a disaster.

Use of nuclear weapons in the Vietnam War was viewed by the Soviet leadership as a fatal event, and Moscow noted any reference to this contingency with apprehension. The United States was not the only source of this danger. Communist China possessed the destructive weapon as well, and it was possible that Beijing would be ready to provide it to its North Vietnamese allies. Although this likelihood was almost negligible, Moscow could not ignore it if it wished to prevent a dangerous turn of the war.

In August 1967 the KGB informed Kremlin leaders that the Chinese had promised to deliver atomic bombs to the DRV for striking American bases in the South in the event the United States initiated the use of nuclear weapons in Vietnam. Soviet intelligence considered it worthwhile to inform American representatives abroad of this Sino-Vietnamese arrangement.[1]

Unfortunately, there is no evidence that Soviet leaders followed the KGB's recommendation and provided Washington with this information. But such a step would have been appropriate for two reasons. First, it would serve as a deterrent against U.S. use of atomic weapons to try to coerce North Vietnam and its allies in the South. Second, the KGB information would prevent collusion between Beijing and Washington, which remained a real nightmare for the Soviet leadership. This problem was aggravated in 1966–1967 when Communist China was paralyzed by the internal struggle between two factions of the Chinese leadership. A collusion between Mao and the United States might bolster the Maoist faction within the Chinese Communist party, thus annihilating the chances for victory of its rivals, who took a more favorable—or at least not so irreconcilable—attitude toward cooperation with the Soviet Union.

The China factor heavily influenced Soviet policy toward a settlement of the Vietnam War, particularly because Moscow had to overcome Hanoi's unwillingness to agree on a diplomatic resolution. At the close of 1965 the North Vietnamese were convinced that the only possible way out of the war lay in a military victory over the American "aggressors" and their "puppets" in Saigon.

In December 1965 the twelfth plenum of the central committee of the Lao Dong party agreed on further mobilization of Vietnamese Communists and all people of Vietnam in order "in any circumstances to inflict a defeat on the aggressive war of American imperialism, to defend the North, to liberate the South, to complete the national democratic revolution in the whole country, to come to a peaceful unification of the motherland."[2] It seems significant that the task of "peaceful unification" was left for the end of the list. The North Vietnamese leadership viewed unification as a result of military success in the war against the United States and the victory of the Communist revolution in the South.

In support of this notion, the central committee of the Workers' party elaborated on concrete actions necessary to achieve these objectives. The committee stressed that the military objectives of the struggle must be the American and "puppet" armies. It was necessary to pay "special attention" to the comprehensive and rapid development of the armed forces, particularly regular forces. Along with the development of guerrilla warfare, three to four battle groups of regular forces were to be created and strategic reserves reinforced.[3] Thus the North Vietnamese leadership devoted most of its attention to war measures, confining itself to a few words on the "political struggle" as an important supplement.

In this atmosphere, Moscow's attempts to put forward ideas of an agreement with the United States at the negotiating table proved to be futile. Moreover, in discussing such matters with their North Vietnamese counterparts, the Soviets had to be careful not to undermine their own position in Hanoi. Initially, in the diplomatic arena, Moscow had to confine itself to various services on behalf of its allies, waiting for an appropriate moment to discuss ways toward a peaceful settlement in Indochina.

The Soviet Union virtually played the role of DRV envoy in its contacts with the West. Soviet officials and diplomats advised their counterparts in the United States, France, England, and other Western countries on Hanoi's position on various problems in settling the war. In turn they provided Hanoi with important information on the Western position as well as confidential information received from intelligence sources. North Vietnamese authorities sometimes instructed their Soviet allies on what actions to take in concrete situations.

The most revealing illustration of this Soviet role lies in documents related to the policy of North Vietnam toward the United Nations. From the outset Hanoi resisted any UN role in the settlement of the Vietnamese conflict, rejecting most of the peace initiatives of U Thant, the UN secretary general. The North Vietnamese refused to accept him as an intermediary.

In the early stages of the Vietnam War, apparently the Vietnamese Communists were afraid that the United States would be able to convince a UN majority to approve its actions in Vietnam and even provide Washington with more than moral support. (The example of the Korean War was too fresh in Hanoi's mind to ignore such a possibility.) Later, perhaps, other considerations prevailed in the DRV's policy toward the UN. The North Vietnamese leadership may have seen no UN role in future developments in Southeast Asia. Hanoi also wished to avoid publicity in this diplomatic sphere (which would have occurred given the character of the UN and the position of its secretary general) and preferred to use more reliable partners like the Soviet Union or Poland. And the DRV did not need the UN in other matters. So it was important for North Vietnamese leaders to prevent the UN from playing a role in settling the war, and they demanded that Moscow see to this task.

In 1966, when the regime in Saigon asked the UN to send independent observers to South Vietnam to attend elections, the DRV chargé in Moscow, Le Trang, met with a high-level Soviet Foreign Ministry official and asked Moscow to "foil the U.S. plot to use the organization in its own interests." The Soviet official informed his colleague that the Soviet Union had already taken certain measures toward this end. He emphasized that his country would continue to try to "foil the provocative maneuver of the Americans concerning dispatching UN observers to attend the elections in South Vietnam."[4]

Several days earlier a similar conversation had occurred between Soviet Ambassador Shcherbakov and North Vietnamese Deputy Foreign Minister Hoang Van Tien. Shcherbakov's counterpart asked the Soviet Union to prevent the inclusion of the Vietnamese question on the agenda of the UN Security Council, even if the Soviet representative at the UN had to use his veto to block the discussion. Shcherbakov promised to send this request to Moscow for consideration.[5]

The UN problem arose again in October of that year, in this case in connection with one of U Thant's recurrent initiatives. North Vietnamese Foreign Minister Nguyen Duy Trinh instructed the Soviet chargé on the steps the Soviet Union should take in this situation. Although Trinh's directives to Moscow were presented in the guise of a request, they recounted in detail the measures the Soviets must take in order to prevent the UN from being converted to an "instrument of the designs of American imperialists."

According to Trinh, the Soviet Union should use "all its influence" to explain to U Thant the DRV attitude toward his initiative and "try to persuade him to speak in support of the DRV." It was necessary to "convince the UN secretary general to take all measures in order to prevent adoption by this session of the UN General Assembly any decision or statement on Vietnam." Finally, if such a document on Vietnam should eventually be adopted, the Soviet Union and other socialist countries "should appropriately condemn it."[6]

The Soviet Union also considered Hanoi's interests in its own relations with other countries. Moscow not only presented and defended the North Vietnamese point of view but also rallied the support of other countries in order to put pressure on the United States in Hanoi's interests. Especially attractive in this respect was de Gaulle's France.

From the beginning of the conflict in Indochina, France reserved a special attitude toward U.S. policy in the region. Unlike other Western powers, such as Britain or West Germany, de Gaulle was in no hurry to ratify Washington's actions that led to escalation of the war. On the contrary, he was highly skeptical of a favorable outcome. According to a CIA memorandum of June 1966, French skepticism was partly explained by de Gaulle's conviction that "if the French, with their experience, finesse, and knowledge of the area, were unable to quash the Communists, then the US, despite all its power, will also be unable to do so."[7] Other reasons for the French attitude could be found in the fear of China's possible involvement in the war, if Beijing were to feel that its security was endangered, and natural jealousy of an American victory in Vietnam (a distinct possibility) "as another example of U.S. hegemony where French hegemony ought to be."[8]

Based on these estimates of France's position, American intelligence concluded that France was "most anxious to see the US pull out of Vietnam. She is realistic enough to know that the US, for reasons of its own prestige and interests, can not simply give up. Therefore, France has always been looking and pushing for ways to bring about a situation that would lead to a US withdrawal."[9] As a result, de Gaulle supported a negotiated settlement of the conflict, even with the Communists eventually overwhelming the region, as long as France occupied a leading position in the negotiations.

Moscow was aware of de Gaulle's "special position" on Vietnam and was prepared to use it in its own and North Vietnamese interests. A Soviet diplomat confided to Le Duc Tho, one of the influential members of the North Vietnamese politburo, during the latter's visit to France in the summer of 1965: "Our joint [i.e., Soviet and North Vietnamese] task is to push France further to a more and more realistic approach toward a solution of the Vietnamese problem by employing to this end all possible channels, and, in particular, diplomatic channels." The Soviet suggested using the "element of anti-Americanism" present in de Gaulle's policy toward various aspects of the international situation. By using this "element," the Soviet Union and the DRV could make France occupy a more decisive position on the Vietnamese problem.[10] Toward this end, Moscow closely followed every turn of French policy toward the United States and the Vietnam War. From 1965 to 1967 the KGB prepared a number of memoranda on de Gaulle's appraisal of the situation in Indochina and his related activities.[11]

Despite Hanoi's intransigent attitude toward a negotiated settlement, Moscow did not abandon its attempts to find ways of resolving the problem of Vietnam by means of diplomacy. Its role as "DRV ambassador" was just one face of Soviet policy toward the conflict. Another face was less conspicuous, especially when the situation offered little hope for success. Nevertheless, Soviet diplomats in Hanoi were prompt to note signs of change in the situation in mid-1966.

The first news of a possible shift in the Vietnamese position toward peace negotiations reached Moscow in late 1965. The Soviet ambassador in Cambodia, Anatolii Ratanov, noted in his quarterly report that the military situation in SouthVietnam seemed unfavorable to the National Liberation Front, though it was not hopeful for the United States either. Nevertheless, difficulties for South Vietnamese patriots and their supporters in Hanoi were increasing. As a result, Ratanov argued, the Vietnamese comrades had begun "to grope for possibilities of negotiation, to change their attitude and tactics on this question."[12]

The Soviet ambassador mentioned that the NLF was now stressing the importance of political struggle, upgrading the role of the peace movement, abandoning its plans for a people's uprising, and putting forward new ideas on negotiations. These developments indicated that, despite Chinese influence, there were changes in NLF policy toward a peaceful settlement. The ambassador's report may have exaggerated these trends and presented more wishful thinking than analysis, but it nonetheless reflects the views of Soviet officials.

Moscow continued to receive information from Soviet diplomats about growing uneasiness among Vietnamese Communist leaders over the course of the struggle. In its political report for 1966, the Soviet embassy in the DRV noted that the NLF was able to continue the war only by relying heavily on aid from the North. In turn, the DRV could not withstand American military pressure without the support of the socialist countries whose aid comprised two-thirds of the DRV's budget. The embassy noted that economic and other difficulties were forcing Hanoi to reevaluate its strategy of protracted war ("five, ten, twenty years," according to Ho Chi Minh) and consider its prospects on the political and diplomatic fronts.[13]

Moscow was glad to use these changes to promote its idea of a peaceful settlement of the Vietnamese conflict. Its efforts were facilitated by the fact that by the end of 1966 the Soviet Union had provided North Vietnam with the bulk of military aid, leaving Communist China far behind.

Soviet leaders began more openly to advise their Vietnamese counterparts on the need to intensify diplomatic activities. They sought to convince Hanoi that peace initiatives would improve the DRV's image in world opinion and win for North Vietnam a moral position that thus far belonged to the United States. To persuade Hanoi, the Soviets used economic leverage. Hanoi often complained that Soviet aid was insufficient and that Moscow was able to send to Vietnam more than it actually did.[14] Although other considerations certainly affected the scale of Moscow's assistance, pressure on Hanoi to induce the DRV to talk with the United States was unquestionably possible.

To avoid undermining its position in the DRV, Moscow combined its own pressure with that of other socialist countries. The Soviets knew that Hanoi, always seeking to augment its aid, sent its emissaries to various socialist countries to rally support for its struggle. Soviet leaders urged the role of "peacemakers" on their European socialist allies who would be freer to talk bluntly with the Vietnamese.

For example, when DRV Minister of the Interior Ung Van Khiem tried to win more aid from East Germany, he was told by his German colleagues that Vietnam was not the only "field of struggle against American imperialism," that the GDR was also a "field" with its own difficulties. Therefore Hanoi could not hope for much support from the GDR.[15]

Despite Soviet efforts to convince Vietnamese Communist leaders of the need for a negotiated settlement of the war, the DRV was initially unresponsive. Hanoi regarded these efforts with suspicion if not disdain. Hanoi still nourished hopes for a military victory over the United States and remained strongly influenced by the Chinese.

These two reasons were put forward by the prominent North Vietnamese General Nguyen Van Vinh, head of the Lao Dong party committee on unification. "It is clear for us," he argued during a conversation with Soviet chargé P. Privalov, "whether to continue the struggle or not. We certainly have to continue the struggle against the aggressor. To answer the question whether to go to negotiations is much more difficult. . . . The present situation is not favorable for the beginning of negotiations. Had we been defeated by the Americans, we would have had no choice but to agree to hold talks. But we are constantly dealing blows to the enemy and winning decisive victories. What would it mean for us to hold talks now? It would mean losing everything, and, *first of all, friendship with China which is utterly opposed to negotiations.*"[16]

This flat statement by a prominent North Vietnamese leader left little opportunity for the Soviet Union to pursue a political resolution of the crisis. In this situation the Kremlin would have preferred to act privately and cautiously, but such an attitude disappointed Washington.

The Johnson administration, while increasing American troop strength in Vietnam and taking the war to the South Vietnamese insurgents and their northern allies, did not exclude the possibility of a diplomatic settlement on American terms. As a consequence, in 1965–1966 Washington proposed several peace initiatives. These were designed to demonstrate U.S. desires for peace and a willingness to negotiate with Hanoi, and to show the intransigence of its enemy. Initially these proposals were viewed by the American leadership largely as propaganda overtures and a supplement to military operations. Their rationale can be seen in the temporary suspension of the bombing of North Vietnam and of operations against the Viet Cong in December 1965 and January 1966, known as the "Thirty-Seven-Day Pause."

When, on December 7, 1965, the clandestine Liberation Radio, voice of the National Liberation Front, broadcast an offer for a twelve-hour truce beginning on Christmas Eve, Washington was annoyed that the Viet Cong were first to propose a holiday cease-fire and thus score a psychological victory. U.S. officials hurried to counterpose this initiative. A suggestion for a cease-fire during Tet, the lunar New Year, which the Saigon regime was about to make, seemed insufficient under the circumstances. As the Joint Chiefs of Staff history of the Vietnam War put it, "State Department officials believed . . . that a GVN [South Vietnam] Tet initiative should be a real response to the VC Christmas offer. However, they were concerned that 'some quarters,' even perhaps a responsible government, might appeal for 'a more forthcoming response' to the VC offer and that the United States should be prepared for this."[17]

After consultation with his advisers Johnson announced a bombing pause beginning December 24. Later extended by the administration, this pause continued to late January, again chiefly for propaganda purposes. According to a memorandum prepared by the National Security Council staff, the extension was "'a matter of our desiring to place full responsibility' on Hanoi and the Viet Cong for the renewal of hostilities" and a "clear demonstration that we have explored fully every alternative but that the aggressor has left us no choice."[18]

Seeking "to turn international public opinion in favor of the United States by placing the onus for the renewal of fighting on the enemy,"[19] the Johnson administration made sure its initiative was acknowledged around the world. The president sent personal messages to Chancellor Ludwig Erhard of West Germany, British Prime Minister Harold Wilson, French President de Gaulle, Italian Prime Minister Aldo Moro, and Pope Paul VI. Johnson's personal representatives traveled to several capitals to explain the purpose of the pause. It was a major U.S. diplomatic offensive.

Even among American officials were there doubts about the effects of such publicity. Chester Cooper, then on the NSC staff, before the pause had raised a problem of distinction "between an attempt to improve our image and a genuine peace probe." Several years later he noted that "the posturing and the overall atmosphere of conspicuous busyness during late December and January seem to lead to the conclusion that the efforts were primarily for the purpose of improving the American image than finding the key to actual negotiations. . . ."[20]

What was the Soviets' role and behavior during the thirty-seven-day bombing pause? First off, it seems that the Soviet Union had almost helped to initiate the "peace offensive." In his memoirs Lyndon Johnson referred to a conversation between Soviet Ambassador Dobrynin and McGeorge Bundy during lunch "one day late in November," and to Dobrynin's query about a possible bombing pause of "twelve to twenty days." U.S. leaders could be assured of "intense diplomatic activity."[21] It is unclear why the Kremlin instructed its ambassador in Washington to offer such an assurance. But Dobrynin's hints coincided with reports from Soviet diplomats in Southeast Asia on a shift in the position of the Vietnamese Communists toward negotiations.[22] If this was the prompt, Moscow took these weak signs more seriously than they deserved. But perhaps Moscow, with U.S. help, had decided to determine how substantial Hanoi's shift was. In any event, Soviet leaders were not to play a decisive role in the enterprise.

When the State Department's Llewellyn Thompson met with Dobrynin on December 28 to give him a statement on the bombing pause, the Soviet diplomat assured Thompson that he would promptly inform his government, but "he wished it understood that he was not undertaking to pass this information to Hanoi."[23] Such reluctance is quite explicable considering Moscow's uncertainty that its steps in favor of settlement would be warmly received in the North Vietnamese capital. Alexander Zinchuk, minister counselor of the USSR embassy in Washington, had made this clear in his conversation with William Bundy of the State Department twelve days earlier. On Bundy's question whether the Soviets were able to have fairly extensive conversations with Hanoi's leaders, Zinchuk answered affirmatively but noted that "they had never found any flexibility whatsoever in Hanoi's statement of the four points."[24]

Conscious of the Soviets' reluctance to raise their voice in support of the peace initiative in their dealings with Hanoi, Washington decided to avoid a request for Moscow's assistance. President Johnson, asking Averell Harriman to visit his old friends in socialist countries, omitted the Soviet Union from the list.[25] Likewise, Defense Secretary McNamara did not find it expedient for Harriman to go to Moscow. The venerable diplomat himself agreed that "it might be a disadvantage to go to Moscow because they might be willing to do something quietly but not otherwise."[26]

Instead the United States chose indirectly to urge the Soviets to bring pressure on Hanoi. Harriman alone visited eleven countries on behalf of the "peace offensive." He talked with Polish President Gomulka, Yugoslav leader Tito, Egyptian President Nasser. He met with Prime Minister Sato in Tokyo, Ayub Khan in Pakistan, the Shah of Iran, Foreign Minister Thanat Khoman in Thailand, and Souvanna Phouma in Laos.[27] In a number of his meetings he touched upon the problem of the USSR's contribution to the cause of peace in Southeast Asia.

During a long conversation with Polish Foreign Minister Adam Rapacki, the American "Ambassador for Peace," as Harriman would later be called, explicitly expressed the hope that "the Soviet Union, yourself [i.e., Poland] and other friends of DRV will urge them to make some response" to the American initiative. Harriman explained that his hope was based on his talks with Kosygin in July 1965. The Soviet premier was "very anxious to bring the war to conclusion. He didn't say he would do anything," noted Harriman, "but my impression is that he wants to end the war."[28]

Harriman also talked with Indian Prime Minister Shastri and Pakistan's President Ayub Khan. Both of them were going to meet with Kosygin in Tashkent. For the American envoy this was a perfect opportunity to convey to the Soviet leader "President Johnson's sincerity in wanting negotiated settlement and yet determination to prevent NVN [North Vietnam] taking SVN [South Vietnam] over by force and to give people of SVN right to determine our [sic] future."[29] Both the Pakistani president and the Indian prime minister promised to carry these words to Kosygin. Thus while the United States did not approach the Soviets directly, they tried to deliver the message through other countries.

Immediately after Harriman's talks with Polish leaders, one of the high-ranking representatives of the Polish Foreign Ministry, Jery Michalowski, visited the DRV. En route to Hanoi he stopped in Moscow where he was encouraged by Soviet officials to urge North Vietnamese leaders to start negotiations for a peaceful settlement. Although nothing of value resulted from his trip,

Michalowski, who was in Hanoi for two weeks, was able to make some progress in convincing the North Vietnamese leadership of the need to settle the conflict. Michalowski also stopped at Beijing and had a "long talk" with three vice-ministers of the Foreign Office there. He was surprised how uncompromising was the Chinese position toward negotiations on Vietnam. According to Michalowski, all three Chinese had been "unbelievably tough in attacking the idea of negotiations for a peaceful settlement of the Vietnamese war. They maintained that the U.S. should be kept deeply involved in this war."[30]

Another plea was made by the Soviets themselves. Soviet politburo member Alexander Shelepin visited the DRV in January 1966, presumably, among other things, to talk with his Vietnamese colleagues about negotiations with the United States. He was not successful. General Vinh criticized this visit in his report at a conference at NLF headquarters later that year. "Soviet Union's Shelepin," said Vinh, "on his visit to our country, seems to have suggested negotiations. Because we have foreseen this, we issued a communiqué containing our determination to fight the U.S. aggressors. Therefore the revisionists' scheme has failed, and they have acquired our opinions."[31]

Eventually the U.S. "peace offensive" led nowhere. Within the framework of this initiative, American diplomats in Moscow and Burma had even been able to maintain direct contacts (code-named Pinta) with their North Vietnamese counterparts, but Hanoi remained unshakable in its determination to win a military victory. Washington was not greatly disappointed. From the outset it had not been optimistic about the whole undertaking. President Johnson admitted in his memoirs that he "had grave doubts about a pause" but was "reluctantly moving" toward acceptance of the risk.[32] He met with strong resistance not only from the military but also from the State Department. As soon as it was clear that Hanoi was unwilling to abandon its military plans in the South and agree on negotiations, Washington ordered a resumption of the bombing of the DRV and the war against the Viet Cong.

Still, the United States continued its search for a settlement in Indochina, hoping to enlist Soviet support in its efforts. Given the reluctance of Moscow to play the role of mediator in a situation where there was little chance of success but a great risk of fierce criticism from Beijing, the Johnson administration courted the

USSR through unofficial channels. Washington authorized private contacts between American diplomats and Soviet officials in Moscow, sent public activists, businessmen, and other accredited representatives to the Soviet capital, and supported the initiatives of foreign diplomats who might convey the U.S. government's views to the Kremlin.

"Special dossiers" in the Communist party archives contain a number of KGB reports on these U.S. approaches. In July 1966, for instance, the KGB sent the Kremlin a report on visiting American trade union leaders who believed it was necessary to hold secret unofficial consultations on the war between responsible representatives of Washington and Moscow.[33] Vietnam was also a subject of Harvard professor Marshall Shulman's conversations in Moscow in October 1966.[34]

The contents of those conversations were probably similar to the discussion that occurred in the Soviet Committee for the Defense of Peace in July 1965 between American publisher and public activist Carlton Goodlett and committee representatives. Goodlett put the substance of this discussion in a memorandum for Soviet authorities. He said he had had much opportunity to meet with President Johnson and to discuss with him the problems of the Vietnam War. His impression was that Johnson did not intend to retreat in South Vietnam. Nevertheless, his appeal for unconditional talks with Hanoi was sincere because the president now found himself in a difficult situation because of the hawks in the American government. Johnson, according to Goodlett, understood that the United States had become entangled in the wrong war at the wrong place at the wrong time; but the intransigence of North Vietnam and the stubbornness of the Saigon regime left him no opportunity to extricate himself from this situation.

Then Goodlett touched upon the position of the Soviet Union. He believed Moscow was anxious to avoid involvement in the conflict which led to its refusal to influence DRV policy. Such a position could be very dangerous, the American warned. If the destruction of North Vietnam by American bombers continued, the Soviet government would have to decide whether to leave the "young socialist country" without support. Thus the situation would be fraught with the danger of a major war. "One would have gotten the impression," Goddlett confided, "that the People's Republic of China alone may gain benefits from a refusal of the

USSR to take an active part in maintaining contacts between Johnson, the National Liberation Front and Ho Chi Minh."[35]

Apparently Washington had not authorized all these approaches. Some people acted from positions of goodwill and a sincere desire to see the fateful conflict in Southeast Asia ended. But these contacts undoubtedly served as useful means to inform the Soviet leadership of U.S. intentions. In this respect a report from the main intelligence directorate of the Soviet General Staff (GRU) to the CPSU central committee on August 23, 1966, is one of the most revealing.

The GRU drew attention to the fact that Colonel Charles G. Fitzgerald, military attaché at the American embassy in Moscow, was, in his talks with officers of the Defense Ministry, "methodically and insistently" maintaining that the USSR could play an important role in settling the Vietnam conflict as the initiator and active mediator of negotiations. The colonel believed that "when two forces meet head on—in this case the U.S. and the Vietnamese communists—a third force is needed, which could help them to come to an agreement. Only the Soviet Union could be this third power." Fitzgerald stressed that the United States would like to leave Vietnam without losing face. That was why the American government continued to look for ways to organize negotiations.[36]

However frank the messages from official and unofficial U.S. envoys, Washington clearly saw they were not enough to encourage Moscow to help in settling the conflict. Concrete stimuli were needed to persuade the Soviets to play mediator. The Johnson administration tried to find such stimuli in concessions to Moscow in the international arena.

In the fall of 1966 the Kremlin received from Budapest a report that, according to Hungarian sources in Washington, a series of high-level conferences had been held in the White House to discuss foreign policy plans and prospects for Soviet-American relations. American policymakers regarded friendly relations with the USSR as a guarantee of U.S. security in the "extraordinarily delicate situation" in Southeast Asia. To maintain such relations, American leaders wished to overcome the usual Soviet view that the war in Vietnam was the main obstacle to fruitful cooperation between the two countries in such areas as the reduction of nuclear arms, cultural and scientific exchanges, and economic ties.

According to the Hungarians, the administration decided to assure the Soviets that the United States would entertain concessions in these and other areas if Soviet involvement in the Vietnam War were diminished or at least not increased. Washington was even ready to consider changes in NATO and its relations with Bonn, for example: (1) recognize the Oder-Neisse border between East Germany and Poland, and (2) limit West Germany's participation in the management of nuclear weapons by its symbolic participation in the McNamara committee of NATO.[37]

This report from Hungary was probably not far from the truth. Some members of the Johnson administration did advise concessions to Moscow in exchange for its support of U.S. peace efforts in Vietnam. On October 3, 1966, in a memorandum "for the President and the Secretary of State," Averell Harriman expressed his belief that "the only real chance" to induce Hanoi to negotiate depended on the influence Moscow would be willing to exert. "If Moscow," continued Harriman, "is to take on the task of persuading Hanoi to move towards a settlement, the USSR will probably have to assume certain risks and obligations. Thus, I believe, we must offer some compensating inducements." These included modification of American cooperation with Bonn on nuclear arms and an offer for mutual reduction of forces in Germany. "In sum," concluded Harriman, "I believe we will have to agree on some arrangements affecting Germany if we are to induce Moscow to act in Vietnam." This should be done despite the political difficulties it might create.[38]

Apparently Harriman was concerned that by the fall of 1966 there were no apparent changes in the Soviet position toward the war. American analysts even noted a significant hardening in Moscow's attitude toward Washington, which they explained as serious anxiety over possible collusion between the United States and the Chinese Communists. As for Vietnam, Soviet policy, according to observers in Washington, was a "combination of continued aid to the North with diplomatic and propaganda strong-arm tactics designed to inhibit us."[39] Yet State Department analysts also noted encouraging nuances in the statements of Soviet leaders, for example Kosygin in one of his speeches indicating that it would be possible to move ahead in negotiations with the United States on such problems as nuclear nonproliferation and a comprehensive test ban regardless of Vietnam. The Soviet premier did not attack President Johnson by name and avoided suggestions that the Kremlin would have no further dealings with his administration.[40]

Llewellyn Thompson was likewise cautious in his appraisal of Soviet-American relations for the president in July 1966. Thompson described Moscow's economic and foreign policy problems and noted that the "Vietnamese affair" had added to the Soviet leadership's difficulties in resolving some of these problems.

Thompson cautioned against any dramatic escalation in U.S. actions against North Vietnam since it would significantly increase the risk of direct confrontation with the Soviet Union. He concluded his memorandum with a rather pessimistic prediction: "Whatever the outcome of Vietnam, I am afraid it will take considerable time for us to get back on the path we were following in our relations with the Soviet Union when the affair began. In any event, we must always be aware that while an important evolution was taking place in the Soviet Union, which over time might have led to real co-existence, the Soviet leaders, as contrasted with the people, are dedicated to a dogma that is implacably hostile to us."[41]

For American officials, the splash of Soviet activity on Vietnam in the fall and winter of 1966–1967 was thus all the more surprising. On the eve of a routine visit to the United States by Soviet Foreign Minister Gromyko, to take part in a session of the UN General Assembly, Johnson's advisers informed the president that in early September a senior member of the Soviet UN delegation had told an American delegate that "Moscow is convinced that US sincerely desires peaceful settlement in Vietnam and believes Gromyko visit to New York in mid-September is a good occasion for discussions on Vietnam."[42] Several days later the same unnamed Soviet delegate again raised the question of Gromyko's imminent visit and stressed the importance of a preliminary meeting between the Soviet foreign minister and UN Ambassador Arthur Goldberg to prepare the ground for a discussion with Secretary of State Rusk. The Soviet proposed an agenda for discussion: Vietnam, outer space, nonproliferation, and nuclear testing.[43]

Johnson's advisers recommended that the president himself meet with Gromyko. Both Walt Rostow and Harriman prepared memoranda for Johnson with almost identical considerations for the meeting. They suggested that the president stress three principal ideas in his discussion with the Soviet foreign minister: the strong

U.S. desire for peace in Vietnam, the belief that the Soviet Union would assist the United States in its search for a peaceful settlement, and U.S. determination to improve relations with the Soviet Union. Rostow recommended the president tell Gromyko that the United States would be "grateful for anything the Soviets may be able to do to enable us to reach a peaceful settlement" of the Vietnam problem.[44]

The conversation between Johnson and Gromyko on October 10 was characterized by a friendly atmosphere. The Soviet foreign minister avoided polemics and was careful not to antagonize the president. The Soviet Union wished to improve relations with the United States, he declared—a change from previous Soviet pronouncements that this could occur only after Vietnam was settled. These remarks led American officials to conclude that the Soviet Union was eager "to see a settlement of the Vietnamese affair," and that Soviet leaders seemed "prepared to reach at least some agreements with us and improve relations despite Viet-Nam."[45]

Likely a shift in Hanoi's attitude influenced Soviet policy at the time. This change manifested itself in a great many contacts with the DRV in late 1966 on the initiative of Polish diplomat Janusz Lewandowski and known in the history of the Vietnam War as Operation Marigold.

Diplomatic historian George Herring has called Marigold "a mysterious and possibly promising initiative."[46] Many documents concerning this diplomatic activity are still unavailable, especially those on the Soviet and North Vietnamese sides. Among the unanswered questions about Marigold are the role of the Soviet Union and why Moscow decided to move toward a peaceful settlement of the war at that time. Nevertheless it is now possible, analyzing Soviet policy during 1965–1967, to shed more light on some aspects of Marigold previously cloaked in mystery.

The history of the Marigold peace initiative has been related in a number of books on the Vietnam War. Its basic outlines are presented in the *Pentagon Papers*. In late June 1966 the Polish representative to the International Control Commission on Vietnam, Janusz Lewandowski, returning to Saigon from Hanoi, met with Giovanni D'Orlandi, the Italian ambassador in South Vietnam. The two men discussed a "very specific peace offer" which Lewandowski was to transmit to the United States on behalf of the North Vietnamese leaders. D'Orlandi communicated the content of his conversation with Lewandowski to the American ambassador in South Vietnam, Henry Cabot Lodge, on instructions from Italian Prime Minister Amintore Fanfani, who was also transmitting it direct to Washington.

What seemed attractive to American policymakers in Lewandowski's offer was that Hanoi, in its proposals as presented by the Pole, did not ask for the immediate reunification of Vietnam. It avoided a demand for a socialist system in the South and for a change in Saigon's relationships with other countries. Nor did North Vietnamese leaders demand "neutralization." They suggested that U.S. withdrawal from Vietnam could be scheduled along a "reasonable calendar" and stated that Hanoi did not seek to interfere with the government in the South.[47]

This first approach by Lewandowski was followed by a series of meetings with D'Orlandi and Lodge. It became clear that Hanoi had significantly altered its stance on a number of principal questions. The North Vietnamese were no longer demanding that the NLF be recognized as the sole representative of the South Vietnamese people and did not oppose the Saigon government's participation in negotiations provided the NLF was also represented. Furthermore, the North Vietnamese were asking only for a "suspension" of the bombing, not its cessation.[48]

However promising this beginning, Marigold did not develop into something more substantial until November. At that time, on the eve of a Lewandowski visit to Hanoi, Washington sought to clarify his role in the initiative and to move it forward by presenting a new concept for negotiations—the so-called Phase A–Phase B plan. Conscious of the DRV's concern over losing face, Washington suggested a mutual deescalation of the war in two phases. As Rusk explained it in instructions to Lodge, "Phase A would be a bombing suspension, while Phase B, which would follow after some adequate period, would see the execution of all the other agreed de-escalatory actions. Hanoi's actions taken in Phase B would appear to be in response to our actions in Phase B rather than to the bombing suspension."[49] Thus the DRV's demand to stop the bombing unconditionally, and Washington's adherence to the principle of mutual deescalation, would both be realized in this plan.

The U.S. proposal, however, elicited not a trace of enthusiasm from Lewandowski. But during his visit to Hanoi in November he formulated and presented to the North Vietnamese leadership ten points (including the A–B plan) that he thought generally reflected the U.S. position on an overall solution of the Vietnam War. In his conversation with Lodge after his return from the DRV on November 30, the Pole discussed these points and stressed that they had been met with interest in Hanoi. He suggested "it would be advisable to confirm them directly by conversation with the North Vietnamese Ambassador in Warsaw."[50] Although there was some delay in receiving authorization of the ten points from Washington, and reservations about the wording of some of the points, the State Department instructed Lodge to inform Lewandowski that the American embassy in Warsaw would contact the DRV embassy there on December 6 or soon thereafter.[51]

Meanwhile the U.S. bombing campaign continued. After a pause because of poor weather, American planes struck targets in the vicinity of Hanoi on December 2 and 4. Despite warnings and protests to the American ambassador in Warsaw, John Gronouski, by Adam Rapacki, the Polish foreign minister, new U.S. air strikes occurred on December 13 and again on December 14. The result was predictable. On December 14 Rapacki summoned Gronouski to inform him that the DRV had requested that all conversations with the United States be terminated. Rapacki expressed his regret that an opportunity to resolve the conflict peacefully had been lost because of U.S. actions and added, "Once again it becomes clear how difficult it is to believe in your words. . . . In future only facts can be taken into consideration."[52]

Not only the Poles were disappointed with the outcome of Marigold. So were the Soviets. Moscow followed closely the developments that unfolded among Poland, the United States, and North Vietnam between June and December 1966. Although it is unclear whether Moscow was informed of Lewandowski's initiative from the outset, the fact that Poland played so important a role was not surprising to the Soviet leadership. The Soviets were aware of the desire of their Polish allies to see the Vietnam War ended as early as December 1965, when the KGB sent to the Kremlin a report from the Polish ICC representative on the possibility of a political settlement in Vietnam.[53]

Polish diplomats met frequently with their Soviet colleagues to discuss a peaceful solution of the conflict and the initiatives of various countries. One such conversation took place in August 1966 at the USSR Foreign Ministry.[54] During this conversation the Poles may have revealed their contacts between Lewandowski and Lodge, which at the time promised to develop into something more substantial than incidental meetings between diplomats in Saigon. The nature of the relationship between the Soviet Union and its Eastern European allies was such that the Europeans were unlikely to take any important step in the area of foreign policy without at least tacit approval from Moscow. But they might propose such a step on their own initiative. Thus Moscow probably sanctioned the contacts between Lewandowski and Lodge, and Rapacki's role in arranging a meeting between the Americans and the North Vietnamese in Warsaw. In any event, at the peak of Marigold, in November 1966, Gromyko met with the Polish ambassador in Moscow who informed the Soviet foreign minister of the conversations between Lewandowski and Lodge and the position taken by the United States. According to the Polish ambassador, Lodge had rejected the DRV's four points but admitted the possibility of a cessation of the bombing of North Vietnam, provided there was reciprocity from Hanoi.[55]

Moscow apparently pressed its Vietnamese allies to agree to contacts with American diplomats. Shcherbakov noted in the embassy's political report for 1966 that the North Vietnamese were receptive to the "advice of the CPSU" and by the end of 1966 had agreed on the need to maintain contacts with the United States and to intensify the political and diplomatic aspects of the struggle.[56] This Soviet ambassador's assertion concurred with that of Soviet chargé in Washington Alexander Zinchuk, who in a conversation with William Bundy confided that during his stay in Moscow in late November he had gained the impression "that Hanoi (or elements in it) were seriously interested in starting something. They had been encouraged by the apparent slackening in the pace of . . . bombing during this period." It was not merely an impression, for Zinchuk emphasized that it was "more than a general sense."[57] He repeated his assurances about Hanoi's intentions in a conversation with John McNaughton, assistant secretary of defense, on January 3, 1967. And Zinchuk implied that Moscow was optimistic about U.S.–North Vietnamese talks. "He said that Ambassador Dobrynin, 'who is very sensitive to the moods that prevail,' was in Moscow early in December and noticed a favorable atmosphere with respect to possibilities for settling Vietnam."[58] Dobrynin himself confirmed Zinchuk's words when he remarked during a conversation with Llewellyn Thompson that the "initial stages of this affair [i.e., Marigold] had given the Soviet Government considerable hope and he said rather cryptically that they had other reasons for some optimism. . . ."[59] By "other reasons" for optimism he clearly implied changes in Hanoi's position.

However considerable were the hopes inspired by Marigold, the American air strikes of December 2 and 4, and then of December 13 and 14, "spoiled everything." The North Vietnamese perceived these attacks as an attempt by the Johnson administration to force Hanoi to negotiate on American terms. Despite assurances by American officials that these strikes represented not an escalation of the bombing campaign but only an execution of previously scheduled raids postponed because of bad weather, and were in no way connected with Lewandowski's initiative, Hanoi remained unconvinced as to the real motives of American policymakers.

The ill-timed strikes stirred negative feelings in Moscow as well. Dobrynin told Thompson that "his Government was frankly baffled" by the American actions in Vietnam and did not know how to judge U.S. policy. Nevertheless, Soviet leaders were not inclined to blame the American government. Rather, they wondered whether some of the U.S. military "were deliberately trying to frustrate a policy of moving toward negotiations" or whether U.S. policy "was one of military victory."[60]

The answer lay somewhere in between. From the beginning of the war in Vietnam, Washington viewed diplomacy as a valuable instrument in achieving U.S. goals in the conflict with the DRV. In this respect there was no difference between the diplomatic and military aspects of American policy in Indochina. They supplemented each other. Like the bombing of DRV territory and the raids by American troops against insurgents in the South, diplomacy was aimed at preserving the Saigon regime and discouraging North Vietnam's support of the Viet Cong. As Wallace J. Thies put it, "Both during the period leading up to the expected talks and then once the talks had begun, it would be necessary to 'orchestrate' military pressures with diplomatic communications so as to enable the U.S., in John McNaughton's words, to 'negotiate' by an optimum combination of words and deeds."[61]

This American strategy was strikingly similar to the North Vietnamese idea of "fighting while negotiating." But it too had serious flaws. American policymakers were sure they could closely control their military action in Vietnam and regulate the bombing. Yet this task turned out to be much more difficult than expected. War has its own logic and, once started, determines people's actions rather than the other way around. And people must be heard to be understood—not a simple matter when words are obscured by the salvos of guns. Soon after the beginning of the war, the Johnson administration found itself in the awkward position of being unable to conduct an "orchestra" of its words and deeds. Marigold only confirmed this failure.

American leaders nonetheless retained a hope of gathering the splinters of what had been destroyed by the air strikes of December 1966. Immediately after the breakdown of Marigold, Washington decided to try a direct approach to the DRV. It was encouraged by signals conveyed by Pham Van Dong in his interview with the American journalist Harrison Salisbury in early January 1967, as well as hints dropped by Soviet diplomats in their conversations with American officials.

For example, during his conversation with Zinchuk on January 3, 1967, McNaughton asked him for suggestions about contacts with Hanoi. The Soviet diplomat replied that "after a little time things might resume again." Referring to forces of moderation in the DRV, Zinchuk noted that these forces could not be active while bombs were falling in Hanoi. According to Zinchuk, the United States had to create "the right atmosphere or 'environment' for the forces of moderation in Hanoi 'who want to get negotiations started.' "[62]

Washington was receptive to signals from Hanoi and Moscow. To facilitate contacts with the North Vietnamese and to placate feelings in the DRV over the bombing raids of December 13 and 14, the Johnson administration ordered a suspension of bombing within ten miles of Hanoi city center. Simultaneously Washington contemplated actions designed to obtain Soviet support for a new U.S. initiative.

With this purpose in mind, President Johnson decided to send signals to Moscow through his new ambassador Llewellyn Thompson. One of the most prominent Soviet experts in the administration, Thompson had already served as ambassador in the Soviet capital in the late fifties and early sixties. Johnson expected that his knowledge of the Soviet Union and his experience in dealing with the Kremlin would facilitate communication between the two governments.

The president and his advisers spent the last months of 1966 in discussions about instructions to the new ambassador, particularly with respect to Vietnam. In addition, the president considered transmitting through his ambassador a letter to Soviet leaders with the administration's views on the development of Soviet-American relations. Johnson's advisers believed Thompson's arrival in Moscow "would be the right time to open up the subject of Vietnam again with Soviet leaders."[63] They were encouraged by Gromyko's conciliatory behavior during his meeting with the president, and they could not fail to note Gromyko's answer to a question from Rusk during their conversation in October. When the secretary asked which Eastern Europeans were closest to Hanoi, Gromyko responded pointedly: "We are."[64] Likewise encouraging was the fact that Foy Kohler, Thompson's predecessor, before his departure had been received by Kosygin himself. The reception testified that the Kremlin attached great importance to its relations with the United States.

Thus American policymakers hoped their Soviet counterparts would more actively help them settle the conflict in Southeast Asia in 1967. This prospect became the subject of a discussion that took place in Averell Harriman's office on December 21, 1966. Among the participants were Harriman, Thompson, the Assistant Secretary of State for Far Eastern Affairs William Bundy, his deputy Leonard Unger, and Joseph Sisco, assistant secretary of state for international organization affairs. They agreed that Thompson "should be given a great deal of latitude and should be able to pursue the question of negotiations as far as the Soviets were willing to go. . . ." As to the letter from the president, the participants were not sure to whom it should be addressed, to Brezhnev or Kosygin, but they were unanimous that the letter should include the assurance that Thompson had the "complete confidence of the President," that the United States was "anxious to resolve the problem of Viet Nam, " and that the Americans "would be prepared to conduct talks with the Soviets to this end either through our Embassy in Moscow or the Soviet Embassy in Washington."[65]

The recommendations of the meeting were apparently taken into account by the president. His letter to Kosygin of January 21, 1967, began with assurances that Johnson attached great importance to the improvement of Soviet-American relations. With this in mind, he had asked Thompson "to return to the Soviet Union" as his ambassador. Johnson noted that he had full confidence in the new ambassador and hoped Kosygin would "feel as free to discuss our mutual problems with him as you would with me if we were able to sit down together." In turn, Johnson would always be available to the Soviet ambassador in Washington "through the channel we have established or directly whenever necessary." Finally, the president said he had "arranged for Ambassador Thompson to have a channel of communication which will be open only to Secretary Rusk and myself."[66] Although the letter defined an agreement on nuclear arms as Thompson's most urgent task, Vietnam was no less important for Washington, especially because it was again seeking a direct channel of communication with Hanoi.

The new U.S. initiative was tagged Sunflower by an amateur gardener in the State Department and went forward in January and February 1967. It involved two interrelated peace moves: a direct American approach to the North Vietnamese through the DRV embassy in Moscow, and an attempt by Prime Minister Harold Wilson of Great Britain and by Premier Kosygin to bring the two rivals to the negotiating table.

George Herring has called Sunflower a "complicated, confusing, and intriguing story."[67] So it was even for those who were closely involved. The published documents leave more questions than answers, and memoirs of the participants do not clarify many problems. The most controversial question is why the United States radically changed its "Phase A–Phase B" formula and hardened its position compared with Marigold. In turn, Hanoi hardened its position, stating that "only after the unconditional cessation [of U.S. attacks of the North] . . . there could be talks." Finally, and perhaps most important, is the question of whether both sides were prepared in January–February 1967 to begin serious talks on a settlement of the war. In any event, Sunflower deserves to be recounted once more with the benefit of new documents from Soviet archives.

In late 1966 the Soviets regarded the prospects of a political settlement in Vietnam somewhat more optimistically than at any earlier stage of the conflict. In its political report for 1966, the Soviet embassy in Hanoi expressed its firm opinion that the "Vietnamese comrades" should develop and intensify their "hard and serious struggle" with the support of the socialist countries and of "all peace-loving forces" so as "*in the current year* [i.e., in 1967] to lead the matter to a settling of the conflict." "We believe," continued the embassy, "all our efforts must be put forth to this end."[68] The embassy based its estimate on clear signs of a rapprochement between the viewpoints of the CPSU and the Workers' Party of Vietnam on the situation in the country and on the development of the political-diplomatic struggle. In addition, Soviet diplomats in Hanoi noted that Chinese influence in the DRV had weakened and that the Vietnamese Communists' faith in China was shaken. At the same time the embassy admitted there was little hope the Vietnamese leadership would take the initiative in suggesting ways for a settlement of the conflict, since "the comrades, apparently, have not grown up to the level of a clear-cut choice." That was why the Soviets, according to the embassy, had to take the lead.[69]

The opportunity for an initiative appeared in January 1967 when Washington instructed the American embassy in Moscow to seek an appointment with the North Vietnamese ambassador and to deliver a message to authorities in Hanoi. The message assured the North Vietnamese that the United States government placed the "highest priority in finding mutually agreeable, completely secure arrangements for exchanging communications with the government of the DRV about the possibilities of achieving a peaceful settlement of the Vietnamese dispute." The Johnson administration stated its willingness to meet any suggestion from the North Vietnamese leadership regarding the time and place of such discussions and to receive information from Hanoi on these questions directly from the North Vietnamese through diplomatic contacts in any world capital.[70]

After several attempts, the American deputy chief of mission in Moscow, John Guthrie, succeeded in arranging a meeting with DRV Minister-Counselor Le Trang on January 10, during which he delivered the message from Washington. The North Vietnamese diplomat accepted it and expressed a desire to preserve their conversation in secrecy.[71] The January 10 meeting proved to be the first in a series of meetings between the two embassies in Moscow in January and February. Despite both sides' intentions to keep their contacts secret, Soviet authorities were aware of them. The American embassy informed the State Department that the movements and telephone calls of American diplomats were being reported to the KGB by chauffeurs and operators, and undoubtedly the DRV embassy was also subject to Soviet eavesdropping.[72] In fact the KGB noted unusual activity between the American and DRV embassies and duly informed its superiors. On January 28 the KGB reported on these contacts to the central committee.[73] Several days later the KGB sent to party authorities information that contacts between the two embassies were continuing.[74]

In light of these facts, American and North Vietnamese preoccupation with the secrecy of their meetings seems purely pro forma. Both countries were more concerned about evading blame for disclosure of the contacts rather than about the Soviets discovering what was taking place under their noses. As a result, Moscow knew almost everything about these developments between the United States and North Vietnam. For example, when Soviet Ambassador Shcherbakov met with DRV Foreign Minister Nguyen Duy Trinh in Hanoi on January 27, he inquired whether North Vietnam was planning to publicize the steps which had been taken earlier *in Warsaw and Moscow.* This question related to an interview which Trinh was about to give to Australian journalist Wilfred Burchett. The North Vietnamese responded that his government intended to preserve the secrecy of the contacts with Americans and would refer only to official information. Shcherbakov was also anxious to find out whether the Vietnamese comrades were prepared to continue an open dialogue with the Americans and at the same time maintain private contacts with them. Yes, Trinh answered, and informed his Soviet colleague that Hanoi planned to deliver its response to the American proposals spelled out during the recent meetings in Moscow. "We can act openly, however we do not decline confidential meetings."[75]

The North Vietnamese response to the American proposals was not encouraging. On January 27, the day of the conversation between Shcherbakov and Trinh, Le Trang asked for a meeting with Guthrie to deliver a "stiffly worded Aide-Memoire" which denounced the United States for intensifying the war in South Vietnam and escalating the bombing of the North, and questioned U.S. sincerity in seeking a settlement. The aide-memoire insisted that Washington "recognize the four-point stand of the Government of the Democratic Republic of Vietnam and the five-point statement of South Vietnam National Front for Liberation," and demanded the unconditional end of the bombing and all other acts of war against the DRV as essential for continuation of the North Vietnamese–American contacts as proposed by the U.S. message delivered January 10.[76]

But Le Trang did not imply that the channel of communication in Moscow should be terminated. On the contrary, he said Hanoi's response to the U.S. clarification of its position, which had been handed to him on January 20, would be delivered "at an appropriate time." The next day, January 28, Trinh's interview with Burchett was published in North Vietnamese newspapers. The text of the interview paralleled that of the aide-memoires. Trinh stressed that "It is only after the unconditional cessation of U.S. bombing and all other acts of war against the DRV that there could be talks between the DRV and the United States."[77] Thus Hanoi revived its insistence on cessation of the bombing, not its "suspension" as indicated in November 1966 when Marigold was under way.

Still, Washington was hopeful about Sunflower, though it expected new complications. In particular, the administration feared that the Soviet Union would join the DRV in pressing the United States to stop bombing in return for talks. The State Department instructed American diplomats in Moscow to counter such efforts by using the "standard position" on this question: a bombing halt *after* North Vietnam stopped infiltrating the South and supporting the Viet Cong. Washington also advised the American embassy in Moscow, in its contacts with the Soviets, "to point to grave practical problem—which we believe Soviets might actually understand although not conceding it—of situation in which we stop bombing, Hanoi continued its actions, and we were thus under great pressure to resume." Furthermore, speculated American policymakers, the cessation of bombings without any reciprocal actions by the DRV would result in rumors that talks were in fact going on. This would jeopardize the secrecy regarded as necessary by both sides. "Aside from this," the State Department continued, "a situation in which the North Vietnamese continue their infiltration of men and materials southward while we are engaging in talks would produce the kind of tensions that would make any constructive steps toward a settlement difficult if not impossible."[78]

Meanwhile, Moscow took its own steps to support the emerging process of negotiations. On January 30 Shcherbakov met with North Vietnamese Premier Pham Van Dong and handed him a packet of Soviet proposals on Vietnam. Presumably the Soviets offered their own plans for talks between Hanoi and Washington and a possible settlement of the war. In the conversation Pham Van Dong repeated the DRV's demand for an unconditional cessation of the bombing and Hanoi's determination to go to the conference table only after all acts of war against the DRV were stopped. The North Vietnamese admitted peace negotiations would be difficult. Therefore, Pham Van Dong emphasized, the Vietnamese Communists must coordinate the military struggle with political and diplomatic efforts. "It is the military struggle which we consider the main at the present time," the premier added, "and the diplomatic struggle must support the military and political ones."[79]

Concluding the conversation, he said Hanoi would not object to the Soviet Union probing U.S. intentions. The meetings between the American and the DRV chargés demonstrated that the United States was "as always very stubborn, and we . . . are not clear on our practical chances as yet."[80]

Having received a report on this conversation with Pham Van Dong, Soviet leaders might have inferred that Hanoi remained wedded to achieving a military victory over the United States. But it was obvious that North Vietnamese confidence in a fast and easy triumph had been shaken. Hanoi now not only admitted the feasibility of talks with the Americans but authorized the Soviet Union to sound out the U.S. position. It was probably the first time that Hanoi had requested such assistance from Moscow.

Soviet leaders sensed an opportunity to implement their peace plans in Soviet Premier Kosygin's scheduled visit to the United Kingdom in early February 1967. The timing of this visit was favorable for a number of reasons. Besides the intense diplomatic contacts between the Americans and the North Vietnamese in Moscow, the visit coincided with a cease-fire announced in connection with the celebration of Tet, the lunar new Year, in Vietnam, so there were no air attacks on DRV territory during the period. And the British were no less determined than the Soviets to facilitate a settlement of the war in Southeast Asia. It might thus be possible to use them to put additional pressure on the United States for early negotiations. Kosygin apparently left Moscow in hopes of employing all these circumstances to induce Washington to begin negotiations with North Vietnam along the lines outlined by Pham Van Dong in his conversation with the Soviet ambassador.

The British were likewise enthusiastic about the prospects of Kosygin's visit to London. Harold Wilson, the British prime minister, also liked the timing of the visit for producing an effective initiative on Vietnam. According to Wilson, "There were straws in the wind to suggest that he [the Soviet premier] might be prepared to change his previous policy of refusing to intervene to get the parties to the conference table."[81] With this in mind, Wilson informed President Johnson of his plans.

Johnson, however, did not share the enthusiasm of his British colleague. Washington's previous attempts to maintain contacts with Hanoi through mediators had proved fruitless, and Johnson did not believe the British would be any luckier than their predecessors. Furthermore, although the direct contacts between the United States and North Vietnam had not been encouraging, the administration still believed that something useful might result from these communications. "Wilson seemed to feel that he and the Soviet leader could serve as mediators and bring about a settlement of the war," Johnson wrote in his memoirs. "I doubted it strongly. I believed that if the Soviets thought they had a peace formula Hanoi would accept, they would deal directly with us rather than through a fourth party."[82]

Washington may also have been concerned with the possible success of the British. As Chester Cooper, then Harriman's special assistant who had been sent to London as a "liaison officer" by the administration to witness almost all events of Kosygin's visit, put it, "There was another, less articulated but more deeply felt attitude about Wilson's imminent meeting that cooled Washington's interest and perhaps even contributed to the failure of the talks. After all the recent frustrations and disappointments of Warsaw and Moscow, the prospect that Wilson might be able to use American chips to pull off peace talks was hard for the President and some of his advisers to swallow. If the time was now ripe to get Hanoi to talk, Johnson, not Wilson, should get the credit."[83]

Nonetheless the administration had little choice but to support its British colleagues. Washington did not wish to appear to oppose a serious peace initiative nor antagonize a consistently supportive ally. Johnson therefore gave Wilson a green light in his negotiations with the Soviet premier on Vietnam and assigned Chester Cooper to serve as a link between London and Washington in the event something substantial resulted from talks between the two leaders.

Kosygin was due to arrive in London on February 6. On the eve of his visit, the Kremlin apparently instructed Ambassador Shcherbakov in Hanoi to meet with Pham Van Dong and secure a response to the Soviet proposals submitted several days before. The Soviet ambassador may also have been instructed to sound out the North Vietnamese premier's position on possible diplomatic action by the Soviets. When the meeting occurred on February 4, Pham Van Dong handed over a formal reply to the Soviet proposals of January 30. It contained a standard denunciation of the American initiative as mendacious and stated that Hanoi was determined to intensify the military and political struggle. The DRV leadership viewed diplomacy only as supplementary. Hanoi asked Moscow to support its four-point program as well as the NLF's five points and to press the United States to cease the bombing of the DRV.[84]

After this unencouraging response, Shcherbakov asked Pham Van Dong about a possible Soviet contribution on the diplomatic front. The DRV leader said it was up to Moscow to decide what methods of the diplomatic struggle should be used and when. The Soviets could, at their own discretion, choose the most appropriate methods of communication with the United States. "It is important," stressed Pham Van Dong, "that in its contacts with the Americans the USSR, with all its might, raise its voice as the powerful socialist country which is supporting Vietnam and is demanding that the U.S.A. take the road of justice."[85]

Obviously Soviet leaders expected more from their Vietnamese colleagues. Yet they had at least been provided with room for maneuver. Not unexpectedly, therefore, the Soviet premier demonstrated his preoccupation with Vietnam from the very moment of his arrival in London. According to Chester Cooper, even on his way into the city from the airport, "Kosygin talked about almost nothing else but the problems the Russians were having in Asia."[86] Wilson was in high spirits. His doubts about Kosygin's willingness to cooperate on Vietnam virtually disappeared.

The events of these Anglo-Soviet talks have been described in detail by Cooper and Harold Wilson, and in his memoirs President Johnson added his own analysis of the British initiative and its results. Here are recounted only the principal moments of Kosygin's visit, focusing on his behavior and motives during the negotiations in London.

Wilson and his colleagues were encouraged by the Soviet premier's willingness to discuss the problems of a settlement in Vietnam, though Kosygin adhered to Trinh's formula as expressed in the interview with Burchett. Kosygin viewed this interview "as key to NVN [North Vietnamese] readiness to negotiate." He repeatedly referred to it during his talks with Wilson and stressed that the Tet cease-fire represented "the big chance" for getting talks between "the principals" started.[87] At the same time Kosygin pointed out that while the Soviets, as well as the British, could help the warring parties find a way out of the conflict, they could not negotiate for them. "The best way to do this is to get the US and NVN together." He suggested that the Soviet Union and the United Kingdom convince President Johnson—"together or separately, privately or publicly, in the communiqué or in a special message"—that Trinh's statement was an acceptable basis for discussion. According to the Soviet premier, "that was the best move for us [i.e., Kosygin and Wilson] to take."[88]

Wilson, in turn, reminded his Soviet counterpart of the Phase A–Phase B plan as it had been presented to Moscow by Foreign Secretary Brown during his November visit to the USSR. Although Kosygin initially showed "no flicker of interest," Wilson repeated the proposal once more in greater detail and finally succeeded in arousing the Soviet premier's attention. His Western counterpart suspected he had not understood it before. Kosygin asked Wilson to repeat it and deliver a written text to him. "He said this would be [a] very important document. . . . He would like to have the proposal in writing so that he could send it to Moscow; the sooner he was given it, the sooner this could be done."[89]

The text of the Phase A–Phase B proposal was prepared by Cooper and two British Foreign Office officials. Then Wilson handed the text to Kosygin. What followed has been extensively described in a number of memoirs and books. Pentagon analysts characterized it as a "battle of tenses." Cooper called the situation a "tragedy of errors."

The point was, Washington had changed its original proposal, significantly hardening it. The first version (which the British followed in their text for Kosygin) said, "The U.S. will stop bombing NVN as soon as they are assured that infiltration from NVN to SVN *will stop*." The same version was included in State Department instructions to Guthrie on the eve of his February 2 meeting with the North Vietnamese chargé in Moscow. But the wording had been changed in a letter Johnson addressed personally to Ho Chi Minh on February 8, 1967. The president wrote, "I am prepared to order a cessation of bombing against your country and the stopping of further augmentation of US forces in South Viet-Nam as soon as I am assured that infiltration into South Viet-Nam by land and by sea *has stopped*."[90] Johnson himself explained that this change was necessitated by a sharp increase in the infiltration of North Vietnamese troops into the South during the Tet truce and thus was justified in order to prevent a similar outcome if negotiations began. The president refused to acknowledge the negative effect this change might have on the Wilson-Kosygin talks.[91]

The opposite opinion has been taken by the British prime minister. He regarded the whole situation as a "total reversal of the policy the US had put forward for transmission to the Soviet Prime Minister. . . . It was a reversal of policy, and it had been deliberately taken just when there was a real chance . . . of a settlement. . . ."[92] Wilson believed the U.S. action had "the worst possible effect on the Russian" who for the first time had shown a willingness to assist the West in finding ways to settle Vietnamese conflict.

In order to placate the injured feelings of his British ally and to save the initiative from failure, Johnson decided to heed some of his advisers,[93] as well as of London, and extend the bombing pause until after Kosygin's departure from London. Then the American government went even further. On February 12 the president sent Wilson a message noting the contribution the British prime minister was making toward peace in Vietnam. Johnson wrote that he felt "a responsibility to give you this further chance to make that effort bear fruit" and that he was "prepared to go the last mile in this week's particular effort. . . ." He authorized Wilson to inform Kosygin that if he could get a North Vietnamese assurance before 10 a.m. the next day that "all movement of troops and supplies into South Viet-Nam will stop at that time," the United States would not resume the bombing of North Vietnam from that time.[94]

This message arrived London after 11 p.m. on the 12th, and Wilson immediately passed it to Kosygin. But nothing came of this new overture, though the Tet cease-fire was extended for six more hours. Kosygin received no response from Hanoi to Washington's proposal. He returned to Moscow without having obtained any decisive results on a settlement in Indochina. As to the Johnson administration, on February 13 it issued final orders to resume naval and bombing operations against North Vietnam. Ho Chi Minh's reply to Johnson's letter which arrived after the resumption only repeated the usual demands to the United States and was no less uncompromising than earlier statements.

In seeking to understand the missed opportunities of Kosygin's visit to London, the historian cannot avoid analyzing the role of the Soviet premier in these events. How sincere was Kosygin in his utterances about effecting negotiations between the United States and North Vietnam, about the "big chance" for peace-loving nations to help settle the conflict? Was he prepared to do everything in his power to facilitate the peace process?

It is scarcely possible to offer definite answers to these questions. More than once Kosygin expressed his desire to see the conflict in Southeast Asia ended. He even planned to raise with the politburo the possibility of Soviet disengagement from the war.[95] His concern probably made him too sensitive to weak signs of change in Hanoi's attitude toward negotiations. Thus information from the Soviet ambassador in the DRV about a shift in North Vietnamese views on talks with the United States in early 1967, coupled with the public statement of the DRV foreign minister that Hanoi could agree to discuss problems of a settlement of the conflict, were perceived by the Soviet premier as a real chance to set the whole affair in motion.

Acting within the limits imposed on him by his colleagues in the Soviet politburo, by Hanoi, and perhaps by his own conviction, Kosygin made every effort to get negotiations started on the DRV terms as they were formulated by Trinh. Apparently the Phase A–Phase B proposal attracted Kosygin's attention as a possible compromise which might pave the way for later reconciliation. Johnson's proposal to extend the cease-fire offered another opportunity for compromise, and was a last chance to keep open prospects for negotiations after the Phase A–Phase B plan had been modified by Washington.[96] When he was informed of the extension of the bombing pause, the Soviet premier immediately called Brezhnev by telephone. In his conversation with Moscow, overheard by British intelligence, Kosygin tried to persuade his colleague that the U.S. proposal on cease-fire represented "a great possibility of achieving the aim, if the Vietnamese will understand the present situation that we have passed to them; they will have to decide. All they need to do is to give a confidential declaration."[97]

Moscow followed Kosygin's request. On February 13 Shcherbakov met with Pham Van Dong and informed him of the U.S. proposal. But the North Vietnamese remained unmoved.[98] The resumption of the bombing clearly left the Soviet premier no chance to change the situation.

Kosygin himself offered an appraisal of the initiative undertaken during his visit in London in a lengthy conversation with Ambassador Thompson after his return to Moscow. He emphasized that it was the first time the Vietnamese had stated publicly that they were ready to negotiate if the bombing was ended unconditionally. He supported the Vietnamese proposal publicly during his visit to London, and though he was highly skeptical of the role mediators might play in settling the conflict, he had joined Prime Minister Wilson in his efforts "because he had seen a basis for US-Vietnamese talks."

Kosygin thought the deadline imposed by Johnson had the "nature of an ultimatum," and noted there was no opportunity for Hanoi to consider the message and conduct necessary consultation. While the United States demanded that Hanoi stop infiltration into the South, the Americans themselves continued to send additional troops, to move their naval vessels to North Vietnamese shores, and to increase the number of their aircraft in the area. In other words, Kosygin said, "US seems believe its infiltration is all right but infiltration by other side is not."

Kosygin expressed doubt that Washington was serious about its proposals and again emphasized that the problem was "to find way toward unconditional cessation of bombings so as to start negotiations." But "he could not venture to propose anything constructive now. He had no basis for doing so and he did not wish to make unrealistic propositions." The Soviet premier was certain, however, that "what should be looked for were constructive steps, certainly not ultimata: US should not send messages stating that something should be done by ten o'clock for it would receive reply that would make it necessary start all over again. . . ."[99]

This remark precisely reflected the situation the American administration found itself in in February 1967. The resumption of bombing made impossible the continuation of contacts between the Americans and the North Vietnamese. During his conversation with Shcherbakov soon after the termination of the cease-fire, Nguyen Duy Trinh informed his Soviet counterpart that there would be no new contacts in Moscow because of the resumption of bombing. The DRV foreign minister made a renewal of talks dependent on a "concrete situation."[100]

Thus Sunflower shared the fate of earlier U.S. peace initiatives. Like Mayflower and Marigold, it was unfruitful. The failure of Washington to orchestrate its diplomatic and military moves resulted in the recurring solo of bombing campaigns that made the whole concert sound out of tune, to the world's annoyance and disappointment.

SIX

Glassboro

The failure to find a political settlement of the Vietnam conflict in early 1967 caused the major participants in the war to turn away from negotiations. For the time being, the prospect of talks gave way to a more irreconcilable military outlook in Southeast Asia. Whatever hopes of ending the war in 1967 had existed in the United States and North Vietnam were now abandoned in favor of new battle plans.

Soviet observers in Hanoi noted that by the spring of 1967 the North Vietnamese leadership had become much more optimistic with regard to the chances of Communist success in an armed offensive against the "American aggressors." The Soviet embassy in the DRV reported that while early that year there had been signs of a "more realistic appraisal" of the situation among the North Vietnamese leaders, including a search for new political and diplomatic initiatives, the picture had now changed. The Vietnamese comrades had dropped the ideas and proposals put forward in the interviews of Pham Van Dong and Nguyen Duy Trinh. The Soviet embassy wondered in fact whether those proposals had been just a propaganda maneuver aimed at world opinion and the weakening of U.S. military pressure during the "dry season" of 1967. But Soviet diplomats did not exclude the possibility that some factors unknown to them might have influenced Hanoi's policy toward a political settlement of the war.[1]

From the start of U.S. bombing raids on the DRV, Hanoi had regarded diplomacy only as a supplement to the military struggle. Even in deciding to intensify diplomatic efforts in early 1967, the thirteenth plenum of the Lao Dong party had emphasized that military and political tactics (i.e., subversion and anti-Saigon propaganda in the South) were principal and decisive factors toward victory over "American imperialism." Diplomacy remained "important, positive, and independent," but it could not be used alone. "On the basis of victories won over the enemy on battlefields," the plenum of the Vietnamese Communists declared, "it is necessary to mount an offensive against him in the diplomatic sphere as well, combining this work with a military and political offensive, striving to expose the crimes and treacherous maneuvers of American imperialists, winning for our side international solidarity and support, creating a united front of peoples of the world against the imperialistic aggressors of the U.S.A."[2] In this view, diplomatic contacts and negotiations were not a means to settle the conflict but purely a propaganda instrument.

Thus the reorientation of Hanoi's policy in the spring of 1967 toward a more militant stance, as noted by the Soviet embassy, was consistent with the views of North Vietnamese leaders on the tactics of the war against the United States and its "Saigon puppets." In this reorientation, however, the DRV leadership obviously received the blessings of its ally in Beijing.

In October–November 1966, at the height of Marigold, Le Duan visited the Chinese capital and met with PRC leaders. Zhou Enlai insistently advised his Vietnamese colleagues to continue the war, at least until 1968. Although Le Duan gave no promises to Zhou, he assured him that the DRV wished to end the war with "maximal advantages for itself."[3] Several months later, during negotiations between Chinese and Vietnamese leaders in Beijing in April 1967, the Chinese leadership, concerned with the recent conciliatory gestures made by Hanoi, increased its pressure on the Vietnamese to prevent a possible settlement of the conflict. They succeeded in obtaining Pham Van Dong's and Vo Nguyen Giap's "solemn promise" to continue the war.[4]

Perhaps this partly explains why in the spring of 1967 the

DRV intensified its military activity. The rate of infiltration of North Vietnamese troops into the South increased, as did material support to the Viet Cong. By midyear more than half the People's Army of Vietnam had been sent to the South, which now comprised 120,000 troops in eleven divisions.[5] Furthermore, Hanoi was now inclined to acknowledge the presence of its troops on South Vietnamese territory,[6] another indication of the growing militancy of Vietnamese Communist leaders.

Beijing's approval of the North Vietnamese war plans did not satisfy all of Hanoi's needs, for China could not meet all its demands for arms and military equipment. For the DRV, Moscow remained the principal source of supplies for the new offensive against the United States. Thus Hanoi dispatched a delegation of its highest officials to Moscow to obtain additional support from its Soviet allies. The delegation that arrived in April was headed by Pham Van Dong and Vo Nguyen Giap, whose mission was to persuade the USSR leadership to provide North Vietnam with all necessary aid for new battles against "American imperialism."

The April talks confirmed Hanoi's rejection of negotiations with the Americans. Pham Van Dong, after listening to Soviet advice and recommendations for a diplomatic settlement, concluded that the "Soviet comrades 'do not yet fully trust' the WPV, are not sure of the final victory of the Vietnamese people. . . ." He avoided discussing Hanoi's plans for a settlement and did not respond to Soviet insistence on greater confidential exchange between the two countries.

"At the present time," the Soviet embassy stated in its report on the talks, "the situation looks as if the Vietnamese comrades would move to a settlement in the following possible situations:

"—If they were convinced that the military struggle took a serious turn for the worse for them, and their internal situation would not allow them to continue;

"—If the United States were to give in and agree to satisfy the main demands of [North] Vietnam;

"—If the Chinese, for some reason, were to change their attitude toward the Vietnam War;

"—If soc[ialist] countries were to declare that they could no longer bear the ever growing burden of the Vietnam War for internal reasons or owing to dangers involved in the protracted and expanded war." None of these incentives, the embassy concluded, now existed to urge the Vietnamese comrades toward an active search for a peaceful settlement.[7]

It is worth noting that while this report included—as a possible means to induce Hanoi to negotiate—a refusal of the Soviet Union and other socialist countries to provide support to the DRV, it avoided even considering it as appropriate leverage, lest it jeopardize Soviet positions in Vietnam which were always precarious because of Chinese influence there.

Meanwhile, Washington too was moving toward a harder line. Early in 1967 the American military pressed for rapid escalation. Although the president was able to resist this pressure while the Moscow and London contacts were under way, once those contacts failed a number of escalatory options came under review. Renewed military pressure against North Vietnam and its allies in the South began almost immediately after the failure of the Sunflower peace initiative. On February 24 U.S. artillery units began firing over the demilitarized zone (DMZ) at targets in North Vietnam; on February 27 U.S. planes began mining internal waterways and coastal estuaries in North Vietnam south of the 20th parallel.[8] In March General Westmoreland asked the administration for a minimum of eighty thousand additional troops for Vietnam. Although this request was not supported by the administration, the war continued to intensify. On April 8 Rolling Thunder 55 was approved, adding to the already authorized list of bombing targets new North Vietnamese airfields and power plants. It began on May 19 with an attack on the power plant in Hanoi.[9]

In this atmosphere there could be little hope for successful negotiations. This was abundantly clear to Soviet leaders who observed these developments with apprehension. In this new stage of hostilities between the United States and the DRV, it seemed that all Moscow's hopes for an early settlement of the conflict in Southeast Asia had been forfeited.

Soviet concern over Vietnam was coupled with misgivings about the Chinese threat, which Moscow perceived as twofold. First, the Soviet leadership feared that Beijing would undermine the USSR's positions in Southeast Asia by exploiting signs of local discontent with Moscow's policy on Vietnam. On the other hand, the Kremlin was no less concerned with a possibility of collusion between China and the United States, which might produce a settlement of the Vietnam War either favorable to Washington or not unsatisfactory to Beijing. In either case Moscow would be deprived of the fruits of the peace.

Soviet officials spared no opportunity to sound out their American colleagues about the "China card." In his conversation with U.S. Ambassador Llewellyn Thompson in March, Vasilii Kuznetsov, the deputy foreign minister, "jokingly" asked about secret U.S. talks with China supposedly in Warsaw,[10] implying the existence of some sort of understanding between the two over Vietnam. Kuznetsov's "joke," in addition to several earlier hints by Soviet authorities as well as information from Thompson and his colleagues, revealed Moscow's poorly concealed suspicion about American-Chinese relations. The State Department was prompt in instructing Thompson to "deny flatly" that the United States had received any approach from Beijing on negotiations with North Vietnam.[11] But this denial scarcely alleviated the suspicions of Soviet leaders.

In these circumstances, one can understand why Moscow was reluctant to threaten the withdrawal of aid to the DRV. It could only forward advice to Hanoi and applaud every turn of DRV policy that might lead to diplomatic contacts between North Vietnam and the United States.

Nguyen Duy Trinh once grouped the North Vietnamese allies according to their support of Hanoi's steps toward negotiations with the United States. In his speech before the DRV Foreign Ministry's staff in February 1967, he observed that there were three clear-cut views. First there were "foreign comrades" who did not support the North Vietnamese diplomatic initiatives. "Second," continued Trinh, "there are comrades who very much welcome our proposals. And, third, there are comrades who welcome everything we are doing." Although the foreign minister did not elaborate on these groups, his subordinates later explained to a Soviet diplomat what Trinh meant. According to them, the first group included China and Albania. The second consisted of the Soviet Union and Eastern European countries. The third group was comprised of North Korea, Cuba, and possibly Rumania.[12]

Clearly Hanoi would have preferred to see the Soviets in the third group. But that would have made the Soviet Union a hostage of the DRV. The opposite policy—putting outright pressure on the North Vietnamese allies—was likewise risky and might bring the loss of Soviet influence over the course of events in Southeast Asia.

Moscow therefore chose a consistent though cautious and sometimes ineffective policy of indirect pressure and persuasion so as not to antagonize its allies or compromise the whole process, and at the same time to obtain as many dividends for itself as possible in international politics.

Accordingly, even when all contacts between Washington and Hanoi had been suspended, Soviet leaders did not abandon their hopes for a political settlement of the war. They noted that Trinh, in his interview with Soviet Ambassador Shcherbakov on February 15, when the United States resumed its bombing campaign against the DRV, did not reject the idea of such contacts, depending on future circumstances.[13] The United States too demonstrated its willingness to proceed along a similar path, despite its escalation in the spring of 1967. The Johnson administration tried to pick up the threads of contacts just after the failure of Sunflower—and this on the instigation of a Soviet diplomat.

On March 12 the State Department informed Ambassador Thompson that N. P. Kulebiakin, a Soviet diplomat at the United Nations, had suggested to the Americans that the time was appropriate for talks between the United States and North Vietnam, and that these talks could take place even without the stoppage of bombing. Kulebiakin linked such an opportunity with the arrival in Moscow of new DRV ambassador Nguyen Tho Chan, and assured his American counterparts that a direct line of communication between the two ambassadors was possible.

The Americans were prompt to pursue Kulebiakin's hint, particularly because they believed it was implicit in earlier Guthrie–Le Trang talks that the North Vietnamese regarded these contacts as preparatory to direct talks at the ambassadorial level. The State Department instructed Thompson to seek a meeting with Le Trang to convey to the Vietnamese that the United States continued to favor prompt peaceful settlement and that the American government was ready, without preliminaries, "to get down to serious substantive and entirely secret discussions on all questions involved in a peaceful settlement itself, in order to bring this matter to a prompt conclusion."[14]

Thompson expressed his doubts about the appropriateness and especially the timing of this approach, but his superiors persisted that a "private talk might be constructive." As to the ambassador's suspicions with respect to Kulebiakin and his overture,

Secretary Rusk assured Thompson that he too was skeptical about Kulebiakin, but the fact that the Russian had been accompanied during his second conversation by a colleague, as well as "his greater detail of suggestion about procedure," convinced Washington that he might be acting under instructions.[15]

The American embassy tried unsuccessfully to reach the North Vietnamese ambassador. It was rebuffed by a subordinate who charged that U.S. efforts to maintain contacts with the DRV at a time of the "grave escalation of aggressive war against people of NVN" was a maneuver by Washington "to deceive world opinion and to cover its criminal acts of war."[16] A similar reaction met an attempt to deliver a letter from President Johnson to Ho Chi Minh in April. The letter was returned to the American embassy in Moscow later the same day. Although it had been opened and Hanoi—as American intelligence discovered—had received the text, the letter was never acknowledged and never answered.[17]

Yet the Johnson administration still nourished hopes that its strategy of "orchestrating" military operations against the Vietnamese Communists alongside a substantial peace initiative would succeed. Some American policymakers questioned this strategy and wanted a reappraisal of the entire American diplomatic approach to Vietnam. In March Chester Cooper, Harriman's special assistant, prepared a memorandum on the possible U.S. steps after the failure of Sunflower. Having witnessed the shortcomings of American diplomacy during the Kosygin-Wilson talks, Cooper called his paper "The Negotiations Track—Another Look," thus emphasizing his dissent from the prevailing views of the president's advisers. He sought "in the aftermath of the Wilson-Kosygin talks and related public charges and counter-charges, the post-Tet resumption of bombing, and the subsequent intensification of military actions" to examine the U.S. negotiating and diplomatic posture and to explore lines of approach for the months ahead.[18]

Cooper criticized Washington's chief demand to North Vietnam, the principle of "mutual de-escalation" or "reciprocal act." "In all our proposals involving 'a reciprocal act' we are asking Hanoi to trade off destruction in the North for a more certain and speedy defeat of Communist forces in the South. . . . While this has important advantages for us, it explains why Hanoi may be unwilling or unable to agree to a 'reciprocal act.'" Cooper doubted the reliability of channels of communication with North Vietnam and claimed that earlier cases of misunderstanding on the part of Hanoi, such as the bombing schedule during Lewandowski's trips to the DRV, were the result of a lack of information conveyed to the Vietnamese Communist leaders from the American side.

Cooper proposed a number of measures to improve communication and enhance the U.S. negotiating position. He suggested reopening a direct channel to Hanoi "as soon as possible" and taking an early opportunity to reaffirm U.S. "standing offers" on mutual deescalation and negotiations. If this could not be done directly, Cooper proposed to ask Moscow to serve as a channel. To make U.S. proposals more flexible and more attractive to the North Vietnamese, Cooper put forward a new, "more elastic" formulation of the Phase A–Phase B offer. He suggested ordering a cessation of all U.S. military action against the DRV in exchange for a private assurance that Hanoi would stop infiltration at an agreed future time. Since Washington regarded a concentration of North Vietnamese troops near the DMZ (as had occurred in January and February) as a substantial threat, Cooper suggested compressing the time between Phase A and Phase B to a few hours, though the period might be extended. Along with this new version of the plan, Washington should indicate to the DRV that it was ready to engage in preliminary and private talks to precede not only Phase B but also Phase A, if need be.

Should this "elastic" formulation prove unsatisfactory to U.S. policymakers, Cooper suggested other initiatives, one of them a mutual withdrawal from the DMZ. According to this initiative, Hanoi and the U.S. government with its Saigon ally agreed not only to pull all forces out of the DMZ but to move them a certain distance north and south of the zone. This would be the first step in a whole range of measures, including inspection by the International Control Commission for compliance with the agreement, U.S.-DRV talks, and a bombing cessation. Cooper did not exclude the possibility that in certain circumstances the United States would stop bombing in exchange for talks.

Several pages of Cooper's memorandum were devoted to the timing of American initiatives. The author favored early negotiations and was against their postponement until after national elections in South Vietnam scheduled for the fall of 1967. Cooper considered the spring most propitious, though not as advantageous as January and February. One reason was that continuous unrest in

China compelled Beijing to concentrate on domestic problems. "The Soviet Union," continued Cooper, "still seems anxious to use its influence in the direction of a political settlement (although not yet on terms which we find acceptable)." American casualties were not yet so large as to deprive the administration of flexibility and an opportunity to seek a solution based on "limited objectives," not on military victory. Finally, a postponement of negotiations until fall might result in a decision by Hanoi to hold out for several more months in order to make the Vietnam War an issue in the 1968 presidential elections. At the close of his memorandum Cooper drew a compelling conclusion: "Over and above these theoretical arguments, there is one practical and compelling one: *We have no choice but to continue to press for a political settlement.*"[19]

Although it is unknown whether Cooper's memorandum reached anyone in the highest echelons of the Johnson administration other than Harriman, similar views were increasingly circulating among high-ranking officials in Washington. Particularly there were growing doubts about the effectiveness of a strategy of "graduated pressure" against North Vietnam as a part of the "fighting while negotiating" policy. Some of the former proponents of this strategy now regarded it as counterproductive, since it increased North Vietnamese determination to withstand U.S. pressure and strengthened Hanoi's will to gain a military victory over the United States. Among those who questioned Vietnam policy were William Bundy, assistant secretary of state for Far Eastern affairs, and John McNaughton, assistant secretary of defense.[20]

But the Johnson administration was not yet prepared to abandon its strategy, and remained hopeful that Moscow would assist the United States toward a negotiated settlement. For example, in April the Canadians suggested that both sides agree once again to respect the demilitarized zone along the 17th parallel. This might lead to further deescalation. The State Department, in turn, used this idea to propose a mutual withdrawal to lines ten miles south and north, respectively, of the DMZ. The new initiative was strikingly similar to that discussed in Cooper's memorandum. As suggested by Cooper, this was to be the first step leading to talks on further deescalation and to an overall agreement.

The State Department initiative was welcomed by a number of American officials. Harriman, among them, planned to meet with a representative of the Soviet embassy to explain the proposal. In a memorandum to the under secretary of state, he explained the need to impress upon the Soviets that mutual withdrawal from the DMZ was a serious proposal and to persuade them to use their influence on Hanoi "to give this thoughtful consideration and a positive response."[21] Harriman did meet with a Soviet diplomat who sent the American proposal on to Moscow, later reporting that the Kremlin had taken the American effort at face value. The next day, however, April 21, the Haiphong power plants were attacked for the first time. Harriman's Soviet interlocutor was greatly disappointed with such a move. "How could Moscow now assure the North Vietnamese that the United States was seriously anxious to de-escalate the war?" he asked Harriman after the event.[22]

Not only the Soviets were perplexed at the inconsistency of the American policy. In a cable to Washington, Ambassador Thompson urged his government to consider "whether in present circumstances our continuing campaign of Vietnam peace moves really serves to further the possibility of peace negotiations."[23]

Thompson's message was inspired by an exchange of views with British Foreign Secretary George Brown on his approaching trip to Moscow. This visit presented a new opportunity for Washington to win Moscow's support of U.S. actions for peace. But the American ambassador was skeptical as to whether such actions would produce a favorable effect. "In present circumstances," he argued, "I believe that initiatives that Soviets know and know that we know have only a remote chance of success may be positively harmful as adding to Soviet suspicion of our sincerity. This is particularly true of our efforts to involve them." Thompson admitted that the Soviets could bring pressure on North Vietnam by threatening to curtail arms shipments or actually doing so. But such a move, the ambassador warned, would throw the Vietnamese into the arms of Beijing, contrary to Soviet objectives in Southeast Asia. Likewise, the U.S. peace initiative was counterproductive, for Hanoi viewed it not only as a propaganda exercise but also as a sign of desperation.

At the same time Thompson added his voice to criticism of American escalation of the war. He could not see it as a solution of the problem. "In fact," the ambassador stated, "I believe that at least in the short run each step-up in bombing reduces the chances of the other side agreeing to negotiate. No government would want to enter negotiations directly connected with the increased use of force against it. . . ."

Thompson proposed a substantial increase of American forces in the South, combined with a reduction of bombing in the North or confining attacks to the infiltration routes. "It is against the foregoing background that I would suggest that rather than have George Brown continue to make peace noises when he comes to Moscow, he should convey to the Soviets a sense of our determination to see this affair through," Thompson concluded.

Thompson's skepticism may have been strengthened by his awareness that Soviet leaders were reconsidering their own foreign policy, especially after the visit of the delegation from North Vietnam. Apparently this process involved not only the Vietnam problem but the entire range of Soviet-American relations. This is why Dobrynin was brought home from Washington for consultations in late April. He confided to Thompson after his arrival in Moscow that "he had known that his government felt strongly about Vietnam but had not realized how strongly until his consultations here."[24]

The Americans received confirmation of this reappraisal in the Kremlin from another Soviet diplomat in Washington. During a reception at the Soviet embassy on April 27, hosted by Soviet military attaché General Valentin Meshcheryakov, the general informed the Americans that U.S. escalation of the war had forced the Soviet leadership to reassess the situation. The general's information may have unsettled the Johnson administration. Meshcheryakov hinted that the Soviet general staff had recommended increasing Soviet military action to assist North Vietnam. Other measures of reprisal supposedly being contemplated by Moscow included refusing to ratify the consular convention with the United States and indefinitely stalling implementation of an airline agreement. According to Meshcheryakov, Dobrynin, who was to return to Washington in early May, would be held in Moscow until approximately May 10 in order to provide Brezhnev an opportunity to instruct the Soviet ambassador on a new hard line and "to make sure he understands Sov[iet] positions." The Soviet military was also insisting that all steps toward détente be halted and aid to North Vietnam increased. These steps, the Soviet military attaché warned, would be apparent in two or three weeks, and even Saigon would feel their effects. Meshcheryakov said "he was speaking seriously and not making idle threats. The U.S. must not underestimate Soviet determination to keep North Vietnam as a viable socialist state, even if it leads to confrontation."[25]

Other facts at the disposal of American policymakers contradicted the Soviet general's remarks. Ten days earlier Averell Harriman had met with Yuri Zhukov, "one of the Soviet Union's most distinguished journalists and an apparent confidant of Kremlin leaders," according to the CIA's biographic register.[26] Although Zhukov strongly criticized U.S. behavior during the Kosygin-Wilson talks and rejected any notion of the Soviet Union serving as mediator in the Vietnam conflict, he favored a quick end to the war and assured his counterpart that "what Kosygin had stated in London still stands."[27]

Still, given the possibility of a hardening Soviet position, the Johnson administration thought it should try to alleviate tension in Moscow, probe the Soviet position, and clarify U.S. objectives in Vietnam for the Kremlin. Brown's visit to Moscow in May would serve this end.

On the eve of the British foreign secretary's trip, Rusk asked for Thompson's recommendations for U.S. actions with regard to this visit. The American ambassador explained that Moscow had not yet completed its policy review, so it was difficult to suggest what line Brown should take. Nevertheless, Thompson believed that it would be useful for Brown to draw the attention of his Soviet counterparts to the "strongest pressure on Administration" that came from the "hawks." "Perhaps most useful line he could take," Thompson continued, "would be to impress on Soviets that in any event military victory for North Vietnam clearly impossible and suggest they use their influence to achieve gradual tapering off of military activities on both sides."[28]

Rusk's message to London took into account Thompson's recommendations. The secretary of state asked his British colleague to convey to Soviet leaders that the United States was prepared to recognize the interest of the Soviet Union in the safety of a Communist regime in North Vietnam. The American government also recognized that U.S. military actions against the DRV presented many problems for the Soviet government. But the Soviets, in their turn, had to recognize the U.S. interest in the safety of South Vietnam and the ability of the South Vietnamese to have their own government. "Surely," stated Rusk, "if we and the Soviets recognize each other's important interests here, we ought to find a way to pull North and South Viet-Nam apart militarily."

According to Rusk, Washington was ready to halt its military actions against the DRV "at any time," but Hanoi had to demonstrate reciprocity in exchange for that gesture of goodwill. Rusk asked Brown to press the Soviets to find out how the North Vietnamese leadership would react to a number of U.S. proposals that included a combination and modified versions of earlier initiatives.[29]

To help ensure a favorable outcome of the reappraisal process in Moscow, the Johnson administration decided to halt the bombing within ten miles of Hanoi. This decision was partly the result of a growing uneasiness within the government about military operations against North Vietnam. Despite the fact that the initiative was a palliative and had no substantial effect on the course of the war, some American officials found it useful, at least in the short run. Harriman strongly advocated the restriction on the grounds that it would bolster Kosygin's supporters who, according to Harriman, favored softer actions. Harriman urged the State Department to send Thompson without delay instructions to seek a meeting with the highest official available, preferably Gromyko or at least his deputy Kuznetsov, to inform the Soviets in confidence of this decision and to indicate that the administration expected the Soviets to use their influence to move Hanoi toward negotiations. Otherwise, Harriman warned, "we must assume that in absence of an approach by us the Soviet decision will be a hard line, at least as far as Vietnam is concerned."[30]

Thompson in Moscow concurred with this opinion. Rusk notified him about the decision on the bombing halt in a cable on May 18. He informed the ambassador that it would be implemented after a strike on the Hanoi power plant, though the administration might decide to forgo this target. Rusk asked Thompson how the bombing restriction should be disclosed privately to the Soviets. The secretary believed the "actions we are considering would be to convey to the Soviets quietly what the future program would be, possibly taking the line that we held off for many months in hitting a series of valid military targets, in deference to possibilities of change in Hanoi's attitude and Soviet efforts and interest." Rusk confided that in the future Washington anticipated that strikes would not be made north of the 20th parallel unless new military targets developed or old ones resumed operation. Following Harriman's recommendation, Rusk asked the ambassador to communicate with highest-level Soviet officials, Gromyko or at least Kuznetsov, in order to convey this decision to the Kremlin.[31]

Thompson "warmly welcomed" the proposed plan. He perceived the decision as in line with his conviction that U.S. military actions should be related to achieving success in the South, and actions north of the 20th parallel must be few and justified only by demands in the South. In this connection, the ambassador regarded the bombing of remaining targets in the Hanoi area before the halt as "unfortunate," especially if the strikes were to coincide with Brown's visit. Since the Soviets were "on verge of reaching major policy decisions not only re Vietnam but on their relations with US across the board," Thompson thought it advisable to send a short letter from President Johnson to Kosygin, which the ambassador would retain until the targets in Hanoi were hit, and then would promptly deliver to the Soviet leader "before Soviet decisions are taken and possibly commitments made to DRV." Thompson reiterated his belief that "Kosygin is in favor of settlement and that message to him will help him with his colleagues."[32]

These U.S. efforts to "appease" Soviet leaders and influence their policy review were endangered by the perilous developments of early June. Growing tension in the Middle East between the Arab states and Israel exploded in war. On the morning of June 5 the Israeli army launched a surprise attack and wiped out the Egyptian air force in one blow. The war ended in six days with Israel occupying territories in Egypt, Syria, and Jordan. It strained relations between East and West, and specifically between the Soviet Union and the United States. Although neither country was inclined to change its sympathies and allies, both recognized the need to find a peaceful way out of the Middle East conflict.

Another incident, though it lacked the scale and importance of the Arab-Israeli conflict, had a potentially serious impact on Soviet-American relations. On June 3 *Pravda* published information that a day earlier American aircraft had attacked the Soviet merchant vessel *Turkestan* off the North Vietnamese port of Cam Pha, damaging the ship and wounding two crewmen. In a note to Washington, the Soviet government stated that this attack represented a "flagrant violation" of the freedom of navigation, an "act of robbery" with "far-reaching consequences." The Soviet government insisted on severe punishment of those guilty in the attack and awaited assurances from the United States that such an incident would not reoccur.[33]

Pravda also carried a commentary on the incident entitled "Provocateurs Playing with Fire." The U.S. embassy conveyed the gist of the article in a message to the State Department and noted that despite its seriousness of tone, *Pravda* implied that the Soviets were treating the affair as an isolated incident rather than as an indication of a U.S. effort to escalate the war. The embassy concluded that the incident further exposed the Soviets to charges that they were not decisive enough in dealing with the United States. Therefore the Soviet decision to publicize it was "probably based on desire avoid risking further charges re US-Soviet collusion and Soviet sell-out to us, as well as difficulties any attempt to hush up such incident could raise internally."[34]

Whatever the reasons, Moscow apparently decided on a demonstration of severity toward the United States. A U.S. reply to the Soviet note only added fuel to the fire. Washington expressed regrets that the *Turkestan* had been damaged and crew members injured but stated that on the basis of information available to the American government, U.S. aircraft had not caused the damage. The reply suggested that North Vietnamese antiaircraft fire might have been responsible.[35]

On June 6 *Pravda* published a new Soviet note rejecting the U.S. explanation of the incident and characterizing it as an attempt to avoid responsibility for the attack. The Soviets declared that the raid had occurred in broad daylight, at a time when there were no other ships in port. "Without doubt American pilots aimed precisely at the *Turkestan*, dropping bombs on her and firing on her." The note ridiculed a U.S. notion that American air operations against "legitimate air targets" in Vietnam necessarily entailed a risk for free international navigation. "U.S. intervention against Vietnam," the Soviet note said, "is the most flagrant violation of all standards of international law and represents in itself a crime against mankind."[36]

The Kremlin obviously scored points on the eve of a party plenum which should have crowned the lengthy policy reappraisal by the Soviet leadership. It was held in mid-June and concentrated almost exclusively on foreign policy problems. Washington was attentive to the results of this Soviet Communist party forum and was concerned with the rather harsh tone of its official documents. Thompson, who on the request of Secretary Rusk prepared an analysis of the plenum's statement, even expressed a fear that in the short run the United States might find itself back in a real cold war atmosphere. It seemed clear to American policymakers that more pragmatic leaders in the Soviet politburo had yielded to the "more ideologically oriented members."[37]

While this policy review continued, the Kremlin announced that Premier Kosygin would participate in the special session of the UN General Assembly devoted to the Middle East crisis. This news stirred excitement in Washington, for it would be the first visit of a Soviet leader to the United States during the Johnson presidency. It opened a great opportunity for the president to meet with Kosygin and discuss various questions of relations between the two countries as well as international problems. Moscow emphasized that Kosygin would be visiting the United Nations, not the United States, but this did not discourage Johnson's advisers.

American diplomats in Moscow were among the first to question the stated motives of Kosygin's visit. On June 16 Chargé John Guthrie drew Washington's attention to the composition of the Soviet delegation to the UN General Assembly. He noted that the delegation was "very thin" on the Middle East side. Absent was Deputy Foreign Minister Vladimir Semenov, who was responsible for the region, and the list included only two middle-level Soviet Foreign Ministry officials. On the other hand, Guthrie noted that the delegation included officials who were experts in fields other than the Middle East. The American chargé concluded that the composition of the Soviet delegation might have been tailored for bilateral talks with the United States, perhaps even on subjects not related to the Middle East. The inclusion of Viktor Sukhodrev, a high-level interpreter, reinforced this idea.

Guthrie speculated that even if Kosygin did not meet with the president, his visit might be highly useful. "Kosygin has never been in US and, in view of his personality, he is more likely to draw appropriate conclusions from what he sees than Khrushchev or any of his colleagues in triumvirate. We hope this benefit will not be negated by Kosygin's tough propaganda posture which we may assume in view [of] present Soviet stance."[38]

Guthrie's analysis was confirmed by the private approaches of

Soviet diplomats on the eve of Kosygin's arrival. On June 14 Walt Rostow, the president's assistant for national security affairs, informed Johnson of a conversation that had taken place between U.S. Information Agency Director Carl Rowan and the press attaché of the Soviet embassy in Washington, Oleg Kalugin. The latter told his counterpart that Kosygin's primary mission in the United States was "to dramatize Soviet support for the Arabs"—but his secondary mission was to have bilateral conversations with the American president.[39]

Whatever the opportunities involved in Kosygin's arrival in the United States, the administration was confronted with what at first glance appeared to be an insoluble problem. The Soviet premier did not wish to go to Washington to meet the president, for officially he had come to the United States to participate in the General Assembly, not to hold talks with Johnson. During his conversation with Rowan, Kalugin hinted that it would be difficult for Kosygin to come to Washington because the Chinese and Arabs would certainly regard such a step with suspicion.

For his part, Johnson was not about to swallow his prestige and hurry to New York to meet with the Soviet premier. His advisers, worried that the meeting might be lost, tried to persuade the president of the great opportunity and of the need to compromise on the problem of venue.

As always, Averell Harriman was persistent in emphasizing to Johnson the advantages of a personal discussion with Kosygin about Vietnam. In his memorandum "Possible Kosygin Talks on Vietnam Settlement," Harriman argued that the president's meeting with Kosygin offered a "unique opportunity for progress towards negotiations for a peaceful settlement in Vietnam," since the direct or indirect cooperation of the Soviets was "essential to get talks going."[40]

Although he was often ignored by the Johnson administration, in this case Harriman's voice was strengthened by Dean Rusk. On June 17 the secretary of state sent the president a memorandum in which he stated that "The most serious question for you to consider is what to do about a meeting with Kosygin." Rusk informed his chief that almost all the major figures of his administration (McNamara, Nicholas Katzenbach, Cyrus Vance, Bundy, Walt Rostow, Thompson, Harry McPherson) were convinced that "there would be enormous political loss" for the president if Kosygin were to go home without the two men meeting.

Rusk reminded Johnson that more than once the president had pledged to "go anywhere, see anybody" in the interest of peace. "If it became generally known . . . ," Rusk warned, "that you had refused to see Kosygin in New York, we believe that you would be under very severe domestic criticism—quite apart from international public opinion." Rusk strongly recommended that the president go to the New York area. To avoid reflections on his prestige, Johnson could meet with other heads of state, announcing such meetings in advance. "If you agree with us," Rusk concluded, "that it is important to see him [Kosygin] before he leaves the United States, it would be better to make the arrangement early rather than appear to be submitting to UN, U.S. or congressional pressure."[41]

Kosygin seemed no less interested in meeting with the American president. Although we have no direct evidence of this, the activity of Soviet officials during his stay in the United States testifies to this effect. Thus Yulii Vorontsov, counselor of the Soviet embassy, "speaking personally and informally" during his conversation with a White House staffer, indicated "strong Soviet interest" in the possibility of a summit. But he pointed out that the Soviet premier could not travel "220 long political miles" to Washington for fear of accusations by the Arabs. "If the President found a way to be in New York or 'in the vicinity,'" Vorontsov was positive a meeting could be arranged without difficulty. When asked how far the "vicinity of New York" extended, Vorontsov did not object to a place as far away as Philadelphia. Besides, Vorontsov assured his counterpart, "Kosygin was a direct and forthright man, and would be prepared to talk about the whole range of subjects of interest," not only the Middle East crisis.[42]

Another report on Soviet interest in a mini-summit reached Washington from New York. A member of the Soviet UN mission, Sveneld Evteev, asked his colleague from the American delegation whether there would be a meeting between Kosygin and the president. Since his interlocutor had no idea, Evteev commented that it would be "your [i.e., American] mistake" if the meeting were not held.[43]

The State Department summarized these and other reports and

concluded that Kosygin's basic purpose in seeing the president was to try to explore Johnson's attitudes and "add the perspective of a face-to-face meeting to his evaluation" of the American leader. On the other hand, the Soviet premier was not likely to confine himself to a purely social meeting. He would no doubt be prepared to discuss many international matters as well as Vietnam. The State Department had no indication that Kosygin would have "anything very new" to say about Southeast Asia.[44] Ambassador Thompson, who was in the United States for consultation, shared this opinion.[45]

While discussions on the substance of possible talks between the Soviet and American leaders unfolded in Washington, the principal question of a site remained unresolved. Rusk met with Kosygin on June 22, after the premier's arrival in New York, to propose McGuire Air Force Base in New Jersey as a possible venue for a meeting. Kosygin flatly objected. He was not persuaded by Rusk's arguments that the base was a quiet and secure place with communications the president needed, and that since Johnson was scheduled to speak in California just after the meeting, he would be able to leave from the base. For Kosygin, it was important to consider public opinion. "People would wonder what we were trying to demonstrate," the Soviet premier reasoned. "Perhaps a place could be found off the base. He was not objecting to the area. He stressed that in his view it was not in the President's interest to meet on a military base. Both countries had [worked] for a peaceful approach, they needed only one room for about four hours and even a hotel room would suffice." If the military base were chosen, Kosygin stressed, people would wonder whether the United States wanted to show him its guns and rockets.[46]

Kosygin's position was not unreasonable. The Soviet leader had to consider how a meeting on an American military base would be viewed in Hanoi and Beijing. Accusations of U.S.-Soviet collusion would undoubtedly be stimulated by the location of the talks, and the reaction of other Soviet allies would be difficult to predict. Nor could Kosygin put aside the reactions of his colleagues in the politburo, such as chief party ideologue Mikhail Suslov, who were watchdogs of Communist purity and vigilance.

Finally a site was agreed upon—the small town of Glassboro, New Jersey, scarcely known even to most Americans and certainly to no one in the Soviet Union. For several days Glassboro became a focus of world attention; forever it remains a part of the history of Russian-American relations.

While preparations for the Glassboro meeting were under way, Kosygin participated in the special session of the UN General Assembly. On June 19 he delivered a speech primarily devoted to the Middle East crisis. Nevertheless Vietnam did not escape his attention. The Soviet premier reiterated his usual denunciation of the United States as waging an aggressive war against Vietnam. He accused Washington of wanting to impose a regime upon the Vietnamese people in accordance with the wishes of "foreign imperialist circles." He emphasized that the only way to resolve the problem was to withdraw U.S. troops from the region. But before that the United States would have to end immediately and unconditionally the bombing of North Vietnam. "No declarations about a readiness to find a peaceful solution of the Vietnamese problem can sound convincing," Kosygin declared, "if this is not realized. Declarations of the United States of America should not differ from its deeds." Kosygin again expressed his and his colleagues' concern that the war in Vietnam increased the risk of a "broad military encounter of powers," implying the Soviet Union and the United States.[47]

Although strong in its language, the speech did not "break a new ground of invective," according to one American diplomat.[48] At the same time it defined Kosygin's negotiating stance on Vietnam in his coming talks with President Johnson. Another indication of the Soviet position was received by Secretary Rusk during a dinner with Gromyko on the eve of the meeting at Glassboro. The subject of Vietnam actually arose after dinner, when the secretary asked his Soviet counterpart whether some of the following steps could be used to bring the conflict in Southeast Asia to an end: bilateral talks, a new Geneva conference, talks under the auspices of the UN, and so forth. Gromyko for the first time spoke in Russian through an interpreter. He said that contacts between the two sides could bring positive developments. But an atmosphere must be created that would be favorable for talks, and this meant the unconditional cessation of the bombing of the DRV. Gromyko added that the Soviets could not conduct negotiations for Hanoi. "The only way to find out what would happen is to stop bombing unconditionally," Gromyko repeated several times, brushing aside Rusk's complaints about North Vietnamese infiltration into the South during bombing pauses and the concentration of DRV troops near the demilitarized zone.[49]

Gromyko was clearly speaking within limits imposed on him by the presence of a Soviet leader to whom he must leave the right to supply details. At the same time he outlined the Soviet position as it had been worked out in Moscow, taking into account Hanoi's attitude as of June 1967.

The DRV favored no peace initiative. After the April visit of Pham Van Dong to Moscow, Hanoi did not budge in its refusal to maintain contacts with the United States, regardless of Soviet appeals. Shcherbakov reported that in his conversations with North Vietnamese leaders the latter confined themselves to "monosyllabic replies" that Soviet recommendations were being studied, that it was necessary to wait for the right moment to put forward a new political or diplomatic initiative. Since Hanoi did not foresee such a moment in the near future, it was not reasonable to expect a North Vietnamese reaction to a U.S. initiative or to a feeler from third countries.[50] Despite such an unencouraging situation, Moscow had not given up hope of moving its Vietnamese comrades toward negotiations.

Johnson and Kosygin met for the first time on June 23, 1967. Most of their talks were devoted to the problems of bilateral relations and the situation in the Middle East. But even during the first session, Johnson tried to involve the Soviet premier in a discussion about Vietnam, though without success. After listening to the president's arguments in support of the U.S. bombing of North Vietnam, Kosygin shifted to the problems of the Middle East.[51]

As it turned out, Kosygin was not being evasive, he was merely awaiting a reply from Hanoi. When the two leaders met again after lunch, Kosygin himself brought up the situation in Indochina. He confided that in anticipation of their talks, he had contacted Pham Van Dong in Hanoi to ask what he could do during his meeting with the president to help bring the war to an end. While they were at lunch, a reply from Hanoi had been received.

The substance of Pham Van Dong's reply was the following: Stop the bombing and the North Vietnamese would immediately go to the conference table. Kosygin urged the president to follow up this proposal. He emphasized that the reply "provided for the first time the opportunity of talking directly with Hanoi at no risk for the United States." The Soviet leader tried to overcome Johnson's visible pessimism. He cited the example of France, which had fought in Algiers for seven years and still ended up at the conference table. He was sure the North Vietnamese had the will to carry on the fight for many years if necessary. "And what would the president accomplish?" asked Kosygin. "He would carry on a war for ten years or more, killing off the best of the young people of his nation." The premier praised the courage of American soldiers and compared it with that of the young people of the Soviet Union who "in similar circumstances would also fight just as well." Nevertheless, Kosygin repeated, it was now time to end the war and sit down at the conference table; then the president could see what would develop.

One of Kosygin's strongest arguments in support of the proposal may have been his reference to China. The Soviet leader insisted that by continuing the war Johnson "was actually helping the Chinese in achieving their very worst designs." Finally, Kosygin stressed the "emergency nature" of his proposal and urged Johnson to weigh it and prepare a reply in two days so that the Soviet premier would be able to transmit it to Hanoi before his departure from the United States.[52]

Apparently Johnson viewed Kosygin's overture with mixed feelings. Although he may have been inspired by the Soviet leader's interest in a peaceful settlement of the conflict and by his obvious apprehension for the effects of the war on the international situation in general and on Soviet-American relations in particular, the president seemed unenthusiastic about a new U.S. approach to the DRV as proposed by Kosygin, especially since the Soviet leader did not guarantee results. In the last resort, Johnson tried to extract from Kosygin a promise to assist the United States at the conference table. But the Soviet premier agreed only to transmit the American proposal to Hanoi and reiterated the usual Soviet position that the USSR could not decide this question "independently without advice from North Vietnam."

Despite his pessimism, the president, in his own words, "studied Hanoi's message carefully." He discussed it at length with Rusk and McNamara.[53] Rusk suggested giving to Kosygin, along with a reply to Hanoi, an oral message in which the president would acknowledge a "very special responsibility" of the United States and the USSR on matters involving peace. The message would inform Kosygin that Washington was prepared to stop the bombing as a step toward peace. But at the same time the United States would retain a right "to resume full freedom of action" if talks did not lead to peace or if Hanoi used protracted talks to achieve a one-sided military advantage. The U.S. government would emphasize the "greatest importance" that Kosygin and Johnson "not misunderstand each other and that no problems of good faith" arise between them.[54]

Johnson delivered this oral message as well as a reply to Hanoi during his meeting with Kosygin on June 25. The premier seemed satisfied with the reply, which declared U.S. readiness to stop the bombing of North Vietnam and assumed that following the cessation of bombing there would be immediate discussions between representatives of the United States and of the DRV "in Geneva, Moscow, Vientiane, or any other suitable location." These discussions, according to the reply, should be accompanied by the mutual restraint of both countries in their military operations in the South, i.e., by the stoppage of North Vietnamese infiltration and by the refusal of U.S. forces and those of South Vietnam to advance to the North.[55]

Kosygin's satisfaction with the results of his talks with the American president expressed itself in his closing words. "The president could rest assured," he declared, "that whatever the circumstances and whatever public pronouncements might be made, the USSR wished peace. The USSR did not wish a confrontation with the US anywhere and the two countries had no conflict in any part of the world. When an acute situation arose somewhere in the world, the two parties should consult." Kosygin could not miss an opportunity to expose the dangerous nature of China's policy. "The US should not believe," he claimed, "those who are trying to raise questions between our two countries. As he had written to the President, there were some in the world who wanted issues to arise between our two countries. Peking was obviously one of those; he certainly did not exclude this possibility. After all, the President had seen what hullabaloo they had raised in Peking in connection with his trip to New York; Peking was saying that he was here to sell out someone, but obviously neither he nor the President had sold out to anyone."[56]

These words clearly revealed Kosygin's principal objectives in his talks with the president. Obviously the Soviet premier, like his colleagues in Moscow, was anxious to see improving relations between the two countries despite all the unfavorable international circumstances at the time. At home a stagnated Soviet economy created an interest in implementing the achievements of American technology in Soviet industry and agriculture, and a desire to cooperate with the United States in scientific and cultural relations. In international politics the Kremlin's goals were more complex. Undoubtedly the Soviets wished to avoid a confrontation with the United States, since they were conscious of the danger such an encounter could entail. But this does not mean they had abandoned their plans to win superiority over "imperialists" in the world-wide struggle. Accordingly the USSR strove to gain advantages over the United States and to increase Soviet influence in various parts of the globe by utilizing the weaknesses of its rival and by preventing the United States from utilizing its own weaknesses. In the late 1960s such a weakness for the Soviet Union was its conflict with China. Because Soviet leaders feared a possible alliance between Washington and Beijing, they were eager to prevent a rapprochement between them.

Thus Moscow's strategy included, at first glance, contradictory goals: to enlist American aid in solving the domestic problems of the Soviet Union, to gain advantages over the United States in international competition, and to prevent the Americans from utilizing Soviet weaknesses. At Glassboro Kosygin operated in accordance with these goals.[57]

President Johnson likewise was interested in clarifying the Soviet position on various international problems, and discussions with the Soviet premier helped him in this regard. But the principal problem of Vietnam, and, more specifically, the Soviet role in it, remained unresolved. Johnson's appeal to Hanoi brought no reaction from the North Vietnamese, and the president's attempts to secure Moscow's services on behalf of the United States in finding ways to settle the conflict proved unsuccessful.

Considering Hanoi's position, the outcome could scarcely have been different. But had Kosygin not been informed of the DRV's attitude before his trip to the United States? Surely he had. He did not deceive the president about his communication with Pham Van Dong on the eve of talks at Glassboro. Soviet documents confirm this exchange.[58] Kosygin probably exaggerated the importance of the North Vietnamese proposal and ignored its background, which was scrupulously analyzed by the Soviet embassy in Hanoi. The embassy's reports clearly demonstrate that the North Vietnamese leadership did not favor negotiations with the United States in the spring and summer of 1967.

One cannot dismiss the possibility that the Soviet premier simply gambled when he confided to Johnson that once the bombing stopped, Hanoi would *immediately* go to the conference table. His scheme may have been to induce Washington to stop the bombing by a promise of early negotiations and to induce Hanoi to agree on negotiations once the bombing stopped. In any event, in June as in February, "the door to peace was still tightly barred."[59] Whatever useful results Glassboro produced in various spheres of international relations, Vietnam was not on the list.

SEVEN

The Road to Paris

The latter half of 1967 was a period of agonizing reappraisal for Washington and Hanoi. The struggle in Vietnam could not continue at the same pace and with the same intensity, for both parties had nearly exhausted their resources of will and perseverance which permitted them to withstand losses and disillusionment. The outcome of the war now depended on a wise choice among existing possibilities and unavoidable risks.

The logical way out of the military stalemate that became obvious in the fall of 1967 was peaceful negotiations on the basis of a less unacceptable compromise for both sides. But while conscious of the need for such a choice, neither Washington nor Hanoi was ready to abandon hope for a military victory. Leaders in both countries seemed to be searching for the slightest chance of success in one more attempt to destroy the enemy by an all-out attack.

The United States' position was more precarious than that of the North Vietnamese. Each day of the war without decisive success contributed to the erosion of domestic support for American participation in the remote Indochina war. Even within the administration, the first signs of this irreversible process revealed themselves among the president's closest advisers. These were the men who had every opportunity to analyze the whole picture of the war in Southeast Asia, not merely isolated fragments of the puzzle presented to the public by officials seeking to avoid unwelcome complications. By the fall of 1967, a man who supported and helped to design the war from the outset, who had directed its course on an everyday basis, and whose name stood second to the president's on almost all military orders during the Vietnam War, appeared on the front line of dissenters and opponents of the war. This was Secretary of Defense Robert S. McNamara.

McNamara's disillusionment with the war, his dissatisfaction with American achievements in the struggle against the Vietnamese Communists, and his understanding of the futility of attempts to undermine North Vietnamese will by bombing DRV territory convinced him of the need to abandon military goals and transform the conflict into a political struggle, with or without negotiations. In August 1967 he proposed a number of measures for gradually limiting U.S. participation in the conflict and for a final disengagement from the war.[1]

McNamara's arguments contradicted optimistic U.S. military reports on the prospects of the war. Throughout the summer and fall of 1967, the Joint Chiefs of Staff, as well as American generals in Vietnam who were directing the military operation—the first among them being William C. Westmoreland—were persuading the administration and the American people that the United States was making "tremendous progress" in the war, that any report of stalemate was a "complete fiction," and that the final victory lay "within our grasp."

The generals' arguments outweighed those of the embattled secretary of defense. They convinced not only members of the Johnson administration who were too eager to be convinced but also the so-called Wise Men, veterans of American politics and diplomacy who met at the president's request in the first two days of November to discuss U.S. policy in Vietnam. Dean Acheson, the former secretary of state; General of the Army Omar Bradley, veteran of World War II; George Ball and McGeorge Bundy, both former members of the Johnson administration; Arthur Dean, the Korean War negotiator; former Treasury Secretary Douglas Dillon; Justice Abe Fortas, close friend of the president; and former Under Secretary of State Robert Murphy—all told President Johnson he should stand firm and reject any suggestion to get out of the war.

Only Averell Harriman remained silent and stone-faced during this "display of unanimity," expressing by his demeanor deep reservations about the war. According to Clark Clifford, then a lawyer and a close associate of the president, and later secretary of defense after McNamara's resignation, only when the discussion turned to the possibility of negotiations did Harriman become animated and argue in support of a diplomatic settlement of the conflict. Negotiation was "inevitable and necessary," he said.[2]

Harriman was among those in official Washington who held serious doubts about the expediency of U.S. policy to continue the war. In the summer and fall of 1967, as always, he remained attentive to any sign of possible talks with Hanoi and considered support from Moscow an essential part of the process of settling the conflict. Just after the meeting at Glassboro, Harriman obtained information from intelligence sources that the North Vietnamese had withdrawn four regiments of troops from the area in and south of the demilitarized zone. In a memorandum to Rusk he suggested this might be a signal from Hanoi to begin a process of settlement, and recommended instructing the American ambassador in Moscow to seek a meeting with Gromyko to clarify the move and to urge Soviet leaders "to obtain from Hanoi . . . a more precise reading of the significance of this withdrawal."[3] A little later Harriman recommended that the secretary of state use a visit by Gromyko to the United Nations as an opportunity "to get Soviet cooperation in achieving any settlement" with the DRV.[4]

Efforts of people like Harriman, as well as the gradual erosion of consensus in Washington, stimulated the Johnson administration to new nonmilitary steps toward settling the conflict. Without abandoning its hopes to win the war on the battlefield, Washington tried to settle it diplomatically. More and more these attempts became a response to demands of time and situation, rather than propaganda moves designed to placate world and domestic opinion. In the latter half of 1967 several such attempts were made by the administration, one through the French scientists Raymond Aubrac and Herbert Marcovich, who were contacted by Henry Kissinger, then a Harvard University professor, and another through the Rumanians. Like all previous attempts, these led nowhere.

Despite this lack of visible success in contacts with Hanoi, Washington's efforts in the summer and fall of 1967 showed a gradual modification of the U.S. position toward negotiations with the North Vietnamese. This modification reflected the changing war situation in Vietnam as well as the domestic political mood, and the growing realization by members of the Johnson administration that it was impossible to bring the North Vietnamese to the negotiating table without sacrificing some points on the U.S. list of conditions for talks.

A shift in the U.S. stance manifested itself in a speech delivered by President Johnson in San Antonio, Texas, on September 29, 1967. Offering an account of the war and the reasons for U.S. involvement, the address contained a peace offer which was the essence of the U.S. proposal sent through the Kissinger channel. Public announcement by the president, it was thought, might underline its significance in the eyes of the North Vietnamese.

At San Antonio Johnson tried to convince his fellow Americans there was a "forward movement" in South Vietnam. And he asserted that "There is progress in the war itself, steady progress considering the war that we are fighting. . . ." According to the president, the Viet Cong had suffered defeat throughout South Vietnam. "The campaigns of the last year," he assured his audience, "drove the enemy from many of their major interior bases. The military victory almost within Hanoi's grasp in 1965 has now been denied them. The grip of the Vietcong on the people is being broken."

In the midst of these victorious declarations, Johnson articulated his peace offer to Hanoi which soon became known as the "San Antonio formula." He said, "As we have told Hanoi time and time again, the heart of the matter is really this: The United States is willing to stop all aerial and naval bombardment of North Vietnam when this will lead promptly to productive discussions. We, of course, assume that while discussions proceed, North Vietnam would not take advantage of the bombing cessation or limitation."[5]

Thus Johnson abandoned his earlier pledge that he would not exchange the bombing of North Vietnam merely for negotiations. Washington also significantly modified its position with respect to North Vietnamese infiltration into the South during the bombing halt. Now American leaders did not demand that the infiltration must cease. Johnson's phrase "We . . . assume that . . . North Vietnam would not take advantage of the bombing cessation" implied that the United States was prepared to agree to the usual volume of the infiltration, but not its increase. Clark Clifford later confirmed this interpretation during confirmation hearings in the Senate in January 1968 on his appointment as secretary of defense. Asked by Republican Senator Strom Thurmond whether "not to take advantage of the pause in the bombing" meant a stoppage by the North Vietnamese of all their military activities, Clifford replied, "Their military activity will continue in South Vietnam, I assume, until there is a cease-fire agreed upon. I assume that they will continue to transport the normal amount of goods, munitions, and men to South Vietnam. I assume that we will continue to maintain our forces and support our forces during that period. So what I am suggesting, in the language of the President, is that he would insist that they not take advantage of the suspension of the bombing."[6]

However substantially the "San Antonio formula" contradicted the determination of the U.S. government to spare no opportunity for military victory, it represented one of the choices American leaders had before them in late 1967. By no means was it the only approach in Washington's plans.

In Hanoi, meanwhile, the North Vietnamese apparently were facing the same kind of agonizing reappraisal. The DRV economy was overburdened with military demands and dangerously undermined by American bombings. Relations with allies and supporters—not only China and the Soviet Union but also the National Liberation Front, which was more autonomous than American officials recognized—were presenting problems. And Hanoi had to consider the patience of its own people who, though indoctrinated and deprived of free opinion by the Communist regime, could not indefinitely endure the burden of the war. While they were more maneuverable with respect to domestic opinion than American leaders, the North Vietnamese were not totally free from the need to care for the primary expectations of their people.

The complex of these and other concerns seems to have pushed Hanoi to revise its plans for the struggle against "American imperialists and their South Vietnamese puppets" and to decide in favor of a negotiated settlement of the conflict. But, much like their American counterparts, North Vietnamese leaders were not prepared to abandon their hope for military victory. They could not afford to neglect a "last chance" to crush the enemy on the battlefield with one decisive blow. As a result, in the summer of 1967 one of Hanoi's responses to growing difficulties on the military, diplomatic, and domestic fronts was to prepare for a general offensive and a general uprising in the South. DRV leaders could not help but understand that their plans for a general offensive ran counter to the views of their powerful allies in Moscow and Beijing. Almost from the outset the USSR viewed the war in Vietnam as an unwelcome development and tried to persuade Hanoi to resolve its problems at the negotiating table. Nor could China applaud designs for an offensive, for it advocated a war of attrition, a guerrilla war limited to isolated assaults by irregular forces against a militarily superior enemy.

But Hanoi nourished plans for a general offensive, convinced that even a partial victory could turn the situation in the South in favor of the Communists, inflict a mortal blow to the Saigon regime, and force the Americans to abandon their war with the North, greatly enhancing Hanoi's prestige in the eyes of the Soviets and Chinese as well as the whole Communist movement. The more impressive a victory the Vietnamese Communists could achieve, the more dividends they would gain.

Hanoi could not expect to defeat the United States but it had every reason to hope for success in undermining the Saigon regime. The Communist leadership of Vietnam had demonstrated common sense and clear vision in its efforts in the South; but plans for a general offensive included such unknown quantities as a mass uprising of the "oppressed" South Vietnamese against the Saigon regime and its American patrons. Here common sense gave way to Communist dogma, which rejected any doubt about popular support for the champions of liberty and peace, that is, the Communists. DRV leaders could not even imagine that this support would be lacking once they began the offensive in the South, and apparently they linked the success of their entire offensive to the popular revolt against the "puppet regime."

Presumably the North Vietnamese had begun serious consideration of a general offensive as early as the spring of 1967. The relatively successful activity of the NLF and North Vietnamese regular troops in the South stimulated Hanoi's desire to broaden the scope of its military operations, coupled with a popular uprising. The Soviet embassy in Hanoi had noted this DRV mood and labeled it as "unjustified optimism concerning the outcome of the military struggle."[7] Soviet diplomats were not likely aware of the reasons for this mood, for Hanoi still enjoyed confusing its Soviet comrades. But the embassy had sufficient indirect evidence to predict that not until after military actions in the spring of 1968 would there be significant change in favor of a settlement of the conflict.[8]

Apparently the process of working out plans for the general offensive was accelerated after the death of Nguyen Thi Thanh, one of the DRV's highest-ranking military authorities. General Thanh, who had been Hanoi's senior military representative in South Vietnam since 1965, knew the situation on the battlefield much better than any official in the DRV capital. His knowledge reportedly made him highly skeptical of plans for a general offensive.[9] Besides, the general was, according to the Soviet embassy in the DRV, one of the leaders of the pro-Chinese faction in the Lao Dong party,[10] and that made him a logical opponent of any plan that ran counter to the Chinese theory of a people's war. In any case, sometime in July 1967 a resolution for a general offensive and uprising was adopted by the politburo of the Lao Dong party,[11] and from that day Hanoi began preparations for the event that was destined to be a turning point in the war in Vietnam.

To achieve the aims of the offensive, the North Vietnamese leadership had to obtain support from its Communist allies. Thus the first task for DRV leaders was to sign new agreements with Moscow and Beijing for supplemental aid. In the fall of 1967 an economic delegation headed by Le Thanh Nghi went on a long journey.

The new demands of the North Vietnamese must have given Moscow the idea that Hanoi was preparing something special for a new season of military activity. The communiqué issued after the talks between the North Vietnamese envoys and Kosygin's deputy Vladimir Novikov not only admitted that aid to the DRV included military supplies but, for the first time since the start of full-scale Soviet assistance to Hanoi, even specified what kind of military assistance was being provided. In response to DRV requests Moscow would deliver in 1968 "aircraft, antiaircraft weapons, artillery and firearms, ammunition and other military supplies." The communiqué added that the Soviet Union would also provide North Vietnam with transportation, oil products, ferrous and nonferrous metals, food, chemical fertilizers, medicaments, and other items "necessary for further enhancement of the DRV defense capability and the development of the people's economy of the DRV."[12]

Such an open declaration of all-out support was unprecedented for Moscow in its relations with allies and proxies. The

Kremlin liked to avoid revealing the quality and scope of its assistance to "friends," though that the Soviet Union did provide them with arms and military equipment was for everyone an open secret. Perhaps the recognition of this fact, as well as a desire to warn Washington indirectly of the DRV's serious intentions, persuaded the Soviet government to specify the character of its military aid.

Soon after the agreement on economic aid had been signed between the Soviet Union and North Vietnam, the first secretary of the Lao Dong central committee, Le Duan, visited Moscow and met with Soviet leaders. One of his conversations in the Kremlin took place on October 31 and included all three members of the Soviet "triumvirate"—Leonid Brezhnev, Alexei Kosygin, and Nikolai Podgornyi.[13] The contents of their conversation is unknown, but presumably the North Vietnamese leader shared with his Soviet counterparts his views about the situation in Vietnam.

It is unlikely that Le Duan revealed all North Vietnamese plans for the offensive in the South. The character of the relationship between Hanoi and Moscow did not allow for such candor between the two countries. But he may have tried to impress on the Soviets that the Vietnamese Communists were on the eve of victory and that a final decisive blow would crush the enemy's resistance. And the Soviets may have allowed themselves to be persuaded about the usefulness of such a move in bringing closer an end to the conflict.[14]

By the end of 1967 Hanoi had apparently prepared its forces for a decisive blow in the South, for in January 1968 North Vietnamese leaders gathered the Lao Dong party's central committee to receive formal approval for their plans. The fourteenth plenum concluded that U.S. efforts in Vietnam had peaked. According to the Vietnamese Communists, from that moment on the Americans would occupy defensive positions and would lose their initiative. The plenum determined that the Communists had won strategically and tactically. The Communist leadership stated that the situation was now favorable for the people's forces and for a new, higher stage of the revolutionary war. The plenum adopted a resolution to begin the general offensive and uprising during Tet, the lunar New Year holidays.[15]

Hanoi saw three possible outcomes of the Tet offensive. At the plenum Vietnamese Communist leaders talked about total victory and the end of the war, but surely they knew this was improbable. Rather, they seemed ready to be satisfied with more modest results, that is, winning predominance in most areas of the South while the war continued and anti-Communist forces were strengthened. But Hanoi did not exclude a third, least desirable outcome: an increase in U.S. forces followed by an invasion of North Vietnam, Laos, and Cambodia.[16] Either way, the plenum stated, the Communists were determined to continue the military offensive until the enemy was defeated.

One event preceded the launching of the general offensive in the South. On the eve of 1968, North Vietnamese Foreign Minister Nguyen Duy Trinh appeared at a reception for a visiting Mongolian delegation in Hanoi. After referring to the "successes of the Vietnamese people in the struggle against American aggressors," Trinh turned to the question of a settlement of the conflict. "The Government of the United States," noted the Vietnamese foreign minister, "appealing to the world community, is constantly saying that it wants to talk to Hanoi but receives no reply. If the Government of the United States really wants to negotiate, then, as noted in the statement of our Government of January 28, 1967, first of all the United States must cease unconditionally the bombing and any other acts of war against the DRV. After the United States ceases, without conditions, the bombings and any other acts of war against the DRV, the DRV will talk to the United States on appropriate questions."[17]

Observers at this reception immediately grasped the new nuance in the otherwise formal remarks of the North Vietnamese leader. For the first time Hanoi had used unequivocal wording in its statement on possible negotiations with the United States. The presence of Pham Van Dong at the ceremony, standing behind Trinh and "smiling enigmatically, as if he knew a little joke he wasn't telling,"[18] seemed to add significance to the foreign minister's remarks. And Hanoi Radio later broadcast the Trinh declaration in English over its international shortwave facility so as to ensure that the United States got the point.

Washington was clearly uncertain how to view Trinh's statement. The Johnson administration was awaiting the results of a new attempt to contact North Vietnam through the Rumanians. Nothing came of this effort. Even before it ended, the North Vietnamese launched their Tet offensive, so Washington later concluded that the Trinh declaration had been nothing more than propaganda.

This conclusion was not far from the truth. Soon after Trinh's appearance at the Mongolian reception, a Soviet diplomat in the DRV, Sergei Divilkovskii, met with Truong Cong Dong, a member of the permanent NLF mission in Hanoi. The latter admitted that Trinh's statement had been designed purely for propaganda purposes, though it had been formulated in new terms. The position of the North Vietnamese remained substantially the same. If the United States halted the bombing of the DRV, the DRV would continue to dispatch aid to the South. Hanoi had given no promises on this. Military operations in the South would also continue. According to Dong, the Trinh declaration was a "propaganda ball" sent to the United States in answer to the "balls" that Johnson had sent to the DRV.[19]

This conversation reaffirmed that the intentions of the Vietnamese Communists in early 1968 were concentrated on a military offensive. The Vietnamese drew Divilkovskii's attention to the fact that Hanoi and its southern allies now regarded negotiations with the United States as impractical. "The talks will begin," Dong claimed, "when the Americans have inflicted a defeat on us or when we have inflicted a defeat on them. Everything will be resolved on the battlefield."[20] The propaganda motives of the Trinh statement notwithstanding, it may have reflected Hanoi's desire not to burn all its bridges on the way to negotiations which might reappear if the military offensive failed.

Thus by early 1968 the war in Vietnam had reached a turning point, and the Tet offensive was to become a decisive event. Undoubtedly the attack was not a complete surprise to the United States. From the beginning of U.S. involvement in Vietnam, each year the so-called dry season was a time of intensified military operations by Viet Cong and North Vietnamese forces against American troops and the South Vietnamese army. Westmoreland and other military and intelligence sources had made early predictions of Communist activity after or even during the Tet celebrations.[21] But no American had foreseen the extraordinary size and scope and, most of all, the psychological impact of the Tet offensive. Considering the optimism that had reigned during the fall of 1967 among members of the Johnson administration and the U.S. military, the effect of Tet was magnified.

The offensive that began on January 31 was unprecedented in the numbers of Communist forces and the size of the operations area. The NLF's armed forces, with the support of its North Vietnamese allies, simultaneously attacked more than one hundred cities and towns, including the capital city of Saigon, thiry-nine of the forty-four provincial capitals, and seventy-one district capitals. Targets included the most important government facilities, military installations, and American military bases and headquarters.[22]

The NLF attack on Saigon, a city considered safe from the threat of the Viet Cong, left an enormous impression not only in the United States but throughout the world. The presidential palace and joint general staff headquarters were besieged for hours by groups of Viet Cong raiders. In the Saigon area the Communist command committed thirty-five battalions to the assault.[23] Smaller Communist forces held another large South Vietnam city, Hue, the ancient capital of Vietnam, for thirty-five-days.

Although American and South Vietnamese forces were able to break the Communist offensive and regain control over most of the lost cities and areas, the blow delivered during the attacks of February and March 1968 proved to be irreparable for the United States. Hanoi and the Front may have suffered a military defeat, but they won an important psychological victory. They demonstrated to the world and, most important, to the Americans, that American military reports had significantly distorted the real situation in Vietnam, and that the war, despite the enormous sacrifices of the United States and its allies, was still far from over. This reality seriously undermined the credibility of the Johnson administration. As Clark Clifford put it many years later, "The most serious American casualty at Tet was the loss of the public's confidence in its leaders. Tet hurt the Administration where it needed support most, with Congress and the American public. . . ."[24]

Yet the cost of this victory for the Vietnamese Communists was likewise enormous. Hanoi lost more than fifty thousand of its best military cadres. More important, the general offensive did not prompt a general uprising in the South. This popular failure revealed the weakness of the Communists' position in the South and undermined Hanoi's pledge that the struggle in Vietnam was being waged by the masses of ordinary people, fighting against an oppressive Saigon regime supported by "American imperialism." As it turned out, most South Vietnamese were tired of the war and equally detested the corrupt and antidemocratic regime of Thieu and the vigorous but no less antidemocratic regime in Hanoi.

Despite the fact that the consequences of Tet clearly dictated changes, neither Washington nor Hanoi was prepared for dramatic action. The Johnson administration was severely split. One faction wished to broaden the scope of the war by invading DRV territory, as well as North Vietnamese strongholds in Cambodia and Laos, and sought a significant increase in American troop strength in Vietnam and an intensification of military operations. Their opponents argued that the problem could not be solved by military means; that it was necessary to halt the bombing of North Vietnamese territory and to begin talks with Hanoi; and that the American public would not support a more aggressive course of war.

President Johnson himself hesitated. The focus of warring opinions in the administration became a televised speech that the president planned to deliver at the end of March.[25] First drafts reflected a hard-line approach, incorporating reasons for sending Westmoreland more troops and calling up reserves. There was no mention of a bombing halt or proposals for negotiations.

But the president continued his appraisal process throughout March. In another meeting the Wise Men, in a total reversal of their position in November 1967, now declared their opposition to the war. The impact of this dissent on the president did not manifest itself until the last days of the month.

North Vietnamese leaders endured a no less complicated process of reappraisal, though no direct evidence of deliberations in Hanoi is yet available. But the results of the first months of the offensive demanded a review of DRV policy toward the war.

The immediate effect of the failure to win a decisive victory in Tet was a turn of the North Vietnamese leadership toward mobilizing its forces for more a protracted campaign of "three or four months." Toward the end of February, the Communist command in the South decided to reduce its level of military activity to small guerrilla-unit operations and harassing fire.[26] The war seemed to be returning to earlier levels.

The Tet offensive also demonstrated to the North Vietnamese leadership that an exclusive reliance on a military solution in Vietnam ceased to be reasonable. It was time to apply a strategy of "fighting while negotiating," which envisaged talks with the adversary and simultaneous armed conflict against him. This combination, according to North Vietnamese policymakers, could bring the victory that was now unattainable by military means alone in the stalemated war.

The "fighting while negotiating" strategy had been outlined by Hanoi long before March 1968. In a speech before a congress of NLF cadres in April 1966, General Nguyen Van Vinh admitted that "The future situation may lead to negotiations. Yet even if there are negotiations, they are [to be] conducted simultaneously with fighting. While negotiating, we will continue fighting the enemy more vigorously. (It is possible that the North conducts negotiations while the South continues fighting, and that the South also participates in negotiations while continuing to fight). Those who are in charge of conducting negotiations negotiate, and those in charge of fighting continue fighting, because the decisive factor lies in the battlefield."[27]

North Vietnamese officials did not conceal from their Soviet allies their intention to continue the military struggle in the South while conducting negotiations with the Americans. Their assertions that the beginning of talks would not change the course of the war in the South reflected the conviction of policymakers in Hanoi that the combination of these two forms of struggle might bring victory to the DRV. The Vietnamese Communist leadership postponed the adoption of the "fighting while negotiating" strategy until after the first waves of the Tet offensive proved the fragility of Hanoi's hopes for military success. Soviet observers from the embassy in Hanoi concluded that "war blows and the political struggle of the Vietnamese comrades in the South during the third 'dry season' did not lead to those maximal results on which they counted: the Saigon army and the Saigon government have not been liquidated, the Americans, in general, have preserved their political base in South Vietnam, the conditions for a seizure of power by the Front and its allies have not been created, and the United States has retained fairly broad possibilities for political bargaining." "These results," continued the Soviet analysts, "again have shown both sides the impossibility of solving the [Vietnamese] question by means of war."[28]

The recognition of this fact was a painful process for both

sides. There can never be an ideal time for negotiations in a situation like Vietnam, as in almost all potential negotiating situations. Arthur Goldberg, in a memorandum to President Johnson in mid-March, observed the uncertainty among politicians in both Washington and Hanoi. "If things are going well militarily," the U.S. ambassador to the UN wrote, "the natural inclination is to look upon negotiations as unnecessary. If, conversely, things are going badly militarily, then the disposition is to look upon negotiations as disadvantageous."[29] Goldberg insisted that the time for negotiations had come and the administration must seize the opportunity.

This and other arguments from his close advisers convinced the president to alter the tone of his March 31 speech. He decided to speak to Americans not about the "grave challenge" that the Communist offensive presented, and about the appropriate U.S. response, but about "prospects for peace in Vietnam and Southeast Asia."[30] Moreover, the president conceived a dramatic announcement which would have important implications for American politics.

As soon as it became known that Johnson would propose a number of decisive measures to get negotiations with North Vietnam started, Averell Harriman suggested contacting Soviet leaders in advance in order to gain their support for the U.S. proposals. In his memorandum to Secretary Rusk, Harriman suggested it would also be useful to request Soviet cooperation in talks with Hanoi.

"It is impossible to predict," Harriman confessed, "what might come from discussions with Soviet leaders, but I am satisfied that informing them in advance of any announcement, and discussing as many aspects of the problem as possible, would have a beneficial effect on their future positions and actions." Then he concluded: "Considering the suspicions that exist between Hanoi and Washington, we need some outside influence to assist in reaching a settlement, and there is no other that could be as effective as the Soviet Union."[31] Following Harriman's advice, just before his speech on March 31, Johnson explained his proposal to Soviet Ambassador Dobrynin and personally emphasized the bid for peace.[32] A short time afterward he delivered his address on nationwide television.

The president reiterated his desire "to find a basis for peace talks." He recalled his San Antonio offer and noted that Hanoi had denounced it. In the hope that a new U.S. initiative would lead to early talks, Johnson announced a unilateral step to deescalate the conflict. "Tonight," the president said, "I have ordered our aircraft and our naval vessels to make no attacks on North Vietnam, except in the area north of the demilitarized zone. . . ." He pointed out that the area in which the United States would stop its attacks included almost 90 percent of North Vietnam's population and most of its territory.

Johnson promised that even this limited bombing would end if the North Vietnamese responded to this U.S. initiative. He stated again that "the United States is ready to send its representatives to any forum, at any time, to discuss the means of bringing this ugly war to an end." As his personal representatives to such discussions the president named Averell Harriman and American Ambassador to Moscow Llewellyn Thompson, who had returned from the Soviet capital for consultations.[33] Johnson concluded his speech with the startling announcement that he would not seek and would not accept his party's nomination for another term as president. He was withdrawing from the presidential campaign in order to devote all his time to the needs of his country.

Johnson's speech of March 31 had strong world repercussions. In Moscow, *Pravda* published news of the speech in its April 2 issue. The tone of the newspaper's comments was restrained. The article characterized the American president's address as "new evidence of the complete failure of American policy in Vietnam." As for Johnson's withdrawal from the presidential campaign, *Pravda* said it might be no more than an "electoral maneuver." "In American political practice," *Pravda* argued, "more than once when potential candidates have refused to seek the nomination, they have later entered the campaign with renewed energy."[34]

Izvestiia was also suspicious of Johnson's announcement. While it admitted that the bombing halt was a laudable step, the newspaper warned that there was no guarantee of it continuing.[35]

The restraint of the Soviet press reflected the Kremlin's attitude toward the new U.S. initiative. Soviet leaders were clearly suspicious about the sincerity of the American moves. Dobrynin, for instance, the day after Johnson's speech, asked Harriman whether the president's decision was final and why he chose the night of March 31 to announce his Vietnam policy.[36] Several weeks later Dobrynin explained to Eugene Rostow, the U.S. under secretary of state for political affairs, that "there were still doubts and hesitations within the Politburo" as to whether the United States was "sincerely interested in a political settlement in Viet-Nam. . . ."[37]

Moscow had every reason to be wary. First, earlier American peace initiatives had usually been followed by a new escalation of the war. In such cases Soviet efforts to gain concessions from Hanoi turned out to be unproductive. In his conversation with Harriman, Dobrynin specifically cited Kosygin's ill-fated negotiations in London in February 1967.

Second, Soviet suspicions may have stemmed from the fact that 1968 was a presidential election year in the United States. Most Soviet observers shared the view that Vietnam would be the leading issue in the presidential campaign, and they surmised that American politicians would change their positions on the war because of the election. Memories of Johnson's position on the war before the 1964 elections served as proof for Soviet leaders that preelection rhetoric was not necessarily indicative of postelection policy, thus changes of policy in Vietnam might not be genuine.[38]

Finally, Johnson's speech did not represent a radical departure from previous U.S. policy on Vietnam. Although in March the president had approved sending to Vietnam fewer ground troops than recommended by his advisers, and had endorsed a reduced level of hostilities and an "early form of what would later be called Vietnamization," he did not change the ground strategy of the war and even quietly authorized the military in April to fight "vigorously while negotiating."[39]

On the positive side, Soviet leaders noted that Johnson did not exclude the possibility of the United States going even further if Hanoi began negotiations—to cease entirely the bombing of DRV territory. This was the main concession the North Vietnamese urged their Soviet colleagues to seek from the Americans. Furthermore, by assigning the two leading Soviet experts, Harriman and Thompson, as chief negotiators in talks with the DRV, the U.S. government implied it was ready to consider Moscow's interests in a settlement in Vietnam. Although the Soviets wished to avoid publicity in their role in the Vietnam affair, they were eager to see a settlement favorable for the USSR's ambitions in Southeast Asia, and hoped to be included in determining the future of the region.

Dobrynin indicated this Soviet concern in his conversation with Harriman on April 1.[40] He explained that Moscow would not oppose any U.S. steps in South Vietnam once America "left North

Vietnam alone." Interestingly enough, just after his discussion with Harriman on Moscow's and Washington's "spheres of interest," Dobrynin turned to the U.S. relationship with China and asked "whether there was any new development in that line." For the Soviets, the China factor always played a major role in Vietnam.

While the White House found the Soviet reaction more or less predictable, Hanoi's response represented an "unknown quantity." Surprisingly, this response came much sooner than expected. On April 3 North Vietnamese radio broadcast a denunciation of the American government that also included the following sentence: "However, on its part, the Democratic Republic of Vietnam Government declares its readiness to send its representatives to decide with the U.S. side the unconditional cessation of bombing and all other war acts against the DRV so that talks can begin."[41]

The speed with which Hanoi responded to the U.S. peace offer seems to have been a surprise not only to Washington but also to Moscow, let alone Beijing, the chief advocate of continuing war.[42] Quite possibly Hanoi did not inform its Soviet allies in advance about its decision to move to negotiations. This lack of consultation was not unusual for the North Vietnamese leadership. But Moscow clearly had information that this step was being prepared.

In addition to forecasts from the embassy in Hanoi about the DRV's strategic shifts and its desire to delay talks with the Americans until after the spring of 1968, the Kremlin undoubtedly had intelligence reports confirming this trend noted by Soviet diplomats. As early as February 16, 1968, the KGB informed the Kremlin of measures undertaken by the DRV leadership and the NLF to prepare the way for a political solution of the Vietnamese problem in 1968.[43] This document remains classified, and we do not know what measures the report described. But the very existence of this document testifies that the Soviet leadership knew something about the intentions of its Vietnamese friends.

Moreover, Moscow was evidently well informed about the situation inside the highest DRV council, the politburo of the Lao Dong party's central committee. The KGB provided the Kremlin with facts about discussions held at meetings of the North Vietnamese politburo on April 2–6 devoted to the DRV response to Johnson's March 31 address.[44] As a result, the Soviets sensed the trend of Hanoi's thinking in the wake of the president's offer.

The American intelligence community, in turn, tried to analyze the substance of DRV policy on the basis of available facts. According to the CIA, Hanoi believed it could achieve military victories even though the cost might be high. The North Vietnamese also expected a crumbling of will to persist among the enemy. In that situation, the CIA argued, the Vietnamese Communists regarded hard bargaining combined with continued military pressure as capable of eventually producing a favorable outcome. The Agency concluded that Hanoi really wanted to talk and that it would not seek pretexts "to back away from establishing contact with the U.S."[45]

U.S. intelligence also appraised the attitudes of North Vietnam's two biggest allies and supporters toward negotiations. The State Department believed that "although the Soviets have probably refrained from exerting pressure on Hanoi to negotiate, they may have tried to point out to the North Vietnamese the advantages of at least a show of greater diplomatic flexibility." State Department analysts were positive that "even if Moscow had not counseled Hanoi's response to the President's speech, the North Vietnamese at least knew that they could count on full Soviet support for the step."[46]

As for China, its influence on North Vietnamese policy was estimated by the CIA as substantially diminished. The Chinese had only two ways of pressuring North Vietnam. They could cut off their supply of rice and wheat—but Hanoi had at least a three-week reserve of these grains, and the Soviet Union could supply needed grain by sea. Or the Chinese could recall their labor battalions from North Vietnam—but the cessation of American bombing would make these forces less essential. The CIA reported that all North Vietnamese officials agreed on China's inability effectively to impose their will on North Vietnam. They even referred to China as "La Grande Impuissance," as compared with "Les Grande Puissances," the French term for the "Great Powers."[47]

Although both Washington and Hanoi declared their determination to go to the negotiating table, they encountered a major problem which threatened to become an insurmountable obstacle on the way to the talks. This problem was a choice of the site for the meetings. Initial suggestions by the United States and North Vietnam were rejected. The United States turned down Phnom Penh on the ground that there were no U.S. representatives in the Cambodian capital. Hanoi refused to accept Geneva because of bad memories about the consequences of the 1954 conference on Indochina. The United States then proposed four possible sites: Vientiane, Rangoon, Djakarta, or New Delhi. After a period of silence from Hanoi, on April 11 TASS announced that the North Vietnamese preferred to meet in Warsaw.

The Polish capital seemed acceptable to several members of the American administration, including Harriman and Cyrus Vance (who had replaced Llewellyn Thompson as conegotiator with Harriman[48]). Harriman regarded the offer as a "slap in the face at the Chinese." He argued that the Eastern Europeans were "frightfully keen to see the war over for the same reasons as the Western Europeans—they don't want to see a confrontation between the U.S. and the USSR,"[49] and this was a good reason for choosing Warsaw.

Aware of the president's reluctance to accept Warsaw as a site for negotiations, Harriman decided to call Johnson to see if he could persuade him otherwise. But Johnson remained adamant. As long as he was president, he declared, the United States was not going to Warsaw. He wanted a neutral place with adequate communications. In reply to Harriman's assurance that it did not bother him to negotiate in an iron curtain country, the president objected that it bothered *him*. "I don't want any part of Warsaw, Czechoslovakia, or any other Eastern European countries," he said. "I think it ought to be in Asia, in neutral territory. We shouldn't be dictated to through TASS."[50] In this case the president went along with advice of the American ambassador in Saigon, Ellsworth Bunker, and his national security assistant, hard-liner Walt Rostow.

Rostow explained Johnson's motives in a message to Rusk."It is clear," Rostow wrote, "that the President regards site as a matter of substance and test of will which could foreshadow character of negotiation. All hands should be aware that policy on site for contacts is matter which rests in President's head and no views are responsible unless checked with him and yourself."[51]

The protracted dispute over a meeting place threatened negotiations even before they began. Beyond doubt, Moscow closely followed developments between the United States and North Vietnam in April and regarded with apprehension the deadlock over a site. The Kremlin knew of Hanoi's plans not to abandon its military goals, especially because the North Vietnamese had not concealed their intentions. They had even submitted to the USSR a request for supplemental aid in two letters signed by Pham Van Dong on March 30 and April 10.[52]

Fearful that the fragile hope for a peaceful settlement in Vietnam might be lost, Soviet leaders took steps to find an acceptable solution to the problem of a site. Possibly Warsaw was suggested by the North Vietnamese on the advice of the Kremlin. The fact that this offer was announced by TASS supports such a hypothesis. The next day, April 12, the Polish government, probably urged by the Soviets, announced its readiness to create the necessary conditions to ensure untroubled American–North Vietnamese contacts.[53]

In spite of a clear indication of U.S. site preferences, conveyed to Dobrynin by Secretary Rusk on Johnson's instructions,[54] the Soviet ambassador tried once more, in his conversation with Harriman and Eugene Rostow, to clarify Washington's position and persuade the White House to accept Warsaw. As a "blue chip" Dobrynin offered an assurance that a South Vietnamese delegation could be received in Poland.[55]

Meanwhile Moscow was searching for an acceptable substitute. Soviet leaders must have noticed that the only city missing from American and North Vietnamese lists of possible sites was Paris. From the Soviet viewpoint, the capital of de Gaulle's France might be an ideal venue for negotiations. The French president had long been a critic of U.S. involvement in Southeast Asia and as such was favorably regarded by Hanoi. Furthermore, North Vietnam maintained some relations with France, and its representative Mai Van Bo had been sent there to keep these relations alive.

The Soviets evidently considered that it would be easier to preserve contacts between Moscow and a North Vietnamese delegation in Paris than in any Asian capital proposed by the United States. In France the Soviet Union had Valerian Zorin as its ambassador, an experienced diplomat who was well known in the United States. This could solve communication problems with the North Vietnamese and Americans, let alone the French. Moscow may also have expected that Washington would not reject the French capital outright, despite tensions between Johnson and de Gaulle. Paris might be the best possible choice.

Exactly when Moscow began to test the idea of Paris with its North Vietnamese friends and the French is unclear. Supposedly it was after it became clear the United States would not agree on Warsaw. The first reaction of Washington to a suggestion of the

French capital was ambivalent. When Arthur Goldberg remarked to Rusk that the omission of Paris from the American list might itself cause Hanoi to choose Paris and put the administration in an "awkward position," the secretary of state had to agree. In such case "it would be almost impossible to explain why we could not accept, particularly since high South Vietnamese officials have apparently told press that South Vietnam would look favorably on Paris."[56] Thus in mid-April, when Rusk informed Walt Rostow of Goldberg's comment, the administration did not regard Paris as a possible choice.[57]

Harriman, on the other hand, quickly perceived the advantages of the French capital as a meeting place for the Americans and the North Vietnamese. He noted a UPI report that French Foreign Minister Couve de Murville had proposed Paris as a site for the talks and wrote to Rusk in support of the proposal. "Before Paris is turned down," Harriman argued, "I would hope that the advantages can be weighed. It seems clear that from de Gaulle down, the French would want to have these first contacts succeed, at least in agreement on the step from contacts to talks." He reminded Rusk that French officials had been helpful in promoting peaceful contacts between the warring parties. "If Hanoi indicates a willingness to go to Paris," he concluded, "I cannot think of a 'credible' reason for our not accepting."[58]

U.S. intelligence supported the choice of Paris as a site. On May 1 the CIA provided the White House with arguments put forth by one of its unnamed contacts, who expressed confidence that "the negotiations would eventually take place in Paris." According to the contact, "Paris was an excellent site" for two reasons. First, the North Vietnamese would accept it, for they knew that de Gaulle's anti-Americanism would guarantee that "any talks undertaken in France would be carried out in an atmosphere and under conditions favorable to North Vietnam." Second, a number of exiled Vietnamese who lived in France could be available for participation in the negotiations as non-NLF representatives of the "National Government" which would be the third party in the talks.[59]

Five days later, as if to bolster the administration in its decision to go to Paris, the CIA presented further arguments in favor of the choice. The CIA memorandum drew attention to de Gaulle's interest in the success of preliminary talks between the two delegations and his desire to make the French capital a site of subsequent negotiations. Intelligence analysts supposed that French officials would probably take a relatively neutral posture during the talks for this reason and to provide de Gaulle with an opportunity to act as a mediator. The CIA also pointed out that French police would be able to maintain the necessary security for the talks.[60]

While the administration considered the pros and cons of Paris, the Soviets paved the way to a solution of the problem. On May 2 Le Duan met with Chargé V. Chivilev in Hanoi and informed him that North Vietnamese leaders, taking into account the opinion of the Soviets as well, planned to propose Paris as a site for the talks. "It is known in Hanoi," Le Duan noted, "*that Soviet comrades have already done some work with the French in this question*, and those, in their turn, also regard favorably the choice of Paris as a meeting place."

Le Duan described the advantages of Paris. First, the North Vietnamese delegation there would have an opportunity to keep in close touch with Moscow. And, considering the relationship between France and South Vietnam, any event in Paris would quickly trigger a reaction in Saigon. Even the fact that the United States and the DRV were sitting down at the negotiating table would weaken the "puppets' power." Ending his conversation, Le Duan asked the Soviet government to persuade the United States to accept Paris as a site for the talks.[61] But Moscow did not need to. As soon as Hanoi announced on May 3 its offer to meet in Paris, as well as the name of its chief negotiator, Xuan Thuy, the White House accepted.

That day President Johnson informed the press that he had sent a message to Hanoi accepting the starting date, May 10, and the site, Paris. He expressed the hope that the agreement would lead to eventual peace in Southeast Asia. The president warned, however, that this was only the first step. "There are many, many hazards and difficulties ahead."[62]

The Soviets were more optimistic. They regarded the beginning of negotiations as a diplomatic success and a hopeful sign that this dangerous conflict, which for so many years had threatened world security, would finally be resolved. "Without acting as an official mediator," the Soviet embassy in the DRV pointed out, "the Soviet Union rendered an important service for the two sides to sit down at the negotiating table and open official talks. The USSR spared no effort to convince world opinion and the countries' governments to come out for an end to bombing raids of the DRV, and exerted pressure on the USA. At the same time it was brought home to the Vietnamese comrades that the year of 1968 was most favorable for a number of reasons for launching the process of the political settlement of the Vietnam issue."[63]

Soviet leaders were no doubt inspired by the surmounting of so many obstacles on the road to Paris. But no one in Washington, Moscow, or Hanoi could anticipate how long and difficult would be the road to peace.

EIGHT

"Very Tough Going"

The start of meetings between representatives of the two warring countries seemed to confirm President Johnson's skepticism. On the eve of the U.S. delegation's departure for Paris, he met with the negotiating team and repeated his doubts regarding the prospects of the negotiations. "I am glad we're going to talk," he told Harriman and other members of the delegation, "but I'm not overly hopeful. I think it is going to be tough going, very tough. . . ."[1]

Although preliminary sessions went smoothly and even inspired hopes of important progress, when official talks began, on May 13 at the old Paris Hotel Majestic, where the Gestapo had made its headquarters during World War II,[2] optimism evaporated. Negotiators from both sides stuck to propaganda-style attacks, for neither Harriman nor Xuan Thuy had received from their respective governments sufficiently flexible instructions to provide them with room for maneuver.

For example, Rusk had emphasized to Harriman that his mission in Paris was only to find out what the North Vietnamese were prepared to do in response to the bombing limitation. No discussions on a U.S. fallback position ever occurred.[3] Negotiating instructions likewise gave the American representatives almost no latitude. Those instructions stated as the basic objective for negotiators, "To make arrangements with the North Vietnamese representative for prompt and serious substantive talks looking towards peace in Viet-Nam, in the course of which an understanding may be reached on a cessation of bombing in the North under circumstances which would not be militarily disadvantageous." This last phrase implied that Hanoi would have to agree to respect the demilitarized zone, not to increase the movement of North Vietnamese troops into South Vietnam, and to reconcile themselves to participation in discussions "affecting South Viet-Nam" or the Saigon government.[4]

Hanoi was going no further than Washington. The assignment of Xuan Thuy as Hanoi's chief negotiator in Paris scarcely reflected a desire to see the talks move quickly on substantive matters. In selecting him, the Lao Dong party leadership had apparently been guided by considerations of political expediency and caution. The fifty-five-year-old poet and revolutionary was a prominent figure in the North Vietnamese hierarchy but not an influential politician.

Socialist diplomats in Hanoi suspected that one reason for Xuan Thuy's assignment to Paris was the DRV's desire to placate Beijing, whose strong opposition to negotiations with the United States was well known in the North Vietnamese capital.[5] Xuan Thuy, who had been president of the Vietnam-Chinese Friendship Association and later minister of foreign affairs of the DRV, had been removed from these prominent positions when to be pro-Chinese was unpopular in North Vietnam. Although later Thuy probably became more nationalist than pro-Chinese, his appointment as head of the DRV delegation may have mollified the Chinese. In sending Xuan Thuy to Paris, Hanoi achieved two goals. First, it avoided unnecessary risk in relations with the powerful Chinese ally. Second, it could rely on the rigidity and intransigence of its envoy while discovering what baggage Washington had sent with its negotiators.

Under these conditions, negotiations quickly reached a deadlock—twice-a-week exercises in polemical posturing and propaganda. Both sides clung to their positions with no hint of compromise. Harriman delivered long speeches laden with quotations from President Johnson, demanding reciprocal steps by the North Vietnamese in response to the partial U.S. bombing halt. Xuan Thuy replied with longer, more doctrinaire denunciations of American aggression. As the talks dragged on without visible results, the excitement surrounding them waned. Media interest disappeared, and the horde of reporters in Paris began to scatter. Officials in Washington gradually became unhappy with the fruitless discussions. Their disdain increased with information of a new attack by North Vietnamese regiments against American troops near Laos. The administration began to consider means of retaliation against the stepped-up military activities of the DRV.

U.S. leaders were not the only ones disappointed by the course of the Paris peace talks. In Moscow, concern about the situation was evident at the highest levels of Soviet leadership. Newspapers, always a mouthpiece of the Kremlin, changed their tone from cautiously optimistic to more and more suspicious. The day before the opening of the "official conversations" between American and North Vietnamese delegations, *Pravda* published an extensive article on the imminent negotiations with profiles of Harriman and Xuan Thuy.[6] It provided its readers with detailed coverage of the ongoing talks, probably reflecting the importance the Kremlin attached to them rather than their interest for *Pravda*'s readers.

Soon, however, the tone of the newspaper coverage changed. On May 17, *Pravda* noted with concern that the first two sessions gave no reason "to believe in the sincere readiness of the United States leaders to deescalate the American aggression in Vietnam."[7] Two days later the newspaper criticized even more gravely the behavior of the American delegation and wondered about such an attitude. "It is clear," the article stated, "that this is done in order to drag out the negotiations as much as possible, to win time for the preparation of military operations of much larger scale and then, having referred to the 'intransigence' of the Vietnamese, to resume the bombing of all DRV territory and again try to achieve a military victory."[8]

Undoubtedly this article, written by Yuri Zhukov who was close to the Soviet leadership, revealed the Kremlin's deepest suspicions. Moscow feared that a deadlock in negotiations could lead to the breakdown of the whole process of peaceful settlement in Vietnam. Although publicly Moscow could blame the Americans, Soviet leaders were aware that Hanoi shared the responsibility for a lack of progress. They were well informed about developments in the talks, first of all because the North Vietnamese apparently provided the Soviets with details of their discussions with Harriman's team. Another stream of information came from Harriman himself, who, soon after his arrival in Paris, spared no effort to maintain contact with Moscow through the Soviet embassy in the French capital. Based on his conviction that only the Soviets could help the United States find ways of reconciliation with the DRV, Harriman, long before Paris, sounded out the possibilities of enlisting Soviet support in conversations with Soviet Ambassador Dobrynin in Washington. For instance, on April 8, after the ambassador's assurances that the Soviet government wanted a peaceful settlement in Vietnam, Harriman "went after him pretty hard on the necessity of the Soviet Union taking real responsibility to achieve this objective."[9] He returned to this subject recurrently, and evidently on May 5, in his last meeting with the Soviet ambassador over lunch before his departure for Paris, he again raised the question of the USSR's cooperation.[10]

In Paris Harriman took it upon himself to act as liaison between the American delegation and the Soviet embassy. He contacted the embassy on May 13, the same day that official conversations between the two delegations began, to invite Ambassador Zorin to his headquarters to meet with him. Two days later Zorin replied that he was waiting for Harriman to visit him, not vice versa. Sergei Bogomolov, the first secretary of the embassy, who called to inform the Americans, explained that since the head of the DRV delegation had called on Zorin, he expected the head of the American delegation to follow this example.[11]

Harriman balked. He did not intend to call on other ambassadors. He pointed out that, on the contrary, the British ambassador and others had come to see him. Therefore he expected Ambassador Zorin to visit him in the next day or two. But Zorin responded that he had other appointments, repeating his invitation to Harriman to visit the Soviet embassy.[12]

This cat-and-mouse game continued two more days until the two men agreed to meet at U.S. Ambassador Shriver's residence on May 19. Valentin Oberemko, minister at the Soviet embassy, visited Harriman to make final arrangements for the meeting and asked about the situation at the talks after the opening sessions. The chief U.S. negotiator expressed his disappointment with the "inaccuracies and falsehoods of North Vietnamese statements which were giving the talks the aspect of a propaganda exercise." Harriman hoped they would soon be able to proceed to matters of substance, "but North Vietnamese arrogance was now predominating."

Oberemko's reply reflected the importance the Soviets attached to the negotiations. He emphasized that "the initiation of discussions had started an irreversible process, that the North Vietnamese recognized this and were determined to carry through in a businesslike manner." Harriman immediately used this statement to present his view on the role the Soviets could play in moving the talks along. The "Soviet Union had a key role to play in these negotiations," he observed, and "he did not believe they could ever be brought to a successful conclusion without assistance from the Soviet Union. He therefore looked forward to *close contact* with Soviet representatives" in Paris.

Harriman then expounded on Washington's objectives at the talks. He confided that at the urging of both Kosygin and Dobrynin he had "carefully" studied the NLF program and found it generally acceptable, though filled with contradictions. He advised that in discussions related to the future of South Vietnam, his government expected the Saigon regime to be present. Harriman also expressed concern that infiltration from the North was continuing at a higher rate and that no restraint of any kind was evident on Hanoi's part.[13]

This preliminary conversation defined the main lines of the discussion between the American representatives and Zorin. In his first meeting with Harriman, apparently Zorin was instructed by Moscow to go no further than restate the well-known Soviet position with regard to the talks. His primary objective was to explore Washington's view of the situation and how far the Johnson administration was ready to go in its negotiations with Hanoi. When the American representatives complained about North Vietnamese intransigence and their increased flow of troops to the South after the partial U.S. bombing halt, Zorin spoke at length and emphasized that the North Vietnamese position was "clear and firm." Its substance was that no further steps could be taken or discussed until the United States ceased bombing North Vietnam without conditions. Zorin underlined the fact that the Soviet government, for its part, understood this position and supported it. The Soviet ambassador repeated this several times, Harriman's arguments and objections notwithstanding.[14]

For the Americans, this first contact with the Soviets did not seem terribly fruitful. Nevertheless Harriman had received some encouraging signs. Zorin, for instance, had not objected to the possibility of future meetings with Harriman. Indeed, he agreed that these contacts *should* continue and outlined a sort of scheme for them. He said he would be glad to meet personally with Harriman and named Oberemko and Bogomolov as other channels of communication. Harriman also had an opportunity to spell out his suggestion for secret meetings between the American and North Vietnamese delegations, "perhaps with the Soviets present if they wished." In the absence of instructions from Moscow, where this proposal may have been greeted with surprise, Zorin "seemed taken aback and said that was 'far off.'"[15] But for the Soviets Harriman's suggestion represented a possible way around the deadlock in the negotiations and was therefore to be viewed positively.

This first conversation between Zorin and Harriman seems to have been favorably assessed in Moscow. The Kremlin instructed Zorin to maintain contact with the American delegation, which the Soviet ambassador admitted during his second conversation with Harriman, on May 25 at the Soviet embassy. The tone of the conversation was much different from that at Shriver's residence. According to Harriman's report, "Zorin was somewhat less argumentative and at least listened courteously."[16] Although he stated that the Soviet position on the principal problems of the talks remained the same, he was more attentive to Harriman's arguments for secret meetings with the North Vietnamese and U.S. views on the problem of reciprocal steps by the North Vietnamese in response to the U.S. bombing halt. As to the possibility of secret talks between representatives of the negotiating teams, Zorin asked about the composition of such meetings, whether they might include two or three delegates from each side.

Discussion of the problem of reciprocity and restraint by Hanoi was more difficult, since each side reaffirmed its position on this question without noticeable modification. Harriman referred to Johnson's March 31 speech and reiterated that the U.S. aim was to negotiate a bombing halt, not just to announce the end of the bombing. He also drew the attention of his Soviet colleague to the North Vietnamese statements of April which seemed to confirm Hanoi's agreement with such an interpretation. In Harriman's view, the North Vietnamese had deviated from their agreement to come to Paris to talk.

Zorin showed particular interest in Harriman's statement that the United States hoped for a sign of restraint from Hanoi and did not require a formal declaration on reciprocity—which the North Vietnamese would certainly oppose. The Soviet ambassador mentioned that the Americans had not said this to the North Vietnamese directly. Harriman referred to the public character of the official conversations which precluded him from making such a statement in plain words. But he promised to inform the DRV delegation that Washington expected the North Vietnamese could do something "by words or by deed" to demonstrate their restraint in response to the U.S. unilateral step.[17]

This conversation at the Soviet embassy demonstrated that Moscow was actively searching for ways of compromise in Paris. The Kremlin apparently posed to Hanoi the idea of secret meetings between the two delegations as well as the problem of restraint. In their communications with the North Vietnamese, Soviet leaders surely referred to the danger of dragging out the fruitless discussions endlessly, drawing Hanoi's attention to Harriman's caution about the strong unfavorable impression it could make on the American public and about the temptation of the Johnson administration to resume full-scale bombing of the DRV.

Perhaps these arguments convinced the North Vietnamese. Two important decisions by Hanoi—to send to Paris its influential representative Le Duc Tho, and to agree on secret meetings between the two delegations—might have been a result of pressure on the DRV leadership from its Moscow colleagues. Soviet leaders were prompt in notifying their ambassador in Paris about these changes in Hanoi's position. Only two days after his first meeting with Harriman at the Soviet embassy, Zorin, asked by Harriman whether he still believed the idea of private talks was "too early," replied no. He advised the ambassador to tell the North Vietnamese about it and see what their reaction would be.[18] Zorin expressed his understanding that private talks would take place alongside public meetings which "could not be suspended."

The Soviet ambassador's wording of the suggestion was cautious. Zorin said that "in his personal opinion, their [North Vietnamese] reaction would probably [be] negative in this time. . . . But with his diplomatic experience, the Governor would understand that conditions changed, and perhaps later on, depending on the pace of the public talks, their answer might be positive."

Zorin could scarcely have had "his personal opinion" on this question. Promoted to a prominent position in the Soviet diplomatic hierarchy under Stalin's regime, he was not used to having his own views and, least of all, conveying them to foreign diplomats without approval from above. He was a diplomat of the "Molotov school," a conscientious executor of his leaders' decisions. And Harriman knew this full well.

In one of his informal conversations with Dobrynin at his home on N Street in Washington, the old "Crocodile" (as Harriman was nicknamed in Washington circles for his penchant for posing uncomfortable questions and making embarrassing remarks) asked his counterpart why the Soviet government did not have a more alert man than Zorin in Paris. "I told him," continued Harriman in the report on this conversation, "I regretted that someone more 'modern' than Zorin was not in Paris. . . ."[19] Thus Harriman no doubt took his Soviet colleague's cautious statement hopefully.

By changes in the conditions of the talks, Moscow clearly meant the decision of the North Vietnamese leadership to send Le Duc Tho to Paris as Xuan Thuy's conegotiator. Contrary to their initial purpose to hold talks about talks, the Vietnamese Communists now intended to transform the meetings from exercises in "suggest and reject," in Harriman's words, into occasions for give and take.[20] As a member of the Vietnamese Communist party politburo, Le Duc Tho was capable, unlike Xuan Thuy, of making decisions and in some respects influencing Hanoi's position toward the negotiations.

Although Moscow knew that DRV leaders viewed the talks as part of their general strategy of "fighting while negotiating," the Soviets also had information about the North Vietnamese approach to the negotiations. As early as January 1968 the Soviet embassy in Hanoi reported that in the first phase of the talks the Vietnamese sought the cessation of bombing and all other acts of war against the DRV accompanied by withdrawal of U.S. navy and air forces from Vietnam. This phase was to be followed by preliminary contacts between the North Vietnamese and Americans to determine all aspects of negotiations. The talks could then begin with the inclusion at a later stage of representatives of the National Liberation Front and the Saigon regime. Finally, the process would be concluded with a Geneva-type conference to provide international guarantees of the settlement.[21]

Whatever doubts Moscow might have entertained about North Vietnamese determination to follow this scheme, Le Duc

Tho's assignment probably dispelled them. On his stopover in Moscow en route to Paris, Le Duc Tho was received by Kosygin, indicating the Soviet's concern for his mission. Kosygin's meeting with the North Vietnamese envoy, on June 2, was followed three days later by a letter from the Soviet leader to President Johnson. In it Kosygin used strong and definite wording to describe the beginning of official talks between representatives of the United States and the DRV as "a real possibility to find a way out of the situation which has developed in Viet-Nam with the aim of halting the many-years-old and bloody war being conducted there."[22] "The peoples of the entire world" expected positive results from American-Vietnamese meetings in Paris, Kosygin said, and he linked their outcome with prospects for the relaxation of international tension.

After complaining that the lack of progress at the talks could be attributed to the continuing U.S. bombing of DRV territory, the Soviet premier reminded the president that the Soviet government had "more than once" expressed its opinion that "a full and unconditional cessation by the United States of bombardments and other acts of war against the DRV can open the path to peaceful settlement." From Kosygin's point of view, the bombing represented "the main obstacle hindering movement forward at the meeting in Paris."

The next part of Kosygin's letter stirred controversy within the Johnson administration and caused heated discussions among the president's advisers. "I and my colleagues believe—and we have grounds for this," Kosygin stated, "that a full cessation by the United States of bombardments and other acts of war in relation to the DRV could promote a breakthrough in the situation that would open perspectives for peaceful settlement." The Soviet leader assured Washington that such a step would not "bring about any adverse consequences whatever for the United States neither in the sense of a loss for the interests of their safety nor even in the sense of a loss for their prestige." Kosygin concluded his appeal to Washington with the information that, on Harriman's request, the Soviet government had alerted the Vietnam representatives to the usefulness of unofficial contacts between the U.S. and DRV delegations, for Moscow was convinced that "all forms of contact between the sides must be used."

Undoubtedly this letter was inspired by Kosygin's talks with Le Duc Tho. During those talks the Soviet premier may have informed his Vietnamese counterpart about conversations that took place in the French capital between Harriman and Zorin, and probably tried to clarify Hanoi's position on the prospects for settlement of the Vietnam War. Having probably received strong assurances from Le Duc Tho that the North Vietnamese would withdraw all their objections to serious talks with the United States once the bombing stopped, the Soviet leadership decided to take a strong hand with Washington on the cessation of the bombing.

But Johnson was not ready to trust unreservedly the signal sent by Moscow. As he wrote in his memoirs, "I still remembered vividly Moscow's assurance late in 1965 that if we stopped bombing the North for twelve to twenty days, 'something good will happen.' On that basis we stopped bombing, not for twelve or twenty but for thirty-seven days—and nothing happened. . . . What was Moscow saying now that it had not said two and a half years earlier?"[23] Rusk and Rostow supported Johnson. During the president's meeting with his foreign policy advisers on June 9, Rusk characterized Kosygin's message as "hard to interpret." The secretary of state wanted a clarification, even guarantees that Hanoi "would do something concrete in response to the bombing halt."[24]

This argument was disputed by Secretary of Defense Clark Clifford, Harriman, and Vance (the latter two had returned to Washington at the time). Clifford regarded the Soviet letter as "a positive gesture that would put Moscow on the spot to produce results."[25] He proposed that the president "accept it in good faith"[26] and announce a bombing pause on all of North Vietnam's territory, making clear to both Moscow and Hanoi that if there were no reciprocal actions by the North Vietnamese, the U.S. halt would be terminated. Clifford, whose views of the war changed radically after his assignment as secretary of defense, believed that bombing would not end the war. "What will stop it is an arrangement with the Soviets so they can use their leverage—which we don't have—to bring the Soviets to force Hanoi to stop it."[27] As for the bad experience with the thirty-seven-day pause, Clifford argued that circumstances were different, and he himself had not favored the earlier pause.

In the discussion of how to respond to Moscow's suggestion, no one supported Clifford. Harriman agreed with the defense secretary that the letter was "extremely important" and thought that positive U.S. reaction to Kosygin's assurances "could be a breakthrough," but he did not risk opposing the president's opinion, aware of his position with Johnson and of the president's regard for Rusk.[28] But later, in an "Absolutely Personal" memorandum for the file, he considered the response of the administration to Kosygin's message as a lost opportunity for a reasonable settlement with North Vietnam in the summer of 1968.[29]

Johnson sent a very cautious reply to the Soviet premier. He informed Kosygin that the United States was prepared to end the bombing of the DRV after it was informed of the steps North Vietnam would take toward further deescalation of the violence. The president assured the Soviet leader that he would be glad to pursue the matters directly with the government of the Soviet Union. "If you are in a position," the letter said, "to tell us privately and *with precision* that there would be no adverse military consequences to our own and allied forces as a result of a bombing cessation, we would be prepared to accept your statement and would issue the necessary orders."[30]

On June 11 Rusk handed Johnson's response to Soviet Ambassador Dobrynin. The level of Soviet disappointment with such an unencouraging message was later demonstrated by Dobrynin during conversations with American diplomats. Moscow had expected a more responsive reply from Washington, the Soviet ambassador noted, and had expected that the U.S. government "would have accepted Kosygin's assurances."[31] In a conversation with Llewellyn Thompson on June 13, Dobrynin emphasized that he thought the United States had missed an opportunity. "He said," Thompson reported, "his Government, as I knew, was quite cautious about not getting into the position of being an intermediary and he thought that in this case they had gone quite far." When Thompson defended the president's skepticism because of Washington's experience with earlier bombing halts, Dobrynin pointed out the difference between Kosygin's latest letter and previous Soviet messages. The Soviet ambassador "observed that in this case his statements had been made in writing by the head of the Soviet Government and moreover that he had spoken in the name of the Government."[32]

One may wonder whether the Soviet leadership had ulterior aims in urging the United States to agree on unconditional cessation of bombings, aside from its usual desire to promote the designs of its Vietnamese "friends." At a meeting with the president on June 9, Charles Bohlen who had participated in the discussion of Kosygin's letter, suggested that if the United States stopped the bombing of all North Vietnam, it would strengthen the Soviet position in Hanoi and allow Moscow to take a more critical stance toward her sister socialist country.

Bohlen confided this idea to Dobrynin several days later, seeking confirmation of his notion from the Soviet ambassador. He told Dobrynin that personally he felt "that one thing the Soviets were trying to tell us was that their commitment to North Vietnam is primarily due to attacks on it by the United States, and therefore logically if the attacks totally ceased then the obligation of the Soviet Union in this regard would be considerably less."[33] Dobrynin joked about Bohlen's experience in Soviet affairs and evaded a direct response to his suggestion. Nevertheless, in a conversation with Harriman on June 22, Dobrynin, who evidently trusted the old diplomat more than his younger colleague, expressed almost in Bohlen's words his belief that "the Soviet Government would be freer to express its opinions to the North Vietnamese after the bombing had stopped completely."[34]

Having rejected Kosygin's assurances, the U.S. government deprived the Soviet leadership of a broader latitude vis-à-vis its Hanoi allies. But undoubtedly such considerations were only part of the equation. The whole truth was that the Soviets wished to settle the war on terms more or less acceptable to their vision of the international situation and the USSR's place in it as well as to the plans of their Vietnamese allies. And the Paris talks represented the only hope for realizing these goals without greater losses.

When Johnson refused to stop the bombing, Moscow, fearing that U.S. intransigence might discourage the North Vietnamese, and hoping to find a compromise, hurried to persuade its allies not to give up. On June 13, in a letter to Hanoi, Soviet leaders reiterated the importance of the negotiations in Paris for a peaceful settlement of the war. The crucial moment was now on the diplomatic front, and it was important to have a clear understanding of how to resolve the Vietnam question. The Kremlin offered its Vietnamese comrades all the power of the USSR's international stature to achieve, as soon as possible, success in this political and diplomatic struggle.[35] Soviet leaders also put forward in this letter an idea that Harriman had insisted on during his meetings in Paris—the need for discussion of issues beyond a bombing halt, such as the question of the DMZ, a schedule of mutual withdrawal of forces from South Vietnam, and participation of the Saigon government in the talks.

The reply from Hanoi to Moscow's appeal was no more encouraging than that from Washington. It came almost a month later and did not contain, as the Soviet embassy reported, "constructive theses aimed at peaceful settlement of the Vietnam question in accordance with the present favorable situation." "The Vietnamese comrades," the embassy continued, "are virtually trying to defend their point of view on events in Vietnam and to keep for themselves a monopoly on the correct assessment and methods of resolution of the Vietnamese conflict." The report concluded that the Vietnamese leadership probably had not yet properly evaluated the importance of the political aspects of the settlement.[36]

According to Soviet diplomats in Hanoi, the China factor continued to play an important role in the DRV's political planning. Beijing's reaction to the early negotiations in Paris was far from positive. Evidently Hanoi had agreed to negotiate with the United States without first asking the Chinese. Even after the DRV announced its readiness to talk, during a visit of North Vietnamese leaders to Beijing in April 1968 the Chinese hosts told them the time had not yet come for Vietnam to enter into negotiations with the United States. "We are too quick with concessions," Chinese leaders complained.[37]

When the negotiations in Paris finally began, Beijing refused to acknowledge them. Chinese newspapers deliberately omitted news of the negotiations. They intensified their criticism of France for providing a venue for the talks.[38] At the same time Beijing took practical steps to undermine a settlement in Southeast Asia.

Chinese leaders tried to thwart Hanoi's determination to negotiate by creating difficulties in various spheres of North Vietnamese activity. They upset the delivery of Soviet aid to the DRV, organizing provocations against Soviet ships that came to Chinese ports en route to North Vietnam, and against Soviet transports bound for the DRV through China's territory. The frequency of such provocations, which had occurred before, visibly increased. According to a report of the Soviet embassy in the PRC, in May and June the Chinese retained on their territory about eight hundred railway cars with arms and military equipment and seven special trains of antiaircraft complexes for North Vietnam.[39]

Clearly these actions were aimed at the Soviet Union as well as at Hanoi, for the Chinese leadership considered Moscow particularly responsible for the DRV's turn toward negotiations. The harassment of Soviet shipments to Vietnam was accompanied by agitation on the Soviet-Chinese border, where such incidents increased from 90 in January–February 1968 to 164 in May.[40]

In their plans to divert the North Vietnamese from negotiations with the United States, Chinese leaders even tried to use the National Liberation Front. Beijing began to broaden its separate (apart from Hanoi) relations with the NLF, convincing its leaders to continue "protracted guerrilla war." Moscow also received information of Beijing's attempts to organize regiments of the local Chinese population in South Vietnam in order to intensify military actions there.[41]

At the same time Chinese leaders continued their efforts to persuade their DRV colleagues that negotiations with the Americans were erroneous and dangerous. When in October 1968 the prospects of an agreement on the U.S. cessation of the bombing seemed imminent at the Paris talks, a high-ranking Chinese official instructed his North Vietnamese colleague in Beijing that China viewed the development as a "compromise between Vietnam and the United States," as a "serious failure and a large loss for the Vietnamese people." He compared such an eventuality with the Geneva Accords of 1954 and declared that Vietnam "should allow the United States to resume bombing and attacks" on its territory. According to the Chinese, the United States would have to disperse its bombing attacks, which would relieve the situation in the South.[42]

The Soviet embassy in Beijing presented its own version of why Chinese leaders so adamantly opposed the Paris talks. According to its report, the continuation of the war in Vietnam allowed the Chinese Communist party to keep China under martial law, stoking the people's fear of encirclement and invasion. The embassy concluded that ideologically a settlement in Vietnam would strike a blow at Mao's military strategy in the protracted war and would lead to the debunking of other ideas of the "great leader." Strategically the war in Vietnam, according to Maoists, weakened the potential of both the United States and the Soviet Union, and increased the chance of a direct military encounter between China's two principal rivals. Besides, the embassy believed, the Chinese were trying to use aggressive tactics and the presence of the United States in Southeast Asia in order to strengthen their own position in the region.[43]

This analysis from Beijing reflected Soviet concern over China's potentially dangerous effect on the Paris negotiations. Although in June some positive signs appeared at the talks in the form of private meetings between representatives of the American and North Vietnamese delegations, there was still no serious step forward in reconciling the positions of Hanoi and Washington.

It took several weeks for the Vietnamese to agree on private meetings. Probably their decision was stimulated by a conversation on June 13 among Zorin, Harriman, and Vance. When the Soviet ambassador informed the Americans of the main points of the North Vietnamese position, which included their refusal to discuss other issues or to initiate private talks until the United States stopped the bombing, Harriman and Vance warned Zorin that the impasse posed a serious danger to hopes for successful negotiations. "There was increasing pressure on the President," they said, "and the longer the Saigon attacks continued and the Paris impasse went on, the sharper the pressure would be." Harriman confided his belief that Moscow's influence had brought Hanoi to Paris against the wishes of Beijing, and if the talks were broken off it would be a defeat for Moscow and a feather in Beijing's cap.[44]

Harriman emphasized that there were certain common objectives among the Soviet Union, the DRV, and the United States. "All three," he said, "wanted North Viet-Nam free of Peking domination." Furthermore, the United States was "quite willing" to see North Vietnam remain a socialist country. As to South Vietnam, its future should be determined by the Vietnamese themselves. Harriman urged Moscow to play a crucial role in arranging private talks—"after dark, if necessary, in the Soviet Embassy or elsewhere, or at the North Vietnamese headquarters . . . presumably with Xuan Thuy and Le Duc Tho" talking to Harriman and Vance. Zorin replied that there should be no illusions about Hanoi's intention to agree to private meetings only after a bombing cessation. Despite Zorin's response, evidently the North Vietnamese negotiators were ripe for a decisive move. The first private meeting between low-ranking members of both delegations occurred on June 17. Eight days later Vance met privately with DRV delegate Ha Van Lau.[45] The same day Shcherbakov informed DRV Foreign

Minister Trinh about the substance of the June 13 conversation in the Soviet embassy in Paris.[46] Hanoi's leaders could feel satisfied that they had preempted the advice of their Soviet comrades.

The beginning of private meetings between members of the two delegations in Paris had no immediate effect on the pace of negotiations. The North Vietnamese took the same position in secret meetings that they did in official conversations. But the Americans did feel freer to suggest various compromises which would have been impossible under the lights of the Hotel Majestic.

In one of his private discussions with Ha Van Lau in late June, Vance offered a possible resolution of the stalemate over the cessation of U.S. bombing and reciprocal steps by Hanoi. Vance formulated it as a "Phase 1–Phase 2" plan. The idea was that the Americans would privately inform the North Vietnamese about the date on which the United States would stop the bombing if, before the public announcement on that date, actions that Hanoi would be ready to undertake were defined during discussions in Paris. The plan thus created the appearance of a unilateral step by the United States and provided the North Vietnamese with a time lag so as to avoid the impression that their reciprocal actions were in any way connected with the bombing cessation. It was a good compromise, but the North Vietnamese refused to retreat from their position that the United States must first stop all bombing before Hanoi would discuss the measures it was prepared to take.

The obstacle seemed insurmountable since President Johnson refused to stop the bombing without advance knowledge about Hanoi's reciprocal steps. In this deadlock, with a compromise seemingly within reach, the Soviets assumed the role they would play more than once until official four-party talks began in January 1969. It was essentially a role as unofficial intermediary, a kind of shuttle between the two parties. The unofficial character of Moscow's efforts allowed the Soviets to free themselves from any responsibility and to assume the functions of go-between only when they perceived an opportunity for compromise and a hopeful attitude from Hanoi.

Publicly the Kremlin repeatedly rejected any suggestion of its involvement as a mediator in Vietnam. Even after the Paris negotiations began, Moscow remained extremely cautious not to appear as a peacemaker, either de facto or de jure, because it knew that both roles involved certain duties and risks. The Soviet leadership wanted neither. It did not wish to compromise its position vis-à-vis North Vietnam and its rivals in the world Communist movement. At the same time, by avoiding publicity it was possible for the Soviets to pursue their goal of a peaceful settlement of the conflict in Indochina.

Thus when the Phase 1–Phase 2 plan, promising though it seemed, failed to move the negotiations forward, Moscow through Zorin suggested a slight modification. The Soviet ambassador proposed to the Americans that they agree unconditionally to stop the bombing while at the same time both sides agreed on a list of military retrenchments to be discussed after the bombing cessation. In other words, as Assistant Secretary of Defense Paul Warnke put it in a memorandum to Clifford, "The key factor is that the reduction in military activity to be discussed would be reciprocal, with each side agreeing on certain de-escalatory measures. The reciprocity thus would occur after, not before, the bombing halt."[47] Warnke believed the United States should try to work out a formula that would satisfy the criteria suggested by the Soviet ambassador.

The American negotiating team in Paris followed the Soviet suggestion, but Harriman and Vance insisted that a list of subsequent mutual actions under Phase 2 would be discussed *before* the United States announced the bombing halt. Although Ha Van Lau showed an interest in the American plan, as it followed from information Harriman gave to Zorin,[48] the North Vietnamese continued to insist on the U.S. stopping the bombing before any such discussions could take place. Again the matter refused to move off dead center.

Rusk explained to Soviet Ambassador Dobrynin that to Washington there was a difference between stopping the bombing and then discussing subsequent acts of deescalation, as against stopping the bombing and *proceeding* to acts of deescalation. "It was a question," he reasoned, "really of de-escalation in return for our execution of the stopping of bombing." Dobrynin remained unconvinced and wondered whether it would really be so difficult for the United States to stop the bombing.[49]

While negotiators in Paris were bogged down in fruitless chicken-and-egg debates, an unmistakable lull settled over the battlefields of South Vietnam. The shelling of Saigon ceased, and troop and supply movement into the DMZ slowed. Had Hanoi sent a signal in a response to the American appeal for reciprocity, or was this just the calm before the next military offensive? Harriman perceived it as an indication of North Vietnamese desire to cooperate in settling the conflict. After consulting with William Bundy and Nicholas Katzenbach, the under secretary of state who happened to be in Paris, he sent a message to Washington recommending that the president stop the bombing on the assumption that the lull was the restraint the United States had asked for.[50]

Surprisingly, even the most vigilant members of the administration were eager to support such an interpretation of the situation on the battlefield. Walt Rostow, for example, prepared a memorandum for the president in which, though he admitted the lull in July might lead to a storm in August, he recommended telling the Soviets the United States was prepared, on the basis of an assessment of the diminishing combat in South Vietnam, to stop bombing on Day X. By making this step, the administration would imply that after the bombing cessation this low level of military activity would be maintained, Saigon would not be attacked, and both rivals would move promptly to reinstall the DMZ. Simultaneously Washington would require from the Soviet Union some broad understanding of this arrangement.

"This is pretty high-risk poker," Rostow admitted, "and the case is good for waiting to see if in fact Hanoi responds directly to the Zorin suggestion. But the fact is that the Kosygin letter [of June 5] gives us an opening for this gambit if you should decide you would like to force this issue."[51]

In an unfortunate coincidence, at the same time Harriman's suggestion, along with a detailed plan of possible U.S. steps, arrived in Washington, the *New York Times* made a similar proposal. And Vice-President Hubert Humphrey added his voice to the chorus of "peace-lovers." According to Harriman, Johnson "went through the roof."[52] He called Harriman's telegram "mush" and labeled it part of a conspiracy designed to force him to stop bombing.[53] He instructed Rusk to hold a press conference on July 30. "This was the hard-line press conference that cut the ground out from all the work Vance and I had been doing in Paris since early May," Harriman complained. "It was interpreted by the DRV as a change in position. In fact, Ha Van Lau asked Vance, since the Secretary of State's statements were at variance with what Vance and I had been talking about, whether we in fact did talk for the President."[54] Under such circumstances, the negotiations again stalled, and the already slim prospects of a compromise based on the Phase 1–Phase 2 plan dwindled. Negotiations dragged on in August and most of September without serious results.

After a splash of activity, Moscow now reduced its involvement in the negotiations. Soviet leaders were too preoccupied with the crisis in neighboring Czechoslovakia to pay much attention to affairs in faraway Southeast Asia.

Events in Czechoslovakia in August 1968 and the ultimate Soviet invasion of the country are connected to the Vietnam War not only because they diverted Moscow's attention from the negotiations in Paris. Because of U.S. involvement in the Vietnamese conflict, the Soviet Union could feel freer to invade a country in its sphere of influence without serious consequences for Moscow's position in the world community or sanctions by the West. The Czechoslovakian crisis also marked a turning point in the growth of Soviet influence in Southeast Asia as compared with that of China, thus providing Moscow with more freedom of action in the region.

This new influence was an outgrowth of Moscow's larger policy, in a bipolar world, to take a leadership role in international events wherever they occurred. The widening gap between Moscow and Beijing only contributed to Soviet desires to strengthen the image of the USSR as the vanguard of the struggle for liberating the world of imperialism. Against Chinese accusations of revisionism, betrayal of Marxism-Leninism and proletarian internationalism, and collusion with the West, the Kremlin had to defend its policy not only by strong words but also by deeds.

Foreign Minister Gromyko, in a speech in early 1966, had warned the world that the "Soviet Union cannot fail but be interested in the situation in any area of the globe." Moscow's policy of noninterference in the affairs of any state and people, Gromyko added, "does not mean a tolerance and neutrality to the interference of others."[55] Clearly the USSR intended to interpret "interference" according to its own system of values. At the same time Gromyko declared pointedly that "The question of boundaries in Europe is settled completely and irrevocably. *The state frontiers of our friends and allies are under the same safety lock as our own frontiers.*"[56] This was a clear warning that the Kremlin would not tolerate any assault on Soviet positions in Europe.[57] As a result, when the Czechoslovkian Communist party lost control of events in that country in 1967–1968, Moscow perceived a threat to the very foundations of socialism in an area close to Soviet borders, and therefore as a threat to its own geostrategic position.

Soviet leaders regarded relations with Czechoslovakia as one of the principal elements of the USSR's European policy and the balance of forces between East and West. Brezhnev, for instance, according to his foreign policy assistant Andrei M. Alexandrov-Agentov, viewed Czechoslovakia, along with Poland and East Germany, as the core of the Warsaw Pact—and as the most reliable and trustworthy of the three.[58] This view was influenced by the personal experiences of the Soviet leaders, particularly Brezhnev.[59]

Although Moscow had closely monitored events in Czechoslovakia since 1967 and had even made several attempts to prevent a blowup and save the Communist party leadership in that country, Soviet leaders did not expect a crisis of such scale and intensity as broke out in the spring and summer of 1968. Under those circumstances, the Kremlin tried to control the situation by means other than military action. It met with the Warsaw Pact countries and tried to rally them to persuade their Czechoslovak fellows to channel developments into a more acceptable direction for the Soviet Union. When this "personal diplomacy" failed, the Kremlin, under pressure from its own hard-liners as well as leaders of other socialist countries who worried that repercussions from Czechoslovakia might jeopardize their own position, resorted to force.

The decision to invade Czechoslovakia was adopted by the Soviet politburo reluctantly. According to documents now available for the first time, Brezhnev almost to the end was unwilling to approve such an action.[60] But the significance of Czechoslovakia for the unity of the socialist camp and for Soviet influence in the region, as well as pressure from some of his colleagues, outweighed other considerations. On the night of August 20–21, armed forces of five Warsaw Pact countries, including those of the Soviet Union, invaded Czechoslovakia. Next day *Pravda* published a TASS report about the "request" of the Czechoslovak Socialist Republic to its allies for assistance and about the "introduction" of troops on its territory.[61]

The Soviet leadership could not help but consider what reaction this step might cause in the West. It was an open violation of the principle of noninterference, though the Soviets insisted on their own interpretation of this principle. In deciding to invade, the

Kremlin demonstrated its confidence that no strong reaction would follow.

Western European countries were obviously in no position to oppose the Soviet move; the only effective countermeasures could come from the United States. But Washington was not about to react with force for two reasons. First, since World War II U.S. leaders had regarded Eastern and Central Europe as a Soviet sphere of influence. Second, the Johnson administration did not wish to sacrifice the normalization of relations with the Soviet Union, and Moscow's help in settling the conflict in Vietnam, to high principles. In other words, American politicians could not allow moral considerations to overrule the realpolitik they so detested.

Washington recognized the danger of a Soviet invasion of Czechoslovakia long before it occurred, but the U.S. government did nothing to prevent it. Did the administration wish to? In his memoirs, Johnson admitted, "There was little we could do except watch and worry."[62] He referred to the absence of treaty commitments with Czechoslovakia, slight hopes for NATO support of military action, and the unwillingness of the Czechs themselves to resist. The only official U.S. reaction to the invasion was Johnson's cancellation of his visit to Moscow to begin strategic weapons talks.

This was a weak response to the Soviet violation of international law. No discussions were initiated in the United Nations, no embargoes imposed on economic or cultural exchanges with the USSR. As to the cancellation of the president's visit to the USSR, it was in Johnson's interest to make such a visit, since he wished to crown his presidency with a dramatic final act, perhaps a summit meeting with the Soviets that would agree on arms-control negotiations. As Clark Clifford testified, the president "hated to lose his last great goal, and looked for ways to avoid a cancellation."[63] After it was finally announced, Johnson nevertheless returned to the idea of a trip to Moscow from time to time.[64]

As soon as the invasion became a fait accompli, the United States made Czechoslovakia a bargaining chip in various areas of Soviet-American relations. On September 17 the administration informed the Soviets privately that "they could take the heat off Czechoslovakia by talks on the Mideast."[65] Washington would obviously use the same tactics in dealing with Vietnam.

While the West chose not to counter the Soviet move against Czechoslovakia, in the East the Kremlin found strong support in

Hanoi for its efforts to preserve the unity of the socialist camp. The DRV's public approval of the invasion signified a decisive turn toward Moscow and a blow to Beijing. The leading newspapers of North Vietnam not only published without deletions the TASS statement on Warsaw Pact troops' "entry" into Czech territory, they accompanied this statement with a preamble that repeated Soviet arguments for the action and statements that it had been done "for a noble purpose."[66]

Against the background of a broad anti-Soviet campaign instigated by Beijing in response to the Soviet invasion, North Vietnamese approval was promptly noticed and assessed in Moscow. On the DRV's twenty-third anniversary, a *Pravda* editorial—always reflective of official government views—praised the "heroic people of Vietnam" and acknowledged Hanoi's position toward the Czech crisis: "The Vietnamese people, through their own experience, are confident of the great strength of proletarian solidarity. The DRV has approved the action of the Soviet Union and other socialist countries to rebuff counterrevolutionary forces in Czechoslovakia. The Vietnamese working people, who wage a severe struggle against the imperialist aggressors, understand full well the perfidy and meanness of subversive activity against socialist countries."[67]

Hanoi's open support of Moscow was a positive sign for Soviet leaders who perceived a reorientation of North Vietnamese policy toward a closer alliance with the USSR and greater independence from China. Although Hanoi was by no means prepared to neglect the opinion of its "great northern neighbor," the Kremlin clearly was pleased by its enhanced influence on Vietnamese policy, particularly in the question of negotiations. Accordingly, Moscow hurried to use this new display of Hanoi's loyalty by more actively promoting the success of the Paris talks as soon as the dust over Czechoslovakia had settled, by the end of September.

Meanwhile, by September the North Vietnamese–American negotiations had taken a small step forward. After the long summer months of unproductive discussions, whether public "official conversations," private meetings between Cyrus Vance and Ha Van Lau, or high-level secret negotiations between Harriman and Le Duc Tho and Xuan Thuy in one of the "safe houses" designated for such sessions, slight shifts occurred in the uncompromising positions of Hanoi's envoys. Harriman and Vance were quick to notice them. On September 17, in Washington, Harriman told the president that in his opinion Hanoi's delegation in Paris "was serious about making progress."[68] Vance confirmed Harriman's impression when he arrived in the United States and met with Johnson on October 3. Vance speculated that the "North Vietnamese might assume that their military situation was likely to deteriorate in the coming months." At a time when South Vietnam was receiving ever greater shipments of arms and equipment, and displaying a strengthened confidence, "Hanoi might wish to settle things sooner rather than later."[69] Despite such optimism, Johnson remained skeptical about near-term prospects for progress in the negotiations.

Nevertheless the continuing secret meetings between the principal negotiators were not entirely fruitless. Harriman and Vance defined the U.S. position on three basic questions, and these points were crystallized during the summer. The United States was prepared to stop the bombing of the DRV if "prompt and serious talks" would follow with the participation of representatives of the Saigon regime, and if Hanoi agreed not to violate the demilitarized zone between North and South Vietnam. But Washington could not sustain a bombing pause if the North Vietnamese and the Viet Cong were to undertake large-scale attacks against South Vietnam's major cities, such as Saigon, Hue, or Danang.

The North Vietnamese delegates appeared ready to accept the U.S. position on the DMZ and on attacks against South Vietnamese population centers. At least they showed an understanding of U.S. concern over these questions. But including the Saigon regime in the negotiations became a real stumbling block. As Vance put it in his conversation with Valentin Oberemko, the DRV attitude toward this question was "totally unrealistic."[70]

During his meeting with Oberemko on September 21, Vance urged the Soviet government to put pressure on Hanoi "to make the DRV realize that they are taking a wholly unreasonable and unrealistic position" with regard to the participation of Saigon in the negotiations. Vance drew Oberemko's attention to the fact that the United States was not opposed to NLF representation at the talks, though the public impression was otherwise. He underlined that the negotiators were "at a critical juncture" and it was very important "that the Soviet Government use its influence at this time to permit us to get around the roadblock and move further."

Oberemko promised to transmit these views to Moscow but

asked whether the inclusion of Saigon representatives was *the* major roadblock to serious discussions. Vance replied yes, since all other problems did not raise North Vietnamese objections. To underscore the importance of the issue, Vance, after conferring with Harriman, sent a letter to Oberemko emphasizing that it was "unthinkable" for the United States to stop the bombing without the inclusion of South Vietnamese representatives in Paris negotiations.[71] Simultaneously the American negotiators asked Rusk to review the U.S. formula on Saigon participation. The American delegation had stated to the North Vietnamese that an understanding on this "crucial issue" "could be a major factor in facilitating a decision to stop the bombing." Le Duc Tho and Xuan Thuy were not satisfied with this wording. They feared it meant there were other factors as well. So did Oberemko. Harriman and Vance concluded that the instructions Washington provided their envoys in Paris were "too narrow" and that it was necessary to broaden them, changing the wording of the previous formula to state "an understanding on this subject *would* be *the* major factor in facilitating a decision to stop the bombing." The American representatives asked that this new wording be authorized as soon as possible, since they expected a positive reaction from Hanoi on this question.[72] The North Vietnamese, however, balked over Saigon's representation for several more weeks.

Meanwhile Moscow was busy backstage trying to solve the problem. It was clearly on behalf of the North Vietnamese that Gromyko, who visited the United States in early October, asked Rusk whether agreement on the inclusion of a South Vietnamese delegation in the talks was a necessary precondition for a cessation of the bombing, and whether it was possible to replace Thieu and Ky with someone more acceptable to Hanoi, as a compromise.[73] Although Gromyko emphasized that his question had no political implications and was just a question, it was certainly inspired by Hanoi whose hatred for the "American puppets" was the main reason why it refused to agree on the participation of the Saigon regime.

Finally, not without Soviet efforts, the North Vietnamese budged. On October 9, during a tea break between the two delegations, and after Harriman and Vance confirmed that the inclusion of representatives of the South Vietnam government was "utterly indispensable," Xuan Thuy and Le Duc Tho informed the Americans that the North Vietnamese were prepared to discuss this subject in a private meeting. They added that what was necessary in regard to the problem was "good will and serious intent," which they had.[74] When the private meeting was held in a CIA-supplied "safe house" in the Paris suburbs, the DRV envoys asked their American counterparts whether the United States would stop the bombing if Hanoi agreed to the participation of the Saigon government.[75] Harriman avoided giving a direct answer and said he would consult with Washington.

In Washington Harriman's report stirred hopes that, as Lyndon Johnson put it, "the ice was beginning to melt."[76] But the administration was careful not to hurry with a decisive move. Washington consulted with its representatives in Saigon, Ambassador Ellsworth Bunker and General Creighton Abrams, the American commander in Vietnam. Both agreed with a proposal to tell the North Vietnamese that the U.S. government was ready to set an early date for total cessation of attacks against the DRV.

The next day Vance's counterpart at the Soviet embassy, Oberemko, delivered an urgent message from Moscow. He told Vance that if the United States stopped the bombing of North Vietnam, Hanoi would agree to the participation of the Saigon government in negotiations that would follow immediately.[77] Again Washington was cautious. Johnson and Rusk wanted confirmation of Oberemko's message directly from Moscow. On October 13 Rusk met with Dobrynin and gave him a text of the message Vance had received from Oberemko the previous day. He told the Soviet ambassador that the administration was interested in its source. "It was one thing," Rusk informed Dobrynin, "if Mr. Oberemko was simply repeating some message which he has received from the North Vietnamese Delegation in Paris and another thing if he were acting on instructions from his government."[78] Apparently Washington wanted an additional guarantee from Moscow. The next day Dobrynin delivered a response from his government. "Our Charge d'Affaires [Oberemko] acted in accordance with the Soviet Government's instructions. The new display of good will on the part of the DRV, of which we are speaking now, is creating, in our profound conviction, a real possibility of speedy progress in this direction."[79]

Upon receipt of this confirmation from Moscow, Johnson met with cabinet members and chief advisers for consultation on the next move. Instructions were sent to Harriman and Vance to tell Hanoi that negotiations should begin within twenty-four hours after the cessation of the bombing.

But after this promising start, the process bogged down, this time not only because of North Vietnamese obstruction but primarily because of objections from the South Vietnamese. Xuan Thuy told Vance that Washington's "next-day requirement" was impractical since, though Hanoi's envoys were ready to meet with the American delegation, they could not guarantee the presence of the NLF delegation within such a short time. For Saigon, the prospect of negotiations with the enemy, as the National Liberation Front was regarded by the South Vietnamese government, was a pretext to postpone the negotiations.

Despite his dark mood over these setbacks in Saigon and Paris, Johnson did not lose hope. Rusk sent a telegram to the American chief negotiator in Paris with instructions not to insist on the "next day" condition and instead to suggest a date within two or three days after the bombing cessation. At the same time Rusk arranged a meeting with Dobrynin to convince the Soviet government of the importance for the administration of the shortest possible interval between a bombing halt and the start of negotiations. Dobrynin promised to report this immediately to Moscow.[80]

It was much more difficult for the Johnson administration to get Saigon to agree on negotiations. While Hanoi might have been stimulated to move toward a settlement because of a possible victory in the 1968 presidential elections by Richard Nixon and the uncertainties involved in a change of administrations in Washington, Saigon, on the contrary, expected that if Johnson lost the White House to Nixon, the new Republican government would be more attentive to the needs of its South Vietnamese allies and more desirous of a settlement on terms acceptable to Saigon. With secret support for these expectations from some members of the Nixon team, Thieu refused to cooperate with Johnson and deliberately stalled the negotiating process.

The second half of October was a period of intense negotiations in Paris addressing a number of impasses between the warring parties. One of the most active players in the drama was the Soviet Union. Always aware of the danger of a breakdown in the talks, Soviet leaders were also apprehensive of the prospects of a Nixon victory. In Moscow's view, Nixon was too unpredictable and reactionary to be a reliable partner in settling the conflict in Southeast Asia. The Soviets preferred to reach an agreement between Washington and Hanoi before the presidential elections. As a result, Moscow was involved at every stage in resolving the problems that threatened to delay and even to disrupt a settlement.

The Kremlin charged its diplomats in Paris, Washington, and Hanoi to search for possible compromise between the negotiating sides. Soviet leaders themselves intervened in the negotiations to urge the Americans and North Vietnamese to make concessions essential for final agreement. American officials were informed that the Soviet press was instructed by the government to play the Vietnam theme in a very low key,[81] so as not to jeopardize prospects for positive results in Paris.

The new obstacle in the way of an understanding between Washington and Hanoi—after the problem of South Vietnamese participation—was the length of time between the announcement of the bombing halt and the beginning of negotiations. The Americans insisted on the shortest possible time lag, not more than three or four days. The North Vietnamese considered "several weeks" as necessary for the National Liberation Front to dispatch its representatives to the French capital. When each party rigidly adhered to its pronounced position, the American negotiators appealed to the Soviets.

On October 18 Harriman and Vance met with Oberemko to urge Moscow to get involved in resolving the problem of the date of negotiations. After being briefed on the status of the talks, the Soviet diplomat suggested that both the United States and the DRV were overemphasizing the importance of the interval. He said "there should be a way to find a compromise." The Americans rejected a compromise, since they had already agreed to change twenty-four hours to two or three days. They advised that "the best thing for both Oberemko and the Soviet Union to do was to use their influence to get the North Vietnamese" to present a date for "serious" talks.[82]

While Oberemko consulted with Moscow, and Moscow presumably sought to convince Hanoi, new problems arose in the negotiations: the structure of the forthcoming talks, and the need for a communiqué of agreement between the United States and the DRV. The Americans proposed a "two-sided" negotiation between four participants, implying that the United States and Saigon would represent "our side," and the DRV and the NLF would talk on behalf of "your side." The North Vietnamese rejected this proposal and instead insisted on a "four-power" conference. Washington could not agree, since a "four-power" format would signify recognition of the Viet Cong as an independent and sovereign power, equal to Saigon. In addition, Hanoi's delegates demanded the issue of a special communiqué, either public or secret, wherein the United States would recognize that it had ceased the bombing of North Vietnam unconditionally. Again the Johnson administration stalled, for recognition of the unconditional character of the cessation would be a blow to U.S. prestige and a clear gain for the North Vietnamese who, from the outset of the war, had declared they would be ready to negotiate with the American aggressor only after an unconditional bombing halt.

Oberemko called Vance on October 22. He was apparently concerned with developments in the negotiations, especially after he found the North Vietnamese "emotional" and "suspicious" after their private meeting with the Americans. But he tried to relieve tensions and to reassure Vance that the reason for this mood was simply a misunderstanding in translation. He said he had had the same difficulty in communicating with the DRV.

Turning to more substantial questions, Oberemko told Vance that it was up to a "third party to try to resolve the situation by putting forward 'a common sense solution.' " After these words, by which he tacitly admitted that the Soviet Union had assumed the role of mediator between the two sides, Oberemko, "acting under the general instructions of his government," proposed that the United States stop bombing on October 24 or 25, with representatives of the four warring parties meeting on November 1 or 2.[83] The Soviets clearly suggested a compromise between the U.S. "two or three days" and the Vietnamese "several weeks," for the interval proposed by Oberemko was seven days.

Referring to the issue of a joint communiqué, the Soviet diplomat said "it was not the business of his government whether the DRV and the U.S. reached an oral or written understanding." As for the structure of the negotiations, Oberemko suggested naming all four parties without referring to "sides," thus avoiding both the American and the North Vietnamese formulas.[84]

This conversation illustrates the role played by the Soviets in helping both sides to reach an agreement without involving themselves as a full-scale intermediary with duties and responsibilities. It is noteworthy that Oberemko, though he confirmed that he represented a "third party," underlined that he acted under the *general instructions* of his government, thus implying that it was his initiative to make concrete proposals to the parties, not Moscow's. Likewise, the Soviet diplomat was careful to avoid involvement in all problems that might have demanded greater responsibility for the USSR in the course of the negotiations. Waving aside the problem of the communiqué, Oberemko implied that it was up to the Soviets to decide what questions required Moscow's participation. As Oberemko declared, the "Soviet Union was trying to get an agreement in principle."

At the same time Oberemko revealed the Kremlin's eagerness for a resolution of all problems. He asked that his proposal be reported to Washington as soon as possible and drew Vance's attention to the need for the American delegation to call a meeting with the North Vietnamese after they had heard from Washington. "Since the DRV had called the last one," the Soviet explained, "it was impossible for them to take the initiative on the next private meeting." In their message to Washington, Harriman and Vance recommended accepting the Soviet proposal "in principle."

Oberemko contacted Vance again later that day, saying he had spoken with the North Vietnamese on the same subject. According to Oberemko, the DRV delegation agreed to the Soviet formula of simply naming the participants of the four-power talks. They also accepted the dates of cessation and the start of negotiations suggested by the Soviets.[85] But the Hanoi negotiators insisted on calling the cessation of the bombing unconditional and complete. Oberemko also confided to Vance that he had recommended against a joint communiqué on the agreement between the United States and North Vietnam, which was a step toward a compromise. But Hanoi still insisted on a secret minute. Concluding his conversation with Vance, Oberemko said the DRV representatives "were taking 'very seriously' the developments of the last 24 hours," hinting that a final compromise between the delegations appeared to be within reach.

Nevertheless debates on the major points continued until October 27. The Soviets intervened often during that time, trying to reconcile the positions of both sides. They made recommendations, pressed the parties, and suggested means for compromise. These interventions occurred even at the highest levels.

In one of his conversations with Vance during this time, Oberemko confided that the Soviet government was "deeply interested in finding a solution" and that he himself "was acting under the instructions of his government."[86] As if to support this assertion, on October 25 Kosygin, obviously concerned that no agreement had yet been reached, sent a letter to President Johnson. The Soviet premier urged an early resolution of these "third-rate details which in reality have no meaning at all."[87] Undoubtedly this letter could be viewed as not only an attempt to persuade the Americans to drop their demands but also as a demonstration of Moscow's considerable involvement in the Paris talks.

Two days after Kosygin's letter, Harriman and Vance reported to Washington that the North Vietnamese had dropped all unresolved demands and proposed a stoppage of bombing on October 30 and the beginning of talks among the United States, the DRV, Saigon, and the NLF on November 3. Upon receiving this news, Johnson summoned his advisers to assess the situation. Rusk noted that the North Vietnamese "made the major step." "If ten steps separated us," he told the president, "they have taken eight and we have taken 2." He and other members of the administration drew the president's attention to the substantial role Moscow played in the negotiating process.

But Johnson was still skeptical. He insisted that the Soviets be fully informed on the three points of the U.S. conditions for cessation of the bombing. Although Rusk assured him that American officials had raised these issues several times during their meetings with the Soviets, Johnson was not satisfied. He wanted guarantees from Moscow that Hanoi would respect all provisions concerning the DMZ and South Vietnamese cities. "Do the Soviets really think this will go?" the president inquired. "Do they understand we'll restart [bombing] if the DMZ and the cities are not respected? . . . Get Soviet assurances the GVN will be accepted."[88]

Johnson decided he would restate the U.S. position to the Soviets. With this purpose in mind he summoned Dobrynin and presented him with a detailed written explanation of Washington's conditions. The president urged the Soviets to transmit this position to the North Vietnamese "so as to avoid any charge of deception and any risk of misunderstanding."[89] The next day Johnson received Moscow's answer. Soviet leaders welcomed the progress in the Paris peace talks. They emphasized that the North Vietnamese were doing everything to reach a settlement and that any doubts with regard to Hanoi's position were "groundless."[90]

Johnson also demanded a report from his negotiators in Paris to see if they were clear enough with their North Vietnamese counterparts on the same questions. Harriman and Vance informed the president that they had raised the issues of the DMZ and indiscriminate attacks against the major cities, and what the United States expected from the DRV on these two matters, in twelve secret meetings. They assured Johnson that the formulation of the American statements was "precisely in accordance" with instructions from Washington. In addition, Harriman and Vance had raised the subject of the DMZ and attacks on the major cities in four meetings with Soviet representatives in Paris. They advised them that a bombing cessation could not be maintained if the DRV acted in bad faith on these matters. Since the Soviets were in regular and frequent contact with the DRV delegation, it is certainly likely that the North Vietnamese understood Washington's points as relayed by the Soviets.

The American envoys in Paris concluded their report with the strong conviction that "the DRV will carry out what we have demanded of them with respect to the DMZ and indiscriminate attacks against major cities. While we have not received direct affirmation that the DRV will abide by our demand—we are convinces [sic] they understand clearly what they are expected to do." Harriman and Vance offered just one reservation: "it is always possible that there will be some minor violations such as moving small numbers of men and supplied [sic] through the DMZ." But they believed such occurrences could be judged in the context of the total circumstances.[91]

Despite this small reservation, Johnson could be satisfied with all the assurances he received. What disappointed him was the intransigence of his allies, since Saigon's refusal to agree on negotiations with the NLF threatened to undermine the compromise the Americans had reached with great effort. President Thieu ignored all warnings and threats from Washington and invented one reason after another for the postponement of talks with his adversary.

Even personal messages from Johnson did not move Saigon from its position.[92]

Washington found itself in an awkward situation. For months its had tried to win concessions from Hanoi on Saigon's participation in the talks and on at least tacit agreement on certain provisions related to the security of South Vietnam once the bombing stopped. Now, when the North Vietnamese had finally given in, the main obstacle to a settlement had been created by Saigon.

Johnson awaited a positive response from Thieu for several days. The date for a start of negotiations was moved to November 4 instead of November 2. But it was not possible to postpone the negotiations endlessly. The president was under strong pressure not only from the North Vietnamese and from Moscow, where Kosygin, according to a Soviet embassy official in Paris, was "waiting to hear."[93] He was also urged by most of his closest advisers to move forward, with or without Saigon's assent. Although Johnson consistently denied it at the time and later, election day, November 5, loomed large in his desire to see negotiations started.

Finally, Johnson decided to take the unilateral step. On October 31 at 8 p.m. an order went to air force and navy units to halt all aerial and naval bombardment of North Vietnam as soon as possible, and within twelve hours at the latest. At the same time Johnson announced this step on nationwide television and noted that a regular session of the Paris talks would be held the following week. As to South Vietnam, Johnson said the Saigon government was "free to participate."[94]

This seemed to be a welcome outcome of innumerable discussions in Paris, as well as in Washington, Hanoi, and Moscow, during the long months since the opening of talks in May 1968. The Soviets could have been well satisfied with the results of their efforts to promote a peaceful settlement of the protracted conflict in Southeast Asia. *Pravda* fully informed its readers of the agreement in Paris. On November 2 the newspaper published the comment of a DRV representative in Paris on the American bombing halt and information about Johnson's televised speech.[95]

The same day the Soviet government issued a statement calling the agreement in Paris an "important success on the way to a peaceful settlement in Vietnam." More favorable conditions had been created for a cessation of bloodshed in South Vietnam, for full withdrawal of American troops, and for political resolution of the whole problem of Vietnam.[96] But realities overturned political expectations. Thieu continued to refuse to negotiate with the National Liberation Front. Weeks went by with no "serious talks" in Paris.

Moscow could not conceal its disappointment with the course of events. On November 7 *Pravda* reminded its readers that a day earlier the new, important phase of the negotiations might have started. But, the newspaper complained, at the last moment Washington had decided to postpone the session because of Saigon's refusal to sit down at the same table with NLF representatives. The organ of the Communist party of the Soviet Union ridiculed this explanation as "groundless."[97] Moscow blamed the Americans for the delay. Just as Washington did not trust Soviet assurances that the Kremlin could not dictate to Hanoi, so Moscow was skeptical of U.S. inability to resolve Saigon's intransigence.

Pravda spelled out this skepticism in an article on November 13. Referring again to American explanations that the negotiations had been postponed because the Saigon authorities refused to talk to the NLF, *Pravda* stated: "Groundlessness of these assertions hardly needs comments. It is clear that the United States could resolve independently the question of termination of [its] aggression in Vietnam, of withdrawal of American military forces, and of liquidation of military bases on the territory of South Vietnam, without consulting with its puppets. Something different puts us on guard. Behind the 'obstinacy' of Saigon's authorities peeps the designs of those militarist forces in the United States who are dissatisfied with the important change that has occurred on the way to a peaceful settlement of the Vietnam question."[98]

Soviet leaders expressed their disappointment not only in the pages of official Soviet newspapers but also conveyed their views directly to U.S. authorities. During a conversation with American senators who were visiting Moscow, Kosygin openly complained that the negotiations in Paris "were not proceeding as swiftly and smoothly as the Soviets hoped." He added: "This is the fault of the United States; the Vietnamese side wants a settlement and we would like to contribute also."[99]

Repeatedly during the last weeks of 1968, Moscow sent signals of its readiness to help through official as well as secret channels. The Soviets did so even at the risk of incurring Hanoi's displeasure, since they knew of the opinion of the DRV's politburo that until Nixon took office after his presidential victory, negotiations in Paris had no practical value.[100] Analyzing results of a recent visit of the DRV delegation to Beijing and Moscow in a speech before North Vietnamese authorities, Foreign Minister Nguyen Duy Trinh noted that in the negotiations in Moscow, Hanoi's envoys consistently felt it was the aim of Soviet leaders "to press us for peace."[101]

Nevertheless Moscow seemed wedded to the idea of getting negotiations started before the inauguration of the new American president. Gromyko stated it clearly to Ambassador Llewellyn Thompson. Touching upon questions that might be discussed during President Johnson's visit to Moscow (still on the agenda in both capitals), the Soviet foreign minister said the Kremlin had no doubt of the usefulness of an exchange of opinions on questions concerning Southeast Asia. "From our point of view," Gromyko continued, "the main problem of this region today remains the stopping of the bloodshed in Vietnam and the achievement there of a political settlement on the basis of respect for the legal rights and aspirations of the Vietnamese people."[102]

What Soviet leaders could not tell their American counterparts officially, they transmitted to them through private channels. In November a U.S. embassy source in London informed the Americans of his conversation with Ivan Koulikov, second secretary of the Soviet embassy, about various problems of Soviet-American relations, including Vietnam. Koulikov confided to his counterpart a future arrangement in Southeast Asia as Moscow envisioned it after the Vietnam War ended. According to him, the Soviets did not wish to precipitate U.S. withdrawal from the region. Specifically they were not opposed to U.S. bilateral defense agreements with such countries as Thailand, Indonesia, the Philippines, and Singapore. Nor did they oppose American bases in those countries. The Soviet diplomat observed that an American presence in Southeast Asia was desirable for Moscow because, "Don't forget we face a common enemy in Asia."[103]

This conversation reveals two dominant ideas in Soviet thinking: to reach an understanding with the United States on spheres of influence in Southeast Asia, and on that basis to build an alliance against China. This scheme obviated the possibility of Washington playing its China card against the Soviets—a continuing fear for

Moscow. Thus in late 1968 Moscow was filled with determination to help Washington clear the way for full-scale talks in Paris.

Even after Saigon finally agreed to send a delegation to Paris, and the South Vietnamese representatives arrived in the French capital on December 8, negotiations did not begin because of numerous procedural questions raised by the reluctant diplomats from Saigon. The biggest problem was the shape of the conference table. Since the South Vietnamese wanted Hanoi and the NLF to sit as a single delegation in Paris, they demanded a seating arrangement, a table shape, flags, and nameplates that reflected this point of view. Hanoi, however, insisted that North Vietnamese and NLF representatives be seated as two separate delegations, at a square table, with two different nameplates and each under its own flag. The United States proposed a compromise: four delegations, a round table, no flags, no nameplates. But such a solution was not acceptable to either Vietnamese side. To resolve this impasse, Harriman and Vance suggested different table arrangements with variations of the table shape: square, rectangular, oval, parallelograms, semicircles, diamonds, and halfmoons. Meetings of the delegations now resembled classes in geometry rather than "serious talks."

The haggling went on for ten weeks,[104] with only one alternative becoming obvious—a large round table. The South Vietnamese were still adamant in their objection to creating an appearance of equality between the NLF and other delegates. The Americans suggested a kind of dividing line between the two sides, but Hanoi's delegation vehemently opposed such a solution, for it reminded them of the abandoned "our side/your side" idea.

The Soviets in Paris, who were apparently informed of all these developments, decided to intervene once more. On January 13 Oberemko told Harriman and Vance that the North Vietnamese would not accept a dividing line. He suggested "some other approach"—a round table with two separate tables for aides and translators. These two tables would be either square or rectangular and placed at right angles to the main table, thus giving the appearance of a separation of the sides. One of the important conditions was that these two additional tables not touch the main table, that there be a distance between them. Vance asked about the distance, and Oberemko suggested, "Perhaps far enough for Bogomolov to walk between."[105] (First secretary of the Soviet embassy Sergei Bogomolov was small and spare.) The prospects of breaking the deadlock over the shape of the table seemed hopeful after Oberemko's promise to discuss this idea with the North Vietnamese. Three more questions remained unresolved, however—speaking order, flags, and nameplates. Vance insisted that all three questions be decided simultaneously.

The next day Oberemko assured Vance that he had good reason to believe the DRV delegation would accept the compromise suggested by the Soviets—a main table plus two smaller ones, no flags or nameplates, and a speaking order determined by the French who would select by lottery a first speaker. Suggesting this package, Oberemko stressed that "time was of the essence and the matter should be settled immediately."[106]

At the January 15 meeting between the U.S. and the DRV delegations, the sides finally reached agreement on these procedural details. The North Vietnamese accepted the Soviet proposal on the shape of the table and dropped their request for flags and nameplates. It was evidently done under Soviet pressure. It was also agreed that procedural meetings of the four delegations would be held in the Hotel Majestic conference room not earlier than January 18.[107]

Johnson could be relieved that the first session of the four-party talks would be held under his administration. Although he regretted, as he confessed in his memoirs, that he was leaving the White House "without achieving a just, an honorable, and a lasting peace in Vietnam," he was at least able to turn over to the successor "a situation more promising and manageable than it had been for years."[108] Undoubtedly Moscow shared some of his satisfaction.

Harriman understood this quite well and was eager to pay tribute to the Soviets, though not publicly. During his farewell conversation with Zorin, the ambassador expressed his appreciation of the Soviet role in the Paris negotiations. Harriman's recommendations and advice about Moscow's attitude toward the Vietnam War seemed fulfilled. "First, he had been telling his friends," Harriman confessed to Zorin, "based on what Kosygin told him three years ago, that the Soviets wanted a settlement and would do what they could within their capabilities to help get talks started; he would like to remind some skeptical friends of this. Second, he was convinced we could not have a real settlement without Soviet help, and he was glad the Soviets had shown this willingness to help. . . ."[109]

Considering Harriman's appraisal, how can we evaluate Moscow's role in the first phase of negotiations on a Vietnam settlement? Cyrus Vance, in his interview for the Johnson Library's oral history collection, rejected the notion that the Soviets acted as an intermediary during the Paris peace talks. "We made clear to the Russians," he said, "what we had told the North Vietnamese, and we asked the Soviets to let us know whether it was clear in their minds that the North Vietnamese understood what had been said and was expected of them. They came back and told us that they did indeed understand precisely what was expected of them, and what the consequences could be if they breached those assumptions. . . ."[110] In other words, according to Vance, the Soviets served as the most reliable channel through which both sides sent information to each other, and no more.

Whether this was Vance's conviction or his fear of revealing the real Russian role at a time when the Paris negotiations were still under way is a matter of speculation. But an acquaintance with the bulk of documents on this period of the talks, as well as with the USSR's policy aims at the time, suggests that Moscow did not confine itself to the distribution of information. It was not just a "postman," to use a favorite expression of Soviet officials, between the Americans and the North Vietnamese. The Soviets were also actively involved in the process of negotiations, seeking to influence their development. At times of crisis in the talks, as in May when the United States pushed for secret meetings, or in October, when the problem of Saigon's participation and the cessation of U.S. bombing was discussed, or in January when procedural matters became paramount, Moscow intervened, suggested compromises, and persuaded both sides to make concessions in order to facilitate an agreement between the two parties.

Undoubtedly Moscow used its leverage with Hanoi to keep the DRV at the negotiating table and to "press them for peace." Thus the Soviet embassy in Hanoi defined its main task for 1969 in the following terms: "To plead our cause in such a manner as in 1969 finally to move the center of gravity in the settlement of the Vietnamese question from the battlefield in South Vietnam to the negotiating table. It is necessary to advise the PTV [Russian acronym for the Workers' Party of Vietnam] to move from 'fighting and negotiating' tactics to negotiations, to renounce delays in Paris, to be more willing to compromise on the principal question—the withdrawal of U.S. forces."[111]

The "serious negotiations" in Paris were a guarantee of sorts for Moscow that the process of settlement had become irreversible. But there remained many uncertainties for the Kremlin in January 1969. And the most important of these was the policy of the new Nixon administration.

NINE

Linkage versus Linkage

Nixon's victory in the 1968 presidential election did not seem to surprise policymakers in Moscow. They followed the campaign for the White House and, noting the disillusionment of Americans with the policies of the Johnson administration, particularly toward the Vietnam War, they were somewhat skeptical of Hubert Humphrey's chances as the Democratic candidate—though they hoped otherwise. A Democratic administration was something the Soviets were used to dealing with. Humphrey's victory would mean for Moscow a basic continuity in U.S. foreign policy, primarily toward the Soviet Union and the Vietnam War. The Kremlin assumed that Humphrey, vice-president in the Johnson administration, would certainly pursue the trend toward closer cooperation with Moscow, especially in arms reduction and economic relations. Soviet analysts took into account Humphrey's criticism of U.S. policy in Southeast Asia, tempered by his loyalty to Johnson, and expected that once he became president he would act more independently to terminate the war as quickly as possible.

Nixon, on the other hand, was an "unknown quantity" for Soviet leaders. Too many factors made him an undesirable partner for Moscow. First and foremost, he represented a Republican party that, in the eyes of Communist ideologists, was more conservative and therefore more reactionary than the Democrats. The history of

Soviet-American relations contained mostly negative examples of interaction under Republican presidents—the policy of nonrecognition, with political and economic boycotts, during the first sixteen years of the Communist regime; confrontation in the 1950s and the showdown following a U-2 spy flight. Although confrontations had occurred under Democratic administrations as well, they were far outweighed in the minds of Soviet leaders by periods when the two countries developed a fruitful collaboration, as during World War II.

Nixon's own background also made the Soviets suspicious. The new president was known in the Soviet Union as a staunch anti-Communist and "anti-Sovietchik," according to Moscow's terminology at the time. He was clearly regarded as a "hawk" and a cold warrior not only on questions of relations with the Communist world but in his attitude toward the Vietnam War. Nixon's advocacy of strong measures against North Vietnam and his appeal to use all possible methods to win the war as soon as possible alarmed Soviet leadership. Perhaps Moscow recognized that these declarations were no more than responses to the demands of the political campaign.[1] But the Soviets could scarcely believe in Nixon's preelection statements about his desire for further cooperation with the Soviet Union and other socialist countries. Instead the Soviet press was eager to note those nuances in Nixon's pronouncements that confirmed the Republican candidate's hawkishness and uncompromising attitude.

In its report of August 4 about preparations for the Republican national convention, *Pravda* cited Nixon's declaration that the war in Vietnam "must be ended." But it also noted his warning that "it must be ended honorably, consistent with America's limited aims and with the long-term requirements of peace in Asia." The newspaper interpreted "Nixon's appeal" to end the war as a way to expand it, which "concurs, as it is not difficult to see, with the demands of the military clique and political 'hawks' in Washington."[2]

When Moscow received news of Nixon's nomination as presidential candidate, *Pravda* published an article that analyzed the convention and its nominee. The newspaper reminded its readers that Nixon was well known as a politician who demanded a military victory in Vietnam and criticized as insufficient "even that gigantic arms race" the Pentagon had conducted under a Democratic administration. "Perhaps those forces that nominated Nixon as a candidate and led him through all the obstacles created by his rivals understood the advantages of such a reputation in the present situation of American politics," *Pravda* concluded.[3] The newspaper added that Nixon had recently adopted a more careful attitude toward foreign policy issues and had even announced that his political views had modified since the early sixties—but the clear implication of this comment was that he was not to be trusted.

In addition, Soviet leaders strongly believed that campaign promises of presidential candidates in the United States usually did not survive their victory. New presidents easily forgot their earlier assurances. So Moscow continued to treat Nixon as the least desirable person for the White House. As in 1964 Soviet leaders had "voted" for Johnson, now they decided to lend indirect support to Humphrey, particularly in that area most sensitive for the Democratic administration, the Vietnam War.[4] This attitude helps to explain Moscow's activity in resolving deadlocks in the Paris negotiations in October 1968, which helped the Johnson administration announce a cessation of bombing several days before election day and thus enhance Humphrey's chances in the contest against Nixon.[5]

Nixon himself not only suspected that the Soviets were behind the October developments that nearly cost him the White House; he was also aware of the fears that the prospects of his victory aroused in Moscow. In his memoirs Nixon wrote: "I was sure that Brezhnev and Kosygin had been no more anxious for me to win in 1968 than Khrushchev had been in 1960. The prospect of having to deal with a Republican administration—and a Nixon administration at that—undoubtedly caused anxiety in Moscow. In fact, I suspected that the Soviets might have counseled the North Vietnamese to offer to begin the Paris talks in the hope that the bombing halt would tip the balance to Humphrey in the election—and if that was their strategy, it had almost worked."[6] Nixon was almost correct, though he exaggerated his own importance by suggesting that the Soviets moved along the Paris peace talks solely to prevent him from being elected president.

The Kremlin had no illusions about the limits of its influence on American political life. Receiving information regularly from the Soviet embassy in Washington as well as from intelligence sources about the public mood in the United States and the election outlook, Soviet leaders could see what the results might be. That same October, when steps to obtain an agreement on the bombing halt were unfolding, the party's central committee secretary and chief of the International Department, Boris Ponomarev, proposed to the politburo that Hanoi be sent an assessment of Nixon's possible victory in the forthcoming elections.[7] By suggesting such a step, Ponomarev might have thought to influence the North Vietnamese leadership to come to an agreement with the United States under the Johnson administration, for Hanoi was obviously no more eager than Moscow to deal with Nixon as president. On the other hand, Moscow evidently foresaw the Republican success and found it expedient to prepare its allies for such a change.

Thus when news of Nixon's election reached Moscow, it caused no sensation. Assessing the results of the presidential election, *Pravda* concluded that "this year the Americans voted not so much *for* as *against* this or that candidate." As to the reasons for the Democratic defeat, the newspaper saw the main ones as popular dissatisfaction with the war in Vietnam as well as in the "explosive domestic problems of the U.S.A."—poverty, inflation, crime. "Even at the beginning of the election campaign," *Pravda* stated, "it was clear that the breach in the people's trust of the present Democratic administration had grown so large that, according to a local journalist, it was possible to move a whole motorized infantry division through it."[8]

From the start of the new Republican administration in January 1969, Nixon's views on Soviet-American relations, as well as the views of his special assistant on national security affairs, Henry A. Kissinger, who played an increasingly important role in U.S. foreign policy, were much more complicated than anticipated. They reflected Nixon's conviction that the United States "can and must communicate and, when possible, negotiate with Communist nations,"[9] but also the idea that the entire international situation dictated a more constructive approach to the socialist countries, and particularly the Soviet Union. By the close of the 1960s the United States found itself in a new environment in which American predominance in the world and Washington's ability to influence developments in various parts of the globe were not as unquestionable as they had been twenty years earlier. One of the most significant factors in this changing political context was the emergence of strategic nuclear parity between the Soviet Union and the United

States. Other developments called for a revision of U.S. foreign policy goals and methods, among them the movement in Europe in the late 1960s toward détente with the East and an increasing rift in Sino-Soviet relations.[10]

Nixon perceived these new trends and was able to take them into account in elaborating his foreign policy program. Just as he had earlier proved skillful in adjusting his views to the realities of the American political scene, after becoming president he grasped the new features of the international situation and worked them into his plans in the world arena. Nixon regarded cooperation with the Soviet Union not as an end in itself but as a useful instrument of American policy. He believed that "it is more sensible—and also safer—to communicate with the Communists than it is to live in icy cold war isolation or confrontation."[11] Cooperation with the Soviet Union might be useful in resolving numerous problems the United States encountered in the late 1960s. Moreover, for Nixon the relationship with Moscow was part of a larger design. According to Raymond Garthoff, Nixon "wanted a foreign policy which would place America in a central and manipulative position of power in the world, just as he sought to consolidate a central, manipulative position of power within the White House."[12] At the beginning of Nixon's presidency, however, the main obstacle for these plans was the war in Vietnam.

By the late 1960s it had become evident to any unbiased observer that U.S. involvement in Vietnam had lost its rational and logical justification. Nixon was not an unbiased observer, and he found good reasons for American participation in the war, at least until it was possible to end it "honorably." But he wanted an "honorable peace" as quickly as possible, for he understood that each day of the war not only moved him further from his desired goals in foreign affairs but also led to the erosion of his domestic policy. So he began looking for a solution of this seemingly insoluble task: to end the war quickly and honorably, and, if possible, to preserve an independent South Vietnam under the Thieu regime.

Nixon recognized that he could not achieve this objective by military means. He understood perfectly well that "total military victory was no longer possible." The only acceptable course, according to Nixon, was "to try for a fair negotiated settlement. . . ."[13] He knew this might not be accomplished by the end of his first year in office, as he admitted in his memoirs. But also he could not exclude the possibility that the war would continue even after that deadline. In this case he would face a loss of credibility at home while trying to preserve it abroad. To avoid such a situation, Nixon decided to link the two tasks of his foreign policy—rapprochement with the Communists and extrication from the Vietnamese conflict—in order to broaden his room for maneuvering both on the domestic scene and in the international arena.

This decision was based on Nixon's conviction that "the key to a Vietnam settlement lay in Moscow and Peking rather than in Hanoi." He believed that "Without continuous and massive aid from either or both of the Communist giants, the leaders of North Vietnam would not have been able to carry on the war for more than a few months."[14] Since the Soviet Union, from Nixon's viewpoint, was more interested in settlement than Beijing, and since to involve the Chinese when no established relations existed between the United States and China seemed problematic, Moscow became an immediate target of Nixon's efforts to resolve the problem of Vietnam.

However strong may have been the new president's inclination toward peaceful resolution, he was never reluctant to resort to military pressure in order to compel the North Vietnamese to agree to a peace on American terms. From the outset Nixon seriously considered threatening to resume the bombing of DRV territory and the mining of principal North Vietnamese ports and lines of communication in the event Hanoi proved intractable and unresponsive. Again the Soviet factor was predominant in the president's thinking, for too much depended on Moscow's reaction to such drastic measures. Thus the Vietnam issue was closely intertwined with détente with the Soviet Union in the new administration's plans.

Nixon believed he would be able to apply sufficient pressure to reach a quick diplomatic settlement with the DRV. He liked to compare himself with a poker player with a good hand. In August 1968, while meeting with Southern delegates to the Republican national convention, he responded to a question about his intention to end the war: "I played a little poker when I was in the Navy. . . . I learned this—when a guy didn't have the cards, he talked awfully big. But when he had the cards, he just sat there—had that cold look in his eyes. Now we've got the cards. . . . What we've got to do is walk softly and carry a big stick."[15] What also encouraged Nixon to adapt his poker rules was a reliable partner in the person of Henry Kissinger, his special assistant on national security affairs.

Almost everyone who has written about the foreign policy of the Nixon administration has not been able to resist the temptation to repeat Nixon's remark about this strange couple—the grocer's son from small-town America and the refugee from Hitler's Germany, the politician and the academic.[16] But the couple was not so curious in their views on foreign policy. There were more similarities than differences in their perception of the world and the role of the United States in it. And where their views did not coincide, they tried to adjust them to find a common ground.

To decide who was the "conceptualizer" and who was "a messenger boy" is beyond the purpose of this book.[17] What is important is that both Nixon and Kissinger shared many ideas on how "honorably" to extricate the United States from the conflict in Vietnam. Even before their association in Washington, Kissinger had spelled out his view of the problem in an article, "The Viet Nam Negotiations," in the January 1969 issue of *Foreign Affairs*, which Nixon could only approve. In it Kissinger emphasized the importance of credibility for Washington, in spite of his conviction that U.S. involvement in Vietnam was disputable from a geopolitical point of view. He explained that a unilateral withdrawal from Vietnam would have grave repercussions for U.S. prestige and even for the whole international situation. "In many parts of the world—the Middle East, Europe, Latin America, even Japan—stability depends on confidence in American promises," Kissinger declared.[18] This appraisal echoed Nixon's own use of the term "credibility." Not surprisingly, in his memoirs Nixon attached the greatest importance to this coincidence of views between the president-elect and his future special assistant. "We also agreed," Nixon wrote, "that whatever else a foreign policy might be, it must be strong to be credible—and it must be credible to be successful."[19]

But Nixon might also have appreciated another idea Kissinger put forward in the article. Drawing attention to the importance for Hanoi of Soviet and Chinese support, he emphasized the conflicting considerations that might have burdened Soviet leaders with regard to the war in Vietnam. He believed that neither a victory nor a defeat of the North Vietnamese would be acceptable to Moscow. He did not call for a direct appeal to Moscow in order to extricate the United States from Vietnam, but he advised that "Washington . . . requires great delicacy in dealing with Moscow on the Vietnam issue," otherwise U.S. approaches to the Soviets might provoke charges from both American and Soviet allies that "the superpowers are sacrificing their allies to maintain spheres of influence."[20]

Walter Isaacson ascribes the authorship of the policy of linkage—the issues of détente and Vietnam—solely to Nixon, repeating Kissinger's own assertion that at first he was skeptical about the Soviet Union as the key to arranging a settlement in Vietnam.[21] True, Kissinger, before his appointment and before his press conference of February 6, 1969, had never explicitly emphasized Moscow's role in a settlement of the Vietnam War; but he had never opposed asking Moscow for help. As Isaacson himself acknowledges, Kissinger "quickly adopted a variation of Nixon's line that the path to peace in Vietnam went through Moscow."[22] The speed of his conversion from a skeptic to a believer is surprising. On November 25, 1968, he met with Nixon personally for the first time; their conversation, if we are to believe Kissinger's account, was devoted to general problems. Less than three weeks later Kissinger, on Nixon's request, was briefing the new cabinet on "our" (i.e., his and Nixon's) approach to foreign policy. Although between these two dates there had been "hours" of discussions on the new course,[23] Kissinger presented himself as a strong proponent of Nixon's policy toward the Soviet Union. He criticized past foreign policy as "'confidence building' for its own sake." Instead, the new administration had to begin working to resolve the differences between the two powers over concrete issues. "A lasting peace," Kissinger claimed, "depended on the settlement of the political issues that were dividing the two nuclear superpowers."[24]

Six days later Kissinger translated these words into concrete demands to the Soviet leadership in a conversation with his contact from the Soviet embassy, Boris Sedov, "the KGB operative masquerading as an embassy counselor." He assured his Soviet counterpart of the sincerity of the new administration's commitment to "an era of negotiations." And he informed Sedov that the administration was prepared to talk about limiting strategic weapons, which, Nixon and Kissinger believed, was Moscow's chief preoccupation. "But we would not be stampeded into talks," Kissinger quickly added, "before we had analyzed the problem." More than that, Washington would "judge the Soviet Union's purposes by its willingness to move forward on a broad front, especially by its attitude on the Middle East and Vietnam."[25]

As one can see, this conversion had taken less than a month. Joan Hoff offered one explanation of Kissinger's transformation when she argued that he was "a geopolitical follower rather than a leader, although his talent for dramatic, back-channel diplomacy may have made the execution of some of Nixon's policies exemplary rather than simply ordinary."[26] This may be true, but the reason why Kissinger accepted Nixon's views so quickly and almost immediately began to translate them into practice was the affinity of the two men's conceptions. It is evident in Kissinger's writings on the Vietnam negotiations, where he emphasized Hanoi's growing dependence on Moscow, particularly after the Soviet invasion of Czechoslovakia, and questioned "the vision of a Titoist Viet Nam."[27] It is also evident in Nixon's memoirs, where the former president wrote: "During the transition period *Kissinger and I* developed a new policy for dealing with the Soviets. Since U.S.-Soviet interests as the world's two competing nuclear superpowers were so widespread and overlapping, it was unrealistic to separate or compartmentalize areas of concern. Therefore *we* decided to link progress in such areas of Soviet concern as strategic arms limitation and increased trade with progress in areas that were important to us—Vietnam, the Mideast, and Berlin. This concept became known as linkage."[28] Knowing Nixon's self-esteem and his jealousy of his special assistant, one can scarcely suspect him of modesty on this question, especially when in his memoirs before and after this passage he writes about "*my* policy," "*my* opinion," "*my* instructions to Kissinger."

In other words, from the beginning of its first term, the new Republican administration regarded policy toward the Soviet Union as an essential part of its efforts to find a solution in Vietnam. As Raymond Garthoff puts it, "The dominant foreign policy preoccupation of Nixon and Kissinger in 1969, and indeed for the entire period through 1972, was not a détente summit meeting with Moscow, but finding an honorable exit from Vietnam. Improvement of relations with the Soviet Union, and a possible parallel rapprochement with China, were at that time seen as much as means to that end as they were ends in themselves."[29] Later, in his memoirs, Kissinger took pains to justify the policy of linkage as based on reality, not on an arbitrary decision by Washington.[30] But in essence it was an attempt to exert pressure on the Soviet Union in order to induce Moscow, in exchange for progress in arms limitation and economic cooperation with the United States, to ease the "honorable" extrication of Washington from the war in Southeast Asia. And Moscow regarded the Nixon administration's efforts in precisely this way.

At the outset the White House apparently tried to determine Moscow's reaction to a policy of linkage through private channels. Kissinger's conversation with Sedov was one such attempt. The response of the Soviet leadership seemed to Nixon and Kissinger positive. Kissinger described Moscow's reply as "soothing." The Soviet leaders admitted that U.S.-Soviet relations would be "favorably affected" by a settlement of the war as well as a constructive approach to the problems of the Middle East and Europe.[31] But it was a standard reply from the Soviet government, which throughout the war in Vietnam spared no opportunity to express its conviction that American withdrawal from the conflict in Indochina would have a positive effect on Soviet-American relations. The Soviets had repeated this statement time and again to President Johnson; they were quite ready to reiterate it to Nixon. It is therefore possible that Moscow did so without first perceiving the substance of the policy of linkage and the importance attached to it by the Nixon administration.

Soon, however, the implications of this policy became clearer to Soviet decision-makers. On January 27, 1969, at his first press conference after the inauguration, Nixon "linked" strategic arms limitation talks with the Soviet Union to "progress on outstanding political problems at the same time."[32] Three days later, on January 31, Kissinger met with prominent Soviet journalist Yuri Zhukov and, as Zhukov reported to Moscow, "clearly and distinctly let [me] understand that Nixon will make development of Soviet-American relations directly dependent on how things will be going with Vietnam settlement." Kissinger hinted to Zhukov, who he knew would inform Soviet authorities of this conversation, that Washington expected "unilateral actions" from Moscow aimed at reaching "acceptable" understandings in Paris, and such actions would be "of great importance."[33] On February 6 the White House took the next step in educating the Soviet leadership. In a briefing for reporters Kissinger explicitly used the term "linkage." He said,

"To take the question of the linkage between the political and the strategic environment . . . [the president] would like to deal with the problem of peace on the entire front in which peace is challenged and not only on the military one."[34]

Moscow did not remain inattentive to these pronouncements from Washington. When Kissinger came to the Soviet embassy on February 14 to attend an official reception, he was invited to the Soviet ambassador's private apartment. Dobrynin, recuperating from a bout of flu, informed his guest that he had a verbal message from Moscow that he wished to deliver personally to the new president.[35] The White House was responsive, and three days later Dobrynin met with Nixon for the first time.

In their memoirs both Nixon and Kissinger offered similar accounts of this first meeting, except that Nixon did not mention Dobrynin's assurance of Soviet willingness to negotiate simultaneously on a number of subjects, as Kissinger did. Instead, according to Nixon, after expressing Moscow's desire to begin talks on arms limitation, Dobrynin had to listen to the president's statement that progress in such talks should be linked to progress in other areas. "History makes it clear that wars result not so much from arms, or even from arms races, as they do from underlying political differences and political problems," Nixon lectured. "So I think it is incumbent on us, when we begin strategic arms talks, to do what we can in a parallel way to defuse critical political situations like the Middle East and Vietnam and Berlin, where there is a danger that arms might be put to use."[36] Kissinger did not mention "an official seven-page note" from Moscow, which Dobrynin handed to Nixon. In this message Moscow indicated, again according to Nixon, that it was prepared to move forward on a whole range of topics, including the Middle East, Central Europe, Vietnam, and arms control.[37] Differences in description aside, based on these accounts it seemed to Nixon and Kissinger that the Soviet leadership in some way agreed on the policy of linkage.

But from other documents it becomes clear this was not the case. Soon after his encounters with Nixon and Kissinger, the Soviet ambassador called on Averell Harriman, with whom he had maintained a good relationship. In their conversation on February 19 Dobrynin could not conceal his concern over the administration's desire to tie nuclear agreements with political settlements. Dobrynin confided to the former American chief negotiator at the

Paris peace talks, who had resigned because of the change of leadership in Washington, that "it had taken Soviet leaders quite a while in discussions over a year to make up their minds whether they wanted to have an agreement on nuclear restraints." According to Dobrynin, a decision had been reached on a majority basis among the Soviet leaders, and they sincerely wished to reach an understanding with the United States. "His Government leaders couldn't understand how it would be possible to tie political settlements with nuclear questions. *They would not be bribed or intimidated.*" Moscow believed that all questions "had to stand on their own feet and be settled accordingly."[38]

Dobrynin tried to persuade Harriman that rumors about how economic problems in the Soviet Union made Moscow eager to talk about arms limitation were far from the truth. He assured Harriman that Soviet leaders would rather face a nuclear race if they could not reach agreement with the United States "on the basis of the merits" of the problem. According to Dobrynin, "Nothing would induce them to give in on some political issue in order to get our agreement on nuclear matters."[39] Later in the conversation the Soviet ambassador returned to the issue of nuclear arms talks and expressed his opinion that the Nixon administration should be candid with Soviet leaders and tell them whether it wanted to move ahead on nuclear discussions or wait. To Harriman, Dobrynin appeared "most anxious" to clarify this question.

Thus, contrary to the optimistic expectations of Nixon and Kissinger, Dobrynin's conversation suggested the Soviet leadership not only had not agreed to talk with Washington "on a whole range of topics" but was prepared to risk the failure of negotiations on nuclear weapons rather than link such negotiations with the problems of Vietnam or the Middle East. Perhaps, having apparently agreed to the linkage, Moscow decided to probe the new administration's commitment to this strategy and even to exert pressure on Nixon for greater flexibility. Dobrynin clearly spelled out his concern to Harriman because he knew the governor would present his case to the White House. And he was correct. On February 21 Harriman met with Nixon and Kissinger and raised the problem of linkage. The veteran diplomat argued against linking political and military negotiations and "urged frankness" on such questions as the timing of talks on nuclear missile restraints.[40]

Although he received assurances from Nixon and Kissinger

that linkage was not U.S. policy, Harriman suspected that neither had been sincere with him. As he and Kissinger were leaving Nixon's office, the president's national security adviser boasted to Harriman: "You will be pleased with our policy with the Russians on Viet-Nam. We want to get hold of them at a top level and come to an agreement with them as to what will happen in Viet-Nam. If we do this, it will be possible to have progress militarily."[41] Harriman did not tell Dobrynin about Kissinger's remark, and the Soviet ambassador seemed "entirely satisfied" with Harriman's information. But he soon found that linkage was still on the agenda of policymakers in Washington.

In his March 4 news conference Nixon touched upon Soviet relations in connection with the problem of Vietnam. He expressed the hope that Moscow would "play, possibly, a peacemaking role in the Mideast and even possibly in Vietnam." He conveyed the "cautious" confidence that "without the Soviet Union's cooperation, it may be difficult to move as fast as we would like in settling the war in Vietnam." Nixon stressed that the USSR ought to agree on such cooperation, since "their interests and ours would not be served by simply going down the road on strategic-arms talks without, at the same time, making progress on resolving these political differences that could explode."[42] Thus he reiterated his desire to link strategic arms negotiations, in which he believed the Soviets were interested most of all, with progress on Vietnam.

Not all Nixon's advisers approved the president's open request for Soviet assistance in a Vietnam settlement. Although they did not oppose linking SALT (strategic arms limitation talks) negotiations with a resolution of the Vietnam War, they questioned the wisdom of making the idea of linkage public. In a memorandum to the president, Nixon's speech writer Patrick Buchanan noted the precariousness of the Soviet position which was "being raked daily by China for collaborating with the West against the world revolution forces." In this situation, Buchanan wondered, "is it not likely to embarrass them to emphasize the hopes we place in their cooperation, or the covert assistance they are providing, for instance, in the Paris talks?" It seemed to entail some risk for the administration itself in case of a reversal of Soviet policy that "would leave the President open to charges of unjustified optimism about Russian intentions."[43]

But Nixon was clearly determined to use all available channels, public and private, to persuade Moscow to take a more constructive position on the question of Vietnam. On March 26 he wrote to Soviet Premier Kosygin along the lines of his February 17 conversation with Dobrynin. Kosygin's reply finally arrived two months later and reiterated the standard Soviet position. The Soviet leadership challenged the administration's linkage concept and insisted on discussing each problem separately.[44] While awaiting a reply from Moscow, the president and his national security adviser were working out plans to involve the USSR in the "honorable" termination of the Vietnam War. One such plan envisaged a mission by Cyrus Vance, Harriman's former conegotiator in Paris, to Moscow. As Kissinger explained the purpose of Vance's mission, it would involve "linking the opening of SALT talks with an overall settlement in Vietnam. Vance would be sent to Moscow to begin SALT discussions and on the same trip meet secretly with a senior North Vietnamese representative."[45] Thus by sending Vance to the Soviet Union the administration would aim at two goals at once: "to make rapid progress in *both* areas, while seeking to keep them in tandem."[46]

On April 14 Kissinger met with Dobrynin to explain to the Soviet ambassador the administration's idea. To enhance its significance, he showed Dobrynin a page of three points initialed by Nixon. Along with a proposal of the mission to Moscow, the page contained a warning (placed under the third point) that "all parties are at a crossroads and that extraordinary measures are called for to reverse the tide of war."[47] This warning was coupled with a hint that without a settlement the United States "might take measures that would create 'a complicated situation.' "[48] The Soviet ambassador asked whether the U.S. administration was making a Vietnam settlement a condition for progress in the Middle East, economic relations, and strategic arms talks. When Kissinger said yes, Dobrynin emphasized Moscow's desire for better relations with the United States whatever happened in Vietnam, and complained that escalation of the war could serve only Chinese desires to see a clash between the Soviet Union and the United States. Nevertheless he promised to inform his government of the American proposal.

Meanwhile Nixon was still waiting for a reply to his letter to Kosygin. The Soviet silence made Washington wonder whether the Soviets were conveying the American proposal to Hanoi.[49] Later

Dobrynin assured Kissinger that the Soviets had informed Hanoi of Vance's mission but had received a negative response from the DRV.[50] Dobrynin's information is confirmed by a Soviet Foreign Ministry USA Department memorandum on American-Vietnamese contacts in that period which reveals the contents of the April 14, 1969, conversation between Kissinger and Dobrynin and the ensuing Soviet steps. According to this memorandum, Moscow brought to the DRV's attention Kissinger's proposal. In a letter of May 5, handed to the Soviets by Pham Van Dong, the North Vietnamese leadership pointed out that negotiators in Paris could quite well reach an agreement and that no other contacts were necessary. More surprising, this Soviet memorandum notes that in its reply to the American proposal, Moscow argued that U.S. refusal to agree on a coalition government in South Vietnam made it difficult for the Soviet Union to help Washington. The question of a coalition government as well as the withdrawal of all foreign troops from Vietnam, the Soviets had noted, was decisive.[51]

It is unclear whether Moscow sent this reply to the U.S. proposal of Vance's mission, or whether Kissinger concealed it in his memoirs in order to show Soviet intransigence. But it is possible that Moscow's response was included in Kosygin's letter to Nixon or transmitted by Dobrynin in one of his private conversations with Kissinger. In either case the Soviets could have omitted a specific reference to Vance's mission, confining themselves to the statement on the North Vietnamese position. If this was so, Kissinger would have seen nothing new in the Soviet attitude and would not have related it to the concrete proposal.

Whatever the case, Washington could not be satisfied with the Soviet position on Vietnam. The administration decided to increase its pressure on Hanoi and Moscow, alternating peaceful offers with threats to escalate the war—and not merely threats. Already in March 1969 Nixon had authorized the secret bombing of Cambodia in order to interdict North Vietnamese supply lines along the Ho Chi Minh Trail and wipe out elusive Communist command headquarters allegedly located in Cambodia. Nor did the president exclude the possibility of resuming bombing strikes against the DRV. At a March 20 cabinet meeting he talked of the need for military strength as a basis for successful negotiations with Hanoi.[52]

Nixon and Kissinger were eager to let Moscow know of their intention to spare no efforts, peaceful or military, to end the war in

Vietnam as quickly as possible. In the first week of May Kissinger warned Dobrynin that the war would be escalated—and violently—if Hanoi failed to respond to American overtures.[53] Some time later the White House decided to couple this threat with a peaceful proposal to demonstrate that it was no less inclined to solve the problem peacefully. On May 14 Dobrynin received an advance copy of the president's Vietnam speech, delivered the same day on national television. It was Nixon's first address as president, was exclusively devoted to Vietnam, and was the first plan to settle the war since Johnson's Manila proposal of 1966. In it Nixon proposed that the bulk of foreign troops—both U.S. and North Vietnamese—withdraw from South Vietnam within one year after an agreement had been signed. An international body would monitor the withdrawals and supervise free elections in South Vietnam.

The speech represented a departure from the "rigid and stale" Manila formula[54] which demanded the unilateral withdrawal of the North Vietnamese forces as a precondition of settlement. But it contained no reference to the question of a political settlement in South Vietnam, on which Hanoi had insisted from the outset of talks in Paris. This omission made the whole plan unacceptable to the North Vietnamese leadership, which perceived it as an invitation to capitulate. Nevertheless one could hardly suspect Nixon of naiveté. The plan not only aimed to score points on the domestic scene but also was part of the diplomatic offensive against Moscow, no less than Hanoi. These efforts included propaganda attacks on both the Soviets and the North Vietnamese, military threats against Hanoi, and private approaches to Moscow through the "back channel."

The so-called "back channel," or more simply the "channel," as Kissinger called his private meetings with Soviet Ambassador Dobrynin in the map room of the White House, was established in February 1969 when the president and his national security adviser considered the problem of how to avoid informing the State Department and Secretary of State William Rogers about the forthcoming first meeting between Nixon and Dobrynin. At the end of his conversation with the Soviet ambassador, Nixon told Dobrynin that in the future matters of special sensitivity should be exclusively taken up with Kissinger.[55] "Intimate exchanges" between Dobrynin and Kissinger continued throughout Kissinger's service in the Nixon administration, first as special assistant to the president on national security affairs, then as secretary of state. In the first half of 1969 most of these exchanges were devoted to discussions of U.S. policy toward the Soviet Union in connection with Vietnam.

Kissinger clearly understood that Dobrynin was no more than a mouthpiece for his bosses in Moscow. Though sociable and skillful in dealing with representatives of American governing circles, Dobrynin obediently followed the line prescribed for him in the Kremlin or in Sennaya Square (the location of the Ministry of Foreign Affairs). "I took it for granted that his effectiveness depended on the skill with which he reflected his government's policies, not his personal preferences," Kissinger wrote in his memoirs.[56] He probably remembered Harriman's opinion of Dobrynin and his advice to the president during their conversation on February 21. An experienced negotiator with Soviet leaders, Harriman told Nixon that "as far as the Russians were concerned, he [Nixon] had to get through to the Politburo leaders." He regarded Dobrynin as "only a high-class cler[k]," and it was a waste of time to talk to him.[57] Therefore when Kissinger found in early June 1969 that Dobrynin was about to fly to Moscow, he saw a meeting with Dobrynin as an opportunity to convey to the Soviet leadership Nixon's and his views on Soviet-American relations and the overall international situation.

The meeting took place on June 12 in Kissinger's office in the White House and, as the Soviet ambassador noted in his report to Moscow, "like all previous meetings with him, this meeting was unannounced."[58] Kissinger began by pointing out that Nixon was aware of the ambassador's departure for Moscow and that he himself had approved the meeting so that Dobrynin "could, if necessary, provide 'first hand' knowledge of the president's point of view on various international questions and especially on Soviet-American relations" in his report to Soviet leaders.[59] Kissinger assured Dobrynin that in foreign policy Nixon considered Soviet-American relations no less important an issue than Vietnam. The American president was eager to avoid confrontation with Moscow and hoped that bilateral relations under his presidency would enter a constructive phase.

Kissinger touched upon the question of Nixon's possible meeting with Soviet leaders and underlined the president's desire to avoid unnecessary publicity on this matter. He preferred to make such meetings, which might take place once a year, businesslike and less sensational. At those meetings an exchange of opinions would be useful so that both sides could better understand each other and avoid dangerous steps that might be misinterpreted.

Kissinger also discussed the situation in Europe, the problem of the U.S.-Soviet joint ratification of a treaty on nuclear nonproliferation, a Middle East settlement, and strategic arms negotiations. He made it clear that the United States was prepared to consider Soviet interests in various regions, for instance in Eastern Europe where the Nixon administration intended to do nothing "which could be evaluated in Moscow as a 'challenge' to her position in the region." Kissinger even cautioned the Kremlin not "to pay much attention 'to President's isolated critical public comments about some Eastern European country, because that is only a tribute to the mood of certain sub-strata of the American population which play a role in American election.' "[60]

Kissinger's comments might seem surprising, but their intention was to introduce the most sensitive and urgent problem for the Nixon administration, Vietnam. It soon became clear to Dobrynin that the main preoccupation of the administration was how, with Soviet help, to bring the war in Southeast Asia to an end. According to the Soviet ambassador, Kissinger said nothing that had not already been said in their previous meetings as well as in Dobrynin's conversation with the president. But on the question of American–North Vietnamese negotiations, Kissinger's appeal for Moscow's assistance in overcoming the deadlock in the Paris peace talks was much sharper. Kissinger noted earlier Soviet efforts in support of the talks as well as their diminished activity in recent months. With the clear purpose of pressing Moscow on this question, Kissinger immediately turned to the problem of China and U.S. intentions to improve relations with Beijing. Although he assured Dobrynin that Washington regarded the Soviet Union, not China, as its main partner in the international arena, and characterized Soviet leaders as more reasonable and reliable than Mao Zedong, Dobrynin had no doubts that the insertion of the China question into the discussion on Vietnam was purposeful. His conviction was only strengthened after Kissinger declared that "it is necessary to stop the Vietnam conflict as soon as possible, and the Soviet Union *must* play a more active role in reaching a settlement, 'without trusting everything to Hanoi, which evaluates the international situation only from its own specific and narrow point of view, which often satisfies first of all the interests of China.' "[61]

The China card was not the only one up Washington's sleeve. Another was the threat to use military pressure against North Vietnam. Dobrynin noted that in the course of their discussion, "Kissinger again (as Nixon had earlier) threw out a comment to the effect that if Hanoi will endlessly 'obstruct' the negotiations, then after a few months it will be necessary for the [U.S.] government to think about 'other alternatives in order to convince Hanoi.'" These alternatives were obvious to Dobrynin, who drew his leaders' attention to "this sufficiently firm-sounding theme of 'other alternatives' in talks with both Nixon and Kissinger. . . ." Dobrynin believed that while such comments were chiefly designed to blackmail the North Vietnamese and, partly, the Soviets with hints of resuming the bombing of the DRV unless the situation at the Paris peace talks changed, he did not entirely exclude "the possibility of such actions by the current administration if the situation, in Nixon's opinion, will justify it."[62]

In his report to Soviet leaders, Dobrynin concluded that "for Nixon foreign policy problem No. 1 remains the question of how to find an exit from the Vietnam War under acceptable conditions, which would guarantee him re-election as President of the U.S.A." The Soviet ambassador believed that "attempts to 'convince' the USSR to help settle the conflict will continue and this will to some extent make itself known in the course of our negotiations with this Administration on other international questions, if not directly, then at least as a definite slowing of the tempo of these negotiations or settlement of other problems."[63]

Soviet leaders who read Dobrynin's report[64] soon found that their ambassador's prediction was well justified. The Nixon administration was increasing its pressure on Moscow. On September 27, during a meeting with Dobrynin, Kissinger warned him that "the apparent failure of all our requests for Soviet help toward ending the war made it very difficult for us to carry on more than basic diplomatic relations between our two countries."[65] To increase this impression of determination, Nixon telephoned Kissinger in the midst of the conversation and asked him to tell Dobrynin that Vietnam was the critical issue in U.S.-Soviet relations.

On October 20 the president himself met with Dobrynin for a "serious talk" on the Soviet position toward Vietnam and the prospects of Soviet-American relations. He stated to the stunned Soviet ambassador, who was about to inform the White House of Moscow's readiness to begin strategic arms negotiations, that an improvement of bilateral relations depended on the desire of the Soviet Union "to do something in Vietnam." Until then, Nixon emphasized, "real progress will be very difficult." He warned about the futility of hopes "to break" him. "I want you to understand that the Soviet Union is going to be stuck with me for the next three years and three months, and during all that time I will keep in mind what is being done right now, today." Nixon repeated threats about his administration's "own way" to bring the war to an end and said "we will not hold still for being diddled to death in Vietnam."[66] Dobrynin apparently was not prepared for such an attack, even though promises and threats were nothing new to him. Nonetheless the Kremlin leadership did not intend to yield to Washington's pressure.

Soviet unwillingness to accept Nixon's policy of linkage did not result from Moscow's desire to benefit from a continuation of the war or to see the United States bogged down in the conflict indefinitely, allowing the USSR to enjoy freedom of action in other parts of the world. Although such considerations were not totally absent from Soviet leaders' foreign policy plans, the factors that influenced Moscow's position on the linkage question were much more complicated. On the one hand, Soviet leaders realized that, notwithstanding Nixon's conviction that he held advantages in his policy toward the Soviet Union, he wanted détente with Moscow no less than Moscow wanted détente with the United States. Nuclear parity left the president no alternatives than to come to an agreement with the Soviets in order to avoid the danger of nuclear war. In these circumstances, efforts to extract concessions from Moscow in exchange for cooperation on the limitation of strategic arms and in economic relations were regarded by the Soviet leadership as bribery and intimidation. Dobrynin confirmed this in his February 19 conversation with Harriman.[67]

Moreover, when Soviet diplomats in Washington analyzed the Nixon administration's policy, they noted the "objective interest of the U.S.A. in positive development of relations with the Soviet Union" as a tendency opposite to the policy of linkage. They concluded that along with its negative aspects, Nixon's policy "inherited from preceding administrations recognition of the military power of the Soviet Union and the necessity for the U.S.A. to avoid aggravations that could lead to direct confrontation with us. . . ." The stabilizing influence of such recognition, in the opinion of Soviet diplomats, would also influence U.S. policy in the future.[68]

In a situation where both countries were almost equally capable of undermining the other's positions in the world, Nixon's threats of military pressure against North Vietnam made no sense either, for Washington had to consider that trying to intimidate Hanoi might provoke a reaction from their allies in Moscow, which could push the world to the brink of nuclear confrontation. In other words, as Stephen Ambrose put it, "The flaw in Nixon's reasoning was that he did not hold the winning cards. . . . The Soviets could match the United States bomb for bomb, which was why the atomic option was not a real option. Nixon thought he could threaten the North Vietnamese into accepting an armistice (really, a cease-fire in place). But any implied threat to destroy Hanoi immediately raised the counter-threat, that the Soviets would destroy Saigon. Nixon was not the only madman in a position to make threats."[69]

On the basis of such an analysis, Moscow countered Nixon's policy of linkage with the Soviet idea of "linkage in reverse." The world really was interdependent, the Kremlin said, and both Nixon and Kissinger were correct in viewing events in different parts of the world as being connected to one another. But they forgot that the United States was not outside these interrelationships, even less above them. Its foreign policy was influenced by numerous factors that American decision-makers, in order to be successful, had to take into account. The Nixon administration was no exception. Soviet leaders quickly recognized this Achilles heel in Washington and resisted attempts to extract concessions from the Kremlin. They based their policy on an assessment of the "correlation of forces," which in the late 1960s they believed was to their advantage. As a result, in response to American efforts to involve the Soviet Union in the process of settlement in Southeast Asia as a condition for negotiations on military questions and problems of bilateral relations, Moscow used differences between the White House and other branches of the U.S. government, and put forward its own proposal on SALT negotiations.[70] Later the Kremlin, aware of Nixon's eagerness for a summit with Soviet leaders, made it dependent on success in negotiations on Berlin.

But another factor influenced Moscow's position on Vietnam. As Dobrynin frequently tried to explain to Kissinger, Soviet influence in Hanoi was limited, given the DRV's skill in maneuvering between Moscow and Beijing and the Kremlin's long-term plans for North Vietnam's role in a regional system in Southeast Asia.

It was difficult for Nixon and Kissinger to accept the idea that the Soviet Union, with all its aid to North Vietnam, still lacked sufficient leverage to dictate to Hanoi on issues of war and peace. Indeed, by 1969 the USSR was clearly the principal supporter of the DRV among the socialist countries. That year the North Vietnamese received from the Soviet Union about half a billion dollars in aid, 50 percent of the assistance provided them by the Communist bloc. Although the amount of military aid declined in 1969, as a result of reduced activity on the battlefield, it still amounted to $200 million. The North Vietnamese armed forces, according to a Soviet embassy report, were rearmed and equipped mostly by the Soviet Union and were one of the most powerful in the region.[71] From 1969 to 1971 Moscow concluded with the DRV seven agreements on aid and economic cooperation, three of them dealing with supplemental help for the North Vietnamese economy and defense.[72]

Still, as in previous years, Soviet assistance to Hanoi was not converted into proportional political influence. Although the North Vietnamese leadership had modified its position toward closer relations with the Soviet Union, as compared with China, it still did not wish to forfeit its independence based on a balancing act between its two powerful allies. Complaints about Hanoi's evasive attitude permeated reports from Soviet diplomats in the DRV to Moscow. As stated in one of the annual reports in those years, "The Vietnamese comrades have remained in the previous position of incomplete confidence in the USSR, basing on the thesis formulated earlier: do not spoil or aggravate relations with the Soviet Union, but do not draw closer to it with complete confidence."[73] Soviet officials had no illusions that this course would change in the near future.

Hanoi's independent policy was felt in various spheres of

Soviet–North Vietnamese relations. Moscow bitterly noted its Vietnamese comrades' efforts to limit Soviet ideological influence in the DRV and to ration information about events in the USSR and other socialist countries.[74] The North Vietnamese treated with suspicion Soviet citizens who worked in Vietnam as civilian or military specialists, sometimes allowing this suspicion to grow to open unfriendliness.[75] They would "forget" to inform Moscow of their foreign policy actions, and Soviet leaders often learned of Hanoi's diplomatic maneuvers from newspapers or international press agencies, as occurred in the case of the exchange of letters between Nixon and Ho Chi Minh.[76] To avoid such confusion, the KGB was seriously considering establishing "confidential contacts" in order to receive timely information on the situation in the Vietnamese leadership and its relations with Beijing.[77]

Notwithstanding these hindrances, the Soviets scored some visible successes in their efforts to strengthen their position in Vietnam. One indication of such success was a shift in the North Vietnamese attitude toward the diplomatic struggle. In January 1970 the eighteenth plenum of the Lao Dong party adopted as its primary goal a combination of all three methods of struggle for the unification of Vietnam.[78] For the first time since the beginning of the war, the Communist leadership placed diplomatic and political efforts on the same level with the military struggle. The same resolution emphasized the importance of the Paris talks for the ultimate victory of the Vietnamese people. Soviet officials, who were informed by intelligence of this change in attitude far in advance, regarded it as a result of their efforts and as a retreat from Hanoi's pro-Chinese positions.[79]

Another positive sign, from the Soviet viewpoint, was the growing number of North Vietnamese contacts with the Soviet Union and other socialist countries, and their participation in international forums on education, medicine, and literature. These exchanges as well as the growth of Hanoi's influence in the region allowed Soviet diplomats to consider coordinating Moscow's policy toward the DRV with that of its allies in order to tie North Vietnam to the Soviet bloc in international affairs. In June 1970 the USSR embassy in Hanoi sent to Moscow a memorandum discussing the possibilities of such coordination. The main purpose of this lengthy note was to assess the prospects of including North Vietnam in the Soviet orbit, of gradually reorienting DRV policy away from Beijing and toward Moscow, and of increasing Hanoi's influence in Southeast Asia.

The embassy suggested involving Hanoi in bilateral and multilateral consultations with socialist countries on various questions of international politics. It found it expedient to intensify North Vietnamese activities in such spheres of foreign policy as disarmament and propaganda. It offered to increase the flow of information to Hanoi about the internal situation in leading Western countries. Summarizing all these measures, the memorandum emphasized that "gradual DRV involvement in the broad and deep process of exchange of information and coordination of foreign policy actions with the socialist countries in the international arena will significantly promote more correct perception and assessment by the Vietnamese of the real situation in the world, an intensification, to our benefit, of the DRV foreign policy activity, utilization in our interests of its present certain international prestige. Broadening the political consultations with the DRV could also ultimately help the Vietnamese get rid of narrow nationalistic errors in the area of foreign policy, and promote the DRV's steady rapprochement with the Soviet Union."[80]

Thus while in 1964–1965 the main task for Moscow was to bridge the gap in Soviet–North Vietnamese relations created by Khrushchev's overcautiousness and to strengthen its position in Vietnam as a counterbalance to the Chinese influence, by the end of the decade the Soviet leadership had moved to the next stage of its policy toward the region. The ultimate goal of this stage was to make Vietnam a partner and Moscow's outpost in Southeast Asia, especially since China, which had played this role in the 1950s, had now resolutely broken with the Soviet system. This idea was put forward even more clearly in another Soviet embassy memorandum a year later, after the twenty-fourth party congress had been held in Moscow. Soviet diplomats in Hanoi believed that "now, when the PTV has been strengthened on the way to independence, when the Party course is developing, in general, (though still slowly) in a favorable direction for us, when the DRV has become the leading force in the struggle of the peoples of Indochina, *we will possess comparatively more possibilities for establishing our policy in this region. It is not excluded that Indochina may become for us a key to all Southeast Asia. In addition, in this region there is nobody, so far, we can lean on, except the DRV.*"[81] That both memoranda were classified as top secret only confirms their importance as policymaking documents.

With such high stakes in North Vietnam, Soviet leaders were eager to avoid any accidents that might jeopardize their policy. As a result, they consistently refused to yield to Washington's pressure and to induce Hanoi to agree on U.S. conditions for peace. They continued to provide North Vietnam and its allies in the South with everything necessary for the military struggle. Despite all the complaints of Vietnamese duplicity, intransigence, and egotism, Moscow never considered disengagement from the war, for Vietnam gradually became for the Kremlin not only an issue of ideology but also a question of geopolitics.

After the negotiations opened in Paris, Moscow could pursue its goals in Vietnam under more secure conditions. Earlier the Soviets feared that the war might spread to other regions of Asia and even lead to a confrontation between the United States and the USSR. After 1968 the talks in Paris became a kind of guarantee that the conflict, if not confined within the boundaries of Vietnam, at least, would not develop beyond Indochina. Therefore it became important for Moscow to prevent a break in negotiations and to keep the participants at the conference table. But even this Soviet role underwent changes. Whereas during U.S.–North Vietnamese "preliminary discussions" Moscow actively involved itself in resolving numerous deadlocks and facilitating an agreement on the cessation of bombing and the four-power talks, as soon as "serious negotiations" began, the Soviet Union reduced its activity, despite U.S. pleas. Soviet Ambassador Zorin explained this position in his farewell conversation with Harriman: "In the first stage of the talks, the subject was the bombing of North Vietnam, a socialist country, which was directly tied to the USSR politically and diplomatically and as a state system, so that the USSR had a direct interest in defending that country. It had to give all necessary assistance, and it did. In the new phase of the Paris talks, the subject would be primarily *South* Vietnam, a country with which the USSR had no direct relations. It did have good and friendly relations with the FLN [National Liberation Front of South Vietnam], so it was interested in the success of the FLN and ready to support its positions and its political ideals generally. But as for Soviet *state* interests, these concerned *peace* in the region assured by a settlement—whereas the internal arrangements [were] a matter for the Vietnamese people themselves to settle in accordance with those forces acting on the South Vietnamese scene. Therefore now, even more than before, the US had an important reason to participate *directly* with the Vietnamese themselves. The character of the talks had changed, and the USSR had less reason to have a concrete interest. Because of the objective facts of the situation, the subjects to be discussed, the *Soviet* role was now more *limited.*"[82] No doubt Zorin expressed Moscow's official position toward the negotiations. But, as is evident from Zorin's words, the Soviets did not totally abandon their role in the negotiations; it only became more indirect and less visible.

It had always been a matter of principle for Moscow that it did *not* negotiate with the North Vietnamese, the United States did. The Soviets followed this course throughout the Paris peace talks, declining Washington's attempts to involve them in the negotiations in any capacity, particularly as mediators. But the Kremlin tried not to miss an opportunity to influence developments in Paris in a direction most desirable for Moscow. In many cases such an opportunity depended on Hanoi's position. Soviet authorities analyzed every turn of North Vietnamese policy with regard to the negotiations, so as to be able to intervene at an appropriate moment and avoid—from their point of view—dangerous consequences. Their efforts were aimed at keeping both sides talking and preventing a resort to drastic measures that might undermine the negotiating process. They considered factors that influenced the attitudes of the DRV—the weariness of the population after many years of war, growing domestic problems, uncertainty about the plans of the Nixon administration—and put forward, in the form of advice and personal opinion, suggestions that might be helpful in the Paris meetings. For this purpose Moscow used various contacts with North Vietnamese officials. High-level negotiations between Soviet and DRV leaders remained an important opportunity for the Kremlin to present its views on the situation and persuade Hanoi of their acceptability. Such negotiations ordinarily took place every year, mostly during visits of North Vietnamese authorities to Moscow. For example, on the eve of Pham Van Dong's 1970 trip to the Soviet capital, when asked by the DRV premier whether Moscow had any advice in connection with the visit, Soviet Ambassador Shcherbakov expressed a desire that political aspects of the negotiations would be "more constructive, more comprehensive, and more sincere." He suggested an exchange of views on "new, additional means and forms of a solution of the Indochinese problem, on new forms of influencing the U.S.A., on the situation in Cambodia and Laos." The ambassador coupled this desire with assurances that while Moscow was always ready to advise its Vietnamese friends, they should make decisions for themselves.[83]

Another level of contacts was represented by meetings of Soviet diplomats abroad with North Vietnamese officials, primarily in Hanoi and Paris. The conversations of Soviet Ambassador Shcherbakov and his colleagues with Hanoi's leaders were especially important. The Soviet embassy in Hanoi was more than a diplomatic mission in a foreign country. People in the embassy were literally plenipotentiary representatives of the Soviet government in the Democratic Republic of Vietnam. In a situation where leaders in Moscow knew little about actual developments in the faraway region, except for a few generalities,[84] the Soviet diplomats there were not only a mouthpiece of the Kremlin but participants in the decision-making process—unlike those at other Soviet embassies. The Kremlin found it expedient to consult with them on specific problems concerning policy toward Vietnam. This was especially important when the DRV, because of the war, became a focus of the aspirations of such powerful countries as the United States, China, and the Soviet Union.

Under these circumstances, Soviet Ambassador Shcherbakov's meetings with North Vietnamese authorities were sometimes no different from their discussions in Moscow, if not more substantive. During these meetings Shcherbakov touched upon various problems of DRV policy, including negotiations with the United States. He received information from DRV leaders on latest developments at the talks, expressed his opinion on them, put forward proposals of possible diplomatic actions by North Vietnam, and explained his own government's position. For example, in his conversation with Xuan Thuy, the North Vietnamese chief negotiator in Paris, in June 1969, the Soviet ambassador advised Hanoi "to avoid any extremes, not adopt a purely propaganda approach, not slip into military methods." Shcherbakov tried to persuade his counterpart that "in the tactics of combining the military, political, and diplomatic struggles, political and diplomatic methods should gradually occupy a more important place. The Paris peace talks should influence events in South Vietnam."[85]

Meanwhile Shcherbakov's colleague in Paris, Valerian Zorin, kept in touch with the Vietnamese Communist delegation to the four-power talks. It became a rule for the DRV negotiators to meet with the Soviet ambassador and provide him with information on the status of the talks. Hanoi was none too eager to follow the advice of its Soviet comrades; least of all were North Vietnamese leaders willing to inform Moscow of their plans. But they did need Soviet support for their actions, and they recognized that Moscow's prestige and power could be used to their advantage. As a result, Xuan Thuy's and Le Duc Tho's visits to the Soviet embassy in Paris had two aims: to show respect for Moscow's role in the negotiations and, in exchange, to request Soviet support of the DRV's policy. Nevertheless the North Vietnamese could not help but pay attention to what Soviet officials were saying, for contempt of their advice might lead to estrangement and jeopardize aid from Moscow.

Thus throughout the period 1969–1972 there were regular meetings between Soviet diplomats in Paris and the Vietnamese Communist delegations to discuss developments in the negotiations. Moscow was informed not only about the official sessions (which, after all, were of secondary importance) but also of the contents of private meetings among Xuan Thuy, Le Duc Tho, and Henry Kissinger. For example, on March 16, 1970, Kissinger met with the North Vietnamese in the private house in Choisy-le-Roi, outside Paris, for a secret discussion, during which Nixon's envoy proposed a precise monthly schedule of total American withdrawal over a sixteen-month period and a mutual deescalation of military operations throughout Indochina.[86] Three days later, on March 19, Le Duc Tho and Xuan Thuy called on Zorin and informed him of all details of the meeting, sharing with the Soviet ambassador their ideas on the negotiations. They noted that if the unproductiveness of unofficial talks undermined Republican chances in the midterm elections, they were ready to drag on the negotiations in order "to make things worse for Nixon." In response, Zorin emphasized that "though Kissinger has put forward excessive demands, he has nevertheless expounded concrete ideas on the military situation." When the North Vietnamese reported Kissinger's agreement to discuss political as well as military problems,[87] Zorin saw this as Washington's readiness to talk with the DRV on all questions, without Saigon's involvement—a retreat from the earlier U.S. position.[88] Thus Zorin tried to emphasize the positive aspects of the negotiations in order to guard against the danger of their breaking up.

A similar discussion took place at the Soviet embassy after the April 4 meeting between Le Duc Tho and Kissinger. It was worth noting that if the March 19 conversation occurred by "mutual agreement," that of April 6 was initiated by the North Vietnamese. Again Le Duc Tho informed Zorin of all details of his discussion with Kissinger, expressing his desire to continue negotiations on Vietnam in spite of the lack of progress. "But we will be patient," Le Duc Tho said.[89]

The Soviets did not confine themselves to dealings with their Vietnamese comrades. They were also prepared to defend the DRV position before the United States. During one of his meetings with Hanoi's delegation, Zorin asked what questions he should put to Henry Cabot Lodge, then the head of the American delegation in Paris, "in order to push the U.S. toward a political settlement."[90] But Moscow was careful not to go too far in that direction. It wished to avoid close involvement in the negotiations as well as Hanoi's suspicion that the Soviets were acting as mediator between the DRV and the United States.

In sum, after 1968 and the advent of the Nixon administration, Moscow did not change its policy toward the Vietnam conflict. The Soviet Union was a reluctant player in the diplomatic settlement in Vietnam and remained mostly behind the scenes, despite the efforts of the Nixon administration and its policy of linkage. Nixon and Kissinger's brainchild turned out to be moribund because of the strong resistance of the Soviet leadership. "On about ten occasions in 1969," Kissinger complained, "in my monthly meetings with Dobrynin I tried to enlist Soviet cooperation to help end the war in Vietnam. Dobrynin was always evasive. He denied that the Soviet Union had any interest in continuing the war; he warned . . . against escalation; he never came up with a concrete proposal to end the war."[91] The Kremlin would continue to withstand this U.S. pressure if, as Andrei Alexandrov-Agentov put it, "it could prevent the Americans from putting on the table their trump card—American relations with China."[92] In the early 1970s this card changed Soviet chances for success in the game, as it changed the entire international situation.

TEN

Between Détente and Vietnam

In the 1960s China became a chief preoccupation for the Kremlin. The split between the two Communist powers was the most serious conflict in the world Communist movement since Moscow's quarrel with Yugoslavia's Tito just after World War II. But in Tito's case the conflict was characterized mainly by ideological accusations and did not represent an insurmountable obstacle to reconciliation after Stalin's death. The Soviet rift with Beijing, on the other hand, rapidly developed into a military rivalry in the late 1960s, and both sides acidly counted a number of clashes on the Soviet-Chinese border. In 1974, when the tension between Moscow and Beijing eased but bitter feelings were still fresh, the Soviets provided an account of Chinese "perfidy" and provocations against the USSR in a book that analyzed Beijing's foreign policy and international relations in the ten years from 1963 through 1973. According to this study, from October 1964 to April 1965, 36 violations of the Soviet border occurred, involving 150 Chinese citizens. The number of such violations increased rapidly and by January–February 1969 had reached 90 intrusions; by May its number was 164.[1] In the spring of 1969 military clashes occurred between the Soviet Union and China with tens of murdered and wounded on both sides. The two countries seemed to be on the verge of open military conflict, with no chance of reconciliation.

In this situation the Soviet Union was extremely sensitive to any prospects of a rapprochement between China and the United States, let alone Chinese collusion with Washington. While Beijing remained a pariah in international relations, without powerful allies or sympathizers, Moscow hoped to reduce the conflict to a purely bilateral problem between the two countries. If other countries were to become involved the situation might turn into a geopolitical issue that threatened to undermine the Soviet world position. Since only the United States, as Moscow's chief rival in the international arena, might profit from the conflict by siding with an adversary of the USSR, most Soviet efforts aimed to prevent such a possibility.

During the Johnson presidency, Washington's preoccupation with the war in Vietnam as well as its strong suspicion of the Chinese Communists and their objectives in Asia precluded any rapprochement between the United States and China. Sino-American contacts in Warsaw bore no visible results and were suspended in May 1968. It was different with Nixon, who even before his election openly expressed his intention to establish relations with Communist China. As early as 1967, during a worldwide trip, he visited Rumania and confided to Nicolae Ceausescu, the Rumanian Communist party's secretary general, that he regarded true détente with the Soviet Union as impossible without "some kind of rapprochement" with Beijing.[2] Although he noted that the United States could scarcely succeed in this approach until after the Vietnam War was ended, Nixon's intention was sufficient to sow anxiety in Moscow.

Soviet leaders probably did not learn about Nixon's plans from Ceausescu, since the Rumanian leader maintained his independence from Moscow and rarely revealed his secrets to the Kremlin. But Nixon published his views in an October 1967 article in *Foreign Affairs*. In it Nixon rejected an anti-Chinese alliance. Instead he talked of prospects for a dialogue with mainland China and efforts aimed at "pulling China back into the world community," as "a great and progressing nation, not as the epicenter of world revolution."[3] As long as Nixon remained a private citizen, Soviet leaders could afford to ignore his utterances. But they probably recalled his views on China after his election to the presidency.

Soon after his inauguration Nixon charged his national security adviser to prepare a study on U.S. policy toward China. On

February 5, 1969, Kissinger translated the president's wishes into a National Security Study Memorandum in which he instructed the secretaries of state and defense, as well as the CIA director, to include in the study an analysis of U.S. relations with both mainland China and Taiwan, the nature of the Chinese foreign policy in Asia, the "interaction between U.S. policy and the policies of other major interested countries toward China" (read the Soviet Union), and alternatives for U.S. policy in this sphere.[4]

Kissinger's directive produced an interagency paper on China which he regarded as unsatisfactory. Kissinger criticized the paper's "excessive emphasis on China's ideology and alleged militancy" to the detriment of "the global implications of Sino-Soviet tensions and the opportunities for us in the triangular relationship."[5] The national security adviser was generally highly critical of the American intellectual community's approach to a Sino-American rapprochement and reserved the credit for the transformation of Washington's China policy for Nixon and himself. But he admitted in his memoirs that he initially regarded relations with China and their role in U.S. policy "as a matter of theory." With Nixon, he "still considered the People's Republic of China the more aggressive of the Communist powers."[6] With such an attitude, the study of a U.S.-China rapprochement might have taken years and might well have been postponed until after the war in Vietnam.

What served as an impulse for the White House's increasing interest in China was the aggravation of Sino-Soviet relations in 1969 and resulting Soviet attempts to obtain diplomatic support in Washington. According to Kissinger, "It was heavy-handed Soviet diplomacy that made us think about our opportunities."[7] When the clashes occurred on the Soviet-Chinese border, Dobrynin met with Kissinger and tried to convince him that China was provoking these incidents. As is usually the case, Dobrynin's assurances had a diametrically opposite effect from what he intended. Nixon and Kissinger concluded that the Kremlin, after the successful Soviet invasion of Czechoslovakia, had decided to use the same methods to resolve problems with China.

Taking into account rumors in diplomatic circles, apparently instigated in some cases by the Soviets themselves, as well as the anti-China propaganda campaign unleashed in Soviet newspapers, the White House regarded Sino-Soviet relations as "approaching a crisis point." It determined to align the United States with China in the event of Soviet attack. Nixon and Kissinger believed China was the victim; all other events were interpreted by American policymakers from this point of view. Even ten years after the events, Kissinger in his memoirs offered a significantly distorted picture of the meeting between Kosygin and Zhou Enlai in Beijing's airport on September 11, 1969. Although he noted that the meeting evidently occurred by Chinese invitation and demonstrated disagreement between the two countries rather than an approach toward accommodation,[8] Kissinger failed to consider such facts as the Soviet premier's readiness to reverse his flight to Moscow in order to meet the Chinese leader, the clear toning down of polemics in the Soviet Union and China after the meeting, and, more significant, reduced tensions on the Soviet-Chinese border. Moreover, on October 7 the Chinese announced that they had agreed to open negotiations on that conflict.[9]

The Soviets protested against rumors of their plans to invade China or their intention to strike Chinese nuclear facilities.[10] If we can believe the assertion of Brezhnev's aide, Andrei Alexandrov-Agentov, there were no serious discussions in Moscow on the appropriateness of war against China. Alexandrov insisted that "neither the Soviet nor Chinese leadership, despite threatening declarations and actions from both sides, wanted war between their countries and seriously prepared for it." Alexandrov recalled that he watched Brezhnev and his colleagues during clashes over Damansky/Chenpao in 1969. "There were neither signs of particular nervousness, nor, moreover, panic."[11] It seems clear that hints in the Soviet media about Moscow's determination to withstand the Chinese attacks, and Soviet diplomatic approaches to American officials about joint efforts against China—that is, developments Nixon and especially Kissinger found so sensitive—were for the Kremlin no more than a war of nerves aimed at restraining and possibly intimidating China's policymakers. The Soviet leaders surely understood the risks involved in a Soviet attack against China, both in terms of military difficulties and political repercussions. Apparently they were not prepared to exceed the limits of a propaganda campaign.

Nevertheless in 1969 American policymakers for the first time saw that their plans vis-à-vis China were moving from the potential to the real. From "nebulous theories," as Kissinger had described the idea of Sino-American rapprochement,[12] it was transformed into an immediate objective of the Nixon administration. In such a rapprochement the White House saw a useful instrument of foreign policy that might quickly replace the failed attempt at linkage. For policymakers in Washington, clashes on the faraway Ussuri River created the basis for approaches to China: a shared fear of the Soviet threat.[13]

In July 1969, in National Security Memorandum 63, Kissinger initiated a study of U.S. policy on Sino-Soviet differences. The memorandum asked agencies to analyze "choices confronting the United States as a result of the intensifying Sino-Soviet rivalry." It specified the need to consider "the broad implications of the Sino-Soviet rivalry on the U.S., Soviet, Communist Chinese triangle" and U.S. options in the event of military clashes between the Soviet Union and China or a Sino-Soviet conflict short of a military clash.[14] At the same time the White House increased its signals to the Beijing leadership about Washington's good intentions.

In July the State Department also announced eased restrictions on trade with and travel to the People's Republic of China. During his around-the-world trip a month later, Nixon spoke with Pakistan's leader Yahya Khan and with Nicolae Ceausescu about his desire to establish contacts with Beijing, knowing that both leaders were friendly with China and would transmit Nixon's hints to Mao's leadership. The president also probed the possibility of their assistance as mediators between Washington and Beijing. Contacts were also made by American diplomats in Hong Kong and Warsaw.

The Chinese did not remain unreceptive to these various signals from Washington. In early 1970 a Chinese representative in Warsaw suggested a resumption of the ambassadorial talks that had been suspended in 1968. That fall the Pakistani "channel" between Washington and Beijing began to function, and in December Zhou Enlai sent through Yahya Kahn a welcome message for the presidential representative's visit to Beijing.[15] Thus in spite of obstacles and difficulties resulting from American actions in Southeast Asia, including the bombing of Cambodia and the invasions of Cambodia and Laos, by 1971 contacts between the United States and China had developed momentum.

The Soviets were too sensitive to signs of a rapprochement between Washington and Beijing to miss these approaches. Moscow probably received information from its intelligence sources, and the prospects of Sino-American collusion against the Soviet Union could not help but stir alarm in the Kremlin. Early on, Moscow launched a diplomatic offensive. The Soviet ambassador in Washington was authorized to meet with the president and deliver a strong message from Soviet leaders concerning U.S. policy toward China. Dobrynin carried out these instructions during a conversation with Nixon on October 20, 1969. "If someone in the United States is tempted to make profit from Soviet-Chinese relations at the Soviet Union expense, *and there are some signs of that,*" Dobrynin read the text of aide-memoire from Moscow, "then we would like to frankly warn in advance that such line of conduct, if pursued, can lead to a very grave miscalculation, and is in no way consistent with the goal of better relations between the U.S. and the U.S.S.R."[16]

Moscow did not confine itself to the diplomatic front. To undermine the emerging reconciliation between the United States and China, it also used secret channels. In May 1970, for instance, the KGB proposed to Soviet authorities that it provide American and Chinese officials with information that would help increase Sino-American antagonisms. At the same time Soviet intelligence planned to inform Beijing of U.S. plans to expand American aggression in Indochina.[17] The Soviets even decided to counter the process of rapprochement between Washington and Beijing by trying to bridge their own gap with China. In these plans, Vietnam would become a basis for reconciliation. Moscow considered using a noticeable improvement of Sino-Vietnamese relations in the early 1970s to plan Sino-Soviet joint actions in Vietnam.[18] Soviet diplomats in Hanoi regarded Zhou Enlai's March 1971 visit to the DRV as a further step toward a Sino-Vietnamese rapprochement and explained this improvement by North Vietnamese leaders' "illusions" about Beijing's more attentive attitude toward its comrades in Hanoi.[19]

Whatever the reason, Soviet officials saw in this rapprochement an opportunity to approach Beijing or, if it failed, to demonstrate the treacherous nature of the Maoist leadership to Hanoi and thus strengthen their own positions in the DRV. Soviet diplomats in North Vietnam recommended that Moscow propose to the Chinese and Vietnamese "joint or parallel actions in support of the struggle of peoples in Indochina." They suggested asking Hanoi to convey this proposal to China, referring to Hanoi's promise "to think about measures which would help an amelioration of Soviet-Chinese relations."[20]

None of these efforts to prevent a Sino-American rapprochement and move closer to Beijing produced desirable results for Moscow. The process of American reconciliation with China proved to be irreversible. The community of interests of the two countries vis-à-vis the Soviet Union was stronger than their mutual distrust and suspicion. The Kremlin may have accelerated the final act of this drama, the summit between Nixon and Mao in Beijing, by repeatedly postponing a meeting of American and Soviet leaders in Moscow.

The idea of a Soviet-American summit had been in the air since 1968. It was seriously discussed in the last months of the Johnson administration, and Johnson was eager to realize it even after his party's defeat in the 1968 presidential elections.[21] He was ready to go to Moscow with the president-elect and proposed such a trip to Nixon. But Nixon was not willing to share the possible fruits of a summit with a defeated president. By this time Soviet leaders had also decided against a meeting with the two American presidents, since they were not sure that the results of such a meeting would survive the transition period.[22] The following year the idea of a summit was repeatedly touched upon in numerous conversations between Dobrynin and Kissinger, but it remained no more than an idea that the Soviets invoked as part of their policy of "linkage in reverse" and as bait for the new administration.[23]

When prospects of a summit with China became more certain, the White House saw its advantage with regard to the Soviet Union. Nixon and Kissinger decided to use a summit in Beijing as leverage against Moscow, hoping, not implausibly, that the Soviets would be more tractable once the Sino-American rapprochement was crowned with a successful meeting between American and Chinese leaders. As Kissinger described his position in a conversation with Dobrynin in June 1971, a month before his secret trip to Beijing, ". . . It was comforting to hold cards of which the other side was unaware. When I told Dobrynin that after fourteen months of exploration the time for setting a date for the summit seemed to have arrived, he must have judged again that he was dealing with an exploitable impatience. In fact, I was in no great hurry; I simply wanted to determine the sequence of the looming summits. I slightly preferred the Peking summit first. Had he responded favorably, we would have had a tricky problem in deciding which summit should have precedence. The Soviets again inadvertently solved the problem for us. I tried to imagine Dobrynin's reaction if I had suddenly told him where I meant to be in a month's time."[24]

The Kremlin's reaction was predictable. Although Moscow had evidently known of developments in Sino-American relations, Soviet leaders did not expect that the process of reconciliation had gone so far. They found themselves caught in their own trap. Now the actors changed roles: the Kremlin became more eager than the White House for the summit. Kissinger remembers that when he saw Dobrynin on July 19, four days after the national security adviser's trip to Beijing, the Soviet ambassador "was at his ingratiating best." He was "all for a Moscow summit." He inquired whether the president would prefer to go to Moscow first.[25] But Nixon and Kissinger were not about to abandon their satisfying position with the "China card" in hand. "To have the two Communist powers competing for good relations with us," Kissinger wrote in his memoirs, "could only benefit the cause of peace. . . ." A few lines later he revealed what he really had in mind: "Geopolitically, it was against *our* interest to have the Soviet Union dominate China or for China to be driven back toward Moscow."[26] That was the strategy the Nixon administration succeeded in executing, and the Kremlin was forced to adjust to new circumstances.

On August 10 Moscow sent a formal invitation to President Nixon to visit the Soviet Union in May or June 1972. Seven days later Kissinger informed Dobrynin that the White House accepted. At the same time the Soviets invited Kissinger to Moscow to discuss preparations for the summit. On October 12 Nixon officially announced his trip to the Soviet Union. Added to his July 15 announcement of a summit in Beijing, the new reality of the international system became apparent, and would define the course of world affairs in the coming years.

North Vietnamese leaders seemed to be most unhappy with this new reality. It was clear to them that the United States was able to split Hanoi from their allies by using "triangular diplomacy." They had recognized this danger long before U.S. policy toward the two principal supporters of the Vietnamese Communist struggle began to produce results. As early as in March 1969 Xuan Thuy declared at the first private meeting with American negotiators that "the United States had nothing to gain by seeking to take advantage of the divisions between the Soviet Union and China."[27] Masters themselves of playing one country against another, North Vietnamese leaders clearly perceived the consequences if both allies of the DRV were to accommodate the United States in their desire for détente. They might press Hanoi to end the war in Vietnam as soon as possible. Under such circumstances, Hanoi would have to make major concessions at the negotiating table—at a time when it planned a new military offensive in the South.

The decision for a offensive had been made by Vietnamese Communist leaders in May 1971.[28] The aim of the new military attack was to break a stalemate in the war and in the Paris negotiations by dealing a severe blow to Nixon's Vietnamization policy and convincing the United States that the Saigon regime had no exclusive sovereignty over South Vietnam. If these two objectives could be achieved, North Vietnamese leaders hoped to receive concessions from the United States on the principal question of the negotiations: a coalition government.[29]

Since Hanoi's strategists always regarded the military struggle as an integral part of their war policy, along with diplomacy, they never abandoned the "fighting while negotiating" strategy, though by 1972 they were placing more emphasis on diplomacy. Nevertheless, when it became clear to the DRV that diplomatic means alone would not achieve desirable results, they looked toward military action. This shift was spotted by Soviet diplomats in Hanoi, who reported to Moscow about the growth of bellicosity among the DRV leadership.[30]

The success of the DRV offensive, as usual, depended on support from the USSR and China, and Hanoi spared no efforts to obtain it. Hanoi's emissaries went to the capitals of both Communist powers to ask for assistance. Two Soviet–North Vietnamese agreements on supplemental aid "for strengthening the DRV defense" were signed in 1971, in addition to the major annual agreement between the two countries.[31] China had to follow the Soviet example, though Beijing was more interested in ending the war in Vietnam because of a changing international situation and the process of rapprochement with the United States.[32] The Soviets estimated China's aid to Hanoi in 1972 at half a billion dollars.[33]

While acceding to North Vietnamese requests for military and economic aid, the Soviets apparently were not enthusiastic about Hanoi's intentions. Informing Moscow of North Vietnamese plans to begin an offensive in the "dry season" of 1972 in order to create "favorable conditions for peaceful negotiations in Vietnam and Indochina," Soviet diplomats judged that "the Vietnamese risk too much." They recommended that Moscow "continue to explain to the Vietnamese comrades the idea that, while warding off American aggression, it is necessary to turn the matter toward a settlement, to constantly keep the diplomatic initiative in hand."[34] The Soviet embassy repeated its recommendation during the preparation for Chairman Nikolai Podgornyi's visit to the DRV in the fall of 1971.[35] But Soviet advice apparently fell on deaf ears in Hanoi, and North Vietnamese preparations for an offensive went ahead full tilt.

Meanwhile preparations for two summit meetings were also under way in the last months of 1971. First was the Sino-American summit in China. Moscow jealously followed developments between Washington and Beijing, cherishing hopes that unforeseen circumstances would reverse this rapprochement to the Kremlin's advantage. Soviet leaders' concern only increased when they received information of Chinese attempts to come to an agreement with the Americans on Vietnam. In early February 1972 the Soviet embassy in the DRV informed Moscow that Beijing had pressed Hanoi for approval of their intention to discuss problems of Indochina with Nixon during his visit to the PRC, and that Le Duc Tho was allegedly preparing for a trip to China to meet with Kissinger.[36] The Kremlin's most dreaded nightmare—China and the United States striking a deal on Vietnam behind the Soviet's back—was about to become a reality. To Moscow's relief, Hanoi resisted the Chinese pressure. Moreover, in conversations with Soviet diplomats, North Vietnamese officials expressed their concern over the possibility of such an agreement in the future.[37]

Reports on the China summit somewhat eased the feelings of Soviet leaders. They noted with satisfaction that the Shanghai communiqué was a result of bargaining between two sides "divided by disagreement which is difficult to overcome."[38] In general the Kremlin may have decided to counter the summit in China with progress in Soviet-American relations, i.e., the summit in Moscow.

From early 1972 Moscow and Washington were actively involved in discussions about the meeting in the Soviet capital. In January Dobrynin returned from Moscow with a letter from Brezhnev outlining a possible agenda for the summit. Dobrynin also raised with Kissinger the question of a possible declaration of principles in addition to a traditional communiqué. They continued to discuss such matters in the following months while the Soviets demonstrated their eagerness to greet the American president in their capital by agreeing to reopen talks to settle lend-lease claims from World War II.[39] At the height of these negotiations, an event occurred that threatened to jeopardize all Soviet plans for the summit.

On March 30 North Vietnamese artillery and infantry units launched a coordinated attack through the DMZ toward Quang Tri city and from the west toward Hue. The spring offensive against South Vietnam involved four basic thrusts by an estimated ten North Vietnamese divisions and two Viet Cong divisions (in all, around 150,000 men), plus Viet Cong local forces. They were equipped with Soviet-supplied tanks, rockets, and a 130mm field gun.[40] Never in the course of the war had Hanoi and its southern allies launched such a massive offensive supported by such well-equipped forces, superior to anything Saigon could muster in the spring of 1972. The South Vietnamese regime quickly lost almost all its northern provinces, large cities like Quang Tri and Loc Ninh, and territory close to Saigon. The offensive shook the very foundations of the Saigon government and demonstrated to the world, once more after Tet, that optimistic reports of American advisers on the success of Vietnamization were far from reality. Although the South Vietnamese army was later able to regain the initiative and eventually beat back the enemy on all fronts, the offensive had a powerful psychological effect on the leadership in South Vietnam and on the Nixon administration.

Yet the price paid by Hanoi and its allies in the South was enormous. The fighting cost Hanoi 100,000 dead compared with the South's 25,000.[41] The Communists had problems handling their modern equipment as well as logistical and organizational difficulties. Air attacks against Hanoi and Haiphong and the mining of North Vietnamese ports, ordered by Nixon in May in retaliation against the offensive, took a heavy toll on the DRV economy from which it took the country several years to recover. But the most devastating blow to the plans of North Vietnamese strategists was dealt by Hanoi's allies in Moscow and Beijing.

The North Vietnamese leadership had good reason to expect strong diplomatic support of the offensive by the Soviet Union and Communist China. DRV leaders even nursed hopes that in the face of such American escalation of the war as the bombing of Hanoi and the mining of DRV ports, both Moscow and Beijing would be prepared to sacrifice at least some fruits of détente with the United States in order to demonstrate its solidarity with the fighting people of Vietnam. They also expected an erosion of domestic support for the Nixon administration as a result of its violent actions in Vietnam. In other words, as Gareth Porter put it, "They expected that the Nixon administration would be forced to pay a price for such escalation in North Vietnam in terms of its diplomatic relations as well as in terms of American domestic opinion, thus eroding its position at the negotiating table and increasing the likelihood of concessions in Paris before the end of the year. What they were not prepared for was a serious American escalation *without* major diplomatic and political setbacks for Nixon."[42]

Neither the Soviets nor the Chinese had been enthusiastic about Hanoi's decision to support its diplomatic efforts by military action. Moscow must have felt especially bitter over the timing of the offensive that occurred on the eve of the summit with Nixon in Moscow and thus rendered it questionable. North Vietnamese leaders so often presented the Soviets with a fait accompli, demanding Soviet support of their actions, that the Kremlin decided to confine itself to propaganda and not to undermine the process of détente with the United States, especially in view of Sino-American reconciliation.[43]

From the outset Washington blamed the Soviet Union for the North Vietnamese offensive. Moscow had provided Hanoi with the bulk of its military aid and knew of North Vietnamese plans without trying to dissuade its friends from such a move. Kissinger expressed this opinion in a number of conversations with Dobrynin in April. As a result, Moscow grew nervous. The prospect of canceling the summit would be most unwelcome for Soviet leaders. Moscow began to press for Kissinger's visit to Moscow, considering it an additional guarantee of a summit. To increase the attractiveness of the visit, the Soviets promised the agenda would include Vietnam.[44]

Nixon was skeptical. He wanted the summit in Moscow no less than the Soviet leaders. He expected the meeting to increase his popularity within the United States, which was an important factor in an election year. At the same time he wanted to extricate the United States from Vietnam, bring back all American prisoners of war, and conclude an "honorable peace." That too was important in an election year. He thought the Soviets could help, but they continued to insist they were unable to influence Hanoi's decisions. Nixon did not believe those assurances. He finally agreed to Kissinger's trip to Moscow on the condition that his envoy concentrate on the problem of Vietnam; only after he received a Soviet assurance of help in Vietnam was Kissinger authorized to discuss issues related to the summit.

In his instructions to Kissinger on the eve of his adviser's departure for Moscow, Nixon, commenting on the briefing book for the visit, emphasized that the goal of Kissinger's talks with Brezhnev was "solely to get action on Vietnam." According to the president, the summit could be arranged through Dobrynin; for this purpose it was not necessary to go to Moscow. "Your primary interest," Nixon stressed, "in fact your indispensable interest, will be get them to talk about Vietnam." Nixon instructed Kissinger to spell out a strong warning that the United States would escalate the war unless Hanoi stopped the offensive and withdrew its troops from South Vietnamese territory. "Brezhnev must directly be told," Nixon wrote, "that as long as the invading North Vietnamese are killing South Vietnamese and Americans in the South the President will have to resort to bombing military installations in the North that are supporting that invasion." As usual, Nixon was preoccupied with public opinion: "If our understanding with the Russians *in any way* indicates that we have been taken in and consequently are letting up on our bombing while the enemy continues its own level of fighting, we will have the worst of both worlds—the contempt of the left and total frustration of the right." He had in mind the same considerations when he insisted that an announcement of Kissinger's visit "*must*, at the very least, include some wording to indicate, directly or indirectly, that Vietnam was discussed and progress made on it."[45]

Kissinger arrived in Moscow on April 21. As he informed Alexander Haig, his deputy in the National Security Council, he was greeted at the airport by First Deputy Foreign Minister Vasilii Kuznetsov who took him to the state guest house. Later the same day Nixon's envoy met with Gromyko. Kissinger reported an atmosphere that was "effusive with endless protestations of eagerness to have Summit and willingness to settle all issues." Gromyko even hinted that the Soviets had some "concrete considerations" for Vietnam.[46]

During his stay in Moscow Kissinger had four meetings with Brezhnev, Gromyko, and Dobrynin. Meetings with Brezhnev convinced him that the Soviet leader "would go to great lengths to avoid cancelling the summit."[47] Brezhnev did not try even to conceal his desire for a summit; he stated plainly that the summit "cannot only be historic but epoch-making." He told Kissinger "it would serve the best interest of the U.S. Government and Soviet people."[48]

Brezhnev made these statements despite Kissinger's repeated threats about "the President's determination to bring about a Vietnam solution at no matter what risk."[49] During his conversations with the general secretary, Kissinger had to listen to "a long emotional discourse on Vietnam." Brezhnev assured him that Moscow was not behind the offensive (that was true), that Hanoi had been hoarding Soviet weapons for two years (that was partly true, since two agreements on supplementary aid had been signed in 1971), and that the Chinese and Vietnamese, who opposed the summit in Moscow, had done their best to prevent détente between the USSR and the United States (that was also true in both cases).[50]

Having received such assurances as well as Moscow's promise to inform Hanoi of the new American proposals on the sequence of plenary and private meetings as well as the agenda of the private session, and not expecting anything more substantial, Kissinger ignored Nixon's instructions and agreed to discuss summit issues. In his memoirs Nixon found a justification for Kissinger's disobedience. "If he had followed my instructions and insisted on a Vietnam settlement as the first order of business," Nixon wrote, "perhaps Brezhnev would have dug in, called his bluff, and told him to go home—and that might have meant the end of the summit, with everything that it could accomplish, while still producing no progress on Vietnam."[51] Although Nixon claimed that at the time he found this risk worth taking, he was evidently satisfied with the results Kissinger brought back from Moscow—on SALT, antiballistic missiles, and the draft of a summit communiqué—and closed his eyes to the absence of progress on Vietnam.

Still, the danger of a canceled summit did not evaporate after Kissinger's trip. When the May 2 private meeting between Kissinger and Le Duc Tho failed to produce results because of the rigidity of the North Vietnamese negotiators, Nixon decided "to go all-out on the bombing front."[52] He was determined to escalate the air war against North Vietnam. But the escalation entailed risks for the summit, and the president feared that if the Soviets canceled the meeting in response to American actions against North Vietnam, Nixon would scarcely be able to survive such humiliation. Instead he was ready to deal a preemptive strike: to cancel the summit himself. Still he hesitated. He wanted to teach the enemy a lesson, but he wanted to go to Moscow too. Finally, on the advice of John Connally, a longtime associate of former President Johnson whose advice Nixon rated highly, Nixon chose to bomb the Hanoi area and to mine North Vietnamese ports.[53]

The Soviet reaction was surprisingly mild. Moscow protested against damage to Soviet vessels caused by American bombers but avoided any reference to the fate of the summit. In its official statement the USSR condemned U.S. actions as "inadmissible" and warned that the Soviet Union would "draw from this appropriate conclusions." The statement placed all responsibility for possible consequences on the government of the United States and insisted that all actions aimed at blockading North Vietnamese ports and disrupting other communications be canceled.[54] The statement implied that the Soviet Union was more indignant at the danger to Soviet ships than at the escalation of the war against a fraternal socialist country. The response from Brezhnev to Nixon's letter of May 8, in which he informed Soviet leaders about U.S. measures against the DRV, convinced the White House that the summit would take place as agreed.[55]

What were the motives behind the calculations of decision-makers in Moscow when they decided on such a mild reaction to the American escalation of the war in Vietnam? Alexandrov-Agentov, one of the few witnesses to events in the Kremlin in those years who has written a memoir, observed that Brezhnev and other members of the Soviet leadership were "shocked and indignant at the provocative character of Washington's actions." But it was not North Vietnam that the Soviet leaders were concerned about. "He [Brezhnev] saw *only* that the Soviet-American meeting, the preparation of which had taken so much effort and energy, was threatened."[56]

Brezhnev had to resist the demands of some of his politburo colleagues who were eager to retaliate and cancel the summit. Agentov attributed such demands to Podgornyi, Ukrainian party boss Pyotr Shelest, and central committee secretary Polyanski. "There was a real possibility," Agentov continued, "that such 'populist' reasoning could elicit a response among a majority of the central committee."[57] In this case all hope for the amelioration of Soviet-American relations would have disappeared. Three days before the summit Brezhnev called a plenary session of the central committee. With the support of Kosygin, Gromyko, Suslov, and Andropov, the most influential members of the Soviet leadership, Brezhnev won approval of his course. His victory was facilitated by the news that the West German Bundestag had ratified the Soviet–West German Treaty of 1970.[58] Thus the summit was saved.

The memoirs of Brezhnev's aide confirm the notion that Moscow did not wish to sacrifice détente for the plans of its Vietnamese friends. But Moscow was not about to abandon its own plans in Southeast Asia, and vis-à-vis China as well. The Soviets could not afford a blatant neglect of their ally in Indochina. To observe at least an appearance of concern for North Vietnamese aspirations, the Kremlin agreed to Hanoi's request to discuss the problem of a peace settlement in Vietnam during the summit with Nixon,[59] but it decided to do this without jeopardizing the principal objectives of the meeting.

Even during his first confidential conversation with the president in Moscow, Brezhnev touched upon the issue of Vietnam. He confided to Nixon that it had been difficult to invite him because of the escalation of the war in Southeast Asia. But Nixon evaded a discussion of this problem, and the first meeting between the Soviet and American leaders finished positively.[60] Nevertheless Brezhnev intended to return to the issue of Vietnam. According to Alexandrov-Agentov, the Soviet leaders had to raise this subject so as "to be justified before their colleagues, before the central committee, before public opinion." But they reserved the discussion for a less official environment, not at the Kremlin but in a state *dacha* in Novo

Ogarevo on the outskirts of Moscow, not in the presence of the two large delegations but in a narrow circle of representatives, or, as Agentov commented, "almost in secret."[61]

We have three accounts of the discussion in Novo Ogarevo, by Nixon, Kissinger, and Alexandrov-Agentov. All three agree on the principal details. After a boat ride on the Moscow River and before a lavish dinner, three Soviet leaders, Brezhnev, Kosygin, and Podgornyi, on one side, and Nixon, Kissinger, and two men of the National Security Council staff, on the other, began a lively discussion of Vietnam which continued about three hours. Most of the talking was done by the Soviet leaders. They bitterly and emotionally condemned the United States and its administration for the war and particularly for its most recent escalation. The tone of the discussion sometimes rose to hysterical levels, when, for example, Podgornyi said to the Americans, "You are murderers. There is blood of old people, women, and children on your hands. When will you finally end this senseless war?"[62]

While these angry Soviet tirades continued, Kissinger mused, "The thought struck me that for all the bombast and rudeness, we were participants in a charade. While the tone was bellicose and the manner extremely rough, none of the Soviet statements had any operational content. The leaders stayed well clear of threats. Their so-called proposals were the simple slogans of the Paris plenary sessions, which they knew we had repeatedly rejected and which we had no reason to accept now that the military situation was almost daily altering in our favor. The Soviet leaders were not pressing us except with words. They were speaking for the record, and when they said enough to have a transcript to send to Hanoi, they would stop."[63]

Kissinger was not far from the truth. As soon as the debate ended, the negotiators returned to their "normal" discussions on problems of bilateral relations, "as if there had been nothing before that." At dinner the "hot" conversation was followed by détente. The mood was joyous. Everyone was "strongly" drunk, and after dinner Nixon could barely find his way out of the room.[64]

The Vietnam subject was again raised during talks between Gromyko and Kissinger which took place within the framework of the summit, on May 27–28. Since in Novo Ogarevo the Soviet leaders had agreed to transmit American proposals to Hanoi and even to send Podgornyi to the DRV as their envoy, Kissinger informed Gromyko of the substance of the U.S. position. He assured his Soviet counterpart that Washington did not consider itself tied to any government in South Vietnam: in the course of events new political forces might come to power in Saigon, and even a Communist government might be established. "The U.S.A. will not stand in the way of it," Kissinger said. "However the U.S.A. cannot do this now by its own hands."[65]

The new wrinkle in the American position was Kissinger's proposal for an electoral commission that would supervise general elections in South Vietnam. He suggested a body of mixed membership: one-third representatives of the Viet Cong, one-third neutrals, and one-third representatives of the Saigon regime. More important, Kissinger did not object to the idea of a coalition government associated with this commission. "Already in the creation of the Electoral Commission," he explained to Gromyko, "there will be laid down the principle of coalition. In fact the Commission itself will be in a sense, a transitional form, similar to a coalition government. It would also be possible to consider how, in a flexible though somewhat camouflaged form, to establish the idea of a coalition government early in the coordination of these issues, though as a whole this problem must be a subject for negotiations between the sides themselves."[66] Thus Thieu's suspicions, as well as those of some scholars later,[67] were justified. Kissinger was ready to agree on a coalition government under the guise of the electoral commission if such a concession would push negotiations with the North Vietnamese toward an agreement to end the war.

It may not have been very hopeful about the mood in Hanoi after the Soviet-American summit, but Moscow kept its promise to Nixon and sent Podgornyi to Hanoi on June 15 for a "friendly unofficial visit."[68] Shortly before, Washington proposed a private meeting between Kissinger and Le Duc Tho on June 28.

Soviet misgivings about the atmosphere in Hanoi were well founded. The summit in Moscow completed the destruction of the international environment in which North Vietnamese leaders had hoped to end the war on their conditions. Their plans to overthrow Nixon had been undermined by the American negotiations in Beijing and Moscow. Although Hanoi might have expected such perfidy from the Chinese, Soviet policy was regarded by the North Vietnamese leadership as the height of cynicism. They understood that Podgornyi would be pursuing three objectives in his visit to

Hanoi: (1) to convey Nixon's position on Vietnam, (2) to explore the attitude of the Vietnamese comrades, and (3) "to press Hanoi for peace."

The North Vietnamese leaders decided to resist this pressure from the Soviets and to demonstrate their indignation with the summit and its results. They planned to express their dissatisfaction with Moscow's conciliatory attitude toward the American aggressors, exemplified in their invitation to Nixon to visit the Soviet Union; to show their disagreement with the Soviet position on Vietnam as stated in the joint U.S.-USSR communiqué in which Moscow had rather routinely repeated its support of North Vietnam; and to criticize their allies for the failure to react strongly to the U.S. bombing of the DRV and the mining of North Vietnamese ports.[69] Not surprisingly, Podgornyi's visit produced no positive results.

However bitter were the North Vietnamese about Soviet and Chinese rapprochement with the United States, Hanoi was prepared to change its attitude in negotiations with Washington. Its plan for the spring 1972 offensive probably considered various scenarios, as was the case with the 1968 Tet offensive. Although the lack of Moscow's and Beijing's diplomatic support weakened North Vietnamese positions, it was not the only reason for Hanoi's decision to adopt a more flexible policy toward the negotiations. According to Gareth Porter, ". . . Hanoi regarded a settlement in 1972 as being in the interests of the revolution. Its leaders realized that American air power had become a major factor in the balance of forces in the South, and that the PRG and its followers needed to be free from the constant threat of B-52 attack in order to permit not only the normalization of the PRG zone but also the strengthening of the PLAF in the South. Furthermore the North itself badly needed a respite from war after seven years of being unable to devote its resources fully to production and economic development."[70] In other words, the North Vietnamese leaders realized that without an American presence in Vietnam it would be easier for them to solve the problem of Thieu and unify the country, particularly after the offensive had revealed the weakness of the Saigon regime and provided the Communists with stronger positions in the South.

As a result, during negotiations between Kissinger and Le Duc Tho in July–October 1972 the North Vietnamese dropped most of their demands and objections concerning the conditions of a settlement, among them the calls for coalition government and for Thieu's replacement, and agreed to sign a settlement with Washington before the U.S. presidential elections. In turn, the Americans agreed to discuss political problems along with the issues of a military settlement. Kissinger declared his readiness to consider the role of a National Council of Reconciliation and Concord whose functions would be confined to administering the election in South Vietnam and promoting the implementation of the peace agreement—an idea developed from the electoral commission.

It seemed that the obstacles to peace in Vietnam had been overcome. But, as in 1968, Saigon resisted the agreement. President Thieu's position was quite explicable. As Stephen Ambrose put it, "The GVN was a government without a country or a people. Its sole support was the U.S. government. It's sole *raison d'être* was the war. For the GVN to agree to peace would be to sign its own death warrant."[71] The prospect of facing armed guerrilla forces supported by the North Vietnamese promised nothing good to Thieu and his corrupt regime. Not surprisingly, he regarded the terms of the agreement that included the withdrawal of all American troops, the establishment of a National Council of Reconciliation, and a cease-fire in place as a guarantee of his eventual defeat. Accordingly he refused to support this agreement despite the considerable pressure that Nixon and Kissinger exerted in order to obtain his approval. Since Nixon himself was hesitant about concluding the agreement with Hanoi before the elections, hoping to take steps to strengthen the regime in Saigon, he instructed Kissinger to comply with Thieu's sixty-nine changes to the agreement and demand additional concessions from Hanoi.

North Vietnamese reaction to the new demands was predictable. They not only rejected them but countered with their own changes. Negotiations dragged on without results from November 20 to December 13, when both Kissinger and Le Duc Tho decided to suspend the talks and return to their respective countries for consultation. Kissinger characterized the North Vietnamese tactics in these negotiations by citing the words of his staff expert on Vietnam, John Negroponte, who labeled them "clumsy, blatant, and essentially contemptuous of the United States" as well as "tawdry, petty, and at times transparently childish."[72] Perhaps the American negotiators, who had spent many hours at the same table with Hanoi's envoys, had grown tired of them and could not see that, despite their alleged intransigence, the North Vietnamese still hoped to resolve the problem of Vietnam peacefully, without resort to military force. According to the Russian version of the transcripts of the last meeting between Kissinger and Le Duc Tho, distributed to members of the Soviet politburo, Hanoi's representative expressed his strong conviction that he and Kissinger would be able to settle the remaining differences. He suggested exchanges of messages while the negotiations were suspended, and was ready to fix the date for a new meeting.[73]

Kissinger's reply was in contrast to Le Duc Tho's conciliatory tone. He spoke of doubts in Washington about the sincerity of Hanoi's position in light of its failure to observe negotiating schedules—though it was the Nixon administration that had broken the schedule by refusing to sign the agreement in October. He complained that progress in the negotiations was not sufficient to bring them to completion. He referred to a "serious temptation" to continue the war and hinted that both he and Le Duc Tho were "more acquainted with the war and more inclined to face the risks related to war than to peace."[74] Again Le Duc Tho tried to persuade Kissinger that negotiations were preferable. "We should act in such a manner," he exhorted Kissinger, "so as not to allow the temperature to increase above the limits of the glass's capacity to resist."[75]

But Nixon and Kissinger decided again to use military pressure to force Hanoi to accept their terms of agreement. On December 14 Nixon ordered the reseeding of mines in Haiphong Harbor and the resumption of aerial reconnaissance and B-52 strikes against the Hanoi-Haiphong area. Three days later tens of U.S. planes took off for the bombing raid against the DRV. Although Washington claimed that the targets were limited to military objectives, many civilian installations were attacked by American forces, among them a water filtration plant for Hanoi, factories manufacturing textiles and noodles, and the Bach Mai Hospital on the southwest edge of Hanoi.[76]

This "unconscionable use of force"[77] seriously undermined U.S. world prestige and Nixon's domestic position. Even governments friendly to the United States raised their voice against the bombing. Both the Soviet Union and China publicly condemned U.S. actions and reaffirmed their support of North Vietnam. In its statement of December 20 TASS warned that "in the governing circles of the Soviet Union the situation created in connection with the intensification of the U.S. military actions against the DRV is being considered most seriously."[78] Brezhnev devoted a substantial portion of his three-and-a-half-hour speech on the occasion of the fiftieth anniversary of the USSR to the Vietnam issue, in which he made the prospects for Soviet-American relations dependent on ending the war in Vietnam.[79]

Privately, however, the Soviets continued their efforts to persuade Hanoi to resume the negotiations and explore possibilities for compromise. On December 23 Soviet Ambassador Shcherbakov met with Pham Van Dong in Hanoi. The North Vietnamese premier expressed his indignation about the U.S. bombing raids. He emphasized that Le Duc Tho, before his departure from Paris, had come to an understanding with Kissinger that the negotiations would resume and that messages would be exchanged. Besides, according to Pham Van Dong, Le Duc Tho would soon be returning to Paris. All this demonstrated the DRV's goodwill and desire to end the war through negotiations. But while the United States was bombing North Vietnam—which should be characterized as an ultimatum and flagrant pressure—it was impossible for Hanoi to agree on the resumption of talks. "Only after the U.S.A. in its relations with North Vietnam returns to that normal situation, which existed in September, October, and November, that is, ceases the bombing while the negotiations are held," Pham Van Dong stressed, "only then will it be possible to talk about the continuation of the Le Duc Tho–Kissinger meetings."[80]

After promising to inform Moscow of the DRV's attitude, Shcherbakov asked whether the United States knew of it. When Pham Van Dong said no, the Soviet ambassador suggested that such a step would be expedient. He also pointed out that pressure on the United States should be aimed at cessation of the bombing and a return to the negotiating table "for the purpose of concluding the agreement *as soon as possible*."[81]

Surprisingly, Hanoi accepted this advice. Four days later Deputy Foreign Minister Hoang Van Tien informed Shcherbakov that the DRV had replied to December 18 and 22 messages from Washington with a proposal to resume the talks. The North Vietnamese asked Moscow to persuade the United States that only a cessation of hostilities north of the 20th parallel and their reduction south of the parallel during the negotiations could lead to a resumption of the talks.[82]

By no means was it only Soviet pressure, on Hanoi and on Washington, that led to the resumption of negotiations between Kissinger and Le Duc Tho on January 8, 1973, and to the conclusion of an agreement to end the war and restore peace in Vietnam, initialed on January 23 by the two chief negotiators. Many other factors, internal as well as external, influenced the decision of the two countries to agree on substantial concessions in order to reach an agreement. As Kissinger admitted in his press conference after the negotiations were over, "It became apparent that both sides were determined to make a serious effort to break the dead-lock. . . ."[83] Doubtless Soviet insistence on the need for a negotiated settlement of the war contributed to that determination.

The Paris agreement was signed on January 27. It marked the end of the war in Vietnam, at least for the United States. Moscow could join Washington in celebrating the end of this bloody, unjust, and brutal conflict which for years had poisoned international relations. At a reception in Moscow in honor of Le Duc Tho and Nguyen Duy Trinh, Brezhnev, after paying tribute to the heroism and courage of the people of Vietnam, emphasized what was now being left behind. "For long years," he said, "this war has been used by the forces of aggression and reaction for the aggravation of international tension and intensification of the arms race. This war created serious obstacles for the maintenance of broad international cooperation. Now new opportunities for deepening détente and strengthening security and world peace are opening. We may expect that the political settlement in Vietnam will have a positive effect on relations between countries that in some way were involved in the events that have taken place in Indochina."[84]

As usual, one must read between the lines to grasp the meaning of Brezhnev's words. For Moscow the end of the Vietnam War marked a new stage of its foreign policy. It meant the elimination of a significant obstacle on the way to détente with the West, an issue often manipulated by Washington for its own purposes. It meant more flexibility in Soviet policy toward China. It meant the chance of a more aggressive Soviet policy in Southeast Asia and in the third world. In this respect the Vietnam War was a watershed in the development of international relations after 1945 and a preface to the last two decades of cold war history.

ELEVEN

The Only Winner?

The signing of the Paris peace agreement in January 1973 and the International Conference on Indochina that followed in March did not bring peace to Vietnam. The war continued between the North and the South for two more years, during which both warring parties received outside support. As it had earlier, the U.S. government tried to strengthen the Saigon regime with military, diplomatic, and moral support. The Soviet Union sent similar assistance to Hanoi. In the new circumstances, however, everything in the war depended on which regime, North or South, proved to be more viable, more capable of converting the aid into decisive results on the battlefield and on the political scene.

Doubtless for Moscow this question was resolved several years before, when in 1971 Soviet diplomats drew up plans to make Vietnam the USSR's key to Southeast Asia. But such confidence had been growing throughout the Vietnam War. When in 1964 Kosygin promised Pham Van Dong Soviet support and assistance, the Kremlin had no solid grounds to expect that in the future Vietnam would be regarded as the Soviet outpost in Indochina. Moscow agreed to close cooperation with Hanoi in the struggle against American aggression largely out of concern for the Soviet image as a reliable partner for its socialist allies in a situation of growing competition with Communist China for leadership of the world Communist movement.

The dynamics of Soviet policy toward the Vietnam War depended on the development of relations between the USSR and the DRV. As the rivalry between Moscow and Beijing intensified, the North Vietnamese leadership was able to exploit the conflict between its powerful Communist supporters and their desire to gain a foothold in Indochina. Skillfully maneuvering between the Chinese and the Soviets, Hanoi preserved its independence in formulating its political aims while becoming more and more dependent on the material assistance of its allies. Moscow had no monopoly in Vietnam; its influence was shared with Beijing throughout the war.

Although Soviet aid to the DRV grew constantly and by 1968 exceeded China's, this assistance was not matched by a growth of influence. On the contrary, Moscow found it sometimes even more difficult to deal with the independent tail that successfully wagged the dog. Since Soviet leaders could not afford to curtail aid in reprisal for disobedience, they preferred to act gradually, to strengthen their positions in Hanoi while undermining Chinese influence there. This is why Moscow was so careful not to jeopardize its relations with the North Vietnamese, not to push them too hard toward settlement but to be ready to seize the slightest opportunity to modify the DRV's attitude toward negotiations.

Aware of its weak positions in North Vietnam vis-à-vis China, the Soviet leadership, on the eve of direct U.S. involvement in the conflict and during the first two years of the second Indochina war, seemed more concerned with avoiding damage to its relations with Hanoi than with pursuing an active policy toward the conflict. Although Moscow was unhappy about the open military struggle between the United States and the Democratic Republic of Vietnam, which threatened to undermine the first positive steps toward détente with the West, it decided to wait until after its influence in Hanoi was strong enough to allow it to promote a negotiated settlement of the war. Meanwhile Soviet leaders adopted a passive posture toward events in Southeast Asia.

Eventually this cautious policy proved to be successful for Moscow. Although Chinese influence remained strong during the war, it diminished markedly by 1973, certainly because of Beijing's rapprochement with the United States. While Hanoi was not enthusiastic about the need to choose between its two allies, its suspicion of China—rooted in history as well as a fear that China's proximity offered Beijing more opportunity to intervene in Hanoi's affairs—increased Moscow's chances in the competition that lasted more than ten years.

This was by no means the only positive result for Moscow of Soviet involvement in the conflict in Indochina. Other benefits were no less important. By supporting Vietnam, Moscow improved its image as a vigilant champion of national liberation movements and proved its credibility in the eyes of allies and clients. And because the war demanded more and more attention from Washington, the Soviet Union could operate more freely in other parts of the world, primarily in Europe. On the other hand, its position as a detached observer in the conflict gave Moscow more flexibility in its relationship with the United States and allowed the Kremlin to win concessions from Washington in exchange for services—or even potential services—on behalf of the United States in contacts with North Vietnam. In addition, military actions in Vietnam provided the Soviets with an excellent opportunity to test their weaponry and to gather data and samples of American arms and equipment for use in developing their military technology.

But it would be a serious distortion of reality to suggest therefore that the Soviet Union favored the continuation of the war and urged North Vietnamese leaders to stand fast against a diplomatic settlement. Although tactically the war in Indochina helped Moscow, strategically it was dangerous, and Soviet leaders understood this full well. They were apprehensive about the conflict spreading to other regions of Asia and even developing into an East-West confrontation and a nuclear disaster. Even short of such consequences, Moscow was not unaware of the negative influence of the war on the general world situation.

As a result, the Soviet leadership soon adopted a two-pronged policy toward the Vietnam War which corresponded generally with the two "faces" of the USSR's attitude toward the world. While supplying Hanoi with the necessary means for war against the United States and the Saigon regime, Moscow undertook behind-the-scene efforts to convince the participants of the need for a negotiated settlement. Initially such efforts failed, for both sides were determined to achieve military victory and bring their winnings to the conference table. Considering the intransigence of the warring parties, the Soviets had to be especially careful, particularly in relations with their North Vietnamese allies. Moscow also had to consider inevitable accusations from Beijing, which spared no opportunity to demonstrate the treacherous nature of Soviet leadership and its eagerness for collusion with imperialism. Therefore the Kremlin rejected any approaches that placed it in the position of mediator in the conflict or threatened to publicize its attempts to find a peaceful solution of the war.

Moscow's dual position toward the war provoked criticism of the Soviet Union in the West and in the United States. American leaders could not understand why the USSR, which provided the DRV with the bulk of its economic and military aid, could not use it as leverage in order to persuade Hanoi to abandon its plans in the South and agree to negotiate. Soviet unwillingness to exceed certain limits in its efforts to find a solution to the conflict created the image of a reluctant diplomat, especially when Moscow avoided active intervention but resorted to half-measures just in order to keep its options open.

Despite its reluctance, Moscow was closely involved in the political settlement of the war. Gradually this involvement increased, reaching a peak at the first stage of the Paris peace talks from May 1968 to January 1969. When the four-power negotiations began, assuring the Soviets that the war would be contained within regional boundaries, Moscow radically reduced its involvement in the negotiations. Instead the Kremlin concentrated on including Vietnam in its orbit and making it the representative of Soviet interests and the channel for Soviet influence in Southeast Asia. Moscow began to assume a more active role in its relationship with the DRV, and this process was accelerated after the conclusion of the Paris Peace Accord of 1973.

At first glance, the Soviet Union might seem to be the only winner in the Vietnam War. Without much sacrifice it gained a strong foothold in Southeast Asia. It skillfully managed the U.S. interest in an "honorable" extrication from the war, earning for itself greater room for maneuver in the international arena and developing détente with the West, which promised new opportunities for Moscow in political and economic cooperation. It accumulated credit in the eyes of its allies and fellows in the world Communist movement for its strict adherence to the principles of proletarian internationalism. And it won sympathies from national liberation movements as a defender of the rights of oppressed peoples against neocolonialists.

But these successes hid the seeds of future failures and shocks in Soviet foreign policy. Inspired by its gains and by the decline of U.S. prestige resulting from Vietnam and domestic upheaval, the Soviet leadership adopted a more aggressive and rigid foreign policy, particularly in the third world. The lessons of Vietnam had a diametrically opposite effect in Moscow. Instead of seeing the U.S. defeat in Indochina as a warning against similar adventures of their own, Soviet leaders, blinded by Marxist-Leninist philosophy and by the conviction that the revolutionary trend of history was on their side, believed that where imperialism had failed they would certainly succeed. Implanted in the "Brezhnev Doctrine" that was formulated to justify the Soviet invasion of Czechoslovakia and Eastern European countries and later was applied to other regions, this belief led in the 1970s to Soviet involvement in turmoil in Africa and the Middle East and eventually to the tragedy of Afghanistan that became one of the reasons for the collapse of the Soviet regime. Such was the chain of events that some would associate with the laws of history and others with its jaws.

Bibliography

Archives

Joseph H. and Stewart Alsop Papers, Library of Congress, Manuscript Division, Washington, D.C.
W. Averell Harriman Papers, Library of Congress, Manuscript Division, Washington, D.C.
Lyndon B. Johnson Presidential Library, Austin, Texas
National Security Archive, Washington, D.C.
Nixon Presidential Materials Project, College Park, Maryland
Storage Center for Contemporary Documentation (formerly CPSU CC archive), Moscow, Russia

Interviews

Anatolii F. Dobrynin, USSR ambassador to the United States, 1962–1985
Oleg A. Troyanovskii, Kosygin's aide, 1964–1967
Cyrus Vance, head of the U.S. delegation to the Paris peace talks, 1968–1969

Newspapers and Periodicals

Izvestiia, 1964–1973
Pravda, 1964–1973

Books and Articles

Rudy Abramson, *Spanning the Century: The Life of W. Averell Harriman, 1891–1986* (New York: William Morrow and Company, 1992).

Andrei A. Alexandrov-Agentov, *Ot Kollontai do Gorbacheva. Vospominaniia diplomata, sovetnika A.A. Gromyko, pomoshchnika L.I. Brezhneva, Yu. V. Andropova, K.U. Chernenko i M.S. Gorbacheva (From Kollontai to Gorbachev: The Memoirs of a Diplomat, Adviser of A. A. Gromyko, Aide to L. I. Brezhnev, Yu. V. Andropov, K. U. Chernenko, and M. S. Gorbachev)* (Moscow: International Relations, 1994).

Stephen E. Ambrose, *Nixon*, Vol. 2: *The Triumph of a Politician* (New York: Simon and Schuster, 1989).

Boyevoi Avangard V'etnamskogo Naroda. Istoriia Kommunisticheskoi Partii V'etnama (Militant Vanguard of the Vietnamese People. History of the Communist Party of Vietnam) (Moscow: Politizdat, 1981).

Clark Clifford, with Richard Holbrook, *Counsel to the President: A Memoir* (New York: Random House, 1991).

William Colby, with Peter Forbath, *Honorable Man: My Life in the CIA* (New York: Simon and Schuster, 1978).

Chester L. Cooper, *The Lost Crusade: America in Vietnam* (New York: Dodd, Mead, 1970).

Dorothy C. Donnelly, "A Settlement of Sorts: Henry Kissinger's Negotiations and America's Extrication from Vietnam," *Peace and Change* 2/3 (Summer 1983): 62.

Raymond L. Garthoff, *Détente and Confrontation: American-Soviet Relations from Nixon to Reagan* (Washington, D.C.: Brookings Institution, 1994), rev. ed.

William Conrad Gibbons, *The U.S. Government and the Vietnam War: Executive and Legislative Roles and Relationships*. Part 3: January–July 1965. (Washington, D.C.: U.S. Government Printing Office, 1988).

Anne Gilks, *The Breakdown of the Sino-Vietnamese Alliance, 1970–1979* (Berkeley: Institute of East Asian Studies, University of California, 1992).

Ted Gittinger, ed., *The Johnson Years: A Vietnam Roundtable* (Austin: Lyndon Baines Johnson Library, Lyndon B. Johnson School of Public Affairs, University of Texas, 1993).

Allan E. Goodman, *The Lost Peace: America's Search for a Negotiated Settlement of the Vietnam War* (Stanford: Hoover Institution Press, 1978).

Allan E. Goodman, *The Search for a Negotiated Settlement of the Vietnam War* (Berkeley: Institute of East Asian Studies, University of California, 1986).

H. R. Haldeman, *The Haldeman Diaries: Inside the Nixon White House* (New York: G. P. Putnam's Sons, 1994).

George C. Herring, *LBJ and Vietnam: A Different Kind of War* (Austin: University of Texas Press, 1994).

George C. Herring, "The Reluctant Warrior: Lyndon Johnson as Commander in Chief," in David L. Anderson, ed., *Shadow on the White House: Presidents and the Vietnam War, 1945–1975* (Lawrence: University Press of Kansas, 1993).

George C. Herring, ed., *The Secret Diplomacy of the Vietnam War: The Negotiating Volumes of the Pentagon Papers* (Austin: University of Texas Press, 1983).

Joan Hoff, *Nixon Reconsidered* (New York: Basic Books, 1994).
Walter Isaacson, *Kissinger: A Biography* (London: Faber and Faber, 1992).
Lyndon Baines Johnson, *The Vantage Point: Perspectives of the Presidency, 1963–1969* (New York: Holt, Rinehart and Winston, 1971).
The Johnson Presidential Press Conferences, Vol. 1–2 (Stanfordville, N.Y.: Earl M. Coleman Enterprises, 1978).
George McT. Kahin, *Intervention: How America Became Involved in Vietnam* (New York: Alfred A. Knopf, 1986).
Paul Kesaris, ed., *Documents of the National Security Council* (Frederick, Md.: University Publications of America, 1987), microfilm ed.
Henry A. Kissinger, *Diplomacy* (New York: Simon and Schuster, 1994).
Henry A. Kissinger, "The Viet Nam Negotiations," *Foreign Affairs* 47 (January 1969): 2, 211–234.
Henry A. Kissinger, *The White House Years* (London: Wiedenfeld and Nicolson, Michael Joseph, 1979).
Gabriel Kolko, *Anatomy of a War: Vietnam, the United States, and the Modern Historical Experience* (New York: Pantheon, 1985).
L. V. Kotov and R. S. Yegov, eds., *Militant Solidarity, Fraternal Assistance* (Moscow: Progress, 1970).
Mark Kramer, "Archival Research in Moscow: Progress and Pitfalls," *Cold War International History Project Bulletin* 3 (Fall 1993): 1, 18–39.
Robert S. McNamara, with Brian VanDeMark, *In Retrospect: The Tragedy and Lessons of Vietnam* (New York: Times Books, 1995).
S. Mkhitarian and T. Mkhitarian, *V'etnamskaia Revolutiia: Voprosy teorii i praktiki (The Vietnamese Revolution: Questions of Theory and Practice)* (Moscow: Nauka, 1986).
Stephen J. Morris, "The '1205 Document': A Story of American Prisoners, Vietnamese Agents, Soviet Archives, Washington Bureaucrats, and the Media," *National Interest* 33 (1993): 28–42.
Richard M. Nixon, *RN: The Memoirs of Richard Nixon* (London: Sidgwick and Jackson, 1978).
Don Oberdorfer, *Tet! The Turning Point in the Vietnam War* (New York: Da Capo Press, 1985).
Daniel S. Papp, *Vietnam: The View from Moscow, Peking, Washington* (Jefferson, N.C.: McFarland, 1981).
F. Charles Parker, IV, *Vietnam: Strategy for a Stalemate* (New York: Paragon House, 1989).
Douglas Pike, *Vietnam and the Soviet Union: Anatomy of an Alliance* (Boulder: Westview Press, 1987).
Gareth Porter, *A Peace Denied: The United States, Vietnam, and the Paris Agreement* (Bloomington: Indiana University Press, 1975).
Gareth Porter, ed., *Vietnam: A History in Documents* (New York: New American Library, 1981).
Gareth Porter, ed., *Vietnam: The Definitive Documentation of Human Decisions* (Stanfordville, N.Y.: Earl Coleman Enterprises, 1979).
Ken Post, *Revolution, Socialism, and Nationalism in Viet Nam.* Vol. 5: *Winning the War and Losing the Peace* (Aldershot, N. H.: Dartmouth, 1994).

Pravda o V'etnamo-Kitaiskikh Otnosheniiakh Za Poslednie 30 Let (The Truth About Vietnam-China Relations Over the Last Thirty Years) (Hanoi: DRV Ministry of Foreign Affairs, 1979).

Peter W. Rodman, *More Precious Than Peace: The Cold War and the Struggle for the Third World* (New York: Charles Scribner's Sons, 1994).

Dean Rusk, with Richard Rusk and Daniel S. Papp, *As I Saw It* (New York: W. W. Norton, 1990).

F. A. Simpson, *Louis Napoleon and The Recovery of France* (London: Longmans, 1960).

R. B. Smith, *An International History of the Vietnam War*. Vol. 2: *The Struggle for South-East Asia, 1961–65* (London: Macmillan, 1985).

R. B. Smith, *An International History of the Vietnam War.* Vol. 3: *The Making of a Limited War, 1965–66* (New York: St. Martin's Press, 1991).

Tad Szulc, *The Illusion of Peace: Foreign Policy in the Nixon Years* (New York: Viking, 1978).

Wallace J. Thies, *When Governments Collide: Coercion and Diplomacy in the Vietnam Conflict, 1964–1968* (Berkeley: University of California Press, 1980).

Richard C. Thornton, *The Nixon-Kissinger Years: Reshaping America's Foreign Policy* (New York: Paragon House, 1989).

U.S. Congress, Senate, Committee on Foreign Relations, *Executive Sessions of the Senate Foreign Relations Committee Together with Joint Sessions with the Senate Armed Service Committee* (Historical Series), 1965, Vol. 17 (Washington, D.C.: U.S. Government Printing Office, 1992).

U.S. Department of State, *Foreign Relations of the United States: Vietnam, 1964–1968,* Vol. 1 (Washington, D.C.: U.S. Government Printing Office, 1992).

USSR Ministry of Foreign Affairs, *Sovetskii Soyuz-V'etnam. 30 let otnoshenii, 1950–1980 (The Soviet Union–Vietnam: Thirty Years of the Relationship, 1950–1980)* (Moscow: Politizdat, 1982).

Brian VanDeMark, *Into the Quagmire: Lyndon Johnson and the Escalation of the Vietnam War* (New York: Oxford University Press, 1991).

Vneshniia Politika i Mezhdunarodnye Otnosheniia KNR (The Foreign Policy and International Relations of the PRC) Vol. 2: *1963–1973* (Moscow: Mysl', 1974).

William Appleman Williams, Thomas J. McCormick, Lloyd C. Gardner, and Walter LaFeber, eds., *America in Vietnam: A Documented History* (New York: W. W. Norton, 1985).

Harold Wilson, *The Labour Government, 1964–1970: A Personal Record* (London: Weidenfeld and Nicolson, Michael Joseph, 1971).

Notes

PREFACE

1. For example, Chen Jian's *China's Involvement with the Vietnam War, 1964–1969*, originally prepared for a Norwegian Nobel Institute research seminar.

2. There are few exceptions in this respect. British historian R. B. Smith, for instance, in his multivolume *International History of the Vietnam War* (New York, 1983–1991), tried to consider Soviet policy toward the conflict within the general context of world developments in those years. Another attempt to analyze Moscow's role in the war, along with that of the United States and China, was made by Daniel Papp in his book based mostly on official publications and press reviews—*Vietnam: The View from Moscow, Peking, Washington* (Jefferson, N.C., 1981). Douglas Pike's study of relations between the Soviet Union and North Vietnam in the 1950s and 1960s, *Vietnam and the Soviet Union: Anatomy of an Alliance* (Boulder, Colo., 1987), reveals the contradictory character of the alliance between Moscow and Hanoi and provides many useful insights into the background of events during that period. An example of how misleading it may be to rely on published sources without a thorough analysis of archival material is F. Charles Parker, IV, *Vietnam: Strategy for a Stalemate* (New York, 1989). The author neglects facts that could have been found in documents from Western archives (in 1989 Russian archives were still tightly closed) and instead takes at face value public utterances by Soviet and Chinese leaders as well as official publications in both countries. As a result, his picture of the policies pursued by those countries supporting North Vietnam resembles a reflection in a mirror, where left becomes right and right becomes left. According to Parker, it was the Soviet Union, not China, who opposed diplomatic settlement of the Vietnam War in the 1960s and urged Hanoi to continue the war regardless of Beijing's efforts toward a peaceful solution. In Parker's book, Moscow plays the role of villain. These four books virtually comprise the historiography of Soviet participation in the Vietnam War. Despite their analysis, many questions about Moscow's activities in the war remain unanswered.

3. George C. Herring, ed., *The Secret Diplomacy of the Vietnam War: The Negotiating Volumes of the Pentagon Papers* (Austin, Tex., 1983).

4. See, for example: Mikhail Il'inskii, *Napalm v Pal'my* (*Napalm to Palms*) (Moscow, 1974); Ivan Shchedrov, *V'etnamskii Reportazh* (*The Vietnam Reportage*) (Moscow, 1972); Yuri Zhukov and V. Sharapov, *Otpor* (*The Rebuff*) (Moscow, 1966).

5. Ia. Pivovarov and Igor' Ognetov, *Demokraticheskaia Respublika V'etnam (The Democratic Republic of Vietnam)* (Moscow, 1975); Evgenii V. Kobelev, *V'etnam, liubov' i bol' moia* (Vietnam, My Love and Anguish) (Moscow, 1971).

6. A. Voronin, *V'etnam: Nezavisimost', Edinstvo, Sotialism (Vietnam: Independence, Unity, Socialism)* (Moscow, 1977); Valentina Liven', *Voina vo V'etname i vnutripoliticheskaia bor'ba v SShA (The Vietnam War and Internal Political Struggle in the U.S.A.)* (Moscow, 1972); Suren Mkhitarian and T. Mkhitarian, *V'etnamskaia Revolutziia: Voprosy teorii i praktiki (The Vietnamese Revolution: Questions of Theory and Practice)* (Moscow, 1986).

7. For details about cooperation between historians and the Russian archives, see Mark Kramer, "Archival Research in Moscow: Progress and Pitfalls," *Cold War International History Project Bulletin* 3 (Fall 1993): 1, 18–39.

8. For Stephen J. Morris's version of the events, see "The '1205 Document': A Story of American Prisoners, Vietnamese Agents, Soviet Archives, Washington Bureaucrats, and the Media," *National Interest* 33 (1993): 28–42.

9. F. A. Simpson, *Louis Napoleon and the Recovery of France* (London, 1960), 246.

1. ON THE EVE

1. *Pravda*, January 4, 1964.

2. *Ibid.* Emphasis added.

3. Mkhitarian and Mkhitarian, *Vietnamese Revolution*, pp. 214–215.

4. *Boyevoy Avangard V'etnamskogo Naroda. Istoriia Kommunisticheskoi Partii V'etnama* (*Militant Vanguard of the Vietnamese People. History of the Communist Party of Vietnam*) (Moscow, 1981), p. 130. This book is a translation from the Vietnamese of the official history of the Lao Dong party from its foundation by Ho Chi Minh.

5. *Pravda o V'etnamo-Kitaiskikh Otnosheniiakh Za Poslednie 30 Let (The Truth About Vietnam-China Relations Over the Last 30 Years)* (Hanoi, 1979), p. 24. Hanoi published this pamphlet at a time of open conflict between the two former Communist allies, evidently in an effort to expose the treacherous nature of the Chinese leadership. Nonetheless, Hanoi could not help but acknowledge the PRC's assistance to the Vietminh in their struggle against the French.

6. This fact is mentioned in the top secret memorandum of the Southeast Asia Department of the Soviet Ministry of Foreign Affairs, "Soviet Moral and Political Support of and Material Aid to the South Vietnam Patriots," March 24, 1966. Tzentr Khraneniya Sovremennoi Dokumentatzii (Storage Center for Contemporary Documentation, hereafter SCCD), fond 5, opis' 50, delo 777, pp. 58–59.

7. *Pravda*, February 9, 1964. Emphasis added.

8. Telegram to the Soviet Ambassador to France. SCCD, f. 4, op. 18, d. 582, St-95/462g, March 14, 1964.

9. *Militant Vanguard of the Vietnamese People*, pp. 134, 137.

10. SCCD, f. 4, op. 18, d. 582, p. 2.

11. *Ibid.*, p. 3.
12. *Ibid.*, p. 5.
13. *Ibid.*
14. *Pravda*, February 12, 1964.
15. *Pravda*, February 26, 1964.
16. International Department to the Central Committee, Secret, July 25, 1964. SCCD, f. 5, op. 50, d. 631, pp. 163–164.
17. Memorandum of Conversation, Krutikov-Spasovski, June 5, 1964. SCCD, f. 5, op, 50, d. 631, p. 130.
18. *Truth About Vietnam-China Relations*, p. 35.
19. SCCD, f. 5, op. 50, d. 631, p. 131.
20. On June 27, *Pravda* published the Soviet government's proposal to call a new international conference on Laos. "The Soviet Union," *Pravda* stated, "on its part, is ready, as before, to assist in efforts to speed up a convocation of an aforementioned international conference. The negative attitude on the part of other states toward this proposal will place the Soviet Government in a position where it will have to consider in general the question of the Soviet Union performing functions of cochairman, since when there are gross and systematic violations of the Geneva Accords the role of cochairman loses its useful meaning and becomes fictitious." *Pravda*, June 27, 1964.
21. *Pravda*, August 3, 1964.
22. *Sovietskii Soyuz–Vietnam. 30 let otnoshenii, 1950–1980 (The Soviet Union–Vietnam: 30 Years of the Relationship, 1950–1980)* (Moscow, 1982), pp. 80–81.
23. *Foreign Relations of the United States, 1964–1968* (hereafter *FRUS*), Vol. 1: Vietnam, 1964 (Washington, 1992), p. 637. R. B. Smith, in his *International History of the Vietnam War*, (vol. 2, p. 293) questions the ignorance of Soviet leaders with respect to the Tonkin Gulf incidents. But if one recalls the status of Soviet–North Vietnamese relations in the summer of 1964, one finds Khrushchev's words quite truthful. Openness has never been a quality of the North Vietnamese leadership. For instance, in a conversation with Soviet Ambassador Krutikov in 1963, Mieczyslav Maneli, Polish representative to the International Control Commission, suggested that Hanoi was deliberately misleading its socialist allies. According to Maneli, the Vietnamese conveyed different information to the Poles in Saigon, the Soviet Ambassador to the DRV, and the Polish Ambassador in Hanoi. "They are sending the most optimistic information and estimates," noted Maneli, "to the Soviet comrades, and the most reserved and precise ones go to the Polish delegation in Saigon, since it is quite obvious that we, at least in part, could check constantly their information." (SCCD, f. 5, op. 50, d. 521, p. 57.) Apparently the North Vietnamese officials were even more reluctant to inform their Soviet "comrades," whom they suspected of the sin of "disengagement."
24. *Pravda*, August 3, 1964.
25. *FRUS*, Vietnam, p. 638.
26. *Ibid.*, p. 648.
27. Pike, *Vietnam and the Soviet Union*, p. 48.
28. USIA Report, April 1965. National Security Archive (hereafter NSA), V-16, Vietnam, G. McT. Kahin Donation, box 4.
29. *Ibid.*
30. Minister-Counselor of the Soviet Embassy in Hanoi Mitrophan Podolski to Moscow, December 17, 1966. SCCD, f. 5, op. 59, d. 327, p. 7.
31. *Truth About Vietnam-China Relations*, p. 40.

32. Memorandum of the Main Intelligence Directorate (Glavnoye Razvedyvatel'noye Upravleniye [GRU]) for the CPSU Central Committee, July 14, 1967. SCCD, f. 5, op. 59, d. 416, pp. 119–122.

33. Top secret letter of the Soviet embassy in Hanoi to Moscow, "On the Political Situation in South Vietnam and the Position of the DRV," November 19, 1964. SCCD, f. 5, op. 50, d. 631, p. 253.

34. See, for example, Parker, *Vietnam,* pp. 48–49.

35. "On the Political Situation in South Vietnam." SCCD, f. 5, op. 50, d. 631, p. 248.

36. That the Soviet leadership had to take such a concern into account is clear from a conversation between Norman Cousins of the *Saturday Review* and the Soviet ambassador in Washington, Anatolii F. Dobrynin, after the start of U.S. bombing of DRV territory. Dobrynin expressed anxiety over the American move and a possible Soviet response. "I believe," he said, "that we are moving into military action ourselves in Vietnam. I don't see how we can avoid it. A Socialist country—a very small country—is being bombed by you. We have to respond. *The Socialist world is looking to us to respond.*" (Lyndon B. Johnson Library, National Security File, Name File, Vice-President, vol. 1, box 4, emphasis added.) Other evidence that socialist countries closely followed the Soviet reaction to events in Vietnam can be found in the memorandum of conversation between W. Averell Harriman and Polish President Gomulka. In his cable to Washington of December 30, 1965, Harriman included the following paragraph on his discussion: "He [Gomulka] struck an ominous note when he said 'we will be there and help them.' He explained by 'we' he meant socialist countries. He maintained that Polish people are wondering how they can rely on USSR in protecting them against [West] Germany if USSR is not defending North Viet-Nam." (Library of Congress, Manuscript Division, W. Averell Harriman Papers, Special Files: Public Service, Trips and Missions, box 548.)

37. *Pravda*, October 20, 1964.

38. Pike, *Vietnam and the Soviet Union*, p. 61. The latter dimension was seriously considered in Shcherbakov's memorandum to Moscow of November 19, 1964. The Soviet ambassador believed that "In the present situation, from our viewpoint, it would probably be more appropriate to further mobilize world public opinion for the soonest political settlement of the problem of South Vietnam on the basis of the Geneva Accords." The danger, according to Shcherbakov, was not in the civil war as an internal affair of Vietnam. "It is in the possibility of either escalation of the direct military involvement of the United States or an ill-considered move on the part of the DRV." Concluding his memorandum, Shcherbakov repeated the idea of a settlement of the conflict: "The Embassy believes that in the present situation the main attention, as always, should be drawn to the search of ways of a political settlement in Vietnam, as well as in whole Indochina." SCCD, f. 5, op. 50, d. 631, pp. 237, 253.

39. *Pravda*, November 10, 1964.

40. *Soviet Union–Vietnam*, p. 85.

41. *FRUS*, Vietnam, vol. 1, p. 990.

42. *Ibid.*, p. 991. Emphasis added.

43. "On the Political Situation in South Vietnam," November 19, 1964, p. 248.

2. TURNING POINTS

1. W. C. Gibbons, *The U.S. Government and the Vietnam War: Executive and Legislative Roles and Relationships.* Prepared for the Committee on Foreign Relations, United States Senate, by the Congressional Research Service, Library of Congress. Part III: January–July 1965 (Washington, 1988), p. 27.

2. *Ibid.*, pp. 27–28.

3. Telegram, Saigon to Washington, January 26, 1965. NSA, V-16, Kahin Donation, box 3.

4. Gibbons, *U.S. Government and Vietnam War*, p. 48.

5. U.S. Congress, Senate, Committee on Foreign Relations, *Executive Sessions of the Senate Foreign Relations Committee Together with Joint Sessions with the Senate Armed Service Committee* (Historical Series), 1965, vol. XVII (Washington, 1992), p. 116.

6. CIA Intelligence Memorandum, "Communist Views on an Indochina Conference," January 15, 1965. NSA, V-16, Kahin Donation, box 3.

7. CIA Memorandum, February 11, 1965. *Ibid.*

8. Intelligence Memorandum, "Situation in South Vietnam," February 3, 1965. NSA, V-16, box 3.

9. *Executive Sessions of the Senate Foreign Relations Committee*, 1965, p. 275.

10. *Ibid.*, p. 180.

11. Statement of Dean Rusk Before the U.S. Senate Committee on Foreign Relations, January 15, 1965. *Ibid.*, p. 232.

12. SNIE 10-3-65, "Communist Reactions to Possible US Actions." NSA, V-16, Kahin Donation, box 3.

13. *Executive Sessions of the Senate Foreign Relations Committee*, pp. 99–100.

14. The United Nations and Southeast Asia, Session of the Committee on Foreign Relations, U.S. Senate, January 15, 1965. *Executive Sessions of the Senate Foreign Relations Committee*, p. 232. Emphasis added.

15. Lyndon B. Johnson Library, National Security File, Name File, Mansfield, Vietnam. Emphasis added.

16. *Pravda*, January 31, 1965.

17. For example, French journalist Madeleine Riffaud told Soviet Ambassador to Cambodia Konstantin Krutikov that "patriots" discussed with excitement how different were the statements of the new Soviet leaders from those of Khrushchev. They noted that these statements were "more definite." They approved Moscow's new political line in the conflict. (Krutikov to Moscow, January 30, 1965. SCCD, f. 5, op. 50, d. 721. p. 45.)

18. *Ibid.*, p. 44.

19. Intelligence Memorandum by the CIA's Office of Current Intelligence, February 1, 1965, in Gareth Porter, ed., *Vietnam: The Definitive Documentation of Human Decisions.* Vol. II. (Stanfordville, N.Y., 1979), pp. 346, 347.

20. CIA Memorandum, "Post-Khrushchev Soviet Policy and the Vietnam Crisis," April 3, 1965. NSA, V-16, Kahin Donation, box 4.

21. Author's interview with Oleg A. Troyanovski, May 1994. At that time Troyanovski was an aide to Kosygin and accompanied the Soviet delegation to China and Vietnam.

22. Chester Cooper, then an NSC staff member, supports the notion that the Pleiku incident gave the administration "an opportunity to put into motion a pol-

icy which they had already decided upon, but needed a fairly conspicuous threshold before they could implement." (Gibbons, *U.S. Government and Vietnam War*, p. 61.) Nevertheless, George McT. Kahin called the U.S. decision "incongruous" since, while Washington deferred De Soto patrols until after Kosygin's visit, it did not defer the "much more provocative bombing." Kahin explains this fact by resistance in the Johnson administration to the strong tendency which became apparent in those days, even in South Vietnam, toward peaceful negotiations to settle the conflict in Indochina. Kosygin had presumably intended to convince Hanoi to agree on such a settlement. "It is clear, however," Kahin supposed, "that this was not what most senior officials desired. They still remained opposed to a negotiated solution until such time as the position of the U.S. and that of its Saigon client were strong enough so they could impose a settlement that would maintain a separate anticommunist South Vietnamese state." Therefore American policymakers used the incident to destroy this opportunity. See George McT. Kahin, *Intervention: How America Became Involved in Vietnam* (New York, 1986), pp. 278–279.

23. For example, Charles Parker put forward such a hypothesis in *Vietnam*, p. 63.

24. Memorandum of Conversation, Counselor Soloviev and Deputy Chief of the First Department, Committee on the Unification of Country, WPV Central Committee Tran Thuc, December 29, 1964. SCCD, f. 5, op. 50, d. 721, pp. 27, 28.

25. Smith, *International History of the Vietnam War*, pp. 368–369.

26. George Ball's words at the National Security Council Meeting, February 8, 1965. He added, "The North Vietnamese action has put the Russians on the spot." (Johnson Library, NSF, NSC Meetings File, tab. 29, box 1). See also William Bundy's statement before the Subcommittee on Far Eastern Affairs of the Senate Committee on Foreign Relations, February 9, 1965. (*Executive Sessions of the Senate Foreign Relations Committee*, XVII, 275.)

27. *Ibid.*

28. *Soviet Union–Vietnam*, pp. 94, 95.

29. *Ibid.*, pp. 95–98. *Pravda*, February 11, 1965.

30. Intelligence Memorandum, CIA Office of Current Intelligence, "Soviet Feelers with Regard to Vietnam," March 20, 1965. NSA, V-16, Kahin Donation, box 4.

31. Summary of the Humphrey conversations with Kosygin in New Delhi, January 17, 1966. Johnson Library, NSF, Name File, Vice President, vol. 1, box 4. Although all of Kosygin's replies have been deleted, it is clear from the context that he complained about the U.S. bombing of North Vietnam while he visited Hanoi. Humphrey had to explain that the U.S. had reasons for bombing North Vietnam and noted that Washington had refrained from bombing the DRV capital or any place near it. "Therefore," Humphrey assured Kosygin, "there never was any threat to the security of Mr. Kosygin while he was visiting Hanoi."

32. *Vneshnyaya Politika i Mezhdunarodnye Otnosheniya KNR. (The Foreign Policy and International Relations of the PRC)* Vol. 2: *1963–1973* (Moscow, 1974), pp. 25–26.

33. Department of State, Sector of Intelligence and Research Note, "Kosygin's Speech Contains Some New Elements on Vietnam But Reiterates Basic Soviet Position," February 26, 1965. NSA, V-16, Kahin Donation, box 3.

34. *Ibid.*

35. "Soviet Feelers with Regard to Vietnam," NSA, V-16, box 4.

36. Johnson Library, NSF, Country File, Vietnam NODIS-LOR, vol. 1(A), box 45.

37. NSA, V-16, Kahin Donation, box 3.

38. Johnson Library, NSF, Country File, Vietnam, vol. 29, box 14.

39. *Executive Sessions of the Senate Foreign Relations Committee*, p. 128.

40. Telegram, Moscow to Washington, March 1, 1965. Johnson Library, NSF, Country File, Vietnam, NODIS-LOR, vol. 1(A), box 45.

41. Bundy's Memo to the President, March 6, 1965. Johnson Library, NSF, Memos to the President, McGeorge Bundy, vol. 9, box 3. Emphasis added.

3. WAR IN THE SADDLE

1. *Pravda*, March 5, 1965.

2. L. V. Kotov and R. S. Yegorov, eds., *Militant Solidarity, Fraternal Assistance* (Moscow, 1970), p. 49; *Pravda*, March 13, 1965.

3. *Ibid.*, p. 50.

4. *Pravda*, March 21, 1965.

5. Parker, *Vietnam*, p. 83.

6. *Pravda*, March 24, 1965.

7. Telegram, Foy Kohler to Washington, March 23, 1965. Johnson Library, NSF, Country File, Vietnam, box 46.

8. Memorandum of Conversation, Shcherbakov–Hoang Van Loi, March 26, 1965. SCCD, f. 5, op. 50, d. 721, p. 117.

9. Memorandum of Conversation between Petrov, an interpreter at the Soviet embassy in the DRV, and a researcher at the Institute of Economy in Hanoi, June 6, 1965. *Ibid.*, p. 178.

10. *Soviet Union–Vietnam*, pp. 103–104, 105; *Pravda*, April 18, 1965.

11. *Pravda*, April 20, 1965.

12. Special Memorandum No. 11-65, "Future Soviet Moves in Vietnam," Office of National Estimates, April 27, 1965. Johnson Library, NSF, Country File, Vietnam, vol. 33, box 16.

13. Memorandum, "The Arrival of Soviet Military Aid to the DRV May Be Imminent," May 7, 1965. Johnson Library, NSF, Country File, Vietnam, Special Intelligence Material, vol. 6(B), box 50.

14. Intelligence Memorandum, "Asian Communist and Soviet Views on the War in Vietnam," May 25, 1965. *Ibid.*

15. Department of State to Moscow, May 26, 1965. NSA, V-16, Vietnam, Kahin Donation, box 4. State Department analysts suggested in this cable that by providing Hanoi with such sophisticated weaponry Moscow hoped to maintain its position in the DRV and to acquire new leverage there, although they were uncertain whether the Soviets would use this leverage to persuade Hanoi to negotiate.

16. Harold Wilson, *The Labour Government, 1964–1970: A Personal Record* (London, 1971), p. 85. Gromyko's position with regard to a Geneva-like international conference on Vietnam was not surprising if one takes into account Hanoi's refusal to agree to Soviet proposals made in February to assist in the convocation of such a conference. The standard North Vietnamese reply to the Soviet suggestion was that the time had not yet come for a conference.

17. Memorandum for the President, Personal and Sensitive, March 6, 1965. Johnson Library, NSF, Memos to the President, McGeorge Bundy, vol. 9, box 3.

18. NSA, V-16, Vietnam, Kahin Donation, box 4. They argued that U.S. acceptance of the idea of the conference on Cambodia "would be a 'victory' for the Soviets (who need such a victory, and *whose victory we need, if they are to [be] a*

useful counter-weight to the Chicoms [Chinese Communists] *in Southeast Asia*). . . ." Emphasis added.

19. See, for example: Kahin, *Intervention*; Wallace J. Thies, *When Governments Collide: Coercion and Diplomacy in the Vietnam Conflict, 1964–1968* (Berkeley, 1980); Brian VanDeMark, *Into the Quagmire: Lyndon Johnson and the Escalation of the Vietnam War* (New York, 1991).

20. VanDeMark, *Into the Quagmire*, p. 134.

21. Cable, Washington to Saigon, May 10, 1965. Johnson Library, NSF, NSC History, Deployment of Major U.S. Forces to Vietnam, vol. 4. See also Herring, *Secret Diplomacy of the Vietnam War*, p. 54.

22. *Ibid.*, p. 57.

23. *Ibid.*, p. 58. Emphasis added.

24. First Secretary of the USSR Embassy to the DRV G. Zverev to Moscow, July 8, 1965. SCCD, f. 5, op. 50, d. 721, p. 181.

25. Herring, *Secret Diplomacy of the Vietnam War*, p. 63.

26. *Ibid.*, p. 63.

27. *Ibid.*, p. 67.

28. *Ibid.*, p. 69.

29. On the shift in Hanoi's negotiating stance in May, see VanDeMark, *Into the Quagmire*, pp. 137–138.

30. Gibbons, *U.S. Government and Vietnam War*, p. 255.

31. *Pravda*, June 5, 1965.

32. *Pravda*, July 13, 1965.

33. *Pravda*, July 24, 1965.

34. Moscow not only knew that its weaponry was being transferred to Viet Cong combat units, it also knew what routes Hanoi was using. On May 3, 1965, the Main Intelligence Directorate (GRU) of the Soviet General Staff informed the CC International Department that a supply of arms and ammunition for "regular troops and guerrilla detachments" under command of the NLFSV was found in depots located in Vinh and Dong Hoi provinces of the DRV. Weapons were being delivered by land through Laotian territory under control of the Pathet Lao; by air through a Cambodian airfield near the South Vietnamese border; and by sea. They were stored in jungle areas controlled by the Liberation Front. GRU to Central Committee, May 3, 1965. SCCD, f. 5, op. 50, d. 721, p. 120.

35. *Pravda*, June 4, 1965.

36. Report on the negotiations between German Chancellor Erhard and Foreign Minister Fanfani in the U.S.A. and on the latter's talks in France, June 1965. SCCD, f. 5, op. 50, d. 690, p. 93.

37. Still-classified report of August 20, 1965, no. 2806. SCCD, First Sector, "Special Dossier." One interesting fact laid a foundation for Soviet concerns. As General William Westmoreland, former head of the U.S. Military Assistance Command in Vietnam, noted during a Vietnam symposium in 1991, when American marines came to Danang in March 1965 they brought eight-inch howitzers that were nuclear-capable, though they did not have nuclear warheads. Therefore it was easy for the United States, once it was decided, to change the character of the war to a nuclear one. See Ted Gittinger, ed., *The Johnson Years: A Vietnam Roundtable* (Austin, Tex., 1993), p. 64.

38. Foy Kohler to Washington, June 25, 1965. Johnson Library, NSF, Country File, Vietnam, vol. 36, box 19.

39. *Ibid.*

40. *Ibid.*

41. Memorandum, H. Sonnenfeldt to L. Thompson, June 26, 1965, "Personal and Confidential." Library of Congress, W. Averell Harriman Papers, Special Files: Public Service, Trips and Missions, box 546.

42. Memorandum of Conversation, Rusk-Dobrynin, July 3, 1965. Johnson Library, NSF, Memos to the President, McGeorge Bundy, vol. 12, box 4. Emphasis added.

43. Rudy Abramson, *Spanning the Century: The Life of W. Averell Harriman, 1891–1986* (New York, 1992), p. 628.

44. *Ibid.*, p. 638.

45. Telephone Conversation, Harriman-McCloy, October 19, 1964. Harriman Papers, Special Files: Public Service, Chronological File, box 583.

46. Memorandum of Telephone Conversation, Harriman-Dobrynin, June 29, 1965. *Ibid.*

47. *Ibid.*

48. Johnson Library, NSF, Memos to the President, McGeorge Bundy, vol. 12, box 4.

49. Memorandum, "Governor Harriman's Trip," from Special Assistant Monteagle Stearns to Assistant Secretary of State for Public Affairs James L. Greenfield, July 6, 1965. Harriman Papers, box 546.

50. Telegram, U.S. Embassy in France to State Department, July 8, 1965. *Ibid.*, Chronological File, box 575.

51. Abramson, *Spanning the Century*, p. 638.

52. *The Johnson Presidential Press Conferences*, Vol. 1 (Stanfordville, N.Y., 1978), p. 342.

53. *Pravda*, July 16, 22, 1965.

54. Telegram, Harriman to Washington, July 23, 1965. Harriman Papers, Trips and Missions, box 546. See also Harriman's memorandum for the president and the secretary of state with excised portions on China, Germany, and Vietnam, in Johnson Library, NSF, Country File, Vietnam, Harriman Talks on Vietnam (July and August 1965), box 193.

55. Harriman's report on his conversation with Yugoslavian Foreign Minister Marko Nikezic, July 27, 1965. Harriman Papers, Trips and Missions, box 546.

56. Harriman's report for Johnson and Rusk. *Ibid.*

57. *Ibid.*

58. McG. Bundy to the President, July 15, 1965. Johnson Library, NSF, Memos to the President, McG. Bundy, vol. 12, box 4.

59. Memorandum, Thomas L. Hughes to Secretary Rusk "Kosygin's Suggestion of an American Counter Proposal to the Four Points," July 24, 1965. Harriman Papers, Trips and Missions, box 546.

60. Memorandum of Conversation, Harriman-Tito, July 28, 1965. Harriman Papers, Trips and Missions, box 546.

61. Gibbons, *U.S. Government and Vietnam War*, pp. 399–407.

62. *Ibid.*, p. 438.

63. Telegram, Kohler to Washington, August 6, 1965. Harriman Papers, Trips and Missions, box 546.

4. "A REAR AREA OF VIETNAM"

1. Directorate of Intelligence Memorandum, "The Vietnamese Communists' Will to Persist," 1966. NSA, V-23-24, Westmoreland vs. CBS, vol. IV, box 2.

2. Memorandum of Conversation, Pavlak–N. Kaliagin, December 18, 1965. SCCD, f. 5, op. 50, d. 777, p. 4.

3. "Vietnamese Communists' Will to Persist."

4. Report, "Socialist Countries' Economic Aid to the Democratic Republic of Vietnam," Research Institute of the USSR Ministry of Foreign Trade, November 1967. SCCD, f. 5, op. 59, d. 329, pp. 125–126. The Chinese shared at that time 44.8 per cent, or 666.2 million rubles.

5. Political Reports of the Soviet Embassy in Hanoi for 1967 and 1968. SCCD, f. 5, op. 59, d. 332, p. 26; *ibid.*, op. 60, d. 375, p. 48.

6. Their chagrin at Beijing's policy in the late 1970s notwithstanding, Hanoi admitted that in the last years of the war against the French, China provided Vietnam with the greatest supplies of military equipment and ammunition. See *Truth About Vietnam-China Relations Over the Last 30 Years*, p. 24. Apparently after 1954 China remained the leading supplier of weaponry for Vietnam; for example, before 1965 South Vietnamese "patriots" had arms mostly of Chinese origin. See Assistant Secretary of Defense McNaughton to General Westmoreland, February 9, 1965. NSA, V-16, Vietnam, Kahin Donation, box 3.

7. Memorandum, "Value of Soviet Military Aid to North Vietnam," October 26, 1965. Harriman Papers, Special Files, Subject File: Vietnam. General. Box 520.

8. Political Report for 1966. SCCD, f. 5, op. 58, d. 263, p. 148.

9. Political Report for 1967. *Ibid.,* op. 59, d. 332, p. 26.

10. Political Report for 1968. *Ibid.,* op. 60, d. 375, p. 48.

11. Monthly Intelligence Report, "The Situation in South Vietnam," June 4, 1965. NSA, V-16, Vietnam, Kahin Donation, box 4.

12. Intelligence Memorandum, "Shutdown of U.S. Aircraft on 24 July by Surface-to-Air Missile," July 26, 1965. Johnson Library, NSF, Country File, Vietnam, Special Intelligence Material, vol. VII, box 50.

13. According to the American intelligence report, one surface-to-air missile battalion, which could be moved from one site to another, normally consisted of six launchers and four missiles per launcher, plus a number of supporting vehicles and pieces of equipment. Because of their mobility, SAMs were almost invulnerable. This was demonstrated during an American air raid on August 9, aimed at destroying SAM sites detected by photo reconnaissance twelve hours earlier. The detected SAMs had been quickly removed, and the strike failed. See Memorandum, "Value of Soviet Military Aid to North Vietnam," and Special Intelligence Report, "Status of Soviet and Chinese Military Aid to North Vietnam," September 3, 1965, in Johnson Library, NSF, Country File, Vietnam, Special Intelligence Material, vol. VII, box 50.

14. Memorandum of Conversations between M. Isaev, an interpreter at the Soviet embassy to the DRV, and PLAF officers, May 14, 17, 20, 1966. SCCD, f. 5, op. 58, d. 264, p. 70.

15. Memorandum, "On Some New Moments in the Attitude of the Workers' Party of Vietnam Toward the Vietnamese Problem," June 30, 1967. SCCD, f. 5, op. 59, d. 327, p. 221.

16. NSA, V-16, Vietnam, Kahin Donation, box 3.

17. Special Report, "Status of Soviet and Chinese Military Aid to North Vietnam," September 3, 1965. Johnson Library, NSF, Country File, Vietnam, Special Intelligence Material, vol. VII, box 50.

18. Political Reports for 1966, 1967. SCCD, f. 5, op. 58, d. 263, p. 150; op. 59, d. 332, p. 27.

19. This opportunity was part of a broader Soviet plan to obtain information on American military hardware whenever possible. Apparently Boris Ponomarev, chief of the International Department, had this plan in mind when he prepared a memorandum to Soviet leaders on the expediency of charging the Ministry of Defense and its Main Intelligence Directorate (GRU) with the task of gathering data on U.S. weapons in Vietnam, the Dominican Republic, the Congo, and on the Indo-Pakistani border. SCCD, f. 5, op. 6, d. 294, "special dossier."

20. Memorandum of the Soviet Embassy in Hanoi on activities of the special group of Soviet experts to study American military hardware, March 14, 1967. SCCD, f. 5, op. 59, d. 329, p. 43.

21. Grechko to Brezhnev, April 17, 1968. *Ibid.*, op. 60, d. 232, pp. 9–10.

22. Papp, in *Vietnam*, considers the question of why Soviet personnel had been covertly sent to Vietnam. He argues that if the Soviet Union had sincerely wished to deter the United States, it would have taken this step publicly. "The Kremlin's reasoning may have gone along the following lines: Since the United States appeared to be strongly committed to achieving its goals in Vietnam and since the Kremlin realized that Hanoi and the Viet Cong were just as intent on achieving their objectives, it was probable that sizable U.S. ground forces in the South and prolonged U.S. air strikes against the North would be forthcoming. Despite Soviet interest in and concern for North Vietnam, Moscow did not desire a confrontation with the United States precipitated by North Vietnam. On the other hand, the Soviet Union found it necessary to fulfill its commitment to North Vietnam and provide effective air defenses. These air defenses, the SAM missiles, required trained personnel to be effective. The only personnel who were trained in their use were Soviet technicians, who therefore had to be sent to the D.R.V. To minimize the possibility of confrontation with the United States, the presence of Soviet personnel at the North Vietnamese missile sites was not publicized. In effect, the Soviet Union signaled the United States that it did not desire a Soviet-American confrontation. At the same time, the lack of official American comment on the Soviet technicians was a U.S. signal to Moscow that the U.S. similarly did not desire a confrontation" (pp. 68, 70).

23. *Soviet Union–Vietnam*, p. 598.

24. Research Memorandum, State Department Bureau of Intelligence and Research, "Volunteers for Vietnam—A Status Report," July 27, 1966. NSA, V-16, Vietnam, Kahin Donation, box 5.

25. *Ibid.*

26. Memorandum of the USSR Foreign Ministry's Southeast Asian Department, "Towards the Question of Sending Volunteers to Vietnam," August 9, 1966. SCCD, f. 5, op. 58, d. 262, pp. 82–85.

27. Intelligence Summary, "No Soviet Volunteers for North Vietnam," July 29, 1966. Johnson Library, NSF, Country File, Vietnam, Special Intelligence Material, vol. X(B), box 51.

28. USSR Ministry of Defense Memorandum, August 8, 1966. SCCD, f. 5, op. 58, d. 262, p. 168.

29. Political Report of the Soviet Embassy in Hanoi for 1968. SCCD, f. 5, op. 60, d. 375, p. 48.

30. "Vietnamese Communists' Will to Persist."

31. GRU to the CPSU CC International Department, December 1, 1966. SCCD, f. 5, op. 58, d. 254, p. 172.

32. Memorandum of Conversation, Shcherbakov–Nguyen Van Vinh, June 13, 1967. SCCD, f. 5, op. 59, d. 331, p. 109.

33. USSR Ministry of Defense Memorandum to the CPSU CC on Vietnam-China military cooperation, July 14, 1967. *Ibid.*, d. 416, p. 121. See also Memorandum of Conversation, G. Zverev, First Secretary of the Soviet Embassy in the DRV, and Vang Chuan, Second Secretary of the PRC Embassy in the DRV, July 1, 1966. *Ibid.*, op. 58, d. 262, p. 112.

34. *Ibid.* See also Intelligence Memorandum, "Chinese Communist Military Presence in North Vietnam," October 20, 1965. NSA, V-16, Vietnam, Kahin Donation, box 4; and "Vietnamese Communists' Will to Persist."

35. Memorandum of Conversation, M. Isaev–Ho Hai Thui, October 25, 1966. SCCD, f. 5, op. 58, d. 261, p. 163.

36. *Ibid.*, p. 164.

37. Douglas Pike argues in his *Vietnam and the Soviet Union*, p. 86: "I have never found plausible the frequently encountered assertion that the DRV did not want Chinese troops in the war because once in they would refuse to leave Vietnam. A contrary case can be built, that the DRV in 1965–1966 schemed to entrap the Chinese into the war but that the Chinese understood the game and refused to play it. In retrospect, it is clear that China saw Vietnam as a trap and had no intention of repeating its Korean mistake. However, to this day the opposite perception . . . persists among Americans." Apparently China did not wish to repeat its Korean mistake, but at the same time Chinese leaders were obviously not reluctant to use an opportunity to acquire additional leverage with Hanoi. And Chinese troops in North Vietnam could help Beijing in this matter. Therefore the Chinese desire to increase its forces in the DRV did not contradict Beijing's efforts to avoid a confrontation with the United States. As to North Vietnamese plans to entrap China, if such plans ever existed they apparently did not envisage large numbers of Chinese troops on Vietnamese territory. North Vietnamese leaders refused to invite even volunteers because of the danger that the numbers of "volunteers" from China inevitably would exceed those from other countries, and this might have "grave political consequences." See Political Letter of the Soviet Embassy in Cambodia, "Further Expansion of the American Aggression in Vietnam and Position of Cambodia," Summer–Fall 1966. SCCD, f. 5, op. 58, d. 324, p. 237.

38. Memorandum of Conversation between Kh. Kalinin, representative of the USSR State Committee of Foreign Trade Relations, and PRC Foreign Ministry official Ling Yuni, July 30, 1966. SCCD, f. 5, op. 58, d. 264, pp. 203–204.

39. Political Report of the Soviet Embassy in Hanoi for 1966. SCCD, f. 5, op. 58, d. 263, p. 140.

40. Memorandum of Conversation, Anatolii Ratanov–Gonzalez Valdez, the Cuban journalist, October 27, 1965. *Ibid.*, op. 50, d. 721, p. 284.

41. *Pravda* correspondent Ivan Shchedrov's memorandum for the CPSU Central Committee, "On the Situation in Indochina and Some Issues of Our Policy in the Region," 1966. *Ibid.*, f. 5, op. 58, d. 264, p. 96. The document had a note from Boris Ponomarev to the International Department: "Please read this memo and submit proposals and measures on issues that call for them."

42. Political Report for 1966, pp. 130, 141.

43. In its Political Letter, "The Soviet-Vietnamese Talks of April 1967" (p. 264), the Soviet embassy in Hanoi recommended constantly emphasizing to the North Vietnamese the danger of imperiling shipments through China, which could damage the struggle of the Vietnamese people because sea routes were becoming increasingly unreliable. The Soviet Union could not afford to confront the United States about U.S. air attacks on Soviet ships, though such a confrontation would have been applauded by Beijing.

44. GRU memorandum to the CPSU Central Committee, April 7, 1967. SCCD, f. 5, op. 59, d. 327, pp. 152–153.

45. Counsellor Podolskii to Moscow, December 26, 1966. *Ibid.*, pp. 18–21.

46. U. Alexis Johnson to Washington, January 26, 1965. NSA, V-16, Vietnam, Kahin Donation, box 3; Special National Intelligence Estimate, "Communist Reactions to Possible US Actions," February 11, 1965. *Ibid.*

47. Pike, *Vietnam and the Soviet Union,* pp. 56–57. This view was ingrained in Le Duan's speech to the twenty-third congress of the Soviet Communist party on March 30, 1966. He declared, ". . . In the present situation the urgent task of Communist and Workers' parties is a struggle in defense of peace in the world. At the same time it is necessary to unfold the revolution aimed at liberation of the working class, the laboring and oppressed peoples. These two tasks are tightly connected; they are to be solved in parallel. . . .

"Our Vietnamese people are waging a decisive struggle against the aggression of American imperialists and for independence of the motherland, and simultaneously we are contributing to the defense of the socialist camp, the independence of peoples, and peace in the world.

"We hope the socialist countries and Communist and Workers' parties are united with us, support us in every way, help us to beat the aggressors—the American imperialists." *Pravda,* March 31, 1966.

48. Political Report of the Soviet Embassy in Hanoi for 1966. SCCD, f. 5, op. 58, d. 263, p. 130.

49. *Ibid,* pp. 137–138.

50. Political Letter, "The Soviet-Vietnamese Talks of April 1967 and the Following Policy of the WPV Toward a Settlement of the Vietnamese Problem," August 1967. SCCD, f. 5, op. 59, d. 327, p. 256.

51. Political Report for 1966, p. 130.

52. *Ibid.*, p. 144.

53. Memorandum, "On Some Cases of Insincere Attitude of the Vietnamese Authorities and the PVA Command Toward the USSR and Soviet Specialists in the DRV," prepared by the USSR Ministry of Defense, July 28, 1966. SCCD, f. 5, op. 58, d. 263, pp. 48, 50.

54. *Ibid.*, p. 49.

55. This was the case when US F-111A was brought down and the Soviets needed to inspect its wreckage for a final report on the effectiveness of the Soviet antiaircraft complex "Dvina." On the report from Marshal Grechko to Brezhnev which, along with an account of the incident, contained complaints that the North Vietnamese denied access to the downed plane, there is a note: "This was used during the negotiations with Com[rade] Pham Van Dong." SCCD, f. 5, op. 60, d. 232, p. 9.

56. SCCD, f. 5, op. 60, d. 368, p. 21.

57. Political Report for 1968, p. 41.

58. Memorandum of the USSR Ministry of Commercial Shipping for the CPSU Central Committee, July 18, 1966. SCCD, f. 5, op. 58, d. 263, pp. 38–41. In

their comments on the facts cited by the Ministry, Soviet Communist party officials characterized some actions of the Haiphong port authorities as "unfriendly" and recommended discussing this problem during the forthcoming visit of the DRV party-governmental delegation to Moscow. K. Rusakov and A. Aggeev to CC Secretary Andrei Kirilenko, August 8, 1966. *Ibid.*, p. 43.

59. Ilyinski's Memorandum to the CPSU Central Committee, January 29, 1968. SCCD, f. 5, op. 60, d. 368, p. 19.

5. WILTED FLOWERS

1. SCCD, First Sector "special dossier," no. 3096, August 12, 1967.

2. *Militant Vanguard of the Vietnamese People*, p. 142.

3. *Ibid.*

4. Memorandum of Conversation, Mikhail S. Kapitsa, Acting Chief of the SEA Department, USSR Ministry of Foreign Affairs, and chargé d'affaires ad interim Le Trang, June 8, 1966. SCCD, f. 5, op. 58, d. 262, pp. 28–30.

5. *Ibid.*, pp. 39–40.

6. *Ibid.*, pp. 292–294.

7. Intelligence Memorandum, "French Involvement in Vietnam," June 17, 1966. Johnson Library, NSF, Country File, Vietnam. Southeast Asia, Special Intelligence Material, vol. X(B), box 51.

8. *Ibid.*

9. *Ibid.*

10. Memorandum of Conversation between Igor Usachev, Soviet chargé d'affaires ad interim in France, and Le Duc Tho, August 29, 1965. SCCD, f. 5, op. 50, d. 721, pp. 221–222.

11. The card file of "special dossiers" (*osobaya papka*) gives scholars an opportunity to note that France occupied the first position after the United States on the list of countries whose policy toward the war was under close scrutiny by Soviet intelligence. The next position belonged to Great Britain. The contents of the "special dossiers" remain classified.

12. Political Letter, "Cambodia and the Problem of South Vietnam," November 4, 1965. SCCD, f. 5, op. 50, d. 721, p. 262.

13. Political Report of the Soviet Embassy in the DRV for 1966. *Ibid.*, op. 58, d. 263, p. 161.

14. Douglas Pike in his book cited North Vietnamese cadres whom he met in POW camps in South Vietnam in 1967. The opinion held by those he interviewed was consistent: "Neither China nor the USSR was supporting 'the revolution' to the extent they should. Such support as that made available was for the wrong reason. Vital weaponry was withheld. The overriding point these cadres made was not how much China and the USSR had done for Vietnam but how much they had not done. This complaint of inadequate commitment was expressed by all without significant deviation. It led to the inescapable conclusion that the same perception, in somewhat more sophisticated form, extended upward to the Hanoi Command and the Politburo itself." (*Vietnam and the Soviet Union*, p. 84). Apparently the Soviet Union and China acted in this manner, pursuing different, sometimes even contradictory goals. Similar views on Soviet aid were relayed to a Soviet diplomat by one of his Vietnamese informants. According to the latter, many Vietnamese, though welcoming Moscow's aid to North Vietnam, were not satisfied with the extent of this aid and viewed it as even weaker than Soviet support of Vietnam in the period

1945–1955. See M. Isaev, interpreter at the Soviet embassy, to Moscow, October 1966. SCCD, f. 5, op. 58, d. 261, p. 166.

15. Memorandum of Conversation, Soviet attaché V. Sviridov–German attaché Klaus Matzke in Hanoi, February 28, 1967. SCCD, f. 5, op. 59, d. 330, pp. 109–112.

16. Memorandum of Conversation, Soviet chargé P. Privalov–Nguyen Van Vinh, August 23, 1966. SCCD, f. 5, op. 58, d. 264, pp. 173–174. Emphasis added.

17. *The History of the Joint Chiefs of Staff: The Joint Chiefs of Staff and the War in Vietnam, 1960–1968*. Part 2, p. 28/18. NSA, V-24, Johnson Library Documents Collections, box 5. (Hereafter *JCS History*.)

18. NSC Memorandum, "The Thirty-Seven Day Pause." NSA, V-16, Vietnam, Kahin Donation, box 5.

19. *JCS History*, p. 28/21.

20. Chester L. Cooper, *The Lost Crusade: America in Vietnam* (New York, 1970), pp. 292, 293.

21. Lyndon B. Johnson, *The Vantage Point: Perspectives of the Presidency, 1963–1969* (New York, 1971), p. 235.

22. See Political Letter, "Cambodia and the Problem of South Vietnam."

23. Memorandum of Conversation, Thompson-Dobrynin, December 28, 1965. Harriman Papers. Special Files: Public Service, Trips and Missions, PINTA, box 549.

24. *Ibid.*, Harriman Papers, Subject File: Vietnam, General, box 520.

25. Telephone Conversation, Johnson-Harriman, December 28, 1965. Harriman Papers, Chronological File, box 583.

26. Telephone Conversation, McNamara-Harriman, December 28, 1965. *Ibid.*

27. Abramson, *Spanning the Century*, p. 640.

28. U.S. Embassy in Warsaw to State Department, December 30, 1965. Harriman Papers, Special Files: Public Service, Trips and Missions, PINTA 3, box 548.

29. Harriman's cable from Teheran, "For President and Secretary of State," January 3, 1966. *Ibid.*, Chronological File, box 576.

30. Memorandum of Conversation, Harriman-Michalowski, February 10, 1969. *Ibid.*, Special Files: Public Service, Trips and Missions, PINTA 3, box 548.

31. First Viet Cong Cadre Report of Vinh Speech at COSVN Congress, March 1966. Library of Congress, Manuscript Division, Joseph H. Alsop Papers, Subject File, box 85.

32. Johnson, *Vantage Point*, p. 235.

33. SCCD, f. 5, op. 6, d. 533, no. 2461, July 21, 1966, "special dossier."

34. SCCD, f. 5, op. 6, d. 533, no. 3384, October 7, 1966, "special dossier."

35. Translated Goodlett's Memorandum, "Thoughts on the Possibility of a Peaceful Settlement of the Vietnamese Conflict." SCCD, f. 5, op. 50, d. 729, pp. 182–185.

36. GRU chief Petr I. Ivashutin to CPSU Central Committee, August 23, 1966. SCCD, f. 5, op. 58, d. 262, pp. 237–238. See also this document translated in English in *Cold War International History Project Bulletin*, 3 (Fall 1993), 61–62.

37. Memorandum, "The American Assessment of the International Situation. Series of Top-Level Conferences in the White House on the Question of the Principal Course of American Policy for the Period up to Summer 1968." Translated from the Hungarian. SCCD, f. 5, op. 58, d. 203, pp. 53–63.

38. Memorandum from Harriman "for the President and the Secretary of State," October 3, 1966. Johnson Library, NSF, Memos to the President, Walt Rostow, vol. 14, box 11.

39. Thomas L. Hughes, Director of Intelligence and Research, Department of State, to Walt Rostow, August 6, 1966. Johnson Library, NSF, Memos to the President, Walt Rostow, vol. 10, box 9.

40. *Ibid.*

41. Thompson's Memorandum for the President, July 15, 1966. Johnson Library, NSF, Memos to the President, Walt Rostow, vol. 9, box 9.

42. Memorandum from Harriman for the President and the Secretary of State, "Negotiations Committee," September 2, 1966. Harriman Papers, Special Files: Public Service, Subject File, Rusk, box 499. By this time Harriman, who had already been given responsibility for all matters concerning American prisoners of war in Vietnam, had been named the president's "ambassador for peace," implying that his task was to seek a peaceful settlement of the Vietnam conflict. Abramson writes: "Harriman never received his assignment in writing, and his mandate was never spelled out by the President. He professed to prefer it that way because he was left to define his own responsibilities. The title had a splendid sound, and he took it to mean that he was free to pursue any diplomatic route to peace." (*Spanning the Century*, p. 643). The "Negotiations Committee" was created as an organ to assist Harriman and explore every possibility to bring about negotiations between the U.S. and the DRV.

43. NSA, V-16, Vietnam, Kahin Donation, box 5.

44. Memorandum from Harriman to the President and the Secretary of State, "Points for President's Talk with Gromyko," October 7, 1966. Harriman Papers. Special Files: Public Service, Subject File, Vietnam, box 520; Memorandum, Walt Rostow to the President, "Meeting with Gromyko, 5 p.m. October 10, 1966." Johnson Library, NSF, Memos to the President, Walt Rostow, vol. 14, box 11.

45. L. Thompson's Memorandum on Johnson's meeting with Gromyko, October 14, 1966. Johnson Library, NSF, Country File, USSR, box 228.

46. George C. Herring, *LBJ and Vietnam: A Different Kind of War* (Austin, Tex., 1994), p. 104.

47. Herring, *Secret Diplomacy of the Vietnam War*, Marigold, Chronology, p. 237.

48. Telegram, Saigon to Secretary of State, July 9, 1966. *Ibid.*, p. 245.

49. Telegram, State Department to American Embassy, Saigon, November 13, 1966. *Ibid.*, p. 264.

50. Telegram, Saigon to Washington, November 30, 1966. *Ibid.*, p. 273.

51. *Ibid.*, p. 274.

52. Telegram, Warsaw to Secretary of State, December 15, 1966. *Ibid.*, p. 304.

53. KGB to CPSU Central Committee, December 13, 1965. SCCD, f. 5, op. 6, d. 341, "special dossier."

54. Memorandum of Conversation with the Minister-Counselor of the Polish Embassy in Moscow, August 18, 1966. SCCD, f. 5, op. 58, d. 262, pp. 178–179.

55. Memorandum of Conversation, Gromyko–Edmund Pszulkowski, November 21, 1966. SCCD, f. 5, op. 58, d. 264, pp. 199–202.

56. Political Report of the Soviet Embassy in the DRV for 1966. SCCD, f. 5, op. 58, d. 263, p. 140.

57. Herring, *Secret Diplomacy of the Vietnam War*, p. 315.

58. Memorandum of Conversation, J. McNaughton–A. Zinchuk, January 3, 1967. Johnson Library, NSF, Memos to the President, Walt Rostow, vol. 18, box 12.

59. Herring, *Secret Diplomacy of the Vietnam War*, p. 321.

60. Memorandum of Conversation, Dobrynin-Thompson, December 30, 1966. *Ibid.*, pp. 321–322.

61. Wallace J. Thies, *When Governments Collide: Coercion and Diplomacy in the Vietnam Conflict, 1964–1968* (Berkeley, 1980), p. 3.

62. Johnson Library, NSF, Memos to the President, Walt Rostow, vol. 18, box 12. Apparently Moscow had reasons for optimism despite the untoward events of December. As yet there is no documentary evidence of the source of this optimism; perhaps it is located in the "special dossiers," still closed, which contain memoranda of the conversations of Le Duc Tho with Brezhnev and Andropov, then secretary of the central committee, on December 15–17, 1966. Soviet leaders could not have helped but touch upon the problem of American–North Vietnamese contact and the prospects for negotiations. And the fact that these conversations took place at the time when American air strikes destroyed what little remained after Marigold added to this certainty. See Memorandum of Conversations between Brezhnev and Le Duc Tho, December 15 and 16, 1966; and Memorandum of Conversation between Yuri Andropov and Le Duc Tho, December 17, 1966. SCCD, VI Sector, no. 0676 and 0677.

63. Memorandum of Meeting, October 14, 1966. Harriman Papers, Special Files: Public Service, Subject File, Vietnam, box 520.

64. Johnson Library, NSF, Memos to the President, Walt Rostow, vol. 19, box 12.

65. Memorandum of Meeting, December 21, 1966. Harriman Papers, Special Files: Public Service, Subject File, Vietnam, box 520.

66. Johnson to Kosygin, January 21, 1967. Johnson Library, NSF, Files of Walt Rostow, box 10.

67. Herring, *Secret Diplomacy of the Vietnam War*, p. 376.

68. Political Report of the USSR Embassy in the DRV for 1966. SCCD, f. 5, op. 58, d. 263, p. 259.

69. *Ibid.*, pp. 259–260.

70. Telegram from the State Department to American Embassy, Moscow, January 5, 1967. Herring, *Secret Diplomacy of the Vietnam War*, Sunflower, Chronology, p. 413.

71. Telegram, Moscow to Secretary of State, January 10, 1967. *Ibid.*, p. 414.

72. Telegram, Moscow to Secretary of State, January 19, 1967. *Ibid.*, p. 418.

73. KGB's Report of January 28, 1967. SCCD, f. 5, op. 6, d. 680, no. 0284, "special dossier."

74. KGB Report of February 7, 1967. *Ibid.*, no. 0398, "special dossier." Unfortunately the exact contents of these two reports are unknown because they remain classified, but it is not difficult to deduce them on the basis of already available documents.

75. Memorandum of Conversation, Shcherbakov–Nguyen Duy Trinh, January 27, 1967. SCCD, f. 5, op. 59, d. 327, p. 92. The memorandum was sent to Gromyko and Andropov.

76. Telegram, Moscow to Secretary of State, January 27, 1967. Herring, *Secret Diplomacy of the Vietnam War*, pp. 419–420.

77. *Ibid.*, p. 424.

78. Telegram, State Department to American Embassy, Moscow and Saigon, January 31, 1967. *Ibid.*, pp. 424–425.

79. Memorandum of Conversation, Shcherbakov–Pham Van Dong, January 30, 1967. SCCD, f. 5, op. 59, d. 327, p. 81.

80. *Ibid.*

81. Wilson, *Labour Government*, p. 345.

82. Johnson, *Vantage Point*, p. 253.

83. Cooper, *Lost Crusade*, p. 356.

84. SCCD, f. 5, op. 59, d. 327, pp. 95–97.

85. Memorandum of Conversation, Shcherbakov–Pham Van Dong, February 4, 1967. *Ibid.*, p. 104.

86. Cooper, *Lost Crusade*, p. 355.

87. Herring, *Secret Diplomacy of the Vietnam War*, p. 434.

88. *Ibid.*; Wilson, *Labour Government*, p. 348.

89. Herring, *Secret Diplomacy of the Vietnam War*, p. 439; Wilson, *Labour Government*, p. 356.

90. Herring, *Secret Diplomacy of the Vietnam War*, pp. 398, 441.

91. Johnson, *Vantage Point*, pp. 253–254.

92. Wilson, *Labour Government*, p. 358.

93. David Bruce, U.S. ambassador in London, strongly recommended postponing the resumption of the bombing until after Kosygin left London. The ambassador was apprehensive about the possible effect of the bombing on the Soviet premier's attitude toward cooperation with the United States on Vietnam. (See telegram from Bruce to Secretary Rusk, February 11, 1967, in Herring, *Secret Diplomacy of the Vietnam War*, pp. 457–458.) A similar recommendation had earlier been sent to the president and the secretary of state by Harriman, who insisted on February 2 that "the pause be extended for the full seven-day Tet period and beyond for a sufficient length of time to permit a reaction from Hanoi." (Harriman Papers, Special Files: Public Service, Subject File, Vietnam, box 520.)

94. State Department to American Embassy, London, February 13, 1967. Herring, *Secret Diplomacy of the Vietnam War*, p. 467.

95. Author's interview with Oleg A. Troyanovski, October 5, 1994. Troyanovski testified that Kosygin's aides dissuaded him from such a step out of concern that it would undermine the premier's position in this Soviet body.

96. Memo of Conversation, Cooper–D. Kraslow and St. Loory of the *Los Angeles Times*, November 8, 1967. Harriman Papers, Special Files: Public Service, Subject File, box 451.

97. Herring, *Secret Diplomacy of the Vietnam War*, p. 400.

98. Memorandum of Conversation, Shcherbakov–Pham Van Dong, February 13, 1967. SCCD, f. 5, op. 59, d. 327, p. 116.

99. Telegram, Moscow to Secretary of State, February 18, 1967. Herring, *Secret Diplomacy of the Vietnam War*, pp. 485–487.

100. Memorandum of Conversation, Shcherbakov–Nguyen Duy Trinh, February 15, 1967. SCCD, f. 5, op. 59, d. 327, p. 149.

6. GLASSBORO

1. Political Letter of the Soviet Embassy in the DRV, "The Soviet-Vietnamese Talks of April 1967 and the Following Policy of the WPV Toward Settlement of the Vietnamese Problem," August 1967. SCCD, f. 5, op. 59, d. 327, pp. 257, 258.

2. *Militant Vanguard of the Vietnamese People*, p. 156.

3. Counselor Podolskii to Moscow, December 26, 1966. SCCD, f. 5, op. 59, d. 327, p. 18.

4. "The Soviet-Vietnamese Talks of April 1967," p. 259.

5. *Ibid.*, p. 255; USSR Foreign Ministry Memorandum, "On Some New Moments in the Position of the WPV Toward the Vietnamese Problem," June 30, 1967. SCCD, f. 5, op. 59, d. 327, p. 221.

6. "The Soviet-Vietnamese Talks of April 1967," p. 255.

7. "The Soviet-Vietnamese Talks of April 1967," p. 263.

8. Thies, *When Governments Collide*, p. 168.

9. *Ibid.*, pp. 170, 171.

10. U.S.-China bilateral talks had begun between consular officials of the United States and the People's Republic of China in 1954 in Geneva. These talks were raised to the ambassadorial level in 1955 and later moved to Warsaw. From 1954 through 1968 representatives of the two countries met 134 times. See Han Nianlong, et al., eds., *Diplomacy of Contemporary China* (Hong Kong, 1990), pp. 119–131.

11. Telegram, Moscow to Secretary of State, March 4, 1967; telegram, State Department to American Embassy, Moscow, March 4, 1967. Herring, *Secret Diplomacy of the Vietnam War*, pp. 497–498. Thompson was able to deliver this denial in his conversation with Gromyko on March 23. *Ibid.*, p. 502.

12. Counselor Podolskii to Moscow, February 11, 1967. SCCD, f. 5, op. 59, d. 327, p. 115.

13. See Chapter 5 above.

14. Telegram, State Department to American Embassy, Moscow, March 12, 1967. Herring, *Secret Diplomacy of the Vietnam War*, pp. 498–499.

15. Telegram, Moscow to Secretary of State, March 13, 1967, and State Department to American Embassy, Moscow, same date. *Ibid.*, p. 499.

16. Telegram, Moscow to Secretary of State, March 21, 1967. *Ibid.*, p. 501.

17. *Ibid.*, pp. 504–505. Johnson, *Vantage Point*, p. 256.

18. Cooper's Memorandum, "The Negotiations Track—Another Look," March 11, 1967. Harriman Papers, Special Files: Public Service, Subject File, Vietnam, box 520.

19. *Ibid.* Emphasis added.

20. Thies, *When Governments Collide*, pp. 173–176.

21. Harriman's Memorandum to Under Secretary of State, April 19, 1967. Harriman Papers, Special Files: Public Service, Subject File, box 478.

22. Cooper, *Lost Crusade*, pp. 373–374.

23. Telegram, Moscow to Secretary of State, April 19, 1967. Johnson Library, NSF, Country File, USSR, box 223. The gist of the telegram is in Herring, *Secret Diplomacy of the Vietnam War*, pp. 506–507.

24. Telegram, Moscow to Secretary of State, April 25, 1967. Herring, *Diplomacy of the Vietnam War*, p. 507.

25. Johnson Library, NSF, Country File, USSR, box 223.

26. Information on Zhukov in CIA's Office of Central Reference Biographic Register. *Ibid.*

27. Memorandum of Conversation, Harriman-Zhukov, April 18, 1967. Harriman Papers, Special Files: Public Service, Subject File, Vietnam, box 520. Zhukov was accompanied in this conversation by Sergei Vishnevskii, Washington correspondent for *Pravda*, and Oleg Kalugin, then press attaché of the Soviet embassy. The American side included Chester Cooper and Vladimir Toumanoff, the Soviet expert from the State Department. Although Zhukov not infrequently undertook his trips to the United States and meetings with American prominent politicians on his own initiative, without the blessings of the highest Soviet authorities (author's

interview with Dobrynin and Nikolai N. Detinov of the CPSU CC, May 1994), the presence of Kalugin, who, as is well known now, was a KGB man, at this particular conversation, added more importance to Zhukov's words than a mere restatement of official attitudes.

28. Telegram, American Embassy, Moscow, to Secretary of State, May 12, 1967. Johnson Library, NSF, Country File, USSR, box 223.

29. Telegram, State Department to American Embassy, London, May 16, 1967. Herring, *Secret Diplomacy of the Vietnam War*, pp. 508–509.

30. Harriman's Memorandum to the President and Secretary Rusk, "Negotiations—Soviet Union," May 15, 1967. Harriman Papers, Special Files: Public Service, Subject File, box 499.

31. Telegram, State Department to American Embassy, Moscow, May 18, 1967. Johnson Library, NSF, Country File, USSR, box 223.

32. Telegram, Moscow to Secretary of State, May 19, 1967. *Ibid.*

33. *Pravda*, June 3, 1967.

34. Johnson Library, NSF, Country File, USSR, box 223.

35. Position Paper, "Bilateral US-USSR Issues," June 20, 1967. Johnson Library, NSF, Country File, USSR, box 229. In his memoirs McNamara explains Washington's reply, though he mistakenly refers to the preceding year. See *In Retrospect*, p. 245 *passim.*

36. *Pravda*, June 6, 1967.

37. Thompson to Katzenbach, June 1967. Johnson Library, NSF, Country File, USSR, box 230.

38. Telegram, Moscow to Secretary of State, June 16, 1967. *Ibid.*

39. Rostow, Memorandum to Johnson, June 14, 1967. *Ibid.*

40. Harriman, Memorandum for the President, "Possible Kosygin Talks on Vietnam Settlement," June 17, 1967. Johnson Library, NSF, Memos to the President, Walt Rostow, vol. 31, box 17.

41. Rusk to Johnson, June 17, 1967. *Ibid.*

42. Norman Davis, Memorandum for the Record, June 20, 1967. *Ibid.*

43. Arthur Goldberg to Washington, June 20, 1967. Johnson Library, NSF, Country File, USSR, box 230.

44. Intelligence Note, "Kosygin's Reasons for Wanting to Meet the President," June 22, 1967. *Ibid.*

45. He dictated over the telephone from New York on June 21, 1967: "I do not think, in view of the high level public declaration of the Central Committee, that a meeting will result in any specific agreement on any specific question. If, however, the President could put the question to Kosygin whether he thought that if our bombing in Viet Nam were cut back to the actual invasion routes in southern Viet Nam, there might be some response from the other side or whether this would enable the Soviets to be more helpful, I believe that this, plus the effect of the President's personality on Kosygin, would enable, when he goes back, to influence his colleagues in a better direction." *Ibid.*

46. Memorandum of Conversation, Rusk-Kosygin, Soviet UN Mission in New York, June 22, 1967. *Ibid.*

47. *Pravda*, June 20, 1967.

48. American UN Mission to Washington, June 20, 1967. Johnson Library, NSF, Country File, USSR, box 230.

49. Memorandum of Conversation, Rusk-Gromyko, June 22, 1967. *Ibid.*

50. Political Letter, "The Soviet-Vietnamese Talks of April 1967 . . . ." SCCD, f. 5, op. 59, d. 327, p. 258.

51. Memorandum of Conversation, Johnson-Kosygin (1), June 23, 1967, Glassboro, N.J. Johnson Library, NSF, Country File, USSR, Addendum.

52. Memorandum of Conversation, Johnson-Kosygin (2), June 23, 1967. *Ibid.*

53. Johnson, *Vantage Point*, p. 257.

54. Rusk's Memorandum to the President, June 24, 1967. Johnson Library, NSF, Country File, USSR, Addendum.

55. *Ibid.*; Johnson, *Vantage Point*, p. 257.

56. Memorandum of Conversation, Johnson-Kosygin, June 25, 1967. Johnson Library, NSF, Country File, USSR, Addendum.

57. During his first conversation with President Johnson, on June 23, Kosygin himself defined the purpose of the meeting by saying that "there was a great deal of clarification needed in order to understand each other's actions, particularly during the recent period of time. The direction that US policy was taking was not clear to him and to his colleagues in the Government of the USSR. Therefore, he proposed to take advantage of this meeting in order to better understand us and to be better understood by us." Memorandum of Conversation, Johnson-Kosygin, June 23, 1967. Johnson Library, NSF, Country File, USSR, Addendum.

58. Shcherbakov mentioned it in his Embassy's Political Letter, "The Soviet-Vietnamese Talks of April 1967. . . ." SCCD, f. 5, op, 59, d. 327, p. 263.

59. Johnson, *Vantage Point*, p. 257.

7. THE ROAD TO PARIS

1. McNamara, *In Retrospect*, pp. 283–290. Allan E. Goodman, *The Lost Peace: America's Search for a Negotiated Settlement of the Vietnam War* (Stanford, 1978), pp. 57–58.

2. Clark Clifford, with Richard Holbrooke, *Counsel to the President: A Memoir* (New York, 1991), p. 455.

3. Harriman's Memorandum, "Is Hanoi Signaling?" July 28, 1967. Harriman Papers, Special Files: Public Service, Subject File, Vietnam, box 520.

4. Harriman's Memorandum to Rusk, September 20, 1967. *Ibid.*, box 499.

5. William Appleman Williams, Thomas J. McCormick, Lloyd C. Gardner, and Walter LaFeber, eds., *America in Vietnam: A Documented History* (New York, 1985), p. 266.

6. Clifford, *Counsel to the President*, p. 471.

7. Political Letter, "The Soviet-Vietnamese Talks of April 1967," p. 257.

8. *Ibid.*, p. 263.

9. Don Oberdorfer, *Tet! The Turning Point in the Vietnam War* (New York, 1985), p. 44.

10. Political Letter, "The Soviet-Vietnamese Talks of April 1967," p. 264.

11. Oberdorfer, *Tet!*, p. 54.

12. *Pravda*, September 24, 1967.

13. Classified Memorandum of Conversation, Brezhnev, Kosygin, Podgornyi–Le Duan, October 31, 1967. SCCD, First Sector, no. 4400, November 13, 1967, "special dossier."

14. Political Report of the Soviet Embassy in Hanoi for 1967. SCCD, f. 5, op. 59, d. 332, pp. 133–137. There is a great temptation to suggest that the whole idea of the Tet offensive belonged to the Soviets. Or at least that during the offensive the North Vietnamese followed Moscow's advice, directing their attacks primarily at the Saigon regime and trying to avoid encounters with the Americans. (See, for

example, Oberdorfer, *Tet!*, p. 180.) No additional facts confirm this hypothesis, but there is sufficient evidence to question Hanoi's obeisance to plans imposed by Moscow. On similar shaky grounds, one could suspect the United States as secretly standing behind the Tet offensive. The government of South Vietnam had such a suspicion. (See *ibid.*) Likewise, one can hardly agree with Parker (*Vietnam*, pp. 184–186) that by supporting the offensive the Soviets were aiming at China. The Soviet government could scarcely use the offensive to nourish a grand design to undermine Mao's positions in the "cultural revolution" in China by means of Viet Cong operations in South Vietnam.

15. *Militant Vanguard of the Vietnamese People*, p. 156.

16. *Ibid.*

17. *Pravda*, January 4, 1968.

18. Oberdorfer, *Tet!*, p. 68.

19. Memorandum of Conversation, S. I. Divilkovskii, First Secretary of the Soviet Embassy–Truong Cong Dong, January 8, 1968. SCCD, f. 5 op. 60, d. 372, p. 10.

20. *Ibid.*, p. 11.

21. Papp, *Vietnam*, p. 89; Clifford, *Counsel to the President*, p. 467.

22. Oberdorfer, *Tet!*, p. 116.

23. *Ibid.*, p. 141.

24. Clifford, *Counsel to the President*, pp. 474–475.

25. See a story about the preparation of the March 31 speech in Clifford, *Counsel to the President*, pp. 508–526.

26. Oberdorfer, *Tet!*, p. 256.

27. Summary of a speech by chairman of the Lao Dong party Reunification Department, Gen. Nguyen Van Vinh, at a COSVN Congress, April 1966. *Vietnam: The Definitive Documentation of Human Decisions*, p. 419.

28. Report of the Soviet Embassy in Hanoi, "Military-Political Results of the Third 'Dry Season' Struggle in South Vietnam," June 23, 1968. SCCD, f. 5, op. 60, d. 372, p. 115.

29. Telegram, Walt Rostow to the President, March 16, 1968. NSA, V-24, LBJ Library Document Collections, box 5.

30. Clifford, *Counsel to the President,* p. 520.

31. Harriman's Memorandum to Rusk, March 29, 1968. Harriman Papers, Special Files: Public Service, Subject File, box 500.

32. Oberdorfer, *Tet!,* p. 319.

33. Williams, et al., *America in Vietnam,* pp. 273–275.

34. *Pravda,* April 2, 1968.

35. *Izvestiia,* April 2, 1968.

36. Memorandum of Conversation, Dobrynin-Harriman, April 1, 1968. Johnson Library, NSF, Country File, USSR, Memos, vol. XIX, box 225.

37. Memorandum of Conversation, Dobrynin–Eugene Rostow, April 27, 1968. *Ibid.*

38. I agree on this point with Daniel Papp, who analyzes the reaction of the Soviet Union toward the March 31 announcement about changes in U.S. policy in Vietnam. See Papp, *Vietnam,* pp. 105–106.

39. George C. Herring, "The Reluctant Warrior: Lyndon Johnson as Commander in Chief," in David Anderson, ed., *Shadow on the White House: Presidents and the Vietnam War, 1945–1975* (Lawrence, Kans., 1993), p. 104.

40. Memorandum of Conversation, Dobrynin-Harriman, April 1, 1968. Johnson Library, NSF, Country File, USSR, Memos, vol. XIX, box 225.

41. Clifford, *Counsel to the President,* p. 529; *Pravda,* April 4, 1968.

42. For example, Douglas Pike believes that "The DRV's decision to go to Paris and begin talks with the United States appears to have caught the USSR off guard, even though Hanoi had been intimating interest for several months." (*Vietnam and the Soviet Union,* p. 94.)

43. SCCD, f. 5, op. 6, d. 787, no. 0644, "special dossier."

44. SCCD, First Sector, no. 1330, April 15, 1968, "special dossier."

45. CIA Memorandum, "Speculation on Hanoi's Motives," April 8, 1968. Johnson Library, NSF, Country File, Vietnam, Talks with Hanoi, box 96.

46. Bureau of Intelligence and Research Report, "Soviet View of the DRV Government Statement on Negotiations," April 3, 1968. *Ibid.*

47. CIA Intelligence Information Cable, "The Views of North Vietnamese Leaders on Peace Negotiations," May 1, 1968. *Ibid.*

48. From the outset Thompson regarded Johnson's decision about his assignment as U.S. representative, along with Harriman, in negotiations with North Vietnam, as undesirable. He told Harriman, when the latter called to inform him about the president's intention, that "it was better that only an independent person, that is not one directly dealing with the Soviets as himself, be named." (Synopsis of Harriman's Telephone Conversation with Thompson, March 31, 1968. Harriman Papers, Special Files: Public Service, Chronological File, box 580.) The same arguments were probably put forward by Thompson in his conversation with Johnson on April 4.

At the same time some members of the administration were suspicious about Harriman's ability to talk to the North Vietnamese along the lines accepted by the White House. Rostow wrote Johnson that he and Maxwell Taylor, the former ambassador to South Vietnam, doubted that the "Ambassador for Peace" was "the man to carry this negotiation—should it develop—beyond its first stage." They believed that Harriman's health would not allow him to sustain such an "arduous effort." Harriman "lacks—and has always lacked—an understanding and sympathy for the South Vietnamese." Therefore Rostow recommended that the president consider "selecting now the man who will carry this negotiation for the long pull, should it develop, and place him in charge of the full-time task force." Rostow's choice was Cyrus Vance. (Johnson Library, NSF, Country File, Vietnam, Talks with Hanoi, box 96.)

Johnson apparently followed Rostow's advice, particularly because he thought highly of Vance.

49. Memorandum of Telephone Conversation, Harriman-Vance, April 11, 1968. Harriman Papers. Special Files: Public Service, Chronological File, box 580.

50. Memorandum of Telephone Conversation, Johnson-Harriman, April 11, 1968. *Ibid.*

51. Johnson Library, NSF, Country File, Vietnam, Talks with Hanoi, box 96.

52. Political Letter of the Soviet Embassy in the DRV, "Soviet-Vietnamese Relations After the April 1968 Negotiations," September 1, 1968. SCCD, f. 5, op. 60, d. 369, p. 107.

53. *Pravda,* April 13, 1968.

54. Cables from Bromley Smith, executive secretary of the National Security Council, to Walt Rostow, April 15, 1968. Johnson Library, NSF, Country File, Vietnam, box 96.

55. In his telephone conversation with Rusk, Harriman informed the secretary that he had met with Dobrynin who told him "very privately" that Moscow was talking with Hanoi about sites. Dobrynin wanted to make sure the Americans op-

posed Warsaw. Memorandum of Telephone Conversation, Harriman-Rusk, April 24, 1968. Harriman Papers, Special Files: Public Service, Chronological File, box 580. See also Memorandum of Conversation, Dobrynin–Eugene Rostow, April 27, 1968. Johnson Library, NSF, Country File, USSR, Memos, vol. XIX, box 225.

56. Rusk to Walt Rostow, April 17, 1968. Johnson Library, NSF, Country File, Vietnam, Talks with Hanoi, box 96.

57. This is contrary to later assurances by members of the administration that Washington deliberately omitted Paris from its list so as to avoid outright rejection by Hanoi and thus to make this city an acceptable alternative. On this point see Clifford, *Counsel to the President*, p. 536; Dean Rusk, *As I Saw It* (New York, 1990), p. 485. It may be revealing that Lyndon Johnson does not mention this foresight in his memoirs. (*Vantage Point*, pp. 503–504.) More likely the president's advisers deliberately omitted Paris because they knew of Johnson's dislike of de Gaulle and French policy toward Vietnam.

58. Harriman's "Memorandum for the Secretary," April 18, 1968. Harriman Papers, Special Files: Public Service, Subject File, Vietnam, box 521.

59. CIA Intelligence Information Cable, "The Views of North Vietnamese Leaders on Peace Negotiations," May 1, 1968. Johnson Library, NSF, Country File, Vietnam, Talks with Hanoi, box 96.

60. CIA Memorandum, "Significance of Paris as Site for Vietnamese Negotiations," May 6, 1968. *Ibid.*

61. Memorandum of Conversation, V. I. Chivilev, Chargé d'Affaires ad interim, and Le Duan, First Secretary of the Workers' Party of Vietnam Central Committee, May 2, 1968. SCCD, f. 5, op. 60, d. 376, pp. 47–50. Emphasis added.

62. *Johnson Presidential Press Conferences*, vol. 2, pp. 937–938; Johnson, *Vantage Point*, pp. 504–505.

63. Political Report of the Soviet Embassy in Hanoi for 1968. SCCD, f. 5, op. 60, d. 375, p. 31.

8. "VERY TOUGH GOING"

1. Johnson, *Vantage Point*, p. 505.

2. Abramson, *Spanning the Century*, p. 661.

3. *Ibid.*, p. 659.

4. Instructions for Governor Harriman, Draft. Harriman Papers, Special Files: Public Service, Subject File, Paris Peace Talks, box 557.

5. Memorandum of Conversation, Soviet chargé in Peking Yuri Razdukhov–Cuban chargé Garcia, May 23, 1968. SCCD, f. 5, op. 60, d. 365, p. 92.

6. Thomas Kolesnichenko, "The Pulse of the Planet," *Pravda*, May 12, 1968.

7. *Pravda*, May 17, 1968.

8. Yuri Zhukov, "Aggressors Must Go Home," *Pravda*, May 19, 1968.

9. Memorandum of Conversation, Dobrynin-Harriman, April 8, 1968. Johnson Library, NSF, Country File, USSR, Memos, vol. XIX, box 225.

10. 1968 Calendar Book. Harriman Papers. Special Files: Public Service, Chronological File, box 577.

11. Memorandum of Telephone Conversation, Harriman-Bogomolov, May 15, 1968. *Ibid.*, Subject File, Paris Peace Talks, box 557.

12. *Ibid.*

13. Memorandum of Conversation, Harriman-Oberemko, May 17, 1968. *Ibid.* Emphasis added.

14. Memorandum of Conversation, Harriman-Zorin, May 19, 1968. Harriman Papers, Special Files: Public Service, Subject File, Paris Peace Talks, HARVAN and HARVAN/PLUS, box 559. The conversation was also attended by Bogomolov, U.S. ambassador in Paris Sargent Shriver, and second secretary of the U.S. embassy Jack Perry.

15. *Ibid.*

16. Harriman to Secretary of State, May 25, 1968. *Ibid.*

17. Memorandum of Conversation, Harriman-Zorin, May 25, 1968. *Ibid.*

18. Memorandum of Conversation, Harriman-Zorin, May 27, 1968. *Ibid.*

19. Memorandum of Conversation, Dobrynin-Harriman, June 22, 1968. Johnson Library, NSF, Country File, USSR, box 229. Dobrynin's reply is sanitized, unfortunately, because Dobrynin would scarcely report his characteristics of Zorin to Moscow.

20. Abramson, *Spanning the Century*, p. 661.

21. Political Report of the Soviet Embassy in Hanoi for 1967. SCCD, f. 5, op. 59, d. 332, p. 14.

22. Kosygin's letter to Johnson, June 5, 1968. Johnson Library, NSF, Files of Walt Rostow, box 10.

23. Johnson, *Vantage Point*, p. 510.

24. Notes of the President's Meeting with Foreign Policy Advisers, June 9, 1968. Johnson Library, Tom Johnson's Notes of Meetings, box 3.

25. Clifford, *Counsel to the President*, p. 546.

26. Notes of Meeting, June 9, 1968.

27. *Ibid.*

28. Abramson, *Spanning the Century*, p. 664.

29. "General Review of Last Six Months," December 14, 1968. Harriman Papers, Special Files: Public Service, Trips and Missions, box 562. In this memorandum Harriman also criticized Rusk for his behavior during the discussion of a response to Kosygin's letter. On the meeting among Rusk, Clifford, and Harriman before their appointment with the president, Rusk took a generally favorable position toward Clifford's arguments—at least he did not oppose them. Later, in the White House, he changed his position and virtually destroyed Clifford's arguments before they were even presented. "What appalled me," Harriman wrote, "was that Rusk took this negative position without telling Clifford that he was going to do it, and without indicating to the President that Clifford had a different point of view. He clearly attempted to cut the ground out from under Clifford before he had a chance to present his position."

30. Johnson's Letter to Kosygin, June 11, 1968. Johnson Library, NSF, Files of Walt Rostow, box 10. Emphasis added.

31. Memorandum of Conversation, Dobrynin-Harriman, June 22, 1968. Johnson Library, NSF, Country File, USSR, box 229.

32. Memorandum of Conversation, Dobrynin–Llewellyn Thompson, June 13, 1968. Johnson Library, NSF, Country File, USSR, box 225.

33. Memorandum of Conversation, Dobrynin–Charles Bohlen, Deputy Under Secretary for Political Affairs, June 12, 1968. NSA, Lyndon B. Johnson Library Collection.

34. Memorandum of Conversation, Dobrynin-Harriman, June 22, 1968. Johnson Library, NSF, Country File, USSR, box 229.

35. Political Letter of the Soviet Embassy in Hanoi, "Soviet-Vietnamese Relations After the April Talks of 1968," September 1, 1968. SCCD, f. 5, op. 60, d. 369, p. 108. The letter analyzes developments in bilateral relations after Pham Van Dong's secret visit to Moscow in April 1968.

36. *Ibid.*, p. 109.

37. *Truth on Vietnam-China Relations,* p. 49.

38. Memorandum of the Soviet Embassy in the PRC, "China's Attitude Toward the Negotiations Between the DRV and the U.S.A.," August 22, 1968. SCCD, f. 5, op. 60, d. 365, pp. 152–153.

39. Soviet Embassy in Beijing, Political Report for 1968. SCCD, f. 5, op. 60, d. 367, p. 89.

40. *Foreign Policy and International Relations of the PRC,* p. 131.

41. Memorandum of the CPSU CC Department on Relations with Communist parties of Socialist Countries, "On New Elements of the Foreign Policy and International Positions of the PRC," June 10, 1968. SCCD, f. 5, op. 60, d. 365, p. 103.

42. *Truth on Vietnam-China Relations,* p. 50. Although these revelations were published by Hanoi after its relations with the DRV's powerful northern neighbor had deteriorated, and the Vietnamese were more than eager to condemn their former allies, they probably were not far from the truth considering Beijing's theory of people's wars and its application to South Vietnam.

43. "China's Attitude Toward the Negotiations Between the DRV and the U.S.A.," pp. 159–160.

44. Memorandum of Conversation, Zorin-Harriman, June 13, 1968. Harriman Papers, Special Files: Public Service, Subject File, box 559. On the Soviet side Oberemko and Bogomolov, and on the American side Vance and Jack Perry, were also present.

45. Bien ban gap rieng giua ta va Ny, 1968. Bo 1, tap. E. (Transcripts of the Report on Private Meetings Between the Vietnamese and American People from the Two Delegations).

46. Memorandum of Conversation, Soviet Ambassador Shcherbakov–Nguyen Duy Trinh, June 26, 1968. SCCD, f. 5, op. 60, d. 373, p. 40.

47. Paul Warnke's Memorandum to Clifford, July 1, 1968. Johnson Library, Papers of Clark Clifford, box 26.

48. Harriman to Secretary of State, NODIS/HARVAN/PLUS, July 16, 1968. Harriman Papers, Special Files: Public Service, Subject File, box 559.

49. Memorandum of Conversation, Rusk-Dobrynin, July 8, 1968. Johnson Library, NSF, Country File, USSR, box 229.

50. Harriman's memorandum, "General Review of Last Six Months," December 14, 1968. Harriman Papers, Special Files: Public Service, Trips and Missions, box 562.

51. Walt Rostow's Memorandum to the President, July 12, 1968. Johnson Library, NSF, Files of Walt Rostow, box 10.

52. "General Review of Last Six Months."

53. Clifford, *Counsel to the President,* p. 567.

54. "General Review of Last Six Months."

55. *Pravda*, April 3, 1966.

56. *Ibid.* Emphasis added.

57. Some American analysts were highly sensitive to the influence of the Vietnam War on the international situation and on Soviet interventionist ardor. In April 1967 a member of the State Department policy planning staff, Zbigniew Brzezinski, prepared a memorandum, "The US, the Soviet Union, and Détente," in

which he expounded his vision of Moscow's policy during U.S. involvement in the conflict in Indochina. Brzezinski believed the Soviet leadership recognized U.S. eagerness to develop friendly relations with the USSR and used it to pursue "with impunity a relatively hard-nosed, conservative foreign policy without jeopardizing those aspects of détente that are in the Soviet interests." The main factor that assisted the Soviets in such a course was, according to Brzezinski, the preoccupation of the American administration with the Vietnam War. "From the Soviet point of view," Brzezinski argued, "the war in Vietnam appears to have increased U.S. eagerness to cultivate cooperative relations with the Soviet Union. This condition, Soviet leaders might reason, can be exploited to stimulate European fears of U.S.-Soviet 'complicity.' At the same time, it reduces the pressure on the Soviet Union to accommodate with the West which otherwise the Sino-Soviet dispute might have generated." From this Brzezinski concluded that the war in Southeast Asia, though it created risks for Moscow, had some "very definite advantages" for the Soviets. "It gives the Soviet Union a free hand for a policy of dividing the Europeans from the United States and of isolating China, while at the same time remaining the object of U.S. efforts to improve U.S.-Soviet relations." Thus the essence of Soviet policy, Brzezinski concluded, was to exploit the U.S. posture, and in so doing "the Soviet Union need not make any basic sacrifices or changes in its policy. It suffices to make occasional peaceful noises about Vietnam, while providing North Vietnam with sufficient aid to keep the war going. . . ." Johnson Library, NSF, Country File, USSR, Memos, vol. 15, box 223.

58. Andrei M. Alexandrov-Agentov, *From Kollontai to Gorbachev: Memoirs of Diplomat, Adviser of A. A. Gromyko, Aide to L. I. Brezhnev, Yu. V. Andropov, K. U. Chernenko, and M. S. Gorbachev* (Moscow, 1994), p. 144.

59. During the last days of World War II Brezhnev participated in the liberation of Czechoslovakia from the Nazis.

60. See, for example, Alexandrov-Agentov, *From Kollontai to Gorbachev*, pp. 152–153.

61. *Pravda,* August 23, 1968.

62. Johnson, *Vantage Point,* p. 486.

63. Clifford, *Counsel to the President,* p. 561.

64. He admitted this and even told of preparations for a Soviet-American summit. See Johnson, *Vantage Point,* p. 489.

65. Notes of Johnson's meeting with top U.S. administration officials, October 14, 1968. Johnson Library, Tom Johnson's Notes of Meetings, box 4.

66. *Pravda,* August 23, 1968.

67. Editorial, "The People of Vietnam Will Win!" *Pravda,* September 2, 1968.

68. Johnson, *Vantage Point,* p. 514.

69. *Ibid.,* p. 515.

70. Telegram from Paris to Washington, NODIS/HARVAN/PLUS, September 21, 1968. Harriman Papers, Special Files: Public Service, Subject File, box 559.

71. *Ibid.*

72. Harriman Papers, Special Files: Public Service, Subject File, box 500.

73. Walt Rostow's Memorandum, October 2, 1968. Johnson Library, NSF, Country File, Vietnam, Memos to the President/Bombing Halt Decision, vol. 1, box 137.

74. Telegram, Harriman and Vance to Washington, October 9, 1968. Johnson Library, NSF, Memos to the President, Walt Rostow, vol. 98, box 40.

75. Clifford, *Counsel to the President,* p. 574.

76. Johnson, *Vantage Point,* p. 515.

77. Clifford, *Counsel to the President,* p. 574.

78. Memorandum of Conversation, Rusk-Dobrynin, October 14, 1968. Johnson Library, NSF, Country File, Vietnam, HARVAN Misc. and Memos, vol. VIII, box 124.

79. *Ibid.*

80. Telegram, Rusk to Harriman and Vance, October 16, 1968. Johnson Library, NSF, Country File, Vietnam, Memos to the President/Bombing Halt Decision, vol. 1, box 137.

81. Johnson Library, NSF, Country File, Vietnam, box 137.

82. Harriman and Vance to Washington, October 18, 1968. Johnson Library, NSF, Country File, Vietnam, Memos to the President/Bombing Halt Decision, vol. 1, box 137.

83. Vance's call to Washington on the secure telephone, 8:00 a.m., October 22, 1968. *Ibid.*

84. *Ibid.*

85. Vance's call to Washington on the secure telephone, 10:25 a.m., October 22, 1968. *Ibid.*

86. Vance's report on his meeting with Oberemko, October 24, 1968. *Ibid.*

87. Quoted in Clifford, *Counsel to the President,* p. 579.

88. Notes on President's Meeting with Group of Foreign Policy Advisers, October 27, 1968. Johnson Library, Tom Johnson's Notes of Meetings, box 4.

89. Johnson, *Vantage Point,* p. 519.

90. *Ibid.,* p. 520.

91. Telegram, Harriman and Vance to Washington, October 28, 1968. Johnson Library, NSF, Country File, Vietnam, HARVAN/DOUBLE PLUS, box 125.

92. For text of the message see, for example, Telegram, Rusk to American Embassy, Saigon, October 30, 1968. Harriman Papers, Special Files: Public Service, Subject File, Paris Peace Talks, box 560.

93. Ben Read to Walt Rostow, October 29, 1968. Johnson Library, NSF, Country File, Vietnam, box 137.

94. Johnson, *Vantage Point,* p. 528.

95. *Pravda,* November 3, 1968.

96. *Ibid.*

97. *Pravda,* November 7, 1968.

98. *Pravda,* November 13, 1968.

99. Memorandum of Conversation, Kosygin–U.S. Senators Albert Gore, Claiborne Pell, and James Lowenstein, November 19, 1968. Johnson Library, Papers of Clark Clifford, Vietnam Files, box 4.

100. GRU on the situation in the world as of 9:00 a.m., December 11, 1968. SCCD, f. 5, op. 60, d. 316, p. 29.

101. Memorandum of Conversation, an official at the Soviet embassy in Hanoi and a North Vietnamese informant, December 10, 1968. *Ibid.,* d. 368, p. 116.

102. Thompson to Secretary of State by telephone, November 29, 1968. NSA, Lyndon B. Johnson Library Collection.

103. Telegram, American embassy in London to Washington, November 1968. Johnson Library, NSF, Country File, Vietnam, Memos to the President/Bombing Halt Decision, vol. 6, box 138.

104. Abramson, *Spanning the Century,* p. 673.

105. Telegram, Harriman and Vance to Washington, January 13, 1969. Johnson Library, NSF, Country File, Vietnam, box 259.

106. Telegram, Harriman and Vance to Washington, January 14, 1968. *Ibid.*

107. Memorandum of the Meeting. *Ibid.*

108. Johnson, *Vantage Point,* p. 529.

109. Memorandum of Conversation . . . , January 18, 1969. Harriman Papers, Special Files: Public Service, Subject File, box 559.

110. Vance's interview, March 9, 1970. Johnson Library, Oral History Collection.

111. Political Report of the Soviet Embassy in Hanoi for 1968. SCCD, f. 5, op. 60, d. 374, p. 180.

9. LINKAGE VERSUS LINKAGE

1. And they were, as Stephen E. Ambrose has clearly demonstrated. See his book *Nixon: The Triumph of a Politician, 1962–1972* (New York, 1989), p. 91.

2. "The Republican Party of the U.S.A. on the Eve of Convention," *Pravda,* August 4, 1968.

3. Georgi Ratiani and Boris Strel'nikov, "The Convention Is Over, the Problems Remain," *Pravda,* August 11, 1968.

4. Brezhnev and Kosygin put forward this idea in their conversation with Pham Van Dong in the fall of 1968, as the North Vietnamese premier confirmed in his conversation with Shcherbakov on October 14, 1970. See SCCD, f. 5, op. 62, d. 489, p. 175.

5. See Chapter 8.

6. Richard Nixon, *RN: The Memoirs of Richard Nixon* (London, 1978), p. 345.

7. Memorandum from Boris Ponomarev to the Central Committee with the draft of resolution, October 22, 1968. SCCD, First Sector, no. 3871, "special dossier."

8. *Pravda,* November 7, 1968.

9. Nixon, *RN,* p. 344.

10. For an analysis of these developments, see Raymond L. Garthoff, *Détente and Confrontation: American-Soviet Relations from Nixon to Reagan* (Washington, 1994, rev. ed.), pp. 10–13.

11. Nixon, *RN,* p. 344.

12. Garthoff, *Détente and Confrontation,* p. 30. Joan Hoff concurs with Garthoff that "From a Nixinger [i.e., Nixon and Kissinger] perspective, détente represented nothing more or less than a political and economic means, strategy, or process (as opposed to goal or condition)", though she limits its goals to the area of Soviet behavior and Soviet attitudes. She rejects the notion that détente under the Nixon administration "was a continuation of the traditional cold war policy of containment." See Joan Hoff, *Nixon Reconsidered* (New York, 1994), pp. 183–184.

13. Nixon, *RN,* p. 349.

14. Nixon, *RN,* p. 345.

15. Quoted in Ambrose, *Nixon,* p. 224.

16. Nixon, *RN,* p. 341. Stephen Ambrose, Joan Hoff, and Walter Isaacson here yielded to the attraction of this comparison. See Ambrose, *Nixon,* pp. 232–233; Hoff, *Nixon Reconsidered,* p. 149; Walter Isaacson, *Kissinger: A Biography* (London, 1992), p. 139.

17. Joan Hoff discusses this question at length. See: Joan Hoff, *Nixon Reconsidered*, pp. 149–157.

18. Henry Kissinger, "The Viet Nam Negotiations," *Foreign Affairs*, 47 (January 1969), 219.

19. Nixon, *RN*, pp. 340–341.

20. Kissinger, "Viet Nam Negotiations," p. 220.

21. Isaacson, *Kissinger*, pp. 165–166. See also Henry Kissinger, *The White House Years* (London, 1979), p. 262.

22. *Ibid.*, p. 166.

23. *Ibid.*, p. 126.

24. *Ibid.*, p. 127.

25. *Ibid.*

26. Hoff, *Nixon Reconsidered*, p. 152.

27. Kissinger, "Viet Nam Negotiations," p. 229.

28. Nixon, *RN*, p. 346. Emphasis added.

29. Garthoff, *Détente and Confrontation*, pp. 77–78.

30. Kissinger, *White House Years*, pp. 129–130.

31. *Ibid.*, p. 128.

32. *Ibid.*, p. 129.

33. Memorandum of Conversation, Zhukov-Kissinger, January 31, 1969. SCCD, f. 5, op. 61, d. 558, p. 18.

34. Kissinger, *White House Years*, p. 129.

35. *Ibid.*, p. 113.

36. Nixon, *RN*, pp. 369–370.

37. *Ibid.*, p. 370; Kissinger, *White House Years*, p. 143.

38. Memorandum of Conversation, Harriman-Dobrynin, February 19, 1969. Harriman Papers, Special Files: Public Service, Subject File, box 455. Emphasis added.

39. *Ibid.*

40. Memorandum of Conversation, Harriman–Nixon and Kissinger, February 21, 1969. *Ibid.*, box 562.

41. Memorandum of Conversation, Harriman-Dobrynin, February 23, 1969. *Ibid.*, box 455.

42. Quoted in Tad Szulc, *The Illusion of Peace: Foreign Policy in the Nixon Years* (New York, 1978), pp. 68–69.

43. Patrick J. Buchanan's Memorandum to the President, March 4, 1969. Nixon Presidential Materials Project, President's Office Files, Memoranda for the President, box 77 (hereafter NPMP).

44. Kissinger, *White House Years*, p. 144.

45. *Ibid.*, p. 266.

46. *Ibid.* Emphasis in original.

47. Nixon, *RN*, p. 391.

48. Kissinger, *White House Years*, p. 268.

49. Kissinger suggested two possibilities: either Moscow passed the proposal to Hanoi and, receiving a negative reply, decided not to reply at all, or the Soviets never transmitted Washington's message for fear of greater involvement in North Vietnamese–American contacts. See Kissinger, *White House Years*, p. 268.

50. *Ibid.*

51. Memorandum of USA Department, USSR Ministry of Foreign Affairs, "On American-Vietnamese Contacts," September 1, 1971. SCCD, f. 5, op. 63, d. 513, pp. 70–71.

52. H. R. Haldeman Notes, March 20, 1969. NPMP, H. R. Haldeman Notes, White House Special Files, Staff Member and Office Files. See also H. R. Haldeman, *The Haldeman Diaries: Inside the Nixon White House* (New York, 1994), p. 42; Ambrose, *Nixon*, p. 257.

53. Szulc, *Illusion of Peace*, p. 63.

54. Dorothy C. Donnelly, "A Settlement of Sorts: Henry Kissinger's Negotiations and America's Extrication from Vietnam," *Peace and Change* 2/3 (Summer 1983), 62.

55. Kissinger, *White House Years*, p. 141.

56. *Ibid.*, p. 140

57. Memorandum of Conversation, Nixon-Harriman, February 21, 1969. Harriman Papers, Special Files: Public Service, Trips and Missions, box 562.

58. Memorandum of Conversation, Dobrynin-Kissinger, undated. SCCD, f. 5, op. 61, d. 558, p. 92. Reprinted in *Cold War International History Project Bulletin* 3 (Fall 1993), 63–67.

59. *Ibid.*

60. *Ibid.*, p. 95.

61. *Ibid.*, p. 101. Emphasis added.

62. *Ibid.*, p. 102.

63. *Ibid.*, p. 103. Dobrynin also included in the report his opinion of Kissinger and his role in the administration. He noted that the president's assistant had "basic, in fact dominant influence" on Nixon and had concentrated in his hands all information on U.S. foreign policy as well as the levers of decision-making in this area. "In this connection," Dobrynin pointed out, "I should mention that Kissinger holds under his own personal control all communications of members of his staff with our Embassy personnel, and sternly requires that all such conversations are reported directly to him, and he considers it necessary that he himself report to the President." The Soviet ambassador took into account Kissinger's tendency to limit the number of communications between Soviet and U.S. officials to his personal contacts with Dobrynin and recommended that Moscow "more and more actively" develop the channel with Kissinger. (*Ibid.*, pp. 104–105.) This recommendation was quite useful. Kissinger's desire to retain a monopoly in contacts with the Soviets had led to a memorandum from John D. Ehrlichman, in which Nixon's assistant on domestic affairs instructed the White House staff to "decline contacts suggested by Soviet Bloc personnel unless you are reasonably convinced that some national advantage or other benefit would result from the meeting." In the latter case it was necessary to submit written notification, "well in advance" of such a meeting, to Kissinger and to the National Security Council, in which a date, time, and place of the meeting must be indicated as well as the name of the person with whom the meeting would be held. Even if someone declined to meet with a Soviet official, the notification had to be sent to Kissinger anyway. See NPMP, White House Central Files, Subject Files, FG 6-6, National Security Council, box 1.

64. There is a handwritten reference to this on the first page of the document.

65. Nixon, *RN*, p. 399.

66. *Ibid.*, p. 407.

67. See note 38.

68. Summary of the Political Report of the USSR Embassy in the United States for 1969. SCCD, f. 5, op. 61, d. 305a, pp. 234–234 rev. Soviet intelligence confirmed this U.S. attitude with information received from other sources. Thus in January 1969 the KGB supplied the Soviet leadership with the summary of a July

1968 memorandum prepared in the French Foreign Ministry which analyzed American policy in Vietnam and toward the Soviet Union under the new administration in Washington. The KGB informed party leaders that French analysts believed "the Johnson administration's desire to ameliorate relations with the Soviet Union may have been preserved almost unchanged with Nixon's coming to power." After the achievement of peace in Vietnam, the memorandum stressed, they would gradually improve. See *ibid.*, d. 458, p. 4.

69. Ambrose, *Nixon*, p. 224. It cannot be said that Washington ignored the limits of their threats to North Vietnam. American officials pointed out that the United States was pursuing a policy in Indochina that would "avoid frictions between great powers in connection with the problems of Southeast Asia." The KGB duly informed the Soviet leadership of this position. See KGB to CPSU Central Committee, August 14, 1970. SCCD, f. 5, op. 62, d. 516, p. 222.

70. Kissinger writes: "Nixon's attempt to tie the opening of strategic arms negotiations to progress on political issues ran counter to the passionate conviction of both the arms controllers, who were eager to limit the arms race, and the Kremlinologists, who were convinced that American foreign policy should strengthen the Kremlin doves against the Kremlin hawks in their presumed policy disputes. The bureaucracy chipped away at the policy outlined in the President's letter [of February 4, 1969, to Cabinet members] by emphasizing arms control as an end in itself in leaks to the press." See Kissinger, *Diplomacy* (New York, 1994), p. 718.

71. Political Report of the Soviet Embassy in the DRV for 1969. SCCD, f. 5, op. 61, d. 459, p. 126.

72. List of Principal Agreements Between the USSR and the DRV, undated. *Ibid.*, op. 66, d. 71, pp. 120–122.

73. Political Report of the Soviet Embassy in the DRV for 1970. *Ibid.*, op. 62, d. 495, p. 103.

74. In the Political Report for 1970, Soviet diplomats noted that in the press and in public statements the North Vietnamese were silent on "almost all issues of the life and activities of the CPSU, its struggle for the unity and cohesion of the Socialist commonwealth and the international Communist movement. The issues of Soviet assistance to and support of developing countries and the national liberation movement have not been well covered, nor issues of the struggle for peace and peaceful coexistence, issues of European security, etc." *Ibid.*, p. 101.

75. On June 29 the KGB provided authorities with facts about the unfriendly attitude of "responsible military leaders" of the People's Army of Vietnam toward Soviet military specialists dispatched to the DRV to accompany special trains with antiaircraft weapons. SCCD, Sixth Sector, no. 2043, "special dossier."

76. Political Report for 1969. SCCD, f. 5, op. 61, d. 459, p. 117. For instance, the creation of the Provisional Revolutionary Government of South Vietnam (PRG) was totally unexpected in Moscow. When Nguyen Duy Trinh informed Shcherbakov of this step, the Soviet ambassador could not conceal his surprise. He noted that creation of the PRG "exceeded the limits of the political situation in South Vietnam," since the Vietnamese requested recognition of this government. Later the embassy drew attention to the fact that on the eve of the announcement of the creation of the PRG, Le Duc Tho made a stopover in Moscow en route to Paris and met with Kosygin, but failed even to mention the planned action. See Memorandum of Conversation, Shcherbakov–Nguyen Duy Trinh, June 9, 1969. SCCD, f. 5, op. 61, d. 458, pp. 92–96; Political Report for 1969, p. 117.

77. The KGB submitted a draft of the decision of the CPSU central committee, which approved KGB activities in maintaining "confidential" relations "on a secret basis" with the Vietnamese in the DRV, Soviet Union, and wherever possible. SCCD, First Sector, no. 4309, December 23, 1970, "special dossier." The document bears only Suslov's approval, but obviously all other members of the politburo shared this influential opinion.

78. *Militant Vanguard of the Vietnamese people*, p. 161.

79. The GRU sent to the CPSU central committee on September 4, 1969, a report on the modification of the DRV leadership's views which proved the efficiency of Soviet intelligence. The report said, ". . . At the present time the DRV leadership [on the issue] of a solution of the Vietnamese conflict has started to show preference for a political settlement, rather than begin a strategic offensive with the aim of delivering a decisive defeat to American and Saigon troops." The GRU attributed such a change to "advocates of sober politics headed by Le Duan." See GRU to Central Committee, September 4, 1969. SCCD, f. 5, op. 61, d. 458, p. 144. Also Political Report for 1970, p. 100.

80. Political Letter of the Soviet Embassy in the DRV, "On Possibilities and Specifics of Coordination of the DRV Foreign Policy with the Soviet Union and Other Socialist Countries," June 25, 1970. SCCD, f. 5, op. 62, d. 492, p. 149.

81. Political Letter, "On the Policy of the Workers' Party of Vietnam Toward the Resolution of Problems of Indochina and on Our Tasks Following Decisions of the XXIV CPSU Congress," May 21, 1971. SCCD, f. 5, op. 63, d. 516, p. 1. Emphasis added.

82. Memorandum of Conversation, Zorin-Harriman, January 18, 1969. Harriman Papers, Special Files: Public Service, Subject File, Paris Peace Talks, box 559. Emphasis in original.

83. Memorandum of Conversation, Shcherbakov–Pham Van Dong, October 14, 1970. SCCD, f. 5, op. 62, d. 489, pp. 176–177.

84. Alexandrov-Agentov, for example, writes in his memoirs about Brezhnev's knowledge of Vietnam: "Brezhnev had never been to Vietnam and knew little about this country except for the most essential facts." See Alexandrov-Agentov, *From Kollontai to Gorbachev*, p. 166. Peter W. Rodman, who as a member of Kissinger's team met Brezhnev on several occasions, also thought that Brezhnev's "grasp of the intricacies of arms control or Third World issues was minimal." (Rodman, *More Precious Than Peace: The Cold War and the Struggle for the Third World* (New York, 1994), p. 145.) It seems that Brezhnev did not care to be involved in formulating Soviet policy toward Vietnam at all. The card file of "special dossiers" contains a card referring to a draft, prepared by the International Department and the Foreign Ministry, of Brezhnev's reply to a letter of Le Duan. A remark on the card, evidently made by one of the general secretary's aides, reads: "To Comrade Chernenko. Leonid Il'ich asked for a vote on this proposal (he has not read the text)." See SCCD, First Sector, no. 4070, December 24, 1971. Like Brezhnev, other members of the Soviet politburo had little knowledge of Vietnam save generalities.

85. Memorandum of Conversation, Shcherbakov–Xuan Thuy, June 1, 1969. SCCD, f. 5, op. 61, d. 460, p. 132.

86. Kissinger, *White House Years*, p. 445.

87. In his own account of the meeting, Kissinger omits this fact. See *ibid.*

88. Memorandum of Conversation, Zorin–Le Duc Tho, Xuan Thuy, March 19, 1970. SCCD, f. 5, op. 62, d. 516, pp. 156–157.

89. Memorandum of Conversation, Zorin–Le Duc Tho, April 6, 1970. *Ibid.*, d. 489, p. 91.

90. Memorandum of Conversation, Zorin–Xuan Thuy and the head of the NLFSV delegation, Tran Buu Kiem, February 21, 1969. SCCD, f. 5, op. 61, d. 460, p. 56. Reprinted in *Cold War International History Bulletin* 3 (Fall 1993), 62–63.

91. Kissinger, *White House Years*, p. 144.

92. Alexandrov-Agentov, *From Kollantai to Gorbachev*, p. 214.

10. BETWEEN DÉTENTE AND VIETNAM

1. *Foreign Policy and International Relations of the PRC. 1963–1973*, pp. 27, 131.

2. Nixon, *RN*, p. 281.

3. Quoted in *ibid.*, p. 285.

4. National Security Study Memorandum 14, February 5, 1969. Paul Kesaris, ed., *Documents of the National Security Council* (Frederick, Md., 1987), microfilm edition.

5. Kissinger, *White House Years*, p. 178.

6. *Ibid.*, p. 172.

7. *Ibid.*

8. *Ibid.*, p. 185.

9. Raymond Garthoff draws attention to these facts in his book. He also notes Kissinger's "surprising unfamiliarity with the facts" concerning the Kosygin-Zhou meeting. See Garthoff, *Détente and Confrontation*, pp. 238–239.

10. *Ibid.*, p. 239.

11. Alexandrov-Agentov, *From Kollontai to Gorbachev*, p. 172.

12. Kissinger, *White House Years*, p. 165.

13. "The new Administration had a notion, but not yet a strategy, to move toward China. Policy emerges when concept encounters opportunity. Such an occasion arose when Soviet and Chinese troops clashed in the frozen Siberian tundra along a river of which none of us had ever heard. From then on ambiguity vanished, and we moved without further hesitation toward a momentous change in global policy." Kissinger, *White House Years*, p. 171. See also Anne Gilks, *The Breakdown of the Sino-Vietnamese Alliance, 1970–1979* (Berkeley, 1992), Chapter 2.

14. National Security Study Memorandum 63, July 3, 1969. *Documents of the National Security Council.*

15. Kissinger, *White House Years*, pp. 167–194; Nixon, *RN*, pp. 545–547.

16. *Ibid.*, p. 405. Emphasis added.

17. SCCD, f. 5, op. 6, d. 989, no. 1573, May 21, 1970, "special dossier."

18. How Beijing's calculations led to this improvement are discussed in Gilks, *Breakdown of the Sino-Vietnamese Alliance*, p. 46.

19. Political Report of the Soviet Embassy in Hanoi for 1970. SCCD, f. 5, op. 62, d. 495, p. 127; Political Letter, "On the Policy of the Workers' Party of Vietnam," p. 29.

20. *Ibid.*, pp. 210, 212. This recommendation contradicts the alleged Soviet plans for war, let alone nuclear war, against China. In fact Moscow would have preferred to find a way to approach Beijing.

21. See Chapter 8.

22. See Nixon, *RN*, pp. 345–346. Nixon explains his refusal by his desire to avoid an unfruitful summit that would leave nothing except the "spirit" of the summit.

23. See an account of the discussion of a possible summit in Kissinger, *White House Years*, Chapter 13.

24. *Ibid.*, p. 731.

25. *Ibid.*, pp. 766, 835–836.

26. *Ibid.*, p. 836. Emphasis added.

27. *Ibid.*, p. 173.

28. *Militant Vanguard of the Vietnamese People*, p. 172.

29. Gareth Porter, *A Peace Denied: The United States, Vietnam, and the Paris Agreement* (Bloomington, Ind., 1975), pp. 102–103.

30. They wrote in May 1971: "As the withdrawal of American troops continues, someone in the DRV has his bellicosity up, and ideas of delivering a 'decisive blow' in 1972 and of 'bringing down Nixon' arise. These ideas may cause the war to flare up anew in full force." See Political Letter, "On the Policy of the Workers' Party of Vietnam," SCCD, f. 5, op. 63, d. 516, p. 25.

31. "Basic Agreements Between the USSR and the DRV." *Ibid.*, op. 66, d. 71, pp. 121–122.

32. The Chinese attitude at this time was surprisingly similar to that of the Soviets. As Anne Gilks puts it, "China's interest in its pivot-wing and alliance relationships with the DRV by mid-1971 were, respectively, to continue to enhance its influence in Hanoi vis-à-vis Moscow, which entailed supplying military aid to Hanoi, and to use its influence to persuade its ally to settle for a compromise negotiated settlement and an early end to the war." See Gilks, *Breakdown of the Sino-Vietnamese Alliance*, p. 73.

33. USSR Foreign Ministry Memorandum, "Vietnam-China Relations," July 4, 1973. SCCD, f. 5, op. 66, d. 71, p. 88.

34. Political Letter, "On the Policy of the Workers' Party of Vietnam," p. 39.

35. Shcherbakov to Moscow, August 5, 1971. *Ibid.*, d. 513, p. 64.

36. "The Diary of Sino-American Relations (January–June 1972)," prepared by the Far Eastern Division of the USSR Foreign Ministry, October 6, 1972. SCCD, f. 5, op. 64, d. 409, p. 134.

37. *Ibid.*, pp. 153–154.

38. *Ibid.*, p. 162.

39. Garthoff, *Détente and Confrontation*," pp. 110–111.

40. Ken Post, *Revolution, Socialism and Nationalism in Viet Nam*, Vol. 5: *Winning the War and Losing the Peace* (Aldershot, N.H., 1994), pp. 201–202.

41. *Ibid.*, p. 204.

42. Porter, *Peace Denied*, pp. 112–113. Emphasis in original.

43. Peter Rodman outlines the dilemma that Soviet leaders faced in April 1972: "For one thing, arms control—especially the Anti-Ballistic Missile (ABM) Treaty that reassured the Soviets against any U.S. breakthroughs in ABM technology. Second, Europe—where Willy Brandt's 'Eastern treaties' accepting postwar borders in Eastern Europe, awaiting ratification, were hanging by a thread in the Bundestag and the Soviets had to fear that a revival of East-West tensions would doom their whole German policy. Next economic relations, about which Brezhnev practically drooled as he imagined vistas of U.S. investment, trade, and technical assistance for the sluggish Soviet economy. Brezhnev had to contemplate all these

potential losses—not to mention leaving the United States in bed with the hated Chinese, whom Nixon had just visited. All of this had to be weighed against the principle of fidelity to a socialist ally several thousand kilometers away who had launched a major offensive at the worst possible time and had embarrassed Brezhnev by pigheaded behavior at a negotiating meeting he had helped set up." See Rodman, *More Precious Than Peace*, p. 127.

44. Kissinger, *White House Years*, p. 1120.

45. Nixon's Memorandum to Kissinger, April 20, 1972. NPMP, President's Personal File, box 74, April 1972, Kissinger's trip to Moscow. Emphasis in original. See also Ambrose, *Nixon*, pp. 531–532.

46. Haig's Memorandum to Nixon, April 20, 1972. NSA, NPMP collection.

47. Kissinger to Haig, April 24, 1972. NPMP, President's Personal File, box 74. See also Kissinger, *White House Years*, p. 1146.

48. Kissinger to Haig, April 21, 1972. NPMP, President's Personal File, box 74.

49. Kissinger commented on the results of his meetings with Soviet leaders: "My approved instructions for this trip were to use stick of bombing and carrot of being forthcoming on summit-related matters in order to get mutual de-escalation in Vietnam. So far we have spent two-thirds of our time on Vietnam during which *I have gone to the brink with repeated declarations that we will continue military operations.*" "Top Secret, Sensitive, Eyes Only" Memo, April 22, 1972. NPMP, President's Personal File, box 74. Emphasis added.

50. Brezhnev informed Kissinger that Hanoi formally asked to cancel the summit. (See Kissinger to Haig, April 24, 1972. NPMP, President's Personal File, box 74.) He complained during his second meeting with Nixon's adviser that "the enemies of the summit in Hanoi and Peking were trying to wreck the summit and we [i.e., the U.S. and the Soviet Union] had to thwart them. (See "Top Secret, Sensitive, Eyes Only," April 22, 1972. *Ibid.*) See also Kissinger, *White House Years*, p. 1151.

51. Nixon, *RN*, p. 592.

52. Nixon's memorandum to Kissinger, April 23, 1972. NSA, NPMP collection.

53. Ambrose, *Nixon*, p. 537.

54. *Pravda*, May 12, 1972.

55. Kissinger, *White House Years*, p. 1194.

56. Alexandrov-Agentov, *From Kollontai to Gorbachev*, p. 223. Emphasis added.

57. *Ibid.*

58. *Ibid.*, p. 224.

59. Dobrynin mentioned such a request in his interview with the author in May 1994.

60. Alexandrov-Agentov, *From Kollontai to Gorbachev,* p. 225. See also an account of the first conversation in Nixon, *RN*, pp. 609–610.

61. Alexandrov-Agentov, *From Kollontai to Gorbachev*, p. 228.

62. *Ibid.*, p. 229.

63. Kissinger, *White House Years*, p. 1227.

64. Alexandrov-Agentov, *From Kollontai to Gorbachev*, p. 230.

65. Memorandum to Members and Candidate Members of the CPSU CC Politburo, "On Conversations Between A. A. Gromyko and Kissinger on the Problem of Vietnam on 27–28 of May." SCCD, f. 5, op. 66, d. 41, p. 115.

66. *Ibid.*, p. 117.

67. See Ambrose, *Nixon*, p. 550.

68. *Pravda*, June 20, 1972.

69. Cable from Nguyen Duy Trinh to Xuan Thuy and Le Duc Tho. Interview with a Vietnamese scholar, February 1995.

70. Porter, *Peace Denied*, p. 115. One cannot, however, agree with Porter's inclination to underestimate the significance of the Soviet and Chinese factors in the decision-making process in Hanoi. He admits the harmful effect on the DRV of the weakening of Soviet and Chinese opposition to American intervention in Vietnam, but immediately adds: "But when the Lao Dong Party leadership finally decided to sacrifice its central demand for the replacement of the Thieu regime by a coalition government in order to get a settlement, it was because of its evaluation of the existing balance of forces and not in response to pressure from the Soviets or Chinese to change its negotiating stance" (p. 115). But the question is how to interpret such pressure. There was not, of course, a direct pressure in the form of threats and arm twisting, at least on the Soviet side. The pressure usually took the form of advice and suggestions, but in combination with many other factors such advice could not be ignored by North Vietnamese leaders.

71. Ambrose, *Nixon*, p. 215.

72. Kissinger, *White House Years*, p. 1443.

73. "Excerpts from the Transcripts of the Meetings Between Kissinger and Le Duc Tho," January 3, 1973. SCCD, f. 5, op. 66, d. 87, p. 4.

74. *Ibid.*, p. 6.

75. *Ibid.*

76. Porter, *Peace Denied*, p. 159.

77. Donnelly, "Settlement of Sorts," p. 72.

78. *Pravda*, December 20, 1972.

79. Porter, *Peace Denied*, p. 163.

80. Memorandum of Conversation, Pham Van Dong–Shcherbakov, December 23, 1972. SCCD, f. 5, op. 66, d. 782, p. 4.

81. *Ibid.* Emphasis added.

82. Memorandum of Conversation, Shcherbakov–Hoang Van Tien, December 27, 1972. *Ibid.*, d. 783, pp. 10–11.

83. Quoted in Goodman, *Search for a Negotiated Settlement,* p. 111.

84. *The Soviet Union–Vietnam, 30 Years . . .*, p. 288.

Index

A NOTE ON THE AUTHOR

Ilya V. Gaiduk is a research fellow specializing in the history of Soviet-American relations at the Institute of World History in Moscow. Born in Krasnovodsk, Turkmenistan, he studied at the Moscow State Pedagogical Institute and at the Russian Academy of Science. Mr. Gaiduk has been a fellow of the Cold War International History Project at the Woodrow Wilson International Center for Scholars and of the Norwegian Nobel Institute. In the opening of previously restricted Soviet archives, he was given exclusive access to most of the secret documents relating to the Soviet Union's role in the Vietnam War.